Men of Steel

MEN OF STEEL

I SS PANZER CORPS
THE ARDENNES AND EASTERN
FRONT 1944–45

by

Michael Reynolds

The story of the 1st and 12th SS Panzer Divisions
in the Ardennes and on the Eastern Front in 1944
and 1945

'Soldiers may not quit the post allotted by the gods'

Tennyson

DA CAPO PRESS

Originally published by Sarpedon

Copyright ©1999 Michael Reynolds.
Maps copyright © 1999 Jay Karamales.

Cataloging-in-Publication Data is available from the
Library of Congress.

ISBN 1-885119-66-6

Printed in the United States of America.

First Da Capo Edition 2001.

EBA   01 02 03   10 9 8 7 6 5 4 3 2

Contents

List of Maps

(pages 323–354)

Author's Note

It is regretted that for commercial reasons it has been impossible to include coloured and pull-out maps in this book; however, for those purists who enjoy knowing the exact location of the places mentioned and their relationship to one another, it is suggested that they photocopy and enlarge the maps provided and have them to hand when reading.

Acknowledgments

Once more I am indebted to my publisher and good friend, Jamie Wilson, for encouraging me to write this book. I hope it will prove a worthy addition to his catalogue of high quality military histories.

Next I must thank most sincerely John Fedorowicz and Mike Olive, President and Vice-President respectively of J. J. Fedorowicz Publishing Inc, for allowing me to quote freely from their publications and Jay Karamales, who not only produced all the maps and Appendices in this book, but spent many hours in the US National Archives on my behalf. Without these gentlemen *Men of Steel* could not have been written.

Others who played important roles in the production of this book were:

Americans

Bill Warnock for producing, from Berlin Document Centre sources, invaluable information on numerous members of I SS Panzer Corps, and for allowing me to use photographs from his personal collection.

Belgians

Georges Balaes for providing information from the Belgian National Archives;

Edouard and Marie-Berthe de Harenne for their generous hospitality during my many visits to the Ardennes;

Joseph Dejardin for providing privileged information concerning atrocities committed in the Ardennes in 1944;

Marie-France Grégoire for translating documents in the French language.

British

Brigadier Tony Baxter for proof reading and suggesting amendments to my first drafts;

Colonel Mike Chilcott for translating documents in the Russian language;

Professor Charles Dick for the provision of Soviet documents and advice on the Red Army;

Jeff Dugdale and Mike Wood for sharing with me their comprehensive knowledge of the German Order of Battle and unit equipment holdings and casualties;

Vic and Lotte Lawson for translating German documents;

Brigadier John Moore-Bick for translating German documents;

Françoise Murcott for translating documents in the French language;

Colonel Howard Stephens for advice concerning my ground reconnaissance in Hungary;

Bill Sumpter for technical assistance.

German

Wolf Detlef Mauder for information on individuals and units in I SS Panzer Corps.

I would also like to thank all those who allowed me to quote from their writings. Their books and publications are listed in the Bibliography.

And finally I must again thank my wife, Anne, for allowing me to spend hours in my study without interruption, to visit the Ardennes many times and enjoy a fascinating ground reconnaissance in Slovakia, Hungary and Austria, and for her ideas and encouragement when I found the 'going' a bit difficult!

MFR
Sussex, England
September 1999

Preface

In March 1943 the three senior Divisions of the Waffen-SS – Leibstandarte Adolf Hitler (Bodyguard), Das Reich (Empire) and Totenkopf (Death's Head) – were fighting against Stalin's armies in the Ukraine under the command of SS Lieutenant General Paul Hausser. His Corps had the title 'SS Panzer Corps'. Aware of the need to create more divisions for his Army and under constant pressure from Heinrich Himmler for more SS troops, Adolf Hitler chose this moment to order the formation of a new SS Panzer Corps. It was to be formed from the existing 1st SS Panzer-Grenadier Division Leibstandarte and a new Division to be created from the Hitlerjugend organisation. These formations were later known as the 1st SS Panzer Division Leibstandarte and 12th SS Panzer Division Hitlerjugend, and their collective title was I SS Panzer Corps Leibstandarte.

The first part of the history of this Corps appeared in my last book, *Steel Inferno – I SS Panzer Corps in Normandy*. This book, after a brief look at the origins of the Corps, tells the rest of the story. For readers who have a particular interest in the actions of the 1st SS Panzer Division Leibstandarte in the Ardennes up to Christmas Day 1944, they should consult my first book, *The Devil's Adjutant – Jochen Peiper, Panzer Leader*. As well as providing more details of the fighting, it goes on to describe the famous trial of the officers and soldiers of the Leibstandarte, and their superiors, who were accused of war crimes in the campaign, in particular the 'Malmédy Massacre', and Peiper's murder in France over thirty years later.

Although other famous formations, such as Panzer Lehr and the Führer Begleit Brigade, were placed under the command of I SS Panzer Corps at various times, this book will describe only the actions of the *designated* Divisions of the Corps and the 101st SS Heavy Panzer and Artillery Battalions which were integral parts of it – only those units whose members were entitled to wear Hitler's name on their sleeves and the 'Dietrich' or 'key' emblem on their vehicles.

In producing my story of I SS Panzer Corps, particularly of its actions on the Eastern Front, I have been forced to rely heavily on the Histories of the 1st and 12th SS Panzer Divisions, compiled by Ralf Tiemann and Hubert Meyer respectively. These Histories, written as tributes to their fallen comrades, have clearly been researched with great care and attention to detail. Nevertheless, as the authors point out, the War Diaries of the 1st and 12th SS Panzer Divisions and their sub-units, with the exception of one Battalion Diary covering only one month, do not exist and they had to place much reliance on human memory – with all its frailty.

Further problems were encountered in the case of Soviet records and accounts of the fighting in Hungary and Austria. These describe the actions mainly at Army level and above and provide little of value at Divisional level and below – as required by this book. Moreover, as John Erickson has pointed out in the preface to his 'tour de force', *The Road to Berlin*, many of the Soviet publications on the 'Great Patriotic War', more than 15,000 volumes, have been doctored or 'dubiously adjusted' in recognition of the various personality cults which followed the death of Stalin. Despite these difficulties and drawbacks, I hope that by coordinating and sometimes interpreting the two German Histories, consulting other reliable sources and carefully relating events to the ground where the fighting took place, the reader will find my descriptions of the fighting, including the complicated series of events on the Eastern Front, both logical and easily understandable.

The word 'Steel' in the title of this book has been chosen with care; first, because steel is a malleable metal which can be hammered into shape; second, because it is hard and strong; third, because it can be blunted by misuse and over-use; and lastly, because it can be broken when subjected to unreasonable stress. It is therefore a suitable description for the men of I SS Panzer Corps.

Guide to Abbreviations and German Words

AA	Anti-Aircraft
AAR	After Action Report
AEAF	Allied Expeditionary Air Forces
Armd	Armoured
Arty	Artillery
Aslt	Assault
Atk	Anti-Tank
Bde	Brigade
Bn	Battalion
Bty	Battery
Cdn	Canadian
CinC	Commander in Chief
Coy	Company
CP	Command Post
Cpl	Corporal
CT	Combat Team
D-Day	Day of Attack
Dead ground	Ground which cannot be seen as you approach it
DF	Der Führer
Div	Division
DR	Das Reich
Engr	Engineer
ETHINT	European Theater Interrogations
FBB	Führer Begleit Brigade
Fd	Field
Flak	Anti-Aircraft
FSD	Parachute/Airborne Division
Gds	Guards
GI	American soldier
Gp	Group
H	Hohenstaufen
Heer	Army
H-Hour	Time of an attack
HJ	Hitlerjugend

How	Howitzer
HQ	Headquarters
Hy	Heavy
I&R	Intelligence & Reconnaissance
Inf	Infantry
IWM	Imperial War Museum
IVMV	Istoriya Vtoroi Mirovoi voiny (Soviet Official History 1939-1945)
IVOVSS	Istoriya Velikoi Otechestvennoi voiny Sovetskovo Soyuza (Soviet Official History 1941-1945)
Jagdpanzer (JgPz)	Hunter tank
Kampfgruppe (KG)	Battlegroup
LAA	Light Anti-Aircraft
LAH	Leibstandarte Adolf Hitler
Lt	Light
Med	Medical
med	medium
Meldung	Status Report
MG	Machine-Gun
Mk	Mark
MMG	Medium Machine-Gun
mor	mortar
Mot	Motorized
NCO	Non Commissioned Officer
'O' Group	Meeting where commander gives orders
OKH	HQ of the German Army
OKW	HQ of German Armed Forces
Op	Operational/Operation
OR	Other Rank
pdr	pounder
PGD	Panzer-Grenadier Division
PIAT	Projector Infantry Anti-Tank
Pl	Platoon
Pnr	Pioneer (engineer)
PRO	Public Record Office
PW or POW	Prisoner of War
Pz	Panzer
Pz-Gren	Panzer-Grenadier (armoured infantry)
PzJg	Panzerjäger (tank hunter)
R & R	Rest & Recuperation
Recce	Reconnaissance
Regt	Regiment
SA	Sturmabteilung (Storm Detachment)
Schwimmwagen	Amphibious vehicle

SHAEF	Supreme Headquarters Allied Expeditionary Force
SP	Self-propelled
Spitze	Vanguard
SPW	German open-topped half track
Sqn	Squadron
SS-VT	Special Purpose Troops
STAVKA	Soviet Supreme Command
StuG	Armoured assault gun
Sturmgeschütz	Armoured assault gun
T-Div	Totenkopf Division
TF	Task Force
Tk	Tank
Tp	Troop
Tpt	Transport
vehs	vehicles
VGD	Volks-Grenadier Division
Werfer	Mortar
Wehrmacht	German Armed Forces
WW II	World War Two (Second World War)
XO	Executive Officer

CHAPTER I
The Leibstandarte: February 1933 – June 1944

(Maps 1 & 2)

The Regiment

On 23 December 1939 the Führer of Nazi Germany went to the Spa Hotel in Bad Ems to take part in the Christmas celebrations of his favourite Regiment – the Leibstandarte SS Adolf Hitler. The field kitchen produced a strong punch and every man was given a bottle of wine, tobacco and a Christmas cake. The officers and men of this elite unit, expanded from the 1933 Chancellery Guard, greeted their charismatic leader with jubilation. They had plenty to celebrate. Their country was militarily the strongest in Europe and they had just taken part in the first, highly successful, Blitzkrieg campaign of the Second World War – the conquest of Poland. After performing well known soldiers' songs, and sketches depicting life in the Leibstandarte, they sat enraptured as Hitler addressed them:

As long as I have the honour to lead the spearhead of this battle, it will be your honour to be that spearhead.[1]

And so it was to be. From August 1939, when the Regiment left its home in Lichterfelde barracks in Berlin, until the final capitulation in Austria in May 1945, it was to be involved almost continuously in some of the most bitter battles of the war. Few present could have visualised the cataclysmic events which were about to engulf them.

The period February 1933 to December 1939 had seen the original Chancellery Guard, formed by Sepp Dietrich on Hitler's instructions, grow into a Regiment of three infantry Battalions and an artillery unit. Additionally, a fourth 'Wach' Battalion was formed for ceremonial and guard duties.

Dietrich was a former personal bodyguard to Hitler and the 117 men he recruited in 1933 for the Chancellery Guard proved to be an extraordinarily successful group of soldiers. Dietrich himself was to become an Army commander; of the others, three became divisional commanders, eight became regimental commanders, fifteen became Battalion commanders

1

and over thirty became company commanders, all within the framework of the Waffen-SS.[2]

Although formally part of the infamous organisation known as the Schutzstaffel (SS), the Leibstandarte always remained separate and unique. As early as July 1933 a special detachment of the SS-Stabswache Berlin, as it was originally known, mounted guard at the Berghof, Hitler's summer retreat above Berchtesgaden. This indicated that the Führer saw it as more than just a guard force for the Chancellery and other important agencies of the Nazi party – it was clearly his personal guard and, as such, its members were issued with distinctive and unique white accoutrements and wore his name on their cuff bands. But the Leibstandarte was also a fully trained military unit. In March 1935 it led the Army in its peaceful occupation of the Saarland and in 1938 it participated in the Anschluss with Austria and the occupation of the Sudetenland.

The individuals who dined with Hitler at Bad Ems in 1939 had no knowledge of the principles he was about to lay down for the use of the Waffen-SS. These were not specified until August 1940 and can be summarised as follows:

1. Since the Greater German Reich will encompass many different peoples, not all of whom will be willing members, there will be a national force with complete authority to execute the authority of the State.
2. This force will have men of the best German blood who take pride in racial and philosophical purity and believe in the basic philosophy which underpins the Greater German Reich.
3. This force will be organised on military lines.
4. This force will earn the respect of the German people by serving at the front and suffering casualties. After returning from the front members of this force will possess the necessary authority to carry out their duties.
5. Since the Wehrmacht is dedicated exclusively and solely for deployment against the external enemies of the Reich, the use of the Waffen-SS at home is in the full interests of both the country and the Armed Forces.
6. In order to ensure the quality of the Waffen-SS, numbers will be limited.

As the war expanded and the casualty figures rose, Hitler's ideal of limiting the size of the Waffen-SS inevitably came to nothing; however, the force never amounted to more than 10% of the total German land forces.

It is also very doubtful if those present at Bad Ems would have recognised themselves in the following description of their organisation given by a senior SS officer:

A tightly knit aristocracy of manhood, whose special service to the Führer combines the strongest SS and military ideals to create a perfect political fighting machine.

On the other hand, the 'Kameraden' were fully aware that they were part of an elite organisation which was quite separate from the Army and the Police, and there is little doubt that they saw themselves as the successors to the Teutonic knights of old. They were certainly encouraged in that belief by the leader of the SS, Heinrich Himmler, when he told them that they were 'the future aristocratic spine of the German nation'. There is also no doubt that they were already aware of Hitler's racist policies, especially towards the Jews – even though the 'Final Solution' had still to be formulated. The existence of concentration camps, such as the one at Dachau, was certainly no secret, and with all new Leibstandarte officers undergoing tactical training courses in the same area (Dachau), they could hardly claim ignorance. This raises the question of just how far one can, or should, differentiate between members of the Waffen-SS, members of the Allegemeine (or general) SS, and those in the Totenkopf Standarten which had been formed by Theodor Eicke for concentration camp duties and from which grew the 3rd SS Totenkopf Division (T-Div). Whilst it is true to say that the Leibstandarte was essentially a military formation and, as such, played no role in Allegemeine activities, it is also true that it received reinforcements from other SS elements as the war progressed and, similarly, if a member of the Leibstandarte became unfit for combat he was fully eligible for transfer to the non-combatant parts of the SS.

The Leibstandarte's motto was 'My Loyalty is my Honour' and members took this very seriously. Their training and environment constantly stressed loyalty to the Führer and to one another, and this led to much emphasis on trust and to a remarkable degree of informality between ranks and between officers and soldiers. Members even addressed each other as 'Kamerad' when off duty.

Growth

Hitler's plans for the expansion of Germany necessitated a huge increase in the size of the Wehrmacht and his Leibstandarte was inevitably caught up in this process. Within four years this unique infantry Regiment had grown into a Panzer Corps with a theoretical strength of some 45,000 men and 400 tanks. The growth was rapid. In the Spring of 1940 the Regiment was expanded into a fully independent Motorized Infantry Regiment and titled 'Reinforced Leibstandarte SS Adolf Hitler'. Following the invasion of the Low Countries and France in 1940 and the Balkans in 1941, it was restructured into a full Division with a strength of nearly 10,000. Hitler ordered that it should be re-titled 'SS Division Leibstandarte SS Adolf Hitler' (LSSAH). By the end of 1942 the Division had been transformed yet again, this time into a 21,000-strong Panzer-Grenadier Division, and in October 1943 it received its final title of '1st SS Panzer Division Leibstandarte SS Adolf Hitler' – usually shortened to 1st SS Panzer Division LAH. The outline organisation of a Waffen-SS Panzer division is shown at Appendix I.

The year 1943 also saw the astounding announcement by the Führer that his Bodyguard Division was to provide the majority of the leaders and several units for a 'clone' SS Division to be formed mainly from Hitler Youths born in the year 1926. It would eventually be called the 12th SS Panzer Division Hitlerjugend (HJ). These two unique Divisions, the only ones to bear Hitler's name, would then form the I SS Panzer Corps Leibstandarte, the Headquarters of which would also be staffed by officers from the LAH. Only when this had happened would the remarkable metamorphosis of the Führer's Lifeguards be complete.

This rapid expansion from Regiment to Corps incurred a high cost. Even if it had been carried out methodically under peacetime conditions, it would almost certainly have involved a dilution of the strict entry standards originally imposed in 1933. These required candidates to be without so much as a filled tooth, to have well proportioned bodies, with no disparity between body and legs and lower leg and thigh, and to provide proof of ancestry back to 1800 for soldiers and 1750 for officers. But as the expansion took place hurriedly during a war in which high casualty rates almost doubled the numbers required, the strain on maintaining standards was severe. In the first five months of the campaign against the Soviet Union for example, the Leibstandarte suffered 5,281 casualties out of a total strength of 9,994.[3] Such losses, when coupled with the need to expand, had two serious repercussions. First, 'ethnic' Germans, i.e., those of German ancestry living outside the borders of the Reich itself, had to be admitted and second, some casualties were replaced by non-volunteers from Waffen-SS replacement units and from Luftwaffe and naval personnel who had not even volunteered for Army, let alone Waffen-SS service. The fact that these men could be quickly assimilated and transformed into enthusiastic and worthy members of the Division, says much for the leadership qualities of those responsible. It was an incredible feat, but then the Leibstandarte was an incredible organisation. In only ten years it developed a reputation second to none and a Divisional spirit equal or even superior to that found in many British regiments; and when one considers that British regiments constitute only one arm of the service and are normally much smaller, the achievement is all the more remarkable. The Leibstandarte, under one emblem, developed into a Division of all arms – infantry, armour, artillery, engineers, signals, etc., and yet it had the same sense of 'family' as a single arm regiment.

Having described the growth of Leibstandarte in general terms, let us look now at the early wartime history of this remarkable formation.

Reinforced Leibstandarte SS Adolf Hitler

The euphoria which had greeted Hitler at Bad Ems was to continue for another eighteen months. The German assault on the Western democracies began on 10 May and the Leibstandarte crossed the Dutch border at 0535 hours. In less than five days, and at a cost of only five dead and seven wounded, the operation was completed and the Regiment moved to join in the equally successful invasion of France. The Leibstandarte suffered a further 501 casualties, but by 25 June General von Bock, the commander of Army Group 'B', was able to issue a Daily Order which started with the unbelievable words, 'The war with France is over!' In only forty-four days a victorious Wehrmacht had forced the Dutch, Belgian and French armies to capitulate and the British to leave the Continent. The Leibstandarte had played its full part and two months later, Himmler, on behalf of Hitler, presented it with the 'Banner of the Führer' – its Regimental Colour.

Adolf Hitler again joined his Regiment for its 1940 Christmas celebrations held in the banqueting hall of a mining company in Metz. The Führer addressed the men in the same vein as the previous year:

> What my fate will be, my men of the Leibstandarte, I do not know. But one thing is clear – you will be at the forefront of every endeavour. You who bear my name will have the honour of spearheading the battle.[4]

In April 1941 the Leibstandarte took part in the conquest of the Balkans. In Greece it fought successfully against the British, Australians and New Zealanders and it distinguished itself particularly in actions at the Klidi and Klissura Passes. Casualties were light.

SS Division Leibstandarte SS Adolf Hitler

In May 1941 SS Division LSSAH moved to the Brünn area of Moravia and preparations began for Operation BARBAROSSA – the attack on the Soviet Union. The heady days of quick victories and glory were over and the Leibstandarte was about to enter into the savagery of the Eastern Front.

In the *History of the Leibstandarte Part II*, Rudolf Lehmann says that the troops were surprised by Hitler's speech justifying the attack on Russia. It records the last sentence of the Führer's Daily Orders for 22 June 1941 as follows:

> German soldiers! With this move, you enter into a hard fight, one full of responsibility; the fate of Europe, the future of the German Reich and the existence of our People lie now in your hands. May the Lord God help us all in this hard battle![5]

Some of the officers noted with alarm that it was the 129th anniversary of Napoleon's attack on Russia!

The new 10,000-strong Leibstandarte did not enter the territory of the Soviet Union until 2 July. Then, as part of von Rundstedt's Army Group South, it took part in the desperate fighting to secure the right bank of the Dnieper river and the pursuit of the Soviet Army along the Sea of Azov. By the end of October the Division was almost on its knees – the infantry companies averaged only sixty-six men, about a third of their authorised strength, and the Corps commander reported:

> The LSSAH [has] been overtaxed for weeks . . . clothing is torn; as socks most of them are wearing foot rags torn from Russian uniforms or Russian bandages. Most of the troops are freezing at night. Morale is down, especially because of the optimistic propaganda given out, which contradicts their experience on the battlefield. The capture of Odessa, Kharkov or anywhere else makes no impression at all if you yourself are lying in the mud. . . . The effect of the Russian air force, rocket launchers and tank platoons on the men's morale is enormous, for they know we are in an inferior position in these respects.[6]

Despite these pessimistic reports and the fact that only 15% of the Division's vehicles were still roadworthy, the III Panzer Corps, of which the LAH was now part, secured Rostov on the Don river on 20 November. But the troops were clearly exhausted and their exposed position dangerously vulnerable. The Russian winter, with temperatures dipping below minus 30° Celsius, had come to the rescue of its peoples. The Germans gave up Rostov on the 29th and went on to the defensive, but even then the fighting was as unrelenting and bitter as ever. The biting weather and sheer immensity of the battlefield resulted in a psychological burden for which few of the soldiers were prepared. The commander of the Leibstandarte's Reconnaissance Battalion wrote later:

> I saw Grenadiers lying behind their machine-guns with tears of despair

running down their faces as, with hands flying, they poured full belts of ammunition into the attacking masses. . . . The company commander led his Grenadiers in the counter-attack without his boots. They were cut from his feet shortly before. Both his feet were seriously frost bitten.[7]

The following day the Corps commander, General von Mackensen, wrote to Heinrich Himmler, the Reichsführer-SS, as follows:

I can assure you that the Leibstandarte is held in high regard, not only by the officers but also by its fellow comrades in the Heer [Army]. Every unit wants to have the Leibstandarte as its adjacent unit, both in the attack and in defence. The unit's internal discipline, its refreshing eagerness, its cheerful enthusiasm, its unshakable calmness in crisis no matter how great, and its toughness are examples to us all. . . . This truly is an elite unit. . . . The Leibstandarte has won this boundless admiration on its own by its power and ability. . . . It can never be said that this high respect just fell into its lap because of the halo of fame which surrounds it as our Führer's Guard unit.[8]

On 6 January Hitler sent the following message to Sepp Dietrich:

I send my heartfelt wishes to you and my valiant Leibstandarte. My awarding you Oakleaves [to the Knight's Cross] is the outward expression of my pride in your accomplishments and those of my Leibstandarte.[9]

Hitler's Bodyguard Division had won its spurs. Before the war its men had been nicknamed 'the asphalt soldiers' by their compatriots in the Army. Now their unit had a new and honourable nickname – 'The Führer's Fire Brigade'. The average age of its soldiers was 19.35 years.

In conditions similar to those suffered by the British and French armies in the Crimean War, the Leibstandarte spent another five miserable months in the Taganrog area before it was brought back to western Europe for rest, rebuilding and restructuring as a Panzer-Grenadier Division. It moved to France in July 1942 and reached its new quarters to the west of Paris by taking part in an extraordinary six-hour parade through the centre of the French capital with Field Marshal von Rundstedt taking the salute.

SS Panzer-Grenadier Division LAH

In October the Leibstandarte moved to Normandy – to the area south of Lisieux. There it carried out intensive training – with an emphasis on night operations – and reconnoitred counter-invasion tasks towards the Channel coast.

The Christmas holiday was spent in France – it was to be the last peaceful one in the Leibstandarte's history. This time Hitler was absent from the celebrations. He was at Rastenburg wrestling with the crisis at Stalingrad. The men listened to the reports from that besieged city on the Wehrmacht news service but knew nothing of the impending disaster. Following an order that everyone was to be medically examined for fitness for service in the tropics, they were hoping that the next move might be to Africa – they were unaware that only a month previously Rommel had urged Hitler, unsuccessfully, to abandon North Africa.

On 30 December any hopes of an agreeable deployment were dashed – the Leibstandarte was ordered to make immediate preparations for a move to the Eastern Front. With the siege of Leningrad about to be raised and the catastrophe of Stalingrad imminent, the 'Fire Brigade' was needed to form part of SS General Paul Hausser's SS Panzer Corps in the Kharkov region. In late January 1943 the men loaded on to 200 trains for the twelve-day journey to the front, but before the refreshed and fully reinforced Leibstandarte could assemble in the Ukraine, von Paulus had surrendered the remains of his Sixth Army. The triumphs of the Greater German Reich were over, but as the *History of the Leibstandarte* puts it, 'The troops rolling off towards this campaign knew and suspected nothing of the kind.'

Arriving in snow storms and bitter cold, the Leibstandarte's initial task was to help defend the line of the Donetz river, covering the vital city of Kharkov. In savage fighting Soviet pressure became too great and, rather than risk losing his SS Panzer Corps in another 'Stalingrad' type disaster, Hausser ordered the abandonment of Kharkov on 15 February. Hitler was furious, but the tactics worked and after two weeks of aggressive defence south of the city, the SS Panzer Corps, now comprising the LAH and the SS Das Reich and Totenkopf Divisions, was able to go over to the attack. During the afternoon of 14 March the Greater Germany Radio made the following special report, preceded by the Horst Wessel:

> The OKW [Headquarters of the Wehrmacht] announces that Army Group South . . . joined by units of the Waffen-SS and valiantly supported by the Luftwaffe . . . has succeeded in recapturing the city of Kharkov. . . . The enemy's losses, in both men and material, are incalculable.[10]

The entire centre of the city had been recaptured by the Leibstandarte and in recognition of this Sepp Dietrich was awarded Swords to his Knight's Cross.

Within another three days Belgorod on the Donetz had been secured in a lightning strike by part of the Division and the line of the river re-established. The crisis created by the fall of Stalingrad had been checked – at least temporarily. But the cost to the Leibstandarte in the three months' fighting had been staggering – 167 officers and 4,373 men. This represented 44% of the Division's strength.[11] Mere figures however, give no real idea of the horrors witnessed by those engaged in the fighting. Even hardened soldiers sometimes find it difficult to come to terms with the realities of the battlefield and the commander of the Divisional Reconnaissance Battalion wrote later:

I hear the wailing of the injured and the heart-rending cries of our burned comrade. He lies on the stretcher and begs me to give him the coup de grâce. His hands lie crippled on his charred body. The hairless head, swollen lips and blackened trunk are his only wounds. . . . I'm too ashamed to speak words of comfort. In such a situation, comfort is a barefaced lie. My other comrades watch me keenly. Again and again the boy begs for relief. The doctor holds out no hope, as he scarcely knows where to give the pain killing injection. A helpless shrug is all the doctor can manage. A blood-curdling scream drives me away from the field dressing station. I am unable to make my farewell. I cannot even lay my hand on his brow. One last glance and I rush away. With the departing day our comrade has fought his last battle.[12]

Atrocities

We must now address the question of atrocities – for one of the most serious accusations against the Leibstandarte arose during the battle for Kharkov. Throughout and after the Second World War various Divisions of the Waffen-SS were accused of violations of the Geneva Convention and the generally accepted Rules of War. The Leibstandarte in particular was accused of killing fifty civilians, including many Jews, in the 1939 Polish campaign, some eighty British soldiers near Dunkirk in June 1940 and then, in the battle for Kharkov, of setting fire to a building containing 300 wounded Soviet soldiers in one incident and shooting some 400 wounded officers in their hospital beds in another. After the war over 100 members of the I SS Panzer Corps were accused of killing civilians in northern Italy in 1943, Canadian troops in Normandy in 1944, and Belgian civilians and American soldiers in the Ardennes during the 'Battle of the Bulge'. Many were found guilty.

On the other side of the coin, the *History of the Leibstandarte* features a photograph[13] taken in July 1941, showing the graves of a whole bicycle company which it says was 'bestially murdered' near Olyka, and it goes on to quote a number of instances when it says its soldiers suffered appalling treatment at the hands of their enemies. One horrifying occasion is described by a member of the 1st SS Panzer-Grenadier Regiment LAH after the capture of Kharkov:

> The bodies of our comrades killed in the fighting to recapture Kharkov and those whose graves were opened by the Russians after we had abandoned the city the first time were assembled in the central park. . . . There greeted us a terrifying picture, the likes of which I had never seen nor later came to see. All the men were naked and most of the bodies had been mutilated. Many of them, and indeed all of the comrades from our company, had not only been beaten and choked, but their limbs severed and their eyes gouged out, such that it was hard to identify them. . . . From that moment on, the fear of being taken prisoner by the Russians haunted us like a ghost.[14]

The whole subject of prisoners of war and civilians in war zones being killed and mutilated has been argued endlessly in the post-war years and it is abundantly clear that war crimes and atrocities were not, and probably never will be, restricted to one side only.

It only remains to be said that there can be no excuse or mercy for the soldiers of any nation who kill or mutilate civilians or prisoners of war, and those who do should always be brought to justice.

Birth Pains

In view of the severely weakened state of the Division in March 1943, the LAH was ordered to move to a so-called 'rest' area to the west of Kharkov. A batch of 600 reinforcements arrived the same day. Whilst the following three-month period was used for limited leave (Hitler lifted the ban on home leave on 19 March following the recapture of Kharkov) and for rest and reorganisation, Dietrich immediately ordered two five-week retraining programmes. But something far more serious and significant was to happen in this same period; when Dietrich returned from Berlin, where he had received his Swords from Hitler on 21 March, he announced the formation of the I SS Panzer Corps Headquarters, which he was to command, and a new 'Hitlerjugend' Division. As already mentioned, many of the personnel for these units were to come from the Leibstandarte. Dietrich was not to hand over command of his beloved 'boys', as he called them, until 4 June, but between the end of March and the end of June, twelve officers, including five SS lieutenant colonels, were removed from the Divisional staff and posted to the new Corps Headquarters[15]. Moreover, the removal of the commanders of both the Division's Panzer-Grenadier Regiments, the commander and entire 1st SS Panzer Battalion, the commander and one of the companies of the Reconnaissance Battalion, a company commander from the Sturmgeschütz (assault gun) Battalion, the Regimental Commander and an entire Battalion from the Artillery Regiment, the Battalion Commander and a battery commander from the Flak Battalion and company commanders from the signals and supply units caused, needless to say, a major crisis. The crisis was then compounded by the arrival of 2,500 Luftwaffe reinforcements and a number of non-volunteers from Waffen-SS replacement units. In any other Western army a Division in this state would have been withdrawn from active duty and rebuilt in the peace and quiet of its home base – not so in the case of the Leibstandarte. On 26 June the second retraining period was interrupted by an order to move. The Division was about to participate in the greatest armoured battle of the war – Kursk.

The German aims in Operation ZITADELLE were to cut off the Soviet salient at Kursk, destroy the forces within it, establish a shorter defensive line and deny the enemy the capability of launching a decisive offensive for the rest of the year. If successful, it was envisaged that more than enough forces would become available to repulse the expected Allied invasion of Europe. In reality it had little chance of success – the Soviets had already established a sophisticated, anti-armour defensive position in great depth, backed by a massive strategic reserve; against it the attacking Panzer divisions would inevitably blunt themselves. Blitzkrieg, in the situation pertaining at Kursk, was an inappropriate tactic.

After numerous delays the German attack was launched on 5 July. The Leibstandarte entered the battle with only one of its two authorised Panzer Battalions. The Division's 114 remaining tanks had been combined in a single unit and the personnel of the other Battalion sent home to help form the SS Panzer Regiment of the new Hitlerjugend Division.

Hitler exhorted his army for the forthcoming battle with the prophetic words:

Soldiers! Today you set out to a great onslaught, the outcome of which could well decide the war. Your victory must serve to convince the world more than ever that any resistance to the German Wehrmacht is fruitless. . . . As a soldier myself, I know exactly what I am asking of you. Despite that, we must fight our way to victory, no matter how bitter and difficult it is in the thick of battle.[16]

Hitler suspended Operation ZITADELLE on 13 July. In the eight days' fighting the Leibstandarte lost 2,753 men, including 474 killed, and sixty tanks. The II SS Panzer Corps, of which the Division was a part, claimed

7,000 Soviet prisoners and 1,167 tanks destroyed.[17] The Russians could afford their losses, the Germans could not.

On 27 July the Division was told to hand over its tanks to the Das Reich and Totenkopf Divisions and prepare for an immediate move by train. The destination turned out to be Innsbruck. Hitler's decision to call off the Kursk offensive is said to have been influenced by the Allied invasion of Sicily and his worry about the southern flank. Accordingly, when the new Divisional commander, Teddy Wisch, reported to Sepp Dietrich in Berlin on 30 July, he was told that the Leibstandarte was to be transferred to Italy. There, following the collapse of Mussolini's fascist dictatorship, it spent the first part of August disarming the Italian army in the Po river valley, and then participating in the defence of northern Italy and Croatia.

No one expected the premier Division of the Waffen-SS to be left in the relatively peaceful and pleasant conditions of Italy for long, and on 20 October the order came for it to return to the Eastern Front. By then the Soviet offensive which had followed the successful defensive operation at Kursk had pushed the Germans back across the Dneiper and caused a major crisis for them in the Ukraine. On 3 November the Russians attacked on both flanks of Kiev with thirty infantry divisions, twenty-four tank brigades and ten motorized infantry brigades.[18] Three days later the city fell, and on 13 November, long before the Leibstandarte under its new name '1st SS Panzer Division Leibstandarte SS Adolf Hitler' could be fully deployed, Russian tanks were in Zhitomir, 100km to its west.

1st SS Panzer Division LAH

The move to the Ukraine took several days and was chaotic. Some elements of the Division did not arrive until 14 November and part of the Panzer Regiment did not receive its new tanks until it arrived in the actual combat zone.[19] Even worse, several companies had to fight their way out of the detraining stations. One SS Panzer-Grenadier reported his experience as follows:

> Our detraining at the Popielnia station, together with the 7th Company, was severely complicated by the presence of four T-34s [Russian tanks] stationed in the vicinity. . . . The Company established an all round defence at the railway station. . . . Shortly after noon our Company commander realised that we could no longer hold that position. . . . Two boys from our reserve troop had knocked off two tanks with magnetic anti-tank hollow charges. When we investigated the crippled tanks, we discovered that there were women in the crews. . . . Disengaging from the enemy ran fairly smoothly but those Russian tanks

which were fit for combat immediately pursued us. . . . Five T-34s
with about fifty Russian infantrymen sitting on them came charging
towards us. There was an exchange of fire and I heard a Russian
commissar shout, 'Don't shoot, SS! There are women and bread waiting
for you in Stalingrad!' The Russian tanks . . . divided into two groups
. . . and then advanced on our column from the rear. . . . With that
we were hopelessly surrounded. Some of our men surrendered at
once and I saw [three senior sergeants] shoot themselves with their
pistols. . . . I took cover in a potato field. . . . Night was falling. I heard
the drunken hollering of the Russians and some pistol shots afterwards.
I learned later that they were shooting my comrades in the back of the
neck.[20]

In the following weeks the LAH took part in many desperate actions to
stem the Soviet advance, and by 28 February 1944 it had been reduced
to little more than a Kampfgruppe (Battlegroup), with only three tanks
and four armoured assault guns still operational.[21]

Two weeks later, after retreating into Galicia, the Division as such had
ceased to exist – its combat strength was forty-one officers and 1,188
NCOs and men.[22] Field Marshal von Manstein wrote:

Our forces had finally reached the point of exhaustion. The German
divisions . . . were literally burnt out. . . . The fighting had eaten away
at the very core of the fighting units. How could we wage effective
counter-attacks, for example, when an entire Panzerkorps had only
twenty-four Panzers ready for battle?[23]

On 18 April the pathetic remnants of the 1st SS Panzer Division LAH
left the Eastern Front and moved into the former billets of its sister
Division, the Hitlerjugend, at Beverloo in Belgium. Its few remaining
veterans would once more become the nucleus around which a new
Leibstandarte would have to be built.

The immediate tasks were, of course, the reception of new equipment
and the training of new soldiers. The former was made easier by a Führer
Order dated 3 May which required the requisition of weapons for his
Leibstandarte Division, but even this high priority could not produce
new tanks and other important equipment until the second half of
the month. Much of it came directly from the factory. Even then a
desperate shortage of fuel, unsuitable terrain and the serious need for
security against the activities of the Belgian 'White Army' (partisans),
made driver training virtually impossible and other types of training
extremely difficult.

The training of the new men, 'Young Marchers' as they were called by the 'Old Hares' (experienced men), was intensive. Many of the 18-year-olds came from the Leibstandarte Replacement Battalion, via the Hitlerjugend Division's training camp at Beverloo and, since the Hitlerjugend Division was over-strength in total manpower, thirteen officers and 2,042 young Grenadiers were transferred from it to the Leibstandarte during May.

While senior officers attended map and signals exercises, carried out 'tactical exercises without troops' and played war games, the young recruits worked hard for the honour of wearing SS runes. They idolised their superiors whose exploits they had heard about from the day they joined the Waffen-SS. But draftees from disbanded Luftwaffe units and the Navy naturally took longer to become effective parts of the machine and many were destined to learn the art of war the hard way – in the battle of Normandy. The 1st SS Panzer Division, despite being at more or less full strength when it was ordered to help defeat the Allied landings in Normandy, would in other armies have been considered unfit for operations. Over half its men had been with the Division for less than a month and the major equipments they would use had, in most cases, been in their hands for an even shorter period – indeed, when the Division started its move on 9 June, some important sub units were ineffective and had to be left behind. Training at any level above that of company had been impossible. The 1st SS Panzer Division of June 1944 was only a shadow of the LAH which had fought the Soviets in the previous winter campaign and it would have to rely more than ever on its battle-hardened officers and NCOs, the majority of whom had already been on active service for nearly five years.

NOTES

1. Lehmann, *The Leibstandarte* I, p. 125.
2. Ibid., p. 1.
3. Lehmann, *The Leibstandarte* II, p. 186.
4. Lehmann, *The Leibstandarte* I, p. 181.
5. Lehmann, *The Leibstandarte* II, p. 7.
6. Ibid., p. 152.
7. Meyer, Kurt, *Grenadiers*, pp. 83–4.
8. Lehmann, *The Leibstandarte* II, p. 199.
9. Ibid., p. 200.
10. Lehmann, *The Leibstandarte* III, p. 175.
11. Ibid., p. 194.
12. Meyer, Kurt, op. cit., p. 54.
13. Lehmann, *Die Leibstandarte im Bild*, p. 123.
14. Lehmann, *The Leibstandarte* III, p. 184.
15. Ibid., p. 194.
16. Ibid., p. 205.
17. Ibid., pp. 247–9.

18. Ibid., p. 307.
19. Ibid., p. 306.
20. Ibid., pp. 309–10.
21. Lehmann & Tiemann, *The Leibstandarte* IV/I, p. 51.
22. Ibid., p. 75.
23. Manstein, *Verlorene Siege*, p. 601.

CHAPTER II

SS Division Hitlerjugend: June 1943 – June 1944

(Map 2)

Hitler ordered the formation of the Hitlerjugend Division following representations by Himmler, who wished to increase the number of SS troops, and in view of the urgent need to create more divisions for the Army as a whole. A Führer Order dated 24 June 1943 said that an SS Panzer-Grenadier Division Hitlerjugend was to be raised at the troop training area Beverloo, south-east of Antwerp, and gave the date of formation as 1 June 1943. This title was amended on 30 October to '12th SS Panzer Division Hitlerjugend'.

The new Division was unique in that it was formed, in the main, from Hitler Youths born in the first half of the year 1926 – this means that the youngest of the 10,000 young men who reported to Lichterfelde Kaserne in Berlin in July 1943 should have been at least 17 years old, and they should all have been over 18 by the time they fought in Normandy a year later. This is an important point because it has become a post-war myth that some members of 12th SS were little more than children. A captured nominal role of the 1st SS Panzer-Grenadier Battalion of the 25th Regiment HJ serving in Normandy in July 1944 shows that 65% of its personnel were 18, 17% 19 and the remainder over 20.[1] Nevertheless, the fact that the HJ Division was *based* on 18-year-olds makes it unique in the Second World War.

In the eyes of Hitler and Himmler the new Division was to be a symbol of the willingness of German youth to sacrifice itself to the achievement of final victory. It was therefore essential that all the new recruits were volunteers. But the idea of sacrifice was not new to members of the Hitler Youth movement – the slogan 'We are born to die for Germany' was to be seen above the entrance to every Hitler Youth training camp! And the notion that war was ennobling and spiritually renewing was an essential ingredient of National Socialist philosophy.

The need for volunteer candidates for the new Division created some

15

initial problems because in many cases parents, teachers and industrialists were reluctant to see young men go off to war before they had finished their education and apprenticeships; this meant the timetable for the establishment of the Division could not be met.

Potential recruits had to be a minimum height of 1.70m for infantry units and 1.68m for Panzer, signals and reconnaissance units, provided they already had special skills. Despite these difficulties and restrictions the HJ Division was 5,718 soldiers over-strength by early April 1944. There was, however, still a desperate shortage of officers and NCOs – over 2,000, and this led to more than fifty officers being transferred in from the Army.

From 1942 onwards all Hitler Youths received 160 hours' simple military training, which included small bore shooting and fieldcraft; this provided them with a reasonable foundation for the full military training they were to receive in Belgium and France, but it differed little from that carried out in the cadet corps of most British public schools at that time. Where their training did differ markedly was in motivation – the Germans were highly indoctrinated in Nazi thinking and its ethnic philosophies. Racialism, German supremacy and the concept of total obedience and loyalty to the Führer were essential ingredients in their upbringing.

The training priorities laid down for the new Division were markedly different from those pertaining in Army training establishments. They were: physical fitness, character training and weapons training – in that order. But since initially there were not nearly enough Waffen-SS camouflaged uniforms to go round, many of the youngsters found themselves doing their training in home clothes or Hitler Youth uniform. Smoking and drinking alcohol was forbidden, as was visiting brothels – in fact any relationship with girls was prohibited for those under 18; though it is interesting to note that the only soldiers in Normandy *not* to have short hair were those of the Hitlerjugend.

A detailed description of the methods used in training the young recruits of the Hitlerjugend Division was given by one of the Regimental commanders:

As the youngsters were still developing, the principles and forms of education had to be somewhat different from those which a unit used to train and educate older recruits. Many established principles of military training were replaced with new ones which, when all is said and done, had their origin in the German youth movement which came into being at the turn of the century [and continued after Hitler came to power with amendments to accommodate Nazi thinking].

There was no dominant superior relationship recognising only orders and unconditional obedience. The relationship between officers, NCOs and other ranks was that between older experienced and younger comrades. The officers' authority existed in the fact that they were the champions and close friends of the young soldiers. They strove for the close relationship of the parental home so far as was possible in the circumstances of war.

The boys were educated to a sense of responsibility, a sense of community, a willingness to make sacrifices, decisiveness, self control, camaraderie, and perception. The leadership of the division was of the conviction that the boys would achieve more if they recognised and approved of the sense of their prospective employment and activity. It was therefore natural practice to develop all orders consistently out of a detailed assessment of the situation. During their training square bashing was frowned upon. March-pasts and similar exercises were not practised. Everything focused on training for battle and this took place under the most realistic battle conditions possible. Physical toughening was achieved through sport; route marches were disapproved of as being unnecessary and harmful. . . . Marksmanship . . . took place exclusively in the countryside. Target exercises in barracks ceased completely. . . . Emphasis was laid on camouflage both in the visual and audible sense, on the masking of radio transmissions, on secrecy and on close combat training by day and night with live ammunition.[2]

The build-up of 12th SS was also plagued by shortages of equipment, fuel and ammunition. At the beginning of January 1944 it had only forty tanks and a third of the armoured personnel carriers (SPWs) and reconnaissance vehicles needed for an SS Panzer division, while many of its trucks were worn out, captured Italian vehicles.

One aspect of motivation which was probably unique was that Panzer crews and officers worked between eight and fourteen days in the MAN tank production factory in Nürnberg.[3]

On 1 April 1944 the 12th SS Panzer Division Hitlerjugend began its move to Normandy where it continued its training; however, due to the Allied air threat, this took place mainly at night. On 1 June 1944 the Divisional commander was able to report 'The Division is ready for offensive actions'[4]; this was despite the fact that the Panzerjäger (tank hunter) Battalion had no Jagdpanzer IVs and the Werfer (mortar) Battalion no tractors. The Division was spread across a large area of Normandy stretching from Louviers, near the Seine, and Dreux in the east, to Vimoutiers in the west.

NOTES

1. First Canadian Army Intelligence Summary No. 46, dated 14 Aug 44.
2. Meyer, Kurt, *Grenadiers*, pp. 115–6.

17

3. Meyer, Hubert, *The History of the 12th SS Panzer Division Hitlerjugend*, p. 7.
4. Ibid., p. 9.

CHAPTER III
I SS Panzer Corps:
6 June – 12 September 1944

Personalities

Despite the carnage of the Eastern Front, the I SS Panzer Corps of June 1944 still contained some of the most famous officers of the Waffen-SS. Its commander, Sepp Dietrich, although contemptuously called 'the Sergeant-Major' by his Wehrmacht colleagues, was greatly admired by his men. His short and broad stature, large, wide nose, rich Bavarian accent and crude sense of humour did not bother them; nor did the fact that his vocabulary, which often shocked the sensibilities of some of his better educated and class conscious superiors, was rich in words more frequently heard in beer cellars and barrack rooms. All that mattered to them was that he had proved himself repeatedly as a Divisional commander. Since the war Dietrich's military ability has been much criticised, usually due to oft-repeated remarks like those of von Rundstedt who called him 'decent but stupid'[1] and Bittrich who recalled, 'I once spent an hour and a half trying to explain a situation to Sepp Dietrich with the aid of a map. It was quite useless. He understood nothing at all.'[2] However, Max Wünsche, a distinguished senior officer in the LAH, who was close to Dietrich in France in 1940 and his adjutant in the 1941 Greek campaign, said of him:

If our men had not been motivated and if Sepp Dietrich had not been at the right places at the right times during the decisive phases, with his orders and decisions, the campaign would have gone a different way.[3]

Rudolf Lehmann, one of Dietrich's principal staff officers from early 1941, wrote of him:

To be sure our old commander (whom we called Obersepp among ourselves) was no strategic genius. But he was a first-class leader of soldiers and of men. As commanding general . . . he would not be using this gift, and knowing that caused him pain. His forte did not lie in formulating a complete tactical evaluation. But he had an extraordinary sense of a growing crisis and for finding the favourable moment for action. His rare and brief speeches to his men contained no flashes of brilliance, but were palpably heartfelt. And the men took them to heart. His brilliance was in his amazing presence. Anyone who experienced it can only recall with wonder and admiration how he, in the darkest night of a crisis, with everything pushing us back, would face the waves of retreating men, his collar pulled up, his hands shoved in his pockets up to the elbows. Uttering sounds incomprehensible, but full of recognisable rage, he could not only bring the men to stop, but even to turn around and head back in. Unforgettable too, was his warning to unit leaders of any rank as they set off to battle: 'Bring my boys back!'[4]

Hitler called Dietrich 'cunning, energetic and brutal', but went on to say, 'For the German people Sepp Dietrich is a national institution.'[5] He was certainly that to his men and it is not without significance that the badge of the Leibstandarte, later to be incorporated into that of both the Hitlerjugend Division and I SS Panzer Corps, was a skeleton key – 'Dietrich' is German for skeleton key.

Dietrich had selected Army Colonel Fritz Kraemer as his Chief of Staff. Kraemer had graduated from the Berlin War Academy in 1934, served on the staff of a Panzer Division until the end of 1942 and had then become the senior administrative officer of I Panzer Corps. He was an ideal choice, although this selection would lead him to stand trial alongside Dietrich in 1946, charged with war crimes.

Turning now to the two Divisions of the Corps – Dietrich's successor as commander of the 1st SS Panzer Division was SS Brigadier Teddy Wisch, one of the original 117-man SS-Stabswache Berlin. He served in every Honour Guard during the years 1934–9, commanded a company in the Polish campaign, was an SS Brigadier and a Panzer-Grenadier Regimental commander in Russia at the age of 35 and had already been awarded the Iron Cross 1st and 2nd Class, Knight's Cross with Oakleaves and the German Cross in Gold.

SS Major General Fritz Witt, the commander of the Hitlerjugend Division, had also been one of the original 117 members of the SS-Stabswache Berlin of 1933. Born in Höhenlimburg in May 1908, he had been awarded an early Knight's Cross for bravery during the French campaign in 1940. He was the first commander of 1st SS Panzer-Grenadier Regiment LAH and added Oakleaves to his Knight's Cross for service in Russia in 1943.

The commander of 1st SS Panzer Regiment LAH, Jochen Peiper, has been called the 'Siegfried' of the Waffen-SS. Apart from a short period during the campaign in France in 1940, during which he won the Iron Cross both 1st and 2nd Class, Peiper was an Adjutant to Heinrich Himmler from April 1938 to July 1941. He rejoined the Leibstandarte in Russia, where he won the Knight's Cross with Oakleaves, German Cross in Gold, and even the Close Combat Badge in Silver. This meant he had been in close combat a minimum of thirty times. Peiper's men idolised him. He was 29.

Max Wünsche, the commander of the 12th SS Panzer Regiment HJ, had been a pre-war Adjutant to Adolf Hitler. Handsome, blue-eyed and fair-haired, Wünsche was everyone's idea of a typical SS officer. He had been commissioned into the LSSAH, along with Jochen Peiper, in April 1936 and soon won recognition on the battlefield. He was wounded and won two Iron Crosses in France in 1940; later he was awarded the German Cross in Gold and the Knight's Cross for his actions in Russia. He was another outstanding leader.

SS Major Max Hansen had been wounded eight times before D-Day! He had joined the Leibstandarte in 1934 and was one of the first training officers at the Jüterbog Training Depot. He never left the LAH, fought in every one of its campaigns – earning the Knight's Cross and Oakleaves in the process – and rose to command the 1st SS Panzer-Grenadier Regiment. Rudolf Sandig, the commander of the 2nd SS Panzer-Grenadier Regiment LAH in June 1944, had also been at the Jüterbog Training Depot in the early days; he was one of the twelve 'Lances', as the sergeant-majors there were known. Another Knight's Cross holder, he was renowned as a hard and unsympathetic trainer.

The commanders of the two SS Panzer-Grenadier Regiments of the Hitlerjugend Division were Kurt Meyer and Wilhelm Mohnke. Kurt 'Panzermeyer' was the commander of the 25th SS Panzer-Grenadier Regiment and became one of the best known Waffen-SS officers. The illegitimate son of a labourer and First World War sergeant-major, Meyer became a policeman before being accepted into the Leibstandarte in May 1934. Being only 1.75m in height and having to wear a raised orthopedic left shoe as a result of a serious leg injury, he was fortunate to be allowed to join, but his enthusiasm and police experience and rank were deciding factors. Meyer 'won his spurs' in Greece in 1941 as the commander of the LAH's Reconnaissance Detachment and was awarded the Knight's Cross. This was followed in 1943 by Oakleaves for his bravery in Russia. A natural and brilliant soldier, Meyer was destined to become Nazi Germany's youngest general at the age of 34 and to be branded a war criminal in 1945.

Wilhelm Mohnke, the commander of the 26th SS Panzer-Grenadier Regiment HJ, was another original member of the 1933 Bodyguard and mounted the first Chancellery Guard in April that year. He took command of an SS infantry Battalion in France in 1940 when his commanding officer was wounded, and it was during this period that his name became linked with a war crime against British soldiers at Wormhoudt. Mohnke lost a foot during an air attack in Yugoslavia in 1941 and was forced to leave combatant duty. Nevertheless, in February 1942 he played an important part in forming, and then became the first commander of the LAH's embryonic Panzer Battalion. However, according to Ralf Tiemann, his Adjutant at that time and the author of *The Chronicle of the 7th Panzer Company 1st SS Panzer Division Leibstandarte*, Mohnke was removed from this appointment after furious arguments with the Chief of the SS Leadership Head Office in Berlin over equipment shortages and was sent to the psychiatric ward of the Würzburg Military Hospital. It was said that his wounds had caused him to lose control of himself! His recovery must have been very swift though, because a month later he was given command of the LAH Replacement Battalion in Berlin. Then in 1943, with the formation of the Hitlerjugend Division, Mohnke saw his chance to return to operational service and was given command of one of its Regiments. He was the only senior commander in the LAH and HJ who did not already wear the Knight's Cross.

Gustav Knittel, the commanding officer of the Leibstandarte's Reconnaissance Battalion with a Knight's Cross earned in Russia, had been wounded four times by June 1944. The commander of the Hitlerjugend Reconnaissance Battalion was SS Major Gerhard Bremer; he had been in the same Battalion in France in 1940 as Kurt Meyer, Jochen Peiper, Max Wünsche and Max Hansen. When he was awarded the Knight's Cross in 1941 he was one of the youngest officers in the Regiment to wear this coveted medal. He went on to fight in all the LAH's campaigns in Russia before being transferred to the HJ in 1943. It is of interest that after the war Army General Heinz Eberbach, who knew the Hitlerjugend Division well, described Witt, Meyer and Wünsche as Waffen-SS idealists, but Mohnke and Bremer as bullies and brawlers.

Other holders of the prized Knight's Cross were Herbert Kuhlmann, commanding the 1st SS Panzer Battalion LAH, and Michael Wittmann who was the Waffen-SS's greatest Panzer ace. After joining the Leibstandarte in 1937, he commanded an armoured car in Poland and France as a sergeant and went on to earn the Iron Cross 2nd Class in Greece. Wittmann was wounded twice and won the Iron Cross 1st Class in Russia in 1941, before being commissioned in December 1942. After only a year as a tank commander he was credited with sixty-six tank 'kills' and had been awarded the Knight's Cross. On Hitler's birthday in 1944 Wittmann was promoted to the rank of SS Lieutenant and ten days later he received Oakleaves to his Knight's Cross. In April 1944 he was given command of the 2nd SS Panzer Company in the 101st SS Heavy Panzer Battalion. By then he and his gunner, Bobby Woll, had been credited with an astonishing 119 enemy armoured fighting vehicles destroyed.

Although, as we shall hear, Normandy took a heavy toll amongst the leaders of I SS Panzer Corps, many of them survived to play leading roles in our story.

The First Campaign
(Maps 2 & 3)

Sepp Dietrich established the Headquarters of I SS Panzer Corps in the Lichterfelde Barracks in Berlin on 26 July 1943[6]; but at that time the LAH was still fighting in the Ukraine, the young soldiers of HJ were only just beginning their training and the other nominated combat elements of the Corps – the 101st SS Heavy Panzer, 101st SS Heavy Artillery, 101st SS Flak and 101st SS Werfer Battalions – had still to be formed.

Nearly a year later, on the eve of the Allied invasion of western Europe in June 1944, Dietrich's Corps was still not an entity. The Hitlerjugend was located in Normandy, to the west of the Seine but nowhere near the invasion beaches, and the Leibstandarte was nearly 400km away, scattered across a wide area of Belgium. This dispersion was due to uncertainty in the minds of Hitler, the OKW and the senior field commanders as to where the invasion would come and how to deal with it when it did. As a consequence the Corps was not involved in the D-Day fighting and was committed to battle piecemeal. Nevertheless, as described in *Steel Inferno – I SS Panzer Corps in Normandy*, parts of it participated in almost every significant action in the campaign from 7 June until the escape from the Falaise Pocket in late August, including the Mortain counter-attack, and the Corps proved to be a – if not *the* – major impediment to the Allied advance.

How was I SS Panzer Corps, with one Division which would have been considered unfit for operations in other armies, and another made up from untried soldiers who were little more than boys, able to perform so dramatically and effectively in Normandy – particularly since it was operating without air support? Without going into too much detail, four factors are significant – tactics, morale, leadership and equipment.

In terms of tactics and communications the Germans were far in advance of the Western Allies. Whereas cooperation on the battlefield between Allied tanks and infantry was still in its infancy and in many cases their infantrymen had no way of talking to the tanks they could see just a few metres away, the Germans had developed a tactical philosophy which stressed the need for close cooperation between tanks, infantry, artillery and engineers, all linked by radio and capable of regrouping whenever necessary to meet a changed situation. This emphasis on flexibility, coupled with an insistence on radio orders and a training system which stressed innovative thinking, produced a very formidable fighting machine.

Turning to morale and leadership, there is no doubt that the men of I SS Panzer Corps still had implicit faith in their Führer and a strong, indeed unshakeable, belief that the war could and would be won. Additionally, the close relationship between the officers, NCOs and soldiers of the Waffen-SS Divisions was a major factor in their fighting ability. This relationship stemmed from both professional competence and the continual sharing of danger and hardship which the Germans had endured throughout the campaigns in Russia. Allied experiences in North Africa and the early months in Italy were simply not comparable, and whereas one often encounters criticism of officers by Allied soldiers, this is something rare amongst their German counterparts. The presence of senior officers, even at four star level, in the forward battle areas, also gave rise to great confidence amongst the junior leaders and young soldiers of I SS Panzer Corps.

With regard to equipment, it is clear that in all classes except aircraft, the Germans enjoyed clear advantages. This was particularly true in the case of tanks. The German Mk IVs and Panthers mounted high velocity 75mm guns and were superior to nearly all the Allied tanks they met in Normandy – the latter were fitted with low velocity guns. The Tiger I, with which I SS Panzer Corps' 101st SS Heavy Panzer Battalion was equipped, weighed a massive fifty-seven tons and mounted the famous 88mm gun. Despite its slow maximum speed and turret traverse, the Tiger had by 1944 already earned the awesome reputation which the German propaganda machine had intended for it.

It is a fact that all Allied tanks could be knocked out by any German tank at any range out to 1000m and often more, whilst it took a lucky hit on the tracks, optics or gun for Allied gunners to disable a German tank; in most cases the Tiger was invulnerable, even at very short ranges, to anything other than a British Firefly (Sherman mounting a 17 pdr) or rocket-firing aircraft.

German self-propelled anti-tank guns were clearly superior to the Allied M-10s and M-36s with their 3-inch and 90mm guns. The vast majority of the Allied anti-tank guns, or Tank Destroyers (TDs) as the Americans called them, were towed. German infantry were equipped with Panzerfausts which could penetrate 200mm of armour. The US equivalent, the 2.36-inch bazooka, could not pierce the frontal armour of any German tank and the British PIAT (Projector Infantry Anti-Tank), although effective up to 100m, was heavy, cumbersome and difficult to fire.

There was little to choose between the Germans and Western Allies in terms of close support and medium artillery, although the Germans had relatively more self propelled guns. However, the German very high velocity 88mm anti-aircraft (AA) gun was used most effectively as a conventional artillery piece and, in particular, as an anti-tank weapon, and their 100mm Kanone had a range of nearly 25km. And in one field they had a unique and terrifying monopoly – multi-barrelled rocket projectors, known as Nebelwerfers. They came in three sizes – 150mm, 210mm and 300mm, firing out to 7500m, 9000m and 5500m respectively.

The SS Panzer-Grenadiers of I SS Panzer Corps were armed with highly effective machine guns, with rates of fire which completely out-classed anything used by the Allies.

In summary it can be said that the members of I SS Panzer Corps had great confidence in their weapons. The same cannot be said for the Allied soldiers they met in Normandy.

The Cost of Normandy

It is no exaggeration to say that without the participation of I SS Panzer Corps in the German defence of Normandy, Montgomery's Armies would have reached the Seine long before D+90. The Hitlerjugend's brilliant actions in the first days of the invasion prevented the early fall of Caen, Michael Wittmann's amazing performance at Villers-Bocage thwarted the early British attempt to outflank the German defence in the same area, and both Divisions of the Corps halted Montgomery's subsequent attempts to outflank Caen in Operations EPSOM and WINDSOR. In the same way the LAH and HJ played major roles in bringing the huge armoured assault, known as Operation GOODWOOD, to a costly halt; and finally, the exemplary delaying actions fought by the LAH and the HJ south-east of Caen between 20 July and 18 August did much to frustrate Allied plans. But the cost had been appalling.

Almost every book written about the Normandy campaign reports that the Leibstandarte had only 'weak infantry elements', and the Hitlerjugend only 300 men after their withdrawal from the Falaise Pocket. These statements are usually based on a Fifth Panzer Army report to Army Group 'B' dated 21 August. But as Hubert Meyer says in his *History of the 12th SS Panzer Division Hitlerjugend*:

> Based on that information, mistaken conclusions regarding the losses in the Falaise encirclement have been drawn. It is completely useless as a basis for such considerations.[7]

Meyer concludes that the Fifth Army figures must refer to those units which had broken out of the Falaise Pocket and were ready for combat. This author agrees. On 22 August the Hitlerjugend numbered approximately 12,500 officers and men, 60% of its authorised strength, of which 2,500 were in the administrative units.[8] Hubert Meyer gives an exact casualty figure of 948 for the overall period of the Falaise Pocket – 15 to

22 August.[9] No comparable figures are available for the Leibstandarte. Nevertheless, it is certain that by 23 August both Divisions were virtually without tanks, Jagdpanzers, assault and AA guns, SPWs (armoured half-tracks) and artillery pieces and had ceased to exist as fighting formations.

And what of the leaders of I SS Panzer Corps? By the end of the campaign Sepp Dietrich was the acting commander of the Fifth Panzer Army – he had taken over after General Heinrich Eberbach had moved to command Panzer Group West on 9 August.

Teddy Wisch, commander of the Leibstandarte, after being wounded in both legs by shell fire on 18 August, was brought out of the Falaise Pocket along what became known as 'The Corridor of Death', in his artillery commander's SPW. He would not fight again. Fritz Witt, commander of the Hitlerjugend, was killed by naval gunfire only seven days after D-Day.

Jochen Peiper, commander of the 1st SS Panzer Regiment, was probably wounded, and certainly disabled, during the fighting against the Canadians south of Caen on 2 August, and two of his Panzer company commanders were killed – one during GOODWOOD and the other during the breakout from the Pocket. Herbert Kuhlmann, commander of the LAH Panther Battalion was also wounded during the breakout, but both he and Peiper would be back within three months to command the Corps' two Panzer Regiments in the Ardennes.

One Panzer Battalion and two Panzer company commanders in the 12th SS Panzer Regiment were killed during the Normandy fighting and the Regimental commander, Max Wünsche, was captured by Canadian soldiers on 24 August as he slept under some bushes waiting for darkness to make his escape.

Albert Frey, commander of the LAH's 1st SS Panzer-Grenadier Regiment, was badly wounded by artillery fire on 20 July; before that, Max Hansen, one of his Battalion commanders, had been wounded for a ninth time during a counter-attack. In Rudolf Sandig's Regiment, the commanders of both the 1st and 2nd SS Panzer-Grenadier Battalions were killed in July. And Hans Scappini, the commander of Kurt Meyer's 2nd SS Panzer-Grenadier Battalion HJ, had his head taken off by a tank shell on the Division's first day in action. Thirteen LAH and HJ Panzer-Grenadier company commanders were killed in Normandy.

The commander of the LAH's StuG Battalion, Heinrich Heimann, was killed in unknown circumstances during the breakout from the Falaise Pocket and his opposite number in the HJ captured; the commanding officer of the HJ Signals Battalion was also killed on 20 August.

And finally, Normandy saw the death of WWII's greatest Panzer ace. Michael Wittmann and the crew of his Tiger I were amongst those listed as 'missing' on 8 August. It was nearly forty years before his remains, and those of his driver, were found near the Caen-Falaise road and identified from dental records.

The overall casualty rate amongst the senior commanders in I SS Panzer Corps (combat Battalion commanders and above) between 7 June and 21 August was more than 53%.

Retreat to the West Wall
(Maps 2, 4 & 5)

Immediately following the disaster of the Falaise Pocket, the German commanders in northern France faced another crisis – how to prevent a further encirclement and the destruction of more than 150,000 troops between the Dives and Seine rivers. Field Marshal Walter Model had taken over as CinC West on 18 August and Sepp Dietrich, it will be recalled, had been made the temporary commander of Fifth Panzer Army. General Heinrich Eberbach had taken over the Seventh Army after SS General Paul Hausser was badly wounded during the breakout from the Pocket.

I SS Panzer Corps existed in name only. Fritz Kraemer, its Chief of Staff, was still running the Corps Headquarters, but neither the 1st nor 12th SS Panzer Divisions existed as coherent entities and the 101st SS Panzer Battalion had long since been destroyed.

In order to achieve the Allied aim of destroying the German forces west of the Seine, General Omar Bradley's 12th US Army Group, which had already reached the line Dreux-Chartres-Orléans by 16 August, was ordered to attack north-east, whilst the British 21st Army Group on its left was to advance as rapidly as possible towards Rouen.

On 18 August, in fulfilment of this directive, an American Division moved on Mantes, which had been left unguarded when the German troops guarding the Seine crossings in that sector had been sent, on Hitler's orders, to cover the direct approach to Paris. It reached the river on the 19th and established a bridgehead the following day – at the very time the men of the LAH and HJ were struggling to cross the Dives river 120km to the west! A second crossing was seized by the Americans 50km south-east of Paris on the 23rd. This meant that the only way out of this second 'Pocket' was across a 60km stretch of the Seine between Louviers and the sea – a stretch on which no bridges were standing except one badly damaged railway bridge at Rouen.

On the 21st Army Group front things did not move so quickly. The British, Canadians and Poles were, to a major extent, still tied up in the Falaise Pocket, and when Bradley suggested that his men should advance into the 21st Army Group sector to cut off the German retreat, Montgomery agreed. An American armoured Division was immediately ordered to strike north from Verneuil into the German flank. It advanced 60km in four days but on the 24th ran into heavy opposition in the Louviers area, where a determined German force was protecting the sixty or so ferries and pontoons being used to evacuate the remnants of the Seventh Army across the lower Seine.[10] The same thing happened to the Canadians. They reached Orbec on the 22nd but when they tried to move north-east the following day, they too ran into strong opposition south-west of Elbeuf.

The three German infantry Divisions which had been defending the coastal areas to the north of Falaise had been forced to withdraw towards the Seine as their left flank was exposed by the Allied advance, and it was principally these troops and some others sent, far too late, from the Fifteenth Army in the Pas de Calais to reinforce the Seventh Army, who were now defending the Seine crossing areas to the west of Rouen.

Where did the few remaining combat elements of I SS Panzer Corps fit into this nightmare scenario? Due to the very confused situation in the period immediately following the breakout from the Falaise Pocket, it is impossible to be certain about the exact sequence of events or indeed which units fought precisely where or when. Nevertheless, from the evidence available from both sides, it is possible to construct a reasonable picture of what happened.

During the breakout General Eberbach had ordered the establishment of two assembly areas for the reception of survivors. One was near Evreux and the other at Pacy, and in these areas those soldiers of I SS Panzer Corps who had become separated from their units were able to obtain food and assistance and re-establish contact. Even so few of these individuals took part in the fighting west of the Seine. On the other hand, certain ad hoc units of the LAH and HJ made significant contributions to the struggle between the rivers.

SS Major Gerd Bremer's weak HJ Reconnaissance Battalion took part in the early fighting on the approaches to Mantes and his sub-units are said to have deceived the Americans as to the real German strength in this area before 18 August. Bremer later received Oakleaves to his Knight's Cross for his part in these actions.[11]

Certainly parts of the Leibstandarte's StuG Battalion, and its 1st SS Reconnaissance Company which had been left behind in Belgium in early July due to a lack of vehicles, also fought against the Americans as they advanced on the Mantes area on 19 August. They formed part of a scratch force, made up from parts of five divisions, including the 10th SS Panzer Division Frundsberg, known as KG Wahl.[12]

The strongest and most important element of the Corps was a KG commanded by Wilhelm Mohnke of the Hitlerjugend. This former commander of the 26th SS Panzer-Grenadier Regiment had been sent back to the Seine area in early August to take charge of those elements of the Division which had been withdrawn for refitting, and to receive reinforcements. On 20 August his KG comprised an infantry Battalion commanded by SS Captain Georg Urabl, some unspecified parts of the 12th SS Panzer Regiment and one StuG and two Flak companies from the LAH. Together these units formed an important part of the force in the Louviers-Elbeuf area.

On 20 August Mohnke set up an initial defensive position to the south of Louviers and claimed later to have destroyed fifteen Shermans during the fighting on that day. He also reported, on the 22nd, that American troops had penetrated his defensive line in three places but that his KG had knocked out twenty-six tanks and ten carriers before it withdrew during the night to positions 6km to the south-east of Louviers.[13] He was joined there on the 23rd[14] by weak, composite Battalions of the HJ's 25th and 26th Panzer-Grenadier Regiments, commanded by SS Majors Hans Waldmüller and Bernhard Siebken respectively, and that night his KG established a strong defence on the line of the road from Louviers to le Neubourg, where the LAH's Reconnaissance Battalion, probably with support from tank crews of the 12th SS Panzer Regiment on their feet, was already in position.[15] It seems probable that KG Wahl also joined up with Mohnke at about this time. The one certainty is that the whole force withdrew successfully across the Seine on the night of the 24th.[16]

The German resistance in the Louviers-Elbeuf area on the 23rd and 24th enabled the majority of the 150,000 German soldiers east of the Dives to escape across the Seine, though most of their heavy equipment had to be abandoned. In that regard, Dietrich is quoted as saying, 'the Seine crossing was almost as great a disaster as the Falaise Pocket.' Nevertheless, the War Diary of the Fifth Panzer Army records that 25,000 vehicles of all types were transported across the Seine between 20 and 24 August.[17] Some 300 barges were destroyed in air attacks between 16 and 23 August, although bad weather after that made it difficult for the Allied Air Forces to maintain their attacks on the ferry and pontoon sites. Nevertheless, the evacuation was a major achievement carried out against enormous odds. Two recollections will suffice to give some idea of the difficulties involved; the first by a member of the 1st SS Panzer Regiment LAH:

On the march to the Seine, little groups formed by chance. Ours was one of them. It contained elements of the Regimental staff and the Signals platoon, about ten SPWs . . . and several personnel carriers and trucks. By bartering with other elements of the Army, we got fuel and supplies. . . . We reached the huge bottleneck at Elbeuf on the Seine. The bridges there were no longer usable. . . . A naval unit had built a ferry out of two barges . . . but they could not be persuaded to take us across in the day. A second attempt, however, with bottles of cognac and other drinks was more successful. By noon we were loaded up and on the river. . . . We were in the middle of the Seine when a Lightning [US fighter-bomber] appeared. The plane flew over us though, and continued on its way. It must have had other orders.[18]

And a member of the LAH's Reconnaissance Battalion remembered:

We arrived at the Seine in Elbeuf at night. . . . Someone said that there was one [a railway bridge] 12km on this side of Rouen. . . . Unfortunately, it was completely destroyed. We set to work fixing it, working almost an entire day and night. A vehicle column almost 9km long was waiting to cross. Thank God it was raining buckets, which kept the planes away. Finally the bridge was ready and we began to move across. Then the artillery fire started . . . some vehicles were hit, but the bridge suffered no damage.[19]

On 25 August Paris was liberated and it was obvious to the German commanders that there was no chance of making even a temporary stand on the Seine. Model ordered an immediate withdrawal to the Somme.

The overall situation facing CinC West at this time was later described by his Chief of Staff, General Günther Blumentritt:

The Seine was expected to hold for at least seven days and then defensive positions to have been taken up through . . . Amiens-Soissons-Châlons. . . . But there were no troops available to man either the Seine or the Somme, and the Allies cut through France with little opposition.[20]

KG Mohnke held a delaying position just to the south of Rouen on the east bank of the Seine on 25 and 26 August but, according to the *History of the Leibstandarte*, it was then 'routed' by the 15th (Scottish) Division and withdrew to another position 15km to the west of Beauvais where it stayed until the 29th.[21] Kurt Meyer, who had taken over command of the 12th SS Panzer Division when Fritz Witt was killed in July, claimed in his book *Grenadiers* that Mohnke's KG continued to resist the advance of Canadian troops until it withdrew on the afternoon of the 29th.[22]

On 28 August SS Lieutenant Colonel Franz Steineck, the acting commander of the Leibstandarte, received orders for all his available units to assemble in the Laon-Marle area. This order stemmed from Model's plan to assemble all mobile troops in the general area Soissons-Reims-Châlons with the intention of checking the rapid advance of George Patton's Third US Army towards the Meuse. But it was too late. The following day, as Patton's armoured columns were approaching Reims, the British Second Army broke out of its bridgehead over the Seine at Vernon and a Corps of the US First Army reached Soissons.

During the night of 28 August a temporary holding area which the Hitlerjugend had set up at Beauvais was moved back to the Hirson area. KG Mohnke caught up with the remnants of the Division on the 29th and Mohnke himself was told that he had been appointed to command a Division which at the time no longer existed – the 1st SS Panzer Division Leibstandarte. One weak Battalion of his KG was sent straight back to Germany and SS Lieutenant Colonel Bernhard Krause took over the other two elements of what had been the 26th Panzer-Grenadier Regiment HJ – they numbered no more than 200 men each.

On 30 August American troops broke through in the Laon area and the three small I SS Panzer Corps KGs which had, in accordance with Model's plan, managed to form up in the Marle area, were engaged against the US VII Corps. The LAH KG, under SS Lieutenant Herbert Rink, fought around Marle; it consisted of elements of the 1st SS Panzer-Grenadier Regiment and two Pioneer Companies.[23] Of the two HJ KGs, made up from the remains of the 25th and 26th Panzer-Grenadier Regiments respectively[24], one repelled an American armoured column 10km west of Rozoy, forcing it to swing east, and the other, under Bernhard Krause, fought on both sides of that town. This latter KG had taken a Luftwaffe Flieger company and two Tigers of the 101st SS Panzer Battalion under command during the withdrawal, and it too is said to have forced a powerful American armoured group to break off its attack. The Tigers claimed eight American Shermans destroyed during this fighting, but they themselves had to be blown up by their crews due to fuel shortages when both KGs made further withdrawals on 1 September, reaching the Beaumont area by nightfall. Krause's KG then continued on directly to Germany. KG Rink had withdrawn to new positions 30km to the east of Mons by 1 September, where it was reinforced by Flak, Pioneer, anti-tank and Nebelwerfer platoons.[25]

Up to fourteen Tigers of the 2nd and 3rd Companies of the 101st SS Panzer Battalion are said to have taken part in the fighting between the Dives and Meuse rivers but none survived to reach Germany – most had to be abandoned by their crews due to breakdowns or shortage of fuel. A surprising re-entry into the fighting on 20 August was SS Captain Rolf Möbius's 1st SS Panzer Company which had been withdrawn from Normandy in early July after handing over its last three Tigers to the other two Companies. It had been issued with fourteen brand new Tiger IIs (King Tigers) in Germany and then moved to the area between Rouen and Paris. Details of this Company's actions are sketchy but can be found in Wolfgang Schneider's *Tigers in Combat II*. Only one Tiger II survived to reach Germany.

On 1 September the Canadians avenged the tragedy of Dieppe by liberating that port and the next day saw the British at the Belgian border near Lille and the Americans near Mons in the north and at Verdun in the south, with patrols on the Moselle. Brussels and Antwerp were liberated by British armoured Divisions on the 3rd and 4th. This lightning thrust split the German Seventh and Fifteenth Armies – 100,000 men of the Fifteenth were cut off with their backs to the sea.

The battle of France was at an end and for the surviving Germans it was now a race to reach the safety of the West Wall. Despite all the criticisms of Montgomery, it had been a brilliant victory for the Allies – the Seine had been reached two weeks ahead of schedule and the whole campaign fought in accordance with *his* original strategy.

On 3 September the 25th Regimental KG of the HJ occupied a final position on the French-Belgian border astride Beaumont, from which it withdrew to the Meuse, blowing the bridge near Yvoir in the face of a pursuing enemy at 0500 hours on the 4th.[26] The HJ's total strength at this time is given as:

three weak Battalions of 150–200 men each,
two Pioneer platoons,
one SP 105mm howitzer,
one mixed battery of three light and two heavy howitzers with 200 rounds,
ten rocket launchers with 251 rounds,
one 75mm anti-tank gun,
one 88mm Flak gun.[27]

Meanwhile, over a period of eleven days , KG Rink conducted an orderly withdrawal through the Ardennes to the West Wall.[28]

Field Marshal Model issued an extraordinary communique to his men on 3 September – few of them were able to read or even hear it:

To the Soldiers of the Western Army
We have lost a battle but I tell you, we will win this war! I cannot say more now, although I know that there are many questions burning on the lips of the troops. Despite everything that has happened, do not allow your firm, confident faith in Germany's future to be shaken. . . . Remember that at this moment the only thing which matters is to gain time for the Führer to bring into action new troops and new

weapons. They will come. Soldiers, we must win this time for the Führer!

Both the 1st and 12th SS Panzer Divisions suffered grievously in Normandy and the retreat to the West Wall. The Hitlerjugend losses in the period 6 June to 11 September, confirmed from named casualty lists, total 8,626 of which a minimum of 1,951 were dead. By estimating the losses in those units for which no lists are available, the Chief of Staff, Hubert Meyer, deduces that his Division must have lost a total of almost 9,000 officers and men.[29]

In the case of the Leibstandarte, the German administrative authorities later compiled a casualty list of 3,901 names for the period 6 June to 30 September, but according to the History of the Division this figure 'is woefully incomplete' and the authors suggest a figure of 'at least 5,000' as more reasonable.[30]

The 1944 campaign in France was a disaster for the Germans. In only three months a quarter of a million men had been killed or wounded and another quarter of a million taken prisoner – twice the casualty rate of Stalingrad and five times the number of men wearing British Army uniform in 1999! In the case of Hitler's designated I SS Panzer Corps, some 43,000 men fought in the Normandy campaign. On 12 September the last of the 29,000 survivors of that Corps crossed into the territory of the Third Reich. Dietrich's 'boys' had been defeated but they had not been annihilated. Herbert Rink, the commander of one of the LAH's small KGs wrote later of his feelings at that time:

At last we would be safe. We were shell-shocked and exhausted. Once behind the West Wall, we could join all the defeated, decimated German units, all those who had made it through 600km of horrifying, crushing battle.[31]

But before they reached the safety of the Reich his group had another unnerving experience:

We crossed the Belgium-Luxembourg border and saw the little town of Trois-Vierges lying 500m in front of us. We could not believe our eyes. Down in the town stood the entire population along the main street, flowers and drinks in hand. They were clearly waiting for the liberation forces. . . . We did not have much time if we wanted to beat the Americans to the town. With an armoured platoon at the head, and the supply vehicles in the middle, we raced out of the forest and into the town. We turned down the main street, keeping a watch to the south, and drove slowly past the waiting people. . . . Never in my life have I seen people so quiet and embarrassed. They did not know what to do with their flowers. They looked at the ground. Their hands sank in a helpless gesture.[32]

Within a week Rink's attitude had changed:

We were able to stabilise the situation at the West Wall after all. We had a continuous front line, sufficient habitable bunkers, and adequate combat installations. And we, who had come depleted and exhausted from the inferno of Caen, through the breakout from the Pocket at Falaise, through the nerve-racking retreat across France and partisan-plagued Belgium – we had gathered our strength and rebuilt our confidence.[33]

Before closing this chapter it has to be recorded that some well known and courageous officers and an unspecified number of NCOs and soldiers were killed and wounded during this retreat at the hands of 'partisans' as the Germans called them, or 'Resistance Fighters' as they were known to the French and Belgians.

A retreating Hitlerjugend column, led by Erich Olboeter, the commander of the HJ's 3rd SPW Panzer-Grenadier Battalion, was ambushed by members of the Belgian Resistance during the night of 1 September. Olboeter's legs were smashed and he died during an operation to amputate them in hospital at Charleville. His fellow Knight's Cross holder Hans Waldmüller, together with a young SS second lieutenant and driver, were similarly ambushed near Basse Bodeux in the Ardennes (Map 10) on the night of the 8th. The driver was found lying in undergrowth, seriously wounded, the young officer was dead from a head wound, and Waldmüller's body was found in the drainage pipe of a small lake, disembowelled and mutilated. Both Olboeter and Waldmüller had fought for five years as platoon, company and Battalion commanders and had led their men with distinction in Normandy.

It has to be said that in defeat the members of the SS, Waffen or otherwise, could expect little mercy from the peoples of occupied Europe. Nevertheless, this author finds it sad that brave soldiers should die away from the battlefield in this manner. It also has to be said that such acts sometimes bring terrible retribution. A total of thirty-one Belgian men and four women died at the hands of German troops at eleven different locations[34] in the area to the south of Spa and west of Stavelot in the period 3 to 11 September 1944 – fifteen of them on the 10th. Since the Germans were leaving Belgium anyway, one has to wonder if some of the actions of the Resistance forces were worthwhile – particularly as when members of the Leibstandarte returned to the same general area only three months later they were to exact a terrible revenge on those they called 'partisans', but who were in fact mainly women, children and old men.

Kurt Meyer, the commander of the Hitlerjugend Division, who not surprisingly had been awarded Swords to his Knight's Cross for his performance in the Normandy campaign, was luckier than the two Battalion commanders just mentioned. He was captured by Belgian Resistance fighters on 6 September in the village of Durnal, 7km to the east of Yvoir (Map 5). He was very fortunate to survive and be made a prisoner of war!

NOTES

1. Shulman, *Defeat in the West*, p. 120.
2. Messenger, *Hitler's Gladiator*, p. 71.
3. Ibid., p. 94.
4. Lehmann, *The Leibstandarte III*, p. 199.
5. Messenger, op. cit., p. 105.
6. Lehmann, *The Leibstandarte II*, p. 310.
7. Meyer, Hubert, *The History of the 12th SS Panzer Division Hitlerjugend*, p. 206.
8. Ibid., p. 204.
9. Ibid., p. 203.
10. Wilmot, *The Struggle for Europe*, p. 433.
11. Meyer, Hubert, op. cit., p. 209.
12. Ibid., p. 205.
13. Ibid., p. 207.
14. Ibid.
15. Lehmann & Tiemann, *The Leibstandarte IV/1*, p. 229.
16. Meyer, Hubert, op. cit., p. 208.
17. Ibid., p. 209.
18. Lehmann & Tiemann, op. cit., p. 230.
19. Ibid., pp. 230–1.
20. Interview Blumentritt-Milton Schulman, Feb 45.
21. Lehmann & Tiemann, op. cit., p. 232.
22. Meyer, Kurt, *Grenadiers*, p. 173.
23. Lehmann & Tiemann, op. cit., p. 234.
24. Meyer, Hubert, op. cit., p. 211.
25. Lehmann & Tiemann, op. cit., p. 235.
26. Meyer, Hubert, op. cit., p. 213.
27. Ibid.
28. Lehmann & Tiemann, op. cit., p. 235.
29. Meyer, Hubert, op. cit., p. 222.
30. Lehmann & Tiemann, op. cit., p. 228.
31. Ibid., p. 237.
32. Ibid.
33. Ibid., p. 238.
34. Lierneux, Bra, Chevron, Rahier, Basse Bodeux, Fosse, Wanne, Stavelot, Spa, La Reid, Creppe.

CHAPTER IV
Rebuilding in the Reich:
22 September – 11 December
(Map 2)

On 11 September Sepp Dietrich was ordered to hand over command of the Fifth Panzer Army to General Hasso von Manteuffel and report to the Führer. When he did so three days later, he received the startling news that he was to form the Headquarters of what, within a few weeks, was to become the Sixth Panzer Army.

Dietrich's new command consisted initially of two SS Panzer Corps – I SS Panzer Corps, now under SS Lieutenant General Hermann Priess, retained the 1st and 12th SS Panzer Divisions, and II SS Panzer Corps, under General Willi Bittrich of Normandy fame, comprised the 2nd SS Panzer Division Das Reich, and the 9th SS Panzer Division Hohenstaufen which had been with him in the defeat of the British and Polish airborne landings at Arnhem in mid-September. Hermann Priess, Dietrich's successor in I SS Panzer Corps, had previously commanded the SS Totenkopf Division in Russia after the notorious Theodor Eicke had been killed in 1943.

Dietrich set up his new Headquarters, initially with just ten officers, at Bad Salzuflen, near Bielefeld, towards the end of September.[1] It had been originally intended that Fritz Kraemer, the Chief of Staff of I SS Panzer Corps throughout the Normandy campaign, should take command of the 12th SS Panzer Division, but after urgent representations by Dietrich it was agreed that he should continue to serve his old master as Chief of Staff of the new Sixth Panzer Army. His substitute as commander of the Hitlerjugend Division was SS Colonel Hugo Kraas. A former member of the Leibstandarte, Kraas had been the first officer to win an Iron Cross 1st Class in the 1940 French campaign, after which he went on to win the Knight's Cross with Oakleaves and to command the 2nd SS Panzer-Grenadier Regiment in Russia where he was wounded. He also held the Infantry Assault and Close Combat Badges.

In late September the Leibstandarte, along with the HJ and two other SS Panzer Divisions of the Sixth Panzer Army, was released by CinC West for re-equipping and rebuilding under Dietrich's command. The ageing

Field Marshal von Rundstedt had just been reappointed to this post and Model made Commander Army Group 'B'.

The towns and villages to the east of Osnabrück in which the 1st SS Panzer Division began assembling in mid-October 1944 will be familiar to all British soldiers who served in the British Army of the Rhine after the Second World War; indeed, the current British 1st Armoured Division is still located in the same area. The LAH Headquarters set up in the attractive town of Lübbecke, the 1st SS Panzer Regimental Headquarters at Rahden and the Divisional units were to be found in nearby towns and villages like Bünde, Herringshausen, Wehrendorf and Hille.[2]

As we have heard, Wilhelm Mohnke, the commander of the original 1933 Chancellery Guard and later of the Hitlerjugend's 26th Panzer-Grenadier Regiment in Normandy, was the new Divisional commander. He had, not unreasonably, been awarded a Knight's Cross for his part in the Normandy battles. It has been said that he was still suffering great pain from the loss of a foot in the 1940 Balkan campaign and regularly took morphia. His critics go on to say that this accounted for some of his failings in the forthcoming operation.

Of the Normandy commanders, only Rudolf Sandig of the 2nd SS Panzer-Grenadier Regiment, Franz Steineck of the 1st SS Artillery Regiment, and Gustav Knittel and Hugo Ullerich of the 1st SS Reconnaissance and Flak Battalions were left. But Jochen Peiper and Max Hansen had recovered from their wounds and returned in early October – the former to reassume command of his Panzer Regiment and the latter to take command of the 1st Panzer-Grenadier Regiment. Karl Rettlinger and Richard Scheler were elevated within their Battalions to command the Jagdpanzers and Pioneers respectively. The commander of the 1st SS Panzer Battalion, Herbert Kuhlmann, had been transferred to the HJ and Werner Poetschke appointed to replace him. The latter had transferred to the Leibstandarte from the 2nd SS Panzer Division Das Reich in 1943 and was already the holder of the Knight's Cross, German Cross in Gold and Iron Cross 1st and 2nd Class.

New commanders had to be found for all except one of the six LAH Panzer-Grenadier Battalions.

By early December the LAH had been brought up to a strength of just under 21,000 men. This meant that over 3,500 reinforcements had been received in just over two months and these inevitably included non-volunteers, more ethnic Germans from the eastern territories and impressed naval and air force personnel, few of whom had received any infantry training. Indeed, few of the new recruits had received more than six weeks' military training of any sort and some of the replacement tank crews had never even been in a tank. The problems of further training in the short time available were immense and it proved quite impossible to provide the correct number of properly trained junior officers and NCOs.

The re-equipment programme saw the arrival of thirty-six Panthers and thirty-four Mk IV tanks. Since this number was less than half the Division's correct establishment, and because of the shortage of trained crews and specialist personnel, a decision was made, probably at Corps level, to concentrate all the tanks in one mixed Battalion under Poetschke's command.

Hansen's and Sandig's SS Panzer-Grenadier Regiments were more or less up to scale in manpower and equipment except for a few AA weapons and a 30% shortfall in trucks which was made up with bicycles. There were no SP guns available for the 1st SS Artillery Regiment so towed 105s and 150s were issued in lieu, and a serious shortage of SPWs and other specialist vehicles saw the Pioneer Battalion with only two mechanized platoons. Knittel's 1st SS Reconnaissance Battalion had to be completely reorganised, with three instead of four companies and VW Schwimmwagens replacing SPWs. The 1st SS Panzerjäger Battalion, built on the remains of the old StuG Battalion, was equipped with its correct number of twenty-one Jagdpanzer IV/L 70s but had towed instead of self-propelled 75mm anti-tank guns. Despite the shortcomings the Division was still very powerful and, in view of the circumstances, surprisingly well equipped.[3]

Thanks to the excellent *History of the 12th SS Panzer Division Hitlerjugend* by Hubert Meyer, its Chief of Staff, we have a very accurate picture of how that Division was prepared for its next campaign.

After the debacles of the Falaise Pocket and retreat across northern France, only six of the senior HJ commanders remained – SS Lieutenant Colonel Oskar Drexler, commanding the 12th SS Artillery Regiment, and two of his commanding officers, and SS Majors Arnold Jürgensen, Gerd Bremer and Willi Müller commanding the 1st SS Panzer, 12th SS Reconnaissance and 12th SS Werfer Battalions respectively. Recall Bremer had been awarded Oakleaves for his part in the Normandy campaign. Hubert Meyer commanded the Division until Kraas arrived in early November. The problem of finding new senior commanders was solved by appointing proven officers from within the Division – Knight's Cross holder Bernhard 'Papa' Krause was confirmed as Mohnke's successor in the 26th Panzer-Grenadier Regiment and SS Major Siegfried Müller, the Pioneer Battalion commanding officer who had still to be awarded his Knight's Cross for Normandy, was given command of the 25th Regiment. Herbert Kuhlmann, who had also proved himself in Normandy as the commander of the 1st SS Panzer Battalion, was brought across from the Leibstandarte to take over the 12th SS Panzer Regiment. The greatest difficulty was finding replacement company commanders. One Battalion of the 25th SS Panzer-Grenadier Regiment ended up with a lieutenant, two second lieutenants and an officer-cadet; few Battalions were better off. Finding new, reasonably trained, platoon commanders was no easier.

The problem of bringing the HJ up to strength in manpower was even greater than that for the Leibstandarte. Some 9,000 replacements were needed and they arrived in small groups. As well as young volunteers, they included convalescent wounded and more than 2,000 non-volunteers from the Luftwaffe and Navy who were also untrained in ground operations. This imbalance was improved to some extent by replacing young HJ soldiers in the Divisional administrative units with older men from the other two services.

By the beginning of October the Division was concentrated in Lower Saxony, to the south of Oldenburg, with its Headquarters in Sulingen. The re-equipment programme began in mid-October. Heavy weapons were provided at a level of 100%, and small arms, automatic weapons, motor-cycles and trucks at 75%. In the case of Müller's so-called 'Motorized' Panzer-Grenadier Regiment, the shortage of trucks was so severe that most men had to walk.

As only thirty-seven Mk IV tanks and the same number of Panthers had been received by the end of November, it was decided, as in the case of the LAH, to concentrate them in one mixed Battalion of four companies. Four command Panthers were also issued – two for the Regimental and two for the Battalion Headquarters. The 12th SS Panzerjäger Battalion received twenty-two Jagdpanzer IV/L 70s for its two armoured companies, but Bremer's 12th SS Reconnaissance Battalion managed only sixteen armoured reconnaissance vehicles and thirteen light SPWs. The SPW Panzer-Grenadier Battalion of the 26th Panzer-Grenadier Regiment was, however, given nearly its full complement – 118 SPWs. All artillery pieces were towed.

When one considers that the time available for training the new men was just over two months and had to be carried out within a re-equipment programme, during the early winter and with the interruption of a Divisional move to a new area, it is remarkable that the HJ was ever considered fit for offensive operations.

We must now consider the state of mind of the officers and soldiers of Hitler's Bodyguard Corps as they were being prepared, unknowingly, for Hitler's last great gamble in the West. And amazingly, despite the recent heavy losses and reverses, morale was still high. Although many of those in the senior echelons of the German hierarchy had by now concluded that it was time to sue for peace, most members of the Waffen-SS considered the war to be far from lost.

In the same way that Winston Churchill had urged the British people to 'wage war against a monstrous tyranny, never surpassed in the dark lamentable catalogue of human crime', so highly effective Nazi propaganda had convinced the Germans that they were defending European civilization against the sub-human hordes of Stalin's Communist Russia. Certainly their experiences on the Eastern Front had strengthened the resolve of the German military to protect their homeland for as long as possible and at whatever cost. Stories circulating at the time concerning the fate of German civilians in the territories captured by the Russians were of course exploited by Joseph Goebbels and did much to strengthen the resolve of both those who had experienced the Eastern Front and the younger members of the Corps who had yet to see battle.

Two other factors played an important part in maintaining the will to go on fighting – the Morganthau Plan and the Allied demand for 'Unconditional Surrender'. The former, named after the adviser to President Roosevelt who initiated it, called for the division of post-war Germany into a few deindustrialised, agrarian states, with the aim of preventing that country from ever again threatening world peace. The Germans learned of its existence in May 1944 and inevitably Goebbels used it to stiffen the nation's resolve. The call for 'unconditional surrender' gave the German soldier little choice other than to fight on, and this was particularly true of the Waffen-SS who knew they could expect little mercy if the war was lost.

Then there was the sense of elitism felt by members of the senior formation in the Waffen-SS and of the only Divisions to bear Hitler's name. It was no accident that in recognition of the HJ's brilliant performance in Normandy, cuff bands bearing the name 'Hitlerjugend' were issued to the members of 12th SS on 19 September, and in October Arnold Jürgensen and two others were presented with their Knight's Crosses in front of the soldiers of the Panzer and Panzerjäger Battalions. Moreover, many of the officers and senior NCOs of the Corps had seen a great deal of active service – service and heroism visible for all to see from medals worn even on combat dress and in action. This led to strong feelings of trust and admiration from those under their command.

And there were other, almost mystical, influences which still pervaded the Corps and gave it a unique character. Some of its leaders had developed a strange philosophy of soldiering which glorified fighting for fighting's sake. They had little regard for life, either their own or that of anyone else. Tales of 'Valhalla', the banqueting-hall of slain heroes, and the 'Valkyrie', the hand-maidens of Odin given the task of selecting the warriors who were to fall in battle, were familiar to Nazi youth. A Leibstandarte captain, in his description of his feelings about the fighting in Russia, spoke for many of his comrades when he said:

We reached a point where we were not concerned for ourselves or even for Germany, but lived entirely for the next clash, the next engagement with the enemy. There was a tremendous sense of 'being', an exhilarating feeling that every nerve in the body was alive to the fight.

And finally there was the oath of loyalty which the members of the

Waffen-SS had sworn to their Führer. As long as he was alive and at their head it was unthinkable that they should stop fighting or surrender. The shameful idea that anyone could have attempted to remove him in the hour of national danger was well described by the Chief of Staff of the Hitlerjugend Division:

> It was incomprehensible that soldiers would attempt a coup against the supreme military leadership while they were themselves involved in bitter defensive fighting against the enemy who demanded 'Unconditional Surrender', not willing to negotiate a cease-fire or even peace.[4]

This type of thinking inevitably permeated through to the new members of I SS Panzer Corps. War was not a 'game' to be played by 'rules'; it was instead a contest which had to be won. The other contestants were seen as inferior and it was unthinkable that the opposition could, or should, be allowed to win. I SS Panzer Corps was therefore still a strange mixture of leaders, hardened and tempered in the crucible of the Eastern Front and Normandy, and soldiers who had been thoroughly indoctrinated in Nazi thinking through their membership of the Hitlerjugend organisation, and who had been led to believe that war was something glorious and honourable.

All these factors combined to produce high motivation and morale. If they could just hold on long enough for their Führer's promise of 'Victory' weapons to be realised, Sepp Dietrich's men firmly believed that victory was not only possible, but inevitable.

On 6 November the 12th SS Panzer Division received orders to move to an area to the west of Cologne and three days later the 1st SS Panzer Division received similar instructions. The moves were not completed until the end of the month and were carried out in the difficult conditions brought about by Allied bombing and strafing. The LAH was located in and around Jülich, Mechernich, Zülpich and Düren, with Jochen Peiper's tanks in the area of Weilerswist, but a reserve Battalion was left behind in the Lübbecke area to hold spare tank crews and to receive, equip and give further training to new recruits still arriving from the basic training establishments. The HJ Headquarters was at Brauweiler and its units located in the general area between Cologne and Grevenbroich.

Although the officers of I SS Panzer Corps would have liked much longer for training, no one was particularly surprised by this move. The Americans had started a major offensive in the Aachen area on 16 November and it was obvious that the Allies were planning an early crossing of the Rhine and an assault on the Ruhr. The positioning of a powerful Panzer Corps to counter this threat clearly made military sense. Little did the members of that Corps realise what their Führer really had in store for them.

NOTES

1. Messenger, *Hitler's Gladiator*, p. 144.
2. Tiemann, *Die Leibstandarte IV/2*, p. 23.
3. All organisational and strength details for the LAH are taken from Tiemann's *Die Leibstandarte IV/2*, supplemented by interviews with LAH veterans and strength and equipment returns held in the Bundesarchiv.
4. Meyer, *The History of the 12th SS Panzer Division Hitlerjugend*, p. 160.

CHAPTER V

WACHT am RHEIN

(Maps 2, 6 & 7)

By the autumn of 1944 it was obvious to the German High Command, and even to Adolf Hitler, that in the long term it would be impossible to conduct a successful defence of the Greater German Reich on three fronts. The Führer resolved therefore to deliver a massive blow on one of the two most important fronts, designed to render that particular enemy incapable of serious offensive action for a considerable period. This, he reasoned, would give him strategic freedom and provide the forces necessary to deliver other decisive blows and, most importantly, buy time for the perfection of his new 'Victory' weapons.

The sheer scale of the Eastern front militated against an attack in that direction. As General Jodl, Chief of the OKW Operations Staff, put it after the war:

The Russians had so many troops that even if we had succeeded in destroying thirty divisions it would have made no difference. On the other hand, if we destroyed thirty divisions in the West, it would amount to more than a third of the whole invasion army [in fact half the Allied Expeditionary Force].[1]

This factor, coupled with the threat to the Ruhr and Hitler's low opinion of the fighting capabilities of both the American and British Armies, turned his eyes again to the Western Front. Once that front was stabilised he believed he would have sufficient forces to resist the inevitable Russian winter offensive. The fact that he was committing Germany's last reserves in men and resources gave the operation an air of finality – even Hitler predicted that the outcome of the offensive would mean life or death for the German nation. Nevertheless, in his eyes this desperate gamble, which invited disaster in the East, was the only course of action which might bring about his own survival and that of his Nazi regime.

On 16 September Hitler revealed his basic plan and strategic goals to a small inner circle including Keitel, the Chief of OKW, and Jodl, the Chief of the OKW Operations Staff. Despite objections by some of his most senior commanders, including von Rundstedt and Model, the final plan was basically unchanged when it was issued in late November. Essentially it called for three Armies under Model's Army Group 'B', to break through the weak American front in the Ardennes and Luxembourg and then, with the main weight on the right flank, cross the Meuse south of Liège and exploit to the great port of Antwerp. This would cut off the British and Canadian 21st Army Group and American Ninth Army, and hopefully cause mass surrenders and deprive the Allies of their most important port. Indeed, Hitler saw it as the basis of another 'Dunkirk', with a loss to the Allies of some twenty to thirty divisions. He even believed it might destroy the British and Canadian Armies once and for all.

Hitler's plan called for a huge force of seven Panzer and thirteen infantry divisions to be used in the initial assault, with a further two Panzer and seven infantry divisions ready to be thrown in later. In all, some 1,460 tanks, assault guns and self propelled anti-tank guns and 2,600 artillery pieces and rocket launchers were to be made available.

Sepp Dietrich's Sixth Panzer Army was destined by Hitler to gain the most honours in the forthcoming campaign and it was given the primary objective of Antwerp. The other two Armies, the Fifth Panzer under von Manteuffel, and the Seventh under General Erich Brandenberger, were seen as very much in support.

Hitler decreed the utmost secrecy in relation to his plan and Dietrich's staff did not receive details of it until 29 November and his Divisional commanders until 6 December – only ten days before the offensive was due to start. Von Rundstedt, Model, Dietrich, von Manteuffel, Priess, Mohnke, Kraas and the other I SS Panzer Corps Divisional commanders were briefed by the Führer himself at the Adlerhof, near Bad Nauheim, on 11 December. The ADC to Model later described the meeting:

Hitler went far back into history before getting to the Ardennes offensive itself. He spoke without notes, without moving his hands and was easy to understand. He was able to describe the objective of the operation – splitting the American and English forces through a lightning advance . . . the destruction of the English armies in an encirclement battle west of Aachen, in a vivid and convincing manner. . . . He said in closing; 'Gentlemen, if our breakthrough via Liège to Antwerp is not successful, we will be approaching an end to the war which will be extremely bloody. Time is not working for us, but against us. This is really the last opportunity to turn the fate of this war in our favour.'[2]

Dietrich had three Corps to command: I SS Panzer Corps with the 1st and 12th SS Panzer plus one Parachute and two Volks-Grenadier Divisions, II SS Panzer Corps with the 2nd and 9th SS Panzer Divisions, and LXVII Corps with two Volks-Grenadier Divisions. The organisation of a Volks-Grenadier division is shown at Appendix II.

The plan called for the Parachute and Volks-Grenadier Divisions to make a break in the crust of the American defences, and then form a hard shoulder on the right flank of the proposed advance. The LAH and HJ would then surge to, and across, the Meuse south of Liège, in one all-powerful wave, followed by Bittrich's II SS Panzer Corps, which would then exploit to the north-west and seize Antwerp. In the meantime, von Manteuffel's Fifth Panzer Army would advance on the left flank and seize Brussels, whilst Branderberger's Seventh Army would advance to protect the left flank of the offensive. The codename for the planning of this operation was WACHT AM RHEIN – Watch on the Rhine. It was chosen to confuse both friend and foe should it be compromised.

Following the devastation caused by Allied fighter-bombers in Normandy and during the retreat across France, Hitler resolved to do everything possible to avoid this happening again. He decided therefore to protect his Panzer forces by launching his attack in bad weather and, despite the apparent contradiction, by ordering two associated air offensives at the same time. The first was designed to provide local air superiority for the Fifth and Sixth Panzer Armies at critical times and the second, codenamed BODENPLATTE, sought to destroy Allied aircraft on the ground by launching some 900 aircraft against eighteen airfields in Belgium and Holland. After the war von Manteuffel recalled Hitler telling him:

> Goering has reported that he has 3,000 fighters available for the operation. You know Goering's reports. Discount 1,000, and that still leaves 1,000 to work with you and 1,000 for Sepp Dietrich.

The real strength of the Luftwaffe in December 1944 was some 1,900 fighters and ground attack aircraft and 100 bombers![3]

In a further attempt to aid his Panzer divisions in their dash to the Meuse and beyond, Hitler ordered one special operation and reluctantly agreed to another. Operation GREIF was the Führer's own brainchild. It was to be led by one of his favourites and a former member of the Leibstandarte, Otto Skorzeny. He was told to form two English-speaking groups who would wear American uniforms and use American equipment. The task of the first group, comprising about fifty men in teams of four or five, was to penetrate US lines and then sabotage important installations and generally cause confusion. The second, much larger, group of some 3,000 men divided into three KGs, was to move at night on parallel lines to the advancing Panzer spearheads and seize bridges over the Meuse.

The second special operation, STÖSSER, involved a night parachute drop of some 800 men, to be carried out before H-Hour, with the aim of disrupting the movement of American units towards the right flank of the advance. Hitler, who would be proved right, did not believe the Luftwaffe was capable of carrying out the drop successfully but, under pressure from Field Marshal Model, he reluctantly gave approval.

The decision to use infantry divisions to make the initial breakthrough was a surprising change of tactics. Maybe Hitler had learned from the lessons of Kursk, reinforced by those of the Mortain counter-offensive? Whatever the reason, in the case of the LAH it turned out to be a mistake – had the assault in its sector been led by tanks, it is most likely that the inexperienced American troops in its path would have fled. Similarly, as events would prove later, if I SS Panzer Corps' request for its attack frontage to be moved farther south[4] had been agreed, and the whole Corps assault then led by tanks, it is more than likely that the Meuse would have been reached in accordance with the planned timetable. Hitler's refusal to listen to his generals when they pointed out that the road network and general topography in the Fifth Panzer Army's planned area of operations was far superior to that in the Sixth's, was to have disastrous results. The members of the Waffen-SS, who were expected to reach the Meuse in three days, would soon find their roads and tracks disintregrating and, unlike in Normandy, they would rarely be able to see as far as the effective range of their weapons.

What forces were deployed in the path of I SS Panzer Corps? Following the victorious advance across eastern France, Belgium and Holland, Eisenhower's Armies had ground to a halt through lack of supplies. Late September and October were spent building up thousands of tons of ammunition, fuel and other essentials, improving the road systems, rebuilding bridges and replacing the many casualties in men and vehicles. Once this had been achieved, Ike ordered the 21st and 12th Army Groups to close up to the Rhine. It proved a costly business. The British did not clear the Meuse until 4 December, the US Ninth Army could not close to the Roer river by that date, let alone the Rhine, and the US First Army became involved in a World War I type slogging match south of Aachen. Patton's Third Army took two weeks and many casualties to take Metz in the south. The unpalatable truth was that the Allies had run up against the West Wall, with all its inherent difficulties for the attacker and advantages for the defender.

After two weeks' fighting in early December, the US First and Ninth Armies reached the Roer valley. It now became essential to capture the great dams at the headwaters of the Roer and Urft rivers, for if the Germans should open the flood-gates they could inundate the Americans in the valley and make the river extremely difficult to cross. It was decided therefore that Lieutenant General Courtney Hodges' First Army, and specifically its reinforced 2nd Infantry Division, should capture them.

South of Aachen, in the Hürtgen Forest, Hodges' Army had seen three of its divisions cut to pieces. Two of them, the 4th and 28th Infantry, were so badly mauled that they had to be withdrawn and sent to quiet sectors in the Ardennes and Luxembourg. They were replaced by the 99th and 106th Divisions, neither of which had been in action before. All four were located right in the path of Hitler's forthcoming offensive. The organisation of an American infantry division is shown at Appendix III.

Looking at the American front opposite I SS Panzer Corps from north to south on 16 December, we find the 99th Infantry Division of Major General Walter Lauer as the right-hand Division of the US V Corps, defending a 25km front from Monschau to Losheimergraben; then a 10km gap before the left-hand Division of Major General Troy Middleton's VIII Corps – the 106th Infantry – occupying a 20km front reaching down to the northern tip of the Duchy of Luxembourg. This 10km gap, known historically as 'The Losheim Gap', was Middleton's responsibility and, when his Corps arrived in sector on 10 December, he gave the job of covering it to Colonel Mark Devine's 14th Cavalry Group. Thus the most vulnerable part of the Allied front, the gap between two Corps and an historical attack route, was occupied by only 450 men of a Cavalry Reconnaissance Squadron[5], the equivalent of a weak Battalion, in village outposts supported by a company of 3-inch Tank Destroyers (TDs).[6]

The extended frontage of the 99th Division meant it had no depth. Lauer's Headquarters was located in Bütgenbach and his three Regiments[7] were deployed in line. The centre Regiment[8] had one Battalion detached, leaving only two Battalions to cover a frontage, much of it heavily forested, of over 5km. A TD Battalion[9] with thirty-six towed guns was in support of the Division but Lauer's only immediate reserve was a single Battalion[10] sited at Buchholz (Map 8) – it was immobile and had one company detached to another Regiment.

The Losheim Gap, and the area just to its north occupied by the untried 99th Infantry, were the precise initial objectives of Hermann Priess's I SS Panzer Corps.

Major General Walter Robertson's seasoned 2nd Infantry Division had begun its task of capturing the Urft-Roer dams on 13 December. It had been well reinforced. In addition to three TD Battalions instead of the normal one, Robertson had an experienced tank Battalion[11] with forty-seven Shermans and the support of CCB, an armoured combat command, of the 9th Armored Division. The organisation of an American armoured division is shown at Appendix IV.

The 2nd Infantry had attacked north-east on a 5km frontage, through the northern sector of the 99th Division towards Wahlerscheid. One

Regiment[12] of the 99th had been attached to provide right flank protection, but by the evening of the 15th little progress had been made. Incredible though it may seem, the 12th SS Panzer Division had no knowledge of the commitment of this powerful formation in its sphere of operations, believing instead that it was located at Camp Elsenborn for refitting.[13]

The only strategic reserve available to General Eisenhower at this time was the XVIII Airborne Corps near Reims in France. It consisted of the 82nd and 101st Airborne Divisions, resting and preparing for a further airborne operation after the ill-fated 'Market Garden' disaster in Holland.

How was it that the Americans were so ill-prepared for an attack in this area? First, because no senior commander believed that the Germans were capable of launching an offensive in the West at this stage of the war; second, because the Allies thought the thick forests, deep valleys and fast flowing rivers of the Ardennes precluded any serious offensive action there during the winter; and third, because although the Allies knew of the existence of the Sixth Panzer Army, they did not realise that by 15 December it had moved south from the Cologne area. They still thought, as Hitler had intended, that it was a counter-penetration force designed to defeat any thrust towards the Rhine and the Ruhr. And because Hitler banned the use of radio and insisted that all communications before the offensive should be carried out on the telephone, ULTRA, the British decrypting organisation, completely failed to detect the build-up of German troops in the Eifel. In fact there were a number of intelligence indicators, including the interception of messages between various Luftwaffe headquarters and bases ignoring the radio ban, which should have alerted the Allies. The trouble was that, due to their preconceived ideas, the senior Allied commanders ignored their intelligence officers when they came up with warnings based on sound indicators. As a result, everyone in the Ardennes sector of the American front, with the exception of the men of the 2nd Infantry and their supporting troops engaged in the Roer dams operation, went to bed contentedly on the night of 15 December – many of them were in for a nasty shock in the early hours of the 16th!

NOTES

1. Jodl, ETHINT 50.
2. Meyer, *The History of the 12th SS Panzer Division Hitlerjugend*, p. 238.
3. Price, *The Last Year of the Luftwaffe, May 1944 to May 1945*, pp. 112–3.
4. Meyer, op. cit., p. 234.
5. 18th.
6. A/820th.
7. 393rd, 394th & 395th.

8. LTC Jean Scott's 393rd.
9. 801st.
10. 3/394th.
11. 741st.
12. 395th.
13. Meyer, op. cit., p. 240.

CHAPTER VI

Preparations for Battle: 12 – 16 December

(Maps 8 & 9)

On 12 December the 1st and 12th SS Panzer Divisions received orders to side-step 60km to their south. No explanation for this move was given and it was carried out, in radio silence and without lights, during the following two nights.

By the morning of the 15th the LAH Headquarters was located in Tondorf, with its Divisional units hidden in villages and forests within a 10km radius of Blankenheim; the HJ Headquarters was in Benenberg, with its units similarly hidden to the east of Hellenthal; and Priess had established his Corps Headquarters in Schmidtheim. Sepp Dietrich's Sixth Panzer Army Headquarters was in Marmagen – he had his 'boys' all round him again.

On 14 December Mohnke and Kraas issued orders for the attack to their Regimental and other senior commanders and they in turn gave their orders on the morning of the 15th. It was therefore well into the evening or even during the night of the 15th-16th that the junior NCOs and soldiers were briefed – twelve hours at best before the start of Hitler's great offensive. So, what was the plan and what orders did they receive?

Taking the infantry first and looking at the front from left to right – the 3rd Parachute (3rd FSD) and the 12th and 277th Volks-Grenadier Divisions (VGDs) were required to break through the thin American defences between Krewinkel and Hollerath, seizing the following immediate objectives: for the 3rd FSD, Lanzerath, Krewinkel, Manderfeld; for the 12th VGD Losheimergraben and Büllingen, and for the 277th, Mürringen, Rocherath and Krinkelt. In order to protect the immediate right flank of the I SS Panzer Corps, the two VGDs of General Hitzfeld's LXVII Corps were to strike on either side of Monschau and then turn north. But there were problems. Major General Wedehn's 3rd FSD had suffered badly in Normandy and was 25% under-strength. Many of his men were Luftwaffe

47

ground personnel with minimal combat training and, to compound his problems, one of his three Regiments had not even arrived in the assembly area by the time the attack was due to start. Major General Engel's 12th VGD was also a rebuilt veteran Division and it too was under-strength – by some 20%. Major General Viebig's 277th VGD had been in defence in the Corps sector since mid-November and it was due to be relieved by LXVII Corps in order to take part in the attack; however, at 0600 hours on the 16th one Battalion of its northern Regiment was still waiting for relief. And perhaps most serious of all, the three Army assault gun Battalions which were meant to support Priess's infantry Divisions had not materialised. This left the 12th VGD with only six StuGs and the 277th with eleven Hetzers (Jagdpanzer 38t). Wedehn's paratroopers had no assault guns.

Turning now to the Panzer Divisions, those of Bittrich's II SS Panzer Corps were positioned behind I SS in the Eifel. We can ignore them because at this stage they play no part in our story.

The master plan for Priess's Panzer Divisions, the LAH and HJ, envisaged two powerful armoured KGs, containing all the Corps' tanks, advancing side by side on parallel routes with secondary, but strong KGs providing flank protection. The routes to be taken have been the subject of much post-war discussion. They are shown on Map 10. As far as this account is concerned only two points require emphasis. First, they were not, as is so often stated, fixed and immutable – they were to be seen as directional. Fritz Kraemer, Chief of Staff of the Sixth Panzer Army, said later:

These roads were to be directional only. If the divisional commanders wanted to take others, they were at liberty to do so . . . these five routes led to the general line Verviers-Spa-Stavelot and from that line new orders were to be given according to the situation at the time.[1]

Hermann Priess, in a post-war interview, described the routes all the way to the Meuse, but he went on to say:

The Corps and, under Corps command, the divisions had freedom of movement within this area. Thus, march routes did not have to be rigidly adhered to. Each division had express permission to deviate from prescribed routes whenever the situation demanded.[2]

The second point requiring emphasis is that only the first part of these routes need concern us at this stage. Routes A and B, allocated to the HJ flank protection KGs, were identical until after Sourbrodt. The combined route ran from west of Hollerath, along an unimproved forest trail for the first 3km and then on a minor road to Rocherath and Krinkelt and finally on to Elsenborn.

Route C, intended for the HJ's armoured KG, started at Udenbreth and went through the northern part of Büllingen to Bütgenbach. Route D, chosen for the Leibstandarte's armoured KG, was clearly the most suitable for tanks; after Losheim and Losheimergraben, it took the main road through Büllingen to Möderscheid, leaving Bütgenbach to the HJ. Finally, Route E – Krewinkel to Manderfeld and on to Amel – was allocated to the LAH's flank protection KG.

What can be said about these routes? Certainly that none of them was suitable for armoured vehicles in the weather conditions likely, indeed almost inevitable, in an Ardennes winter; and that those chosen for the Hitlerjugend were totally unsuitable for a Panzer Division. In the case of the Leibstandarte's Route D, statements by some commentators that it ran through Lanzerath and Honsfeld are incorrect. It is inconceivable that the strongest armoured KG in I SS Panzer Corps would not have been allocated the best route, the N-32, to get it on its way; and the fact that Jochen Peiper, the commander of that KG, positioned himself before H-Hour at the Headquarters of the Division (the 12th VGD) tasked with taking Losheimergraben, clearly indicates that his intended route ran that way and not through Lanzerath, which was an objective of the 3rd FSD. Further confirmation that Route D ran through Losheimergraben and not Lanzerath comes from reports by veterans of KG Peiper and Hubert Meyer in his description of the fighting on the first day of the offensive:

> The failure of the first attack by the 12th VGD on the heavily fortified positions at Losheimergraben led to a decisive delay in the action by Panzergruppe Peiper.[3]

The organisation of the Panzer Divisions was dictated by I SS Panzer Corps. The LAH's armoured KG was, as already mentioned, commanded by Jochen Peiper. In addition to his own mixed SS Panzer Battalion of seventy-two Mk IV and Panther tanks under Werner Poetschke, he was given the forty-five Tiger IIs of SS Major Hein von Westernhagen's 501st SS Heavy Panzer Battalion[4] as a second Panzer Battalion. Also in Peiper's KG were the 3rd SS (SPW) Panzer-Grenadier Battalion and the 150mm Infantry Gun Company of Sandig's 2nd Regiment under SS Captain Jupp Diefenthal, an artillery Battalion with eighteen towed 105mm guns and, as well as his own 9th SS Pioneer and 10th SS Panzer AA Companies, part of the 84th Luftwaffe Flak Battalion under a Major von Sacken – probably with about twenty 37mm and 20mm guns. All in all it was an extremely powerful Kampfgruppe, comprising some 4,800 men and 800 vehicles including 117 tanks, 149 SPWs, twenty-four artillery pieces and nearly forty AA guns. It lacked a bridging capacity, but this was deliberate – it was intended that the speed and surprise of the advance would ensure that the necessary bridges would be captured intact.

Behind KG Peiper on Route D, Rudolf Sandig's motorized 2nd SS Panzer-Grenadier Regiment – about 3,000 men and 400 vehicles, but less Diefenthal's 3rd Battalion – moved in front of the Divisional units not allocated to the four KGs.

On Route E, Max Hansen had his own motorized 1st SS Panzer-Grenadier Regiment, reinforced by Karl Rettlinger's 1st SS Panzerjäger Battalion with twenty-one Jagdpanzer IVs and eleven 75mm anti-tank guns, a towed 105mm artillery Battery and the twenty-four Nebelwerfers of the SS Major Klaus Besch's 1st SS Werfer Battalion – over 4,500 men and 750 vehicles. Behind KG Hansen came a 'Fast Group' of 1,500 men and 150 vehicles commanded by Gustav Knittel. It consisted of his own 1st SS Panzer Reconnaissance Battalion, reinforced by a 105mm artillery Battery and a truck mounted SS Panzer Pioneer Company.[5] Knittel had the option of switching routes so that he could, if the opportunity presented itself, race ahead and seize a bridge over the Meuse.

The Hitlerjugend's organisation was similar. The armoured KG commanded by Herbert Kuhlmann was due to advance on Route C. Its 1st SS Panzer Battalion had thirty-seven Mk IVs, thirty-seven Panthers, four command and two recovery tanks, all under the command of Arnold Jürgensen, a Knight's Cross winner from the Normandy campaign. Its second Panzer Battalion was provided by the Army's 560th Heavy Panzerjäger Battalion with forty-two Jagdpanzers, including fourteen Jagdpanzer Vs (Jagdpanthers). This unit had been attached to the Corps by an OKW order of 5 December. Kuhlmann's KG also included the rest of his own 12th SS Panzer Regiment with its AA and Pioneer Companies, the 3rd SPW SS Panzer-Grenadier Battalion and 150mm Infantry Gun Company of 'Papa' Krause's 26th Regiment under SS Captain Georg Urabl, and a towed 105mm artillery Battalion – more or less the same total strength as KG Peiper of the LAH.

Behind KG Kuhlmann on Route C came Gerd Bremer's 'Fast Group', similar to KG Knittel, followed by the Divisional Tactical Headquarters, and then the rest of Krause's Regiment and the 12th SS Werfer Battalion. The unallocated Divisional units, together with the balance of the Divisional artillery and a Luftwaffe Flak Battalion, followed on.

The leading unit on Route A-B was the 1st SS Panzer-Grenadier Battalion of Müller's 25th Regiment, commanded by SS Captain Ott. This Battalion was due to branch off and link up with the paratroopers of Operation STÖSSER in the Baraque Michel area on the right flank of the advance. It was followed by KG Müller, comprising the 12th SS Panzerjäger Battalion with twenty-two Jagdpanzers, the rest of the 25th Regiment and a towed artillery Battalion and Pioneer Company.[6] The KGs of I SS Panzer Corps are summarised at Appendix V.

Although it has been said that it was hoped to seize the bridges required for the advance, two army bridging columns were in fact allocated to I SS Panzer Corps. However, due to the poor roads and close country, there was no possibility of them being anywhere near the front of the attacking columns and they followed on some considerable distance to the rear of both Divisions.

The two SS Panzer Divisions were obviously well organised for their mission of slicing through the thin American defences, causing panic in the rear areas and 'bouncing' crossings over the Meuse. However, it has to be pointed out that neither of the units provided as second Panzer Battalions in the two armoured KGs – the 501st SS Heavy Panzer and 560th Heavy Panzerjäger Battalions – was particularly suitable for the type of Blitzkrieg operation envisaged. The Tiger IIs, at 69 tons, were far too cumbersome and unreliable, and the crews of the Jagdpanzers were inexperienced and untrained for assault operations in cooperation with infantry. Any chance of cohesion within the two Panzer Regiments was therefore minimal and the resulting mixture of armoured vehicles inevitably produced serious maintenance and supply problems.

The infantry Divisions of I SS Panzer Corps, charged with making the necessary breaches for the Panzer spearheads, were neither equipped, manned nor in many cases, trained to carry out their missions successfully.

At 1100 hours on 15 December Hermann Priess held a conference for his senior commanders. He stressed the vital importance of the offensive and his Chief of Staff repeated the basic attack order and then stated that two train loads of fuel had not arrived. This was serious news – the Corps' objectives were over 150km away from the assembly areas and the tanks had only enough fuel for some 100km at best. Details of known American fuel dumps were given and all commanders told to seize as much as they could until resupply could be arranged. Ammunition was sufficient for four or five days at intense combat rates.

Whatever optimism Priess may have shown at his conference, his real feelings, like those of his superiors, were very different:

The area assigned for the Corps attack was unfavourable. It was broken and heavily wooded. Wartime experience had tended to show that particularly good troops were needed for woodland fighting and that, as a consequence of the state of training of the infantry divisions, a rapid breakthrough in terrain such as this was very doubtful. . . . Therefore the following requests were made by the Corps to the Army:
1. To transfer our attack sector farther to the south because the territory in that region was more open and because more and better roads were available.
2. In the event of a disapproval of this first request, the commitment

51

of the two SS Panzer divisions, or at least parts of these, to the actual breakthrough itself in order to force this as quickly as possible. Both requests were refused.[7]

Priess's point about the unfavourable ground for the attack was completely valid. As well as being broken and heavily forested, the roads and tracks in the area were generally poor and the prevailing weather conditions made cross-country movement impossible for wheels, extremely difficult for tracked vehicles and painfully slow for foot soldiers.

It was dark by 1700 hours on 15 December and dawn would not break the next morning until about 0745 hours. The metal of the armoured vehicles was so cold that it was painful to touch; inside they were as cold as refrigerators, making sleep for the men of I SS Panzer Corps unthinkable. Meanwhile, with the exception of the men of the 2nd Infantry, most of the Americans in front of them settled down in their warm, timber covered bunkers or Belgian billets, for a good night's sleep.

When dawn broke on 16 December, low cloud covered the Ardennes, mist enveloped the forests and the temperature hovered around zero. Occasional snow flurries further restricted visibility but, except on the highest ground, little snow fell and even that soon turned to sleet and rain. Thin ice covered the puddles and men sank into thick, clawing mud the moment they stepped off the roads. It could not have been more miserable.

At the Adlerhof, Hitler and his generals were already aware that not everything was going according to the master plan. Operation BODENPLATTE, the air offensive against the Allied airfields, had had to be postponed due to poor visibility, and when the paratroopers of Operation STÖSSER had tried to move to their mounting airfields at Paderborn and Bad Lippspringe, they found insufficient transport to move them. That operation too had to be postponed. In addition, it had been impossible to find more than a handful of fluent English speakers for Skorzeny's commandos and in the same way, the American tanks and vehicles with which his so-called '150th Panzer Brigade' was to be equipped had not materialised. In the end it had only one Sherman, together with five Panthers and five StuGs disguised to look like Shermans.

At precisely 0535 hours an intense German artillery barrage broke the silence of the dark winter's morning – Hitler's final offensive in the West had begun. Its codename was AUTUMN MIST (HERBSTNEBEL).

NOTES

1. Interview with Robert Merriam, Aug 45.
2. *Commitment of I SS Pz Corps during the Ardennes Offensive, Gruppenführer Herman Priess*, MS # A-877 dated Mar 46.

3. Meyer, *The History of the 12th SS Panzer Division Hitlerjugend*, p. 281.
4. The 101st SS Hy Pz Bn was re-numbered 501st on 22 Sep 44.
5. All organisational details are taken from Tiemann's *Die Leibstandarte* IV/2, supplemented by interviews with LAH veterans and strength returns held in the Bundesarchiv.
6. All organisational details are taken from Hubert Meyer's *The History of the 12th SS Panzer Division Hitlerjugend*, p. 236 and strength returns held in the Bundesarchiv.
7. MS # A-877 dated Mar 46.

CHAPTER VII

AUTUMN MIST: 16 December

(Map 8)

On the Sixth Panzer Army front the artillery barrage was fired by the massed guns and Nebelwerfers of two artillery corps and two Volks Werfer brigades. There are conflicting reports about its duration, ranging from ten minutes on the German side to one and a half hours by the American.[1] The Germans insist they had only enough ammunition for a short fire plan, but the point is not important anyway. Although some serious disruption was caused to communications due to the severance of telephone wires, American casualties were few. The effect of those shells and rockets which did land on troop targets was largely negated by the overhead protection provided for most of the American foxholes and bunkers and the fact that some soldiers slept in Belgian houses.

The Leibstandarte Front

Taking the attack front from left to right, we will start with the Leibstandarte's sector. The 5th Regiment of General Wedehn's 3rd FSD took longer than expected to rout the men of the 14th Cavalry Group in the Krewinkel area, but by 1430 hours the way to Manderfeld was wide open. All that stood in the way on Route E was an old German minefield, forgotten by the planners.

Farther north on Route D, General Engel's 12th VGD was much less successful. Despite the use of StuGs, the 1st Battalion of the US 394th Infantry Regiment could not be evicted from the Losheimergraben crossroads and an attempt to take Buchholz, where the 99th Divisional reserve Battalion was based, also failed. Although the American Regiment suffered 959 casualties, including thirty-four dead and an astonishing 701

53

missing during the first day of the offensive, Route D was still blocked at last light.

Jochen Peiper had expected to start his advance soon after first light but he knew, not least from the radio nets at Engel's Headquarters, that the Volks-Grenadiers were failing in their attempts to clear a way for his tanks. At about 1400 hours he rejoined his KG as it crawled forward on the few roads and tracks available to it, with KG Hansen following on behind. From just outside Stadtkyll there was only one metalled road available to the LAH – through Hallschlag, where Hansen was due to turn south onto Route E at Ormont, and then onto the old International highway just south of Losheim. Progress was painfully slow with the road and all adjacent tracks cluttered with the vehicles, horses and equipment of two infantry Divisions and the Corps artillery.

At this moment there appears to have been either a breakdown in communications or more likely a lack of initiative on the part of the German commanders, for by 1400 hours it should have been obvious to Mohnke, or even Priess, that there was more chance of a breakthrough on Route E than on Route D. The Americans at Losheimergraben were holding firm, and the fact that the road bridge over the railway to its south was demolished added to the problems in that area. However, apart from the old minefield which would have to be gapped, the way to Manderfeld was clear and, as Hansen was to prove on the 17th, it was a simple matter to drive from there to Amel or Honsfeld via Herresbach or Holzheim (Map 11). An order to Peiper to take Hansen's Route E at this time would have had the added advantage of avoiding a further bottleneck near Scheid, between Hallschlag and Losheim, where another demolished bridge blocked the road. Uncharacteristically, the German commanders and staffs displayed none of the flexibility demanded by the situation and, by sticking rigidly to the original plan with Peiper on Route D and Hansen on Route E, a great opportunity was wasted.

It was 1700 hours before Peiper's Spitze (vanguard) reached Losheim, and since Losheimergraben was still in American hands, the KG was ordered to divert through Lanzerath; it had taken the 9th Parachute Regiment all day to capture the village and its immediate environs.[2] However, since another old German minefield barred the way, this diversion was easier said than done. In a rushed attempt to clear a path the Spitze lost three of its seven tanks and it was 2200 hours before the remainder reached the village; after being told by the Wedehn's paratroopers that the woods to the north and west of the village were full of Americans, the Spitze commander decided to await further orders.

Peiper himself reached Lanzerath at about 2300 hours. He was not impressed by what he found – sleeping paratroopers and no one taking any offensive action.

The problem of forgotten German minefields was also affecting KG

Hansen. While LAH Pioneers assisted those of the 3rd FSD to clear a route, Rettlinger's 1st SS Panzerjäger Battalion had to wait at Ormont. This in turn held up Knittel's Fast Group, which was concentrated on the road to the east of Stadtkyll; and Skorzeny's three KGs, of the so-called 150th Panzer Brigade, were also held up just to the west of Dahlem. KG Sandig was still in its assembly area near Tondorf.

Midnight on Day One found Peiper, Hansen and Mohnke angry and frustrated – the advance was over twelve hours behind schedule and, as far as they were concerned, they were still in Germany.

The Hitlerjugend Front
(Map 9)

Kraas, Priess and Dietrich were equally furious – Wilhelm Viebig's 277th Volks-Grenadiers, attempting to make breaches for the Hitlerjugend, had been even less successful.

The attack from the Hollerath area by the 989th Grenadier Regiment, lacking one of its Battalions but reinforced by a Pioneer company and some Hetzers of the Divisional Panzerjäger Battalion, met with limited success. Its immediate objective was Rocherath, but by last light it had advanced only 2km and was still 4km short of the village; nevertheless, it was halfway through the forest, having bypassed most of an American infantry Battalion[3] which had suffered some 300 casualties in the day's fighting.

We come now to a puzzling aspect of the fighting in this sector. According to the Chief of Staff of the Hitlerjugend, Hubert Meyer, at around noon on this first day Priess ordered the leading KG on Route A-B, SS Captain Ott's 1st SS Panzer-Grenadier Battalion of the 25th Regiment, reinforced by anti-tank and infantry heavy gun platoons, to 'enlarge the breach along Advance Route A [Hollerath-Rocherath-Krinkelt]'.[4] It is puzzling for several reasons: first, this KG failed to establish contact with the 989th VG Regiment which it was meant to support; second, it failed to make radio contact with its parent 25th Regiment; third, it seems to have played little or no part in the fighting in this sector; and fourth, Ott apparently 'gained the impression' that the Americans were trying to outflank his force and 'decided during the course of the night to withdraw to the most forward German positions'.[5] Since there are no details of Ott's KG in the fighting on the 17th either, one has to question whether it ever arrived in the 989th Regiment's sector at all.

Farther south, the 990th Grenadier Regiment, reinforced by Fusilier and Pioneer companies and with the support of at least four Hetzers, assembled in the bunkers of the West Wall near Udenbreth and Neuhof. This was the strongest of Viebig's Regiments and its objective was not

Krinkelt, as recorded by many writers, but Mürringen. This misunder-standing stems from a passage in the Official US History, *The Ardennes: Battle of the Bulge*, by Hugh M. Cole, which states:

> In front of the 393rd, across the frontier, were entrances to the two forest roads which ran through the regimental sector, one in the north at Hollerath, the second in the south at Udenbreth. . . . At the western edge of the woods the roads converged, funneling along a single track into Rocherath-Krinkelt. The twin villages, therefore, had a tactical importance of the first order.[6]

Whilst it is certainly true that the 'twin villages' were tactically important and dominated the direct approaches from the north-east, east and south-east, it is certainly *not* true that the track from the Udenbreth road 'converged, funneling along a single track into Rocherath-Krinkelt'. The tracks today are the same as they were in 1944 and although it was, and still is, quite possible to follow a track running north-west from the Udenbreth-Neuhof road towards Rocherath, the *main* forest trails from the Udenbreth-Neuhof road run west and south-west (through the Honsfelder Wald and Langelenfenn) to Mürringen and the vital Losheimergraben-Büllingen road. These tracks are clear on pre-war maps but are not shown on MAP II in Cole's Official History and consequently they have been ignored by most historians. It would have made no military sense to target *both* the 989th and the 990th Regiments at the Twin Villages and ignore the shortest and most direct route to Büllingen – a route which as far as Mürringen could not be observed from the Twin Villages. This thesis would seem to be confirmed by Hubert Meyer who points out in his *History of the 12th SS Panzer Division Hitlerjugend* that 'the 277 Division had its focal point to the left'. When one adds the fact that KG Kuhlmann, the strongest in the Division, was poised to take Route C, it is clear that the main attack in the 277th VGD sector should have been, and was, directed towards Mürringen and the Büllingen road and certainly not towards the Twin Villages.

The 990th Regiment's projected advance straddled the boundary between two American infantry Battalions[7], and involved crossing a kilometre of open ground before fighting through thick forest. The Germans suffered serious casualties from artillery, mortar and machine-gun fire as they crossed the open ground in daylight and, although the Americans were pushed back some 300m, the assault soon bogged down.

It was during this first day's fighting that we get a number of references by members of the 99th Division to German tanks – especially Tiger tanks. One commanding officer and two of his company commanders[8] stated in a combat interview in January 1945, that a Tiger was knocked out by one of their 57mm anti-tank guns near the Losheimergraben crossroads on the first morning of the attack; and another Battalion reported German tanks in the fighting near Neuhof on the same day.[9] The only Tigers on this front on the 16th were those of KG Peiper and they were certainly nowhere near Losheimergraben that morning. In both cases the so-called tanks were in fact the StuGs or Jagdpanzers of the relevant VGDs. The simple explanation is that the inexperienced soldiers of the 99th had heard about the dreaded Tiger and expected to see one every time they heard the noise of tracks. References to Tigers and '88s' in personal interviews and unit After Action Reports should therefore be treated with caution. In the same way, post-war interviews with German commanders like Jochen Peiper and Hermann Priess are also open to question – they were often intent on providing excuses for their failures, exaggerating their achievements or emphasising the heroics of their men.

In an attempt to restart the attack in his southern sector, Viebig threw in his reserve 991st Regiment; it was no more successful and at the end of the day the Americans, although by then reduced to half strength, were still holding most of their positions.[10] It is interesting that Viebig used his reserve Regiment to support his southern thrust, rather than the one against Rocherath. This would again indicate that the direct route through Mürringen towards Büllingen was seen as the most important.

By last light on the first day of the offensive the Germans had completely failed to make their breakthrough and had suffered heavy casualties, particularly in junior leaders. The Americans were able to take advantage of this situation by deploying part of the reserve and uncommitted Regiment of the 2nd Infantry Division to back up their weakened, but unbroken, defences. One Battalion occupied a prepared position to the north-east of Rocherath[11], one remained north of that village, and another was moved to cover the vital Losheimergraben-Büllingen road in the Hünningen area.[12]

The main problem facing the German commanders at last light on 16 December was how to launch their two most important KGs, Peiper and Kuhlmann, down Routes D and C respectively. We have heard how Peiper was ordered to divert through Lanzerath. What were the options in the case of Kuhlmann? There were four: first, continue to try to break through in the north in order to open up a route through Rocherath; second, strike again directly towards Mürringen and clear the shortest and most direct way to Route C; third, continue the attempt to break through in the north and at the same time order the 12th VGD to attack north-west towards Hünningen; and fourth, send Kuhlmann via the Losheimergraben crossroads. This last option was found to be unrealistic. The crossroads area was still in American hands and it would have involved the KG moving down the main road from Hollerath at right angles to the American front, or taking a very much longer route via

Hallschlag and Losheim (Map 8). In the first case the Americans were still in a position to cause severe attrition on many parts of the road, and in the second it meant getting entangled with the KGs of the Leibstandarte and having to repair, or bypass, a demolished bridge over the railway between Losheim and Losheimergraben.[13]

The first option had two advantages – it would build on what little success had already been achieved and, if it succeeded, the Americans blocking the way to Mürringen would almost inevitably be forced to withdraw. The second option, the simplest, involved fighting through 3km of thick forest. Option three offered the possibility of cutting off all the Americans to the east of a line drawn through the Twin Villages and Hünningen, and of thus opening up Route C. Not surprisingly Priess chose the third option and KG Müller, with its twenty-two Jagdpanzer IVs, was ordered to take the Twin Villages. The necessary orders were given to 12th VGD and during the night General Viebig moved the 990th Regiment in behind the 989th so that it too could engage in the attack on Rocherath.

The decision to implement the third option presented much greater opportunities to the Germans than they realised. If the operation were successful it would not only cut off the 99th Division, but it would also threaten the lines of communication of the 2nd Infantry Division. Indeed, due to the disquieting news from his southern flank, General Robertson was already making plans to withdraw that Division by the time the German decision was made.

Mention must now be made of the special operations designed by Hitler to assist Operation AUTUMN MIST. As previously mentioned, the parachute drop on the Baraque Michel area had already been postponed, but just before midnight on 16 December sixty-eight Junker 52 troop carriers with 870 real and 300 dummy paratroopers took off heading for their drop-zone north of Malmédy. The commander was Colonel von der Heydte.

In the second special operation Skorzeny's armoured KGs had been unable to advance as planned owing to the failure of the break-in battle, but a number of his commando teams had been more successful. Using US jeeps and uniforms, they had managed to penetrate American lines and by last light on the 16th one group had even reached Huy (Map 10) on the Meuse. After the war Skorzeny said that forty-four of his men got through; whatever the correct number, there is no doubt that they achieved some success in that they made the Americans very jittery and security conscious; although as von Manteuffel said later: 'The importance of Operation GREIF has been grossly exaggerated since the war.' The exploits of these commandos have been recounted many times before and need not be repeated. Twenty-three of them were captured and eighteen executed for contravening the Rules of War by wearing enemy uniforms.

How did the higher American echelons of command react to the events of 16 December? Apart from the Supreme Allied Commander himself, nobody seemed to appreciate the seriousness of the German attack. It was fortuitous that General Bradley, the commander of the Twelfth US Army Group, happened to be in Paris conferring with Eisenhower on that vital day. He was there to discuss the general problem of replacements. When, that afternoon, they received a message from Bradley's Headquarters in Luxembourg City giving word of the German attack, Ike suggested that he should perhaps, as a precaution, move the 7th Armored Division down from the north and the 10th Armored up from the south.[14] Bradley agreed and at 1730 hours Brigadier General Bob Hasbrouck's 7th Armored Division at Heerlen (Map 6) in Holland received a warning order for a move south.

Another important event early on the 16th was when Hodges, commanding the US First Army, telephoned Lieutenant General William Simpson of the US Ninth Army to discuss the overall situation. The result was a reinforcement from north to south starting the same day and continuing into the 17th; this included the 26th Infantry Regiment of the uncommitted 1st Infantry Division – the 'Big Red One'. It was alerted as early as 1100 hours on the 16th and, starting at 0230 hours on the 17th, it set out for Camp Elsenborn where it arrived at 0700 hours. Simpson's further offer of the 30th Infantry Division was to have a profound effect on the forthcoming battle.

The one puzzling decision on the American side on the first day of AUTUMN MIST was Hodges' refusal to call off the 2nd Infantry's attack towards the Roer dams.

NOTES

1. Meyer, *The History of the 12th SS Panzer Division Hitlerjugend*, p. 242 and Cole, *The Ardennes: Battle of the Bulge*, p. 82.
2. According to German records, the 9th Parachute Regiment suffered forty-three killed and twenty-four wounded on 16 Dec 44. Following the withdrawal of four US TDs and a Recce Pl of A/820 TD Bn from the village soon after first light, the way past Lanzerath was denied to the paratroopers until nearly last light by the I&R Pl/394th Inf Regt and a four-man arty observation party from C/371st Fd Arty Bn. This group of two officers and twenty men was positioned on a hill some 300m to the north-west of the village. One American was killed and the rest captured. All received medals.
3. 3/393rd.
4. Meyer, op. cit., p. 243.
5. Ibid., p. 244.
6. Cole, op. cit., p. 95.
7. 1/393rd & 2/394th.
8. 1/394th.
9. 2/394th.

10. 1/393rd.
11. 3/23rd.
12. 1/23rd.
13. Meyer, op. cit., p. 243. It was, and still is, reasonably easy to bypass this bridge.
14. Merriam, *The Battle of the Ardennes*, p. 111.

CHAPTER VIII
AUTUMN MIST: 17 December
The Leibstandarte Front
(Map 11)

The 17th of December 1944 was the most significant day in Jochen Peiper's life. As a result of what happened on that fateful Sunday, he was to be sentenced to death by hanging, serve nearly eleven years in prison as a war criminal and be murdered in France nearly thirty-two years later.

Peiper's advance from Lanzerath towards Buchholz did not begin until about 0330 hours. The four-hour delay was due to the need to close up the column, negotiate the minefield to the west of Losheim in the dark and overcome the difficulties of assembling and organising the paratroopers who were dispersed throughout Lanzerath and its adjacent woods. Peiper took one Parachute Battalion under command and, while one company led his column and provided flank protection, the remainder rode on his tanks – mainly on the Tigers at the rear of the column. His KG was some 25km in length and, in the difficult, forested country ahead, with little or no chance of cross-country movement, he was forced to advance on a one-vehicle front.

To Peiper's great relief there were no Americans in the woods to the north-west of Lanzerath. Most of the reserve Battalion at Buchholz[1] had been used to reinforce the Losheimergraben defences and the sixty or so men left in the hamlet were nearly all asleep. The Spitze drove straight through towards Honsfeld while Panzer-Grenadiers mopped up without trouble.

Honsfeld contained a large number of troops and was ostensibly defended by five TDs and some miscellaneous minor units. In fact virtually all the Americans were asleep in the village houses and the leading German tanks were again able to drive through without trouble. One TD man wrote later:

> I was sleeping in the attic with three or four other buddies when I was awakened . . . and told to get up as the Germans had us completely

surrounded. . . . We all jumped up and began looking out of the various windows and saw that German soldiers were everywhere we looked.[2]

Later on, after daylight, US troops in the outlying farms and houses began to offer some resistance; two Panthers were damaged and the rear elements of the KG, mainly paratroopers, lost some fifty men. Nevertheless, Honsfeld was a disaster for the Americans. They lost seventeen TDs, some fifty reconnaissance vehicles and over 300 men as prisoners. One Troop (company) of the 14th Cavalry, which had unfortunately moved there after withdrawing from the Losheim Gap, lost all its vehicles and equipment and only forty-four men escaped.[3] It was later alleged that fifteen American prisoners were killed by Peiper's men. Photographic evidence would suggest that this allegation was not without some foundation.

At about 0600 hours, whilst it was still dark, the advance continued. Peiper was in a hurry to get to Büllingen where he knew there was a fuel dump. Leaving most of his paratroopers to clear up in Honsfeld, he ordered SS Lieutenant Werner Sternebeck's depleted Spitze and SS Captain Georg Preuss's 10th SS Panzer-Grenadier Company, reinforced with Mk IV tanks, anti-tank guns and Pioneers, to get on as quickly as possible. At least one company of paratroopers stayed with the KG.

Büllingen was a major administrative centre for both the 2nd and 99th Infantry Divisions and, as well as fuel and ammunition dumps, it contained a large number of administrative units. At the south-west edge of the town there were two air-strips on each of which were based a dozen L-5 light observation aircraft. The only combat unit in the area was an Engineer Battalion[4] belonging to V Corps and, in view of the confused and threatening situation, it was released to General Lauer at midnight on the 16th. He immediately ordered the engineers to form a defensive line to the south and east of Büllingen. An indication of the confusion at that time can be gathered from the fact that the Battalion commander was told that all roads leading into the town were covered by TDs or tanks and he was to protect these road blocks. In fact there were none; but the engineers moved quickly and by 0500 hours they had a company on each of the main roads leading in from Losheimergraben, Honsfeld and the south-west.

At about 0630 hours Peiper's Spitze approached the road block set up by the engineer Company[5] on the Honsfeld road, just to the south of Büllingen. What happened next is disputed. The Americans claim the SS Panzer-Grenadiers were beaten back four times before tanks overran some of the engineers and the rest were outflanked and forced to withdraw. The commander of the Spitze, Werner Sternebeck, had no recollection of any of this when he revisited the area with the author in October 1985. He remembered receiving fire from automatic weapons about 2km south of the town and from west of the road, and said part of the Spitze group 'veered off, returned the fire and attacked an airstrip containing light reconnaissance aircraft'. Nevertheless, there seems little doubt that the Spitze Company group was indeed forced to deploy at this point and that some delay was caused – even if the casualties claimed by the Americans may seem a little exaggerated.

There is certainly no disputing the fact that the Spitze lost one Mk IV to bazooka fire as it reached the outskirts of Büllingen, and that it then lost its way in the darkness and exited the town to the north, where it lost a second Mk IV to TD fire somewhere south of Wirtzfeld. Little did Sternebeck realise that at that moment he was within 750m of the commander of the 2nd Infantry Division, Major General Walter Robertson, whose Command Post was in the village![6]

Meanwhile Preuss's Spitze Company Group fought its way into Büllingen and in a very confused battle the Germans suffered a number of casualties including two platoon commanders. Preuss himself became separated from his Company and later claimed he was unable to rejoin it until the following day because he became involved in 'brief firefights with withdrawing American infantry groups'.

The fighting in Büllingen was mainly against the engineers who suffered eighty-seven casualties, including fifty-five missing, before they were forced to withdraw to the high ground just to the east of a manor house on the Bütgenbach road known to the Americans as Dom (short for Domäne) Bütgenbach. The Germans took a large number of prisoners in Büllingen but about half of the light aircraft managed to take off from the air-strips before the arrival of Preuss's men.

By 0900 hours Peiper's column was ready to resume its advance. Despite intermittent shelling many of the tanks and SPWs had managed to refuel at the US fuel dump.[7]

The engineers at Dom Bütgenbach (Dom B), had by now been joined by stragglers from other units and some Headquarters staff from the 99th Division, and they were both surprised and relieved when they saw Peiper's column leave the town, not on the Bütgenbach road as expected, but to the south-west. They were even happier when they saw eleven P-47 aircraft attack the German column. The Thunderbolts had been called in by the 99th Division and thirty-nine sorties were flown in the Büllingen area between 0900 and 1100 hours.[8] Peiper admitted to the loss of one Tiger but otherwise his KG seemed to suffer little, and between 0930 hours and midday it advanced through Möderscheid, Schoppen and Ondenval to Thirimont, meeting no opposition on the way. Sternebeck with his depleted Spitze had by now rejoined the column but was no longer in the lead.

Peiper's running mate, KG Hansen, had a much easier time on the 17th.

By first light the minefield east of Krewinkel had been breached and the column, led by Rettlinger's Jagdpanzer IVs with SS Panzer-Grenadiers mounted, set off soon after dawn. Barring the way were troops of the 14th Cavalry Group, including seventeen light tanks, near Andler and at Herresbach, Wereth and Heuem. These units, although only lightly armed, should have been able to impose some delay on the Germans but they simply melted away, most of them without firing a shot, to St Vith, Meyerode and Born.

Hansen decided to split his KG, and while the Jagdpanzer group moved via Andler and Herresbach, another Battalion group went via Holzheim and Honsfeld, and yet another by way of Manderfeld and Lanzerath.[9] By midday Hansen's leading elements were 5km to the south of Peiper's and only a short distance behind them. The Leibstandarte had made its breakthrough.

The Hitlerjugend Front
(Map 9)

The situation on the Hitlerjugend front was very different. The 12th VGD renewed its attack at Losheimergraben soon after dawn and by early afternoon the crossroads area was in German hands. At the same time the reserve 89th Regiment of the 12th VGD, with StuG support, advanced through the woods to the north of Buchholz and attacked the American Battalion[10] positioned just to the east and south-east of Hünningen in the late afternoon. After heavy fighting the Americans were forced to withdraw and the survivors reached Wirtzfeld the following day.

The third option chosen by Priess for opening up Route C seemed to be working, for on the northern flank too the Germans were having some success. During the morning the Americans[11] on the approaches to the Twin Villages were hit hard by SS Lieutenant Colonel Richard Schulze's 2nd SS Panzer-Grenadier Battalion[12] and, despite the appalling ground conditions, by SS Captain Brockschmidt's Jagdpanzers, supported by artillery and SS Pioneers. By 1400 hours the defenders had been forced back, but not before inflicting severe casualties on the SS men. A Platoon commander in Schulze's Battalion described some of the fighting:

> The woods were mined, the mines connected by above-ground wires. . . .
> Our attack initially progressed well. The fighting spirit of the men
> was excellent. Enemy resistance increased constantly. All sorts of
> shells exploded around us, not only on the ground but also in the
> treetops.[13]

His Battalion commander later recalled:

Since the men were largely without combat experience, only the deployment of the officers at the front could help. In the first hours, all the Company commanders were lost, either killed or wounded [and the Adjutant and technical officer]. Senior NCOs took over the Companies.[14]

And the commander of the 1st SS Panzerjäger Company, SS Lieutenant Zeiner, said later:

We followed a narrow, occasionally winding forest track to a spot where it split and dropped off. There all hell broke loose. . . . The enemy had armour-piercing weapons, snipers in the trees and a few Shermans in ambush positions. SS Senior Sergeant Roy . . . was driving behind me. He was killed by a shot in the head. Roy had been awarded the Knight's Cross during the invasion. . . . The death of our comrade surely provoked great rage in us all, and I drove ahead recklessly.[15]

This advance by KG Müller, as expected, outflanked the two American Battalions covering the approaches to Mürringen[16] and they too began to pull back.

It will be recalled that permission to call off the 2nd Division's attack towards the Roer dams on the 16th had been refused. The V Corps commander, Major General Leonard Gerow, renewed his request early on the 17th and was finally told to act as he thought fit. He immediately contacted General Robertson of the 2nd Division and orders were issued to pull back from the Wahlerscheid salient (Map 8).

KG Peiper's sudden appearance at Honsfeld and Büllingen and Sternebeck's Spitze on the Wirtzfeld road, even if it was a mistake, had done much to focus the minds of the senior American commanders. It was clear that the Twin Villages were threatened and that major elements of the 2nd and 99th Infantry Divisions might soon be cut off. Fortunately for the Americans, Peiper's orders were to strike south-west and no one on the German side had the vision or initiative to change those orders. If they had, and Peiper had taken the Bütgenbach road, it is more than possible that the Americans would have panicked and the whole front south-east of Elsenborn might have collapsed. Even so it would be fair to say that during the morning of the 17th it seemed that Priess's third option was beginning to work and that the way to the west would soon be open for the Hitlerjugend.

The order to withdraw the 2nd Division was quickly implemented and began at midday. By 1700 hours, in fog which reduced visibility to less than 100m, one Battalion of just over 400 and part of another[17], supported by three TDs – all told about 600 men – had taken up positions just to the north-east of the Twin Villages. They were in time to see the sad remnants of two other Battalions[18] streaming back from their forest battles with the 277th Volks-Grenadiers and KG Müller, but they did not panic and in fierce fighting the Jagdpanzers and Schulze's SS Panzer-Grenadiers were brought to a halt.

The situation at last light on 17 December can be summarised therefore as follows: the Twin Villages were held by four 2nd Division infantry Battalions[19], supported by tanks and TDs[20]; an engineer and four infantry Battalions[21] were in position 2km to the north and north-east of the Twin Villages; three infantry Battalions were defending the Wirtzfeld area[22], and three US infantry Battalions had been decimated and the survivors were on their way back to Elsenborn.[23]

(Map 10)

It will be remembered that Luftwaffe Colonel Freiherr von der Heydte's parachute operation (STÖSSER) finally went ahead in the early hours of the 17th; however, high winds, inexperienced pilots and both friendly and enemy AA fire led to a very dispersed drop and by last light only some 300 of the 800 men, without heavy weapons or radios, had managed to form up in the Baraque Michel area to the north of Malmédy. The mission had failed – von der Heydte had arrived with too little, too late. The Regiment of the US 1st Infantry Division which he might have delayed or disrupted was already taking up its assigned positions – one Battalion to the south-west of Wirtzfeld, one at Dom B and a third in Bütgenbach itself.[24]

In some respects though, STÖSSER was a success. Due to the dispersed drop the Americans gained the impression that there had been a very large parachute operation, with the result that hundreds of men were wasted looking for mythical paratroopers instead of getting on with their proper jobs. It is a fact that many veterans, and indeed many Belgians, together with most After Action Reports, talk about numerous incidents with German airborne troops. Clearly, the few who landed behind American lines had an effect out of all proportion to their numbers. All were eventually captured.

(Map 9)

In darkness and with snow falling, Brockschmidt's Jagdpanzers and Schulze's SS Grenadiers renewed their assault on the Twin Villages sometime around 1900 hours on the 17th. One group of four Jagdpanzers from the 1st Company with a platoon of Grenadiers, led by Helmut Zeiner, taking advantage of the darkness and very confused situation, managed to get through the Americans on the outskirts of Rocherath[25] without loss. After entering the village along the track coming in from due east, they claimed three Shermans knocked out, one within a few metres of the

65

church, and in a bizarre situation they remained there all night without reinforcement. Zeiner described the scene as follows:

> We tried, time and again, to establish radio contact with our Battalion. . . . We set up a hedgehog position. . . . The small village was larger . . . than we had originally thought. Enemy infantry were still sitting in its western section. . . . I only had some forty Grenadiers, and each of my Jagdpanzers had only some ten high explosive shells left. Also, our fuel supply was very low. As well, we had taken approximately eighty prisoners. Tactically, our situation in the village centre was hopeless in case of an enemy infantry attack.[26]

Another larger group of some six Jagdpanzers from the same Company took a different route, which ran towards the village from the north-east. All but one of the Jagdpanzers were lost to mines, bazookas and artillery. A further attack by the 2nd Panzerjäger Company with at least seven Jagdpanzers, commanded by SS Lieutenant Wachter, supported by the rest of Schulze's Panzer-Grenadiers, was halted by intense artillery fire and the men of the 9th Infantry Regiment. The German column was said by one US artillery observer to be a thousand yards long. Three Jagdpanzers reached Rocherath but four were knocked out by artillery fire and Wachter and one of his platoon commanders killed. All four artillery Battalions of the US 2nd Division and the three heavy howitzer Battalions of the V Corps were used to break up this attack – a total of 112 guns. By 2315 hours the Hitlerjugend assault on the Twin Villages had been halted, with casualties amongst the Panzer-Grenadiers being particularly heavy – one Company in Schulze's Battalion had been reduced to twenty-seven men.[27] An American officer described the silence which descended on the battlefield as 'almost frightening'.

The Leibstandarte Front

(Map 11)

Meanwhile, what had happened to the Leibstandarte's KGs? We left KG Hansen at noon with its Spitze in the Heppenbach area. By 1430 hours Rettlinger's Jagdpanzers and the 1st SS Panzer-Grenadier Battalion had reached Born. The 14th Cavalry was still withdrawing in front of them, but at Recht, shortly before last light, the Germans ran into a company of Shermans.[28] There was a forty-five minute engagement, in which Hansen's men say they knocked out four or five tanks before the Americans withdrew, setting fire to the wooden bridge on the Poteau road as they did so. Hansen decided to remain where he was for the night.

By this time Fast Group Knittel was just to the east of the Kaiserbarracke crossroads and well poised to switch to Route D if necessary.

One incident had occurred on the southern route during this period which again soils the reputation of the Leibstandarte. Eleven black US prisoners from an artillery unit[29] were brutally murdered just outside the village of Wereth sometime after dark on the 17th. The mutilated bodies of these soldiers were found by Belgian civilians the following morning. The perpetrators of this crime were never identified but they must have been members of either KG Hansen or Fast Group Knittel.

KG Sandig remained in its assembly area behind the West Wall all day on the 17th.

(Map 12)

This leaves the main KG of the Leibstandarte – KG Peiper. At midday there were no American combat units deployed anywhere on Peiper's planned route to prevent him reaching the Meuse river. The only elements which might have given him trouble, a Combat Command of the 9th Armored Division which had been located across Route D in the Faymonville area, had moved south during the night towards St Vith (Map 11).

Peiper knew from a captured American officer that some sort of US Headquarters was situated in Ligneuville and he was anxious to get there as quickly as possible in the hope of seizing maps and other intelligence papers which might tell him when and where he could expect opposition. To this end his Spitze Company Group tried to take a short cut along a forest track from Thirimont to the main Malmédy-St Vith road, but it proved impassable even to tracked vehicles and many became mired. Werner Sternebeck with what was left of the original Spitze, two Mk IVs and two Pioneer SPWs, therefore took over the lead again and followed the road via Bagatelle and the Baugnez crossroads. As he approached Bagatelle he saw, to his left on the main N-23 road leading south from the Baugnez crossroads, a column of some thirty American jeeps and trucks heading towards Ligneuville.[30] Both German tanks opened fire with their 76mm guns, five or six rounds each, and they then drove rapidly to the crossroads where they turned left and headed south, firing their machine guns at the Americans, who had by now abandoned their vehicles and were taking cover. As the terrified Americans stood up to surrender, Sternebeck waved them back towards the crossroads and then halted his small force at the next bend in the road, awaiting further instructions. He did not have long to wait for Peiper's voice soon came over the radio ordering him to advance with all speed to Ligneuville, 4km to the south. After the war Peiper recalled following closely behind the Spitze and seeing three groups of Americans – those with their hands up, those on the ground and in the ditches pretending to be dead and a third group who, after pretending to be dead, got up and tried to run to nearby woods. He said his men had fired warning shots at the latter two groups.[31]

While over 100 Americans were being assembled in a field close to the Baugnez crossroads, the Spitze, Peiper in an SPW and the 11th SS Panzer-Grenadier Company moved on towards Ligneuville. It was now about 1330 hours.[32]

What happened next at those infamous crossroads has been the subject of numerous articles, books and films. The incident became known as the 'Malmédy Massacre'. The results of this author's investigations, and his opinions, are set out in his book, *The Devil's Adjutant – Jochen Peiper, Panzer Leader*, but bearing in mind that the subject of this present book is the history of the I SS Panzer Corps, it is sufficient to say here that eighty-four Americans died and twenty-five were wounded as a result of this confrontation with KG Peiper. Of the 113 unarmed prisoners in the field near the crossroads, sixty-seven died in or within 200m of that field, and forty-six managed to escape – although four of them died later. Fifty-six men survived the whole affair, of which seven became normal prisoners of war. There were no German casualties.

Ligneuville contained the Headquarters of a 90mm AA Brigade and the echelons, or 'trains' as the Americans called them, of the 9th Armored Divisional units which had moved south the previous night.[33] The personnel of these units were unaware of the incident at Baugnez but someone, probably a survivor, gave warning of the German approach and most of the Americans, including the artillery Brigadier-General, managed to escape before Sternebeck's tanks and SPWs entered the village and halted at the bridge over the Amblève river. Sternebeck then sent his SS Pioneers forward to check the bridge for demolitions and they came under fire from the south side. At about the same time the next tank to arrive in the village, a Panther commanded by Poetschke's Adjutant, was hit in the rear by anti-tank fire and burst into flames. A short battle followed before the 11th SS Panzer-Grenadiers cleared up the situation. The Americans lost two armoured vehicles and half a dozen trucks; and at least twenty-two men were taken prisoner, eight of whom were later shot.

Peiper's order of march had become very muddled by the various events of the day and some unsuccessful cross-country movement attempted between Büllingen and Möderscheid, and so he decided to delay any further advance and reorganise before moving on towards Stavelot after last light. When the KG did move off, at about 1700 hours, a Panther Company formed the Spitze and the column was led by two captured American jeeps containing two Belgians under guard who were being forced to show the way. Preuss's Spitze Company Group, which had attempted the short cut to Ligneuville, had now caught up and von Westernhagen's Tigers were beginning to arrive in the village, near which they remained for the night – many had broken down or become mired on the way.

(Map 13)

The advance towards Stavelot continued at a walking pace with commanders leading their tanks in the pitch dark along the narrow, icy, tree-lined and twisting road. No one had any idea when or where they might meet the enemy and with no possibility of deploying off the road, the column was extremely vulnerable. Peiper did not accompany his KG at this time but remained in Ligneuville where, as well as having a meal, he discussed the overall situation with his Divisional commander, Wilhelm Mohnke, who had come forward with a small tactical Headquarters.

By about 1900 hours the German Spitze had reached a point about one kilometre short of Stavelot, where there are a series of bends with a cliff on one side and a sheer drop down to the Amblève river on the other, and it was at this point that it ran into a hastily established American road block. This road block had been ordered by the commanding officer of an engineer Battalion[34] in Malmédy when he learned that a German armoured column had moved south from Baugnez and, although it comprised only a few anti-tank mines laid on the road and twelve men[35] with a bazooka and a machine-gun, it was well sited and sufficient to stop the Germans. After a short exchange of fire the engineers, unknown to the Germans, withdrew; but they had done their job – they had halted, albeit temporarily, the strongest Kampfgruppe of the I SS Panzer Corps and this enforced delay was to have dramatic consequences.

Jochen Peiper reached the head of his stationary column at about 2300 hours. He was told about the road block and could see vehicles transitting the town below with their headlights on; the headlights were in fact those of American vehicles in full retreat from the Malmédy area and beyond. Stavelot gave every appearance of being well defended, but in reality the way through was completely clear. The only combat troops in the town, a Company of engineers[36], had hurriedly left about half an hour before Peiper's arrival, joining all the other Americans pulling out to the west. Whether by mistake or misunderstanding they had failed to prepare the stone bridge over the Amblève for demolition – a bridge Peiper *had* to cross to get into the town.

After the war Peiper gave the following description of the situation as he remembered it that night:

At 1600 . . . we reached the area of Stavelot, which was heavily defended. We could observe heavy traffic moving from Malmédy toward Stavelot and Stavelot itself seemed clogged up completely with several hundred trucks. That night we attempted to capture Stavelot but the terrain presented great difficulties. The only approach was the main road and the ground to the left of the road fell very sharply and to the right of the road rose very sharply. There was a short curve just at the entrance to Stavelot where several Sherman tanks and anti-tank guns were zeroed in. Thereupon, we shelled Stavelot with heavy infantry howitzers and mortars, resulting in great confusion within the town and the destruction of several dumps. . . . At 1800 a counter-attack circled around a high hill 800 metres east of Stavelot and hit my column from the south . . . the counter-attack consisted entirely of infantry. After the counter-attack was repulsed, I committed more Panzer-Grenadiers to attack Stavelot again. We approached the outskirts of the town but bogged down because of stubborn American resistance at the edge of Stavelot. We suffered fairly heavy losses, twenty-five to thirty casualties, from tank, anti-tank, mortar and rifle fire. Since I did not have sufficient infantry, I decided to wait for the arrival of more.[37]

This account belies nearly all the real facts – the timings are wrong, the description of the ground is inaccurate, Stavelot was not shelled or mortared that night, there were no US tanks in the town until 1600 hours the following day, there were no US infantry there either until 0345 hours on the 18th, and no Americans capable of launching counter-attacks on the 17th.

Nevertheless, one part of Peiper's statement is true – he did decide to delay his attack on Stavelot until the following morning. Why? There were several valid reasons. First, it was of course inconceivable to the Germans that the only bridge leading into Stavelot would not be prepared for demolition and defended; second, the KG was spread out all the way back to Ligneuville and its artillery was not deployed; third, more Panzer-Grenadiers and Pioneers would be needed for the assault on the bridge and they would have to be brought forward; fourth, and perhaps most importantly, everyone was tired out. Maybe the Panzer-Grenadiers had managed to 'cat-nap' in the back of their freezing SPWs, but commanders, like Peiper and Poetschke and Diefenthal, and many drivers and vehicle commanders had not slept for over forty hours.

There is little doubt that if Peiper and his weary men had realised that at 2300 hours they could have driven straight through Stavelot, their tiredness would have disappeared – there is also little doubt that if they had done so they would have reached the Meuse the following day, with potentially catastrophic results for the Americans in particular and the Allies in general.

The 17th of December had seen a dramatic breakthrough by the Leibstandarte KGs but gains of less than 5km on the Hitlerjugend front. It is clear that had the request to move the I SS Panzer Corps' attack front a mere 10km to the south been granted, both armoured KGs – over 230 Mk IVs, Panthers, Tigers and Jagdpanzers, not accounting for breakdowns – would almost certainly have reached a line drawn from Stavelot to St Vith by midnight on the 17th. It would be unwise to attempt to assess the consequences.

I SS Panzer Corps had suffered remarkably few casualties in the first two days of the offensive. KG Peiper had lost three Panthers, three Mk IVs and at least one Tiger to mines and enemy action. At least eight Panthers, four Mk IVs and upwards of twenty Tigers had broken down, but many of these would be repaired and rejoin within a relatively short time. Considering the depth of the penetration, some 50km, personnel casualties in KG Peiper had been remarkably light and KG Hansen was virtually unscathed.

Of the Hitlerjugend KGs, only KG Müller had been engaged. Its 2nd SS Panzer-Grenadier Battalion had suffered badly and at least nine of its Jagdpanzers lost. Suggestions that HJ Panthers and Mk IV tanks took part in the fighting on the second day of the offensive and suffered casualties can be discounted. There were no tanks in KG Müller and those of Jürgensen's 1st SS Panzer Battalion were still well to the east of the West Wall.

Readers may be wondering what had happened to Otto Skorzeny's 150th 'Panzer' Brigade. The simple answer is nothing. During the evening of the 17th Skorzeny attended a staff conference at Dietrich's Sixth Panzer Army Headquarters[38], where he explained that due to poor roads, traffic conjestion and the overall lack of progress, he had been unable to launch any of his three KGs. He suggested that they should be combined and used as a conventional unit. This was agreed and he was ordered to assemble them to the south of Malmédy as soon as conditions permitted and report to Wilhelm Mohnke at Ligneuville for further orders.

NOTES

1. 3/394th.
2. Letter from W.T. Hawkins to author 23 Mar 89.
3. A/32nd.
4. 254th Engr Combat Bn.
5. B/254th.
6. Citation for award of DSC to Robertson dated 28 Dec 44 signed by Gerow.
7. Letter from Arndt Fischer to author dated 29 May 85.
8. OPSUMs held in the Office of Air Force History at Bolling Air Base.
9. Tiemann, *Die Leibstandarte*, Part IV/2 and LAH veterans to author loc cit., 2 Oct 85.
10. 1/23rd.
11. 3/23rd & 3/393rd & five Shermans C/741st.

12. Schulze had won a German Cross in Gold and been wounded in Russia. After being Adjutant to Hitler, he was released for the Ardennes offensive. Rather than serve on the staff, and although he was senior to Müller, he accepted a Battalion in his Regiment.
13. Meyer, *The History of the 12th SS Panzer Division Hitlerjugend*, p. 245.
14. Ibid., p. 246.
15. Ibid.
16. 1/393rd & 2/394th.
17. 1 & 3/9th respectively.
18. 3/393rd & 3/23rd.
19. 1, 2 & 3/38th and (the depleted) 1/9th.
20. 741st Tk, parts of 612th & 644th TD.
21. 2/393rd, 395th Regt, 324th Engr.
22. 2 & 3/9th & 2/23rd.
23. 1 & 3/393rd & 3/23rd.
24. 3, 2 & 1/26th respectively.
25. 1 & 3/9th Inf & 644th TD.
26. Meyer, op. cit., p. 251.
27. Ibid., p. 249.
28. 17th Tk Bn.
29. 333rd Fd Arty Bn.
30. B Bty, 285th Fd Arty Observation Bn.
31. Tiemann, op. cit., p. 64.
32. Sternebeck to author loc. cit., 1 Oct 85.
33. 149th AA Bde, 14th Tank, 16th Fd Arty and 27th Armd Inf Bns.
34. LTC David Pergrin of the 291st Engr Combat Bn.
35. Sgt Hensel and a squad of C/291st Engrs.
36. C/202nd.
37. Interview with Maj Ken Hechler, US Army, Sep 45.
38. Skorzeny, *Skorzeny's Special Missions* and ETHINT 12.

CHAPTER IX
The Other Side of the Hill: Night 17 – 18 December
(Maps 10 & 11)

Whilst the American intelligence staffs had a reasonably clear picture of what was going on in the 2nd and 99th Divisional areas on the afternoon of the 17th, they were completely in the dark about the situation in the vast area to the south of a line drawn from Büllingen to Stavelot. The locations and strengths of the Leibstandarte's leading KGs were completely unknown – indeed, even I SS Panzer Corps was unaware of their exact whereabouts at this particular time.[1]

One of the few officers in the entire First US Army who knew there were German tanks near Malmédy on the afternoon of the 17th was Lieutenant Colonel Dave Pergrin, the commanding officer of the few engineers[2] who had stayed in that town when everybody else had fled. One of his officers had spotted Peiper's column just before it reached Baugnez at midday, and a short time later the sound of firing had been heard from the crossroads area. Pergrin guessed that a US convoy[3], which he had warned not to proceed via Baugnez on its way to St Vith, had run into trouble. Sometime between 1500 and 1600 hours he decided to drive up towards the crossroads to see what had happened and to his amazement he encountered three semi-hysterical survivors of the 'Malmédy Massacre'. He rushed them back to his Command Post and at 1640 hours sent a message to the Chief Engineer at First Army Headquarters in Spa, and to his direct superior[4] in Trois Ponts, saying that there had been some sort of massacre of prisoners of war at Baugnez and that a Nazi armoured column had moved south from that area. This was the first firm information that anyone in the senior echelons of command had received of just how far the Germans had reached, and it did not take a military genius to work out that the column would almost certainly turn west at Ligneuville, threatening both the strategic town of Malmédy and Hodges' own Headquarters at Spa.

This new intelligence electrified the Americans. As well as the serious situation in the Bütgenbach and St Vith areas, General Courtney Hodges was now faced with a breakthrough between the two by enemy armour. He became so concerned that he asked his Army Group commander, General Omar Bradley, to press Eisenhower to release the Strategic Reserve to him. Under this combined pressure Ike agreed and at 1900 hours the XVIII Airborne Corps, near Reims in France (Map 2), received a warning order for a move to the First Army area. The acting Corps commander, Major General Jim Gavin, immediately drove to Hodges' Headquarters in Spa where he arrived early on the Monday morning. The place was in a state of chaos with the staff pulling out in any vehicle they could find. On learning that a German armoured column was probably only some 15km away, Gavin readily agreed to redirect his 82nd Airborne Division to the Werbomont area. The 101st Airborne Division would continue on to Bastogne (Map 6) as previously ordered.

The other major formation which was on its way to the northern shoulder of the German breakthrough at this time was the 30th Infantry Division. At 1625 hours on the 17th its first Regiment moved south, heading for Aywaille, to be followed a short time later by the two others, directed on Malmédy.

The only troops immediately available to First Army on the Sunday afternoon were two infantry Battalions and a TD Company[5], nicknamed 'The Praetorian Guard' since their main duties were guarding the Headquarters of Bradley's 12th Army Group and Hodges' First Army. They were ordered to Malmédy ten minutes after Pergrin's message was received in Spa at 1650 hours.

At a much lower level, the news that a Panzer column was probably heading towards Stavelot and Trois Ponts caused the Engineer Group commander in the area[6] to send for an extra company[7] to come to Trois Ponts in order to prepare the two vital bridges over the Amblève and Salm rivers for demolition. It started to arrive in Trois Ponts just before midnight.

Recall that the only troops who might have resisted KG Peiper in Stavelot on the Sunday night were a company of engineers[8] and that their commander had decided, in the absence of any orders to the contrary, to join the general exodus to the west. Sadly for him and his men they were intercepted as they moved through Trois Ponts at around midnight by none other than their Group commander and he ordered them back to Stavelot with orders to 'defend' the vital bridge over the Amblève. The only other troops in the Stavelot area were about sixty men of the 5th Belgian Fusilier Battalion who were guarding the nearby First Army fuel dumps which contained millions of gallons of petrol and oil. The largest one, with over one million gallons of fuel, was just 4km north of the town.

By 0300 hours on 18 December the first reinforcements reached Dave Pergrin and his 180 engineers in Malmédy. It was the 'Praetorian Guard' – a Battalion of truck-borne infantrymen and most of an armoured infantry Battalion and an attached TD Company. Part of this 'Guard', an armoured infantry Company and a TD platoon[9], had been diverted to Stavelot during the move from west of Spa; they arrived at about 0345 hours to find that the vital bridge over the Amblève had still not been prepared for demolition. The Company commander of the returning engineers had decided that placing a few mines on the southern ramp of the bridge and covering them with a machine-gun fulfilled his mission of 'defending' the bridge.

Farther south, in front of KG Hansen at Recht, there were hardly any American defences at all. Command of what remained of the 14th Cavalry Group at Poteau – the remnants of four Troops (companies) and three TDs[10] – changed four times during the night. Behind them, at Petit Thier, an ad hoc force of stray tanks, infantry, cavalry and engineers, nicknamed Task Force (TF) Navaho, was all that stood in Hansen's way.

In summary, it can be said that during the early hours of the 18th a fairly strong, if rather chaotic, American defence had been built up in front of the Hitlerjugend Division, but to all intents and purposes, the way was wide open for KGs Peiper and Hansen of the Leibstandarte. Admittedly a very primitive defence was being established at Malmédy, Stavelot and Trois Ponts but few of the defenders had been in action before and, except for the engineers, no one had seen the places they were defending in daylight.

NOTES

1. Hermann Priess, MS # A-877 dated Mar 46.
2. 291st Engr Bn.
3. B Bty, 285th Fd Arty Observation Bn.
4. Col Wallis Anderson of the 1111th Engr Gp.
5. 99th (Separate) Inf & 526th Armd Inf Bns and A/825th TD.
6. Col Wallis Anderson.
7. C/51st.
8. C/202nd.
9. A/526th Armd Inf & 1st Pl, A/825th TD.
10. C/32nd Sqn, C, E & F/18th Sqn and A/820th TD.

CHAPTER X
AUTUMN MIST: 18 December
The Leibstandarte Front
(Map 11)

We left Max Hansen preparing to advance at first light with the Salm river bridge at Vielsalm as his objective; as we have seen, there was little to oppose his KG. Nevertheless, the latest commanding officer of the 14th Cavalry Group was determined to try to do something positive, and he ordered what was left of his command to form a Task Force (TF) and advance with the aim of recapturing Born. Accordingly, the remnants of four Troops of Cavalry and three TDs[1] set off from Poteau in the early morning of the 18th. After only 300m they ran into Hansen's Jagdpanzers and SS Panzer-Grenadiers moving south-west from Recht. The result was the destruction of the main part of the American TF. The survivors withdrew to Poteau, where they continued to resist until midday; from there they were ordered back to Vielsalm. Although many of the Americans eventually reached there on foot, only three armoured cars, two jeeps, one TD, and a solitary light tank survived the encounter. The road to the Salm was wide open, with only TF Navaho in the way.

It is understandable therefore that Hansen felt both frustration and anger when, at 1400 hours, he received orders[2] to withdraw to Recht and secure it for the further advance of the 9th SS Panzer Division Hohenstaufen, part of the reserve II SS Panzer Corps. Hermann Priess, commanding I SS Panzer Corps, makes no mention of this extraordinary order in his post-war interrogation, but it was clearly illogical and wasted an opportunity which would not recur. If Hansen had been allowed to strike for Vielsalm on the Monday afternoon there is little doubt that he would have been successful – with potentially catastrophic results for the Americans in the St Vith sector. The whole of the 7th Armored and 106th Infantry Divisions and CCB of the 9th Armored would have been put at risk. But instead, having broken contact, Hansen was told to be prepared to advance, via Logbiermé and Wanne, to Trois Ponts in support of KG Peiper. Maybe Sixth Panzer Army's idea of bringing in another Panzer Division on the Leibstandarte's left flank was sound in theory, but in the event a golden opportunity was wasted and it was to be five more days before 9th SS finally advanced beyond the Salm river. This is yet another example of the many serious errors of judgement made during the Ardennes offensive by German commanders at all levels, from Hitler himself down through Army, Corps, Division and KG. Hansen himself said later:

> I became very angry with this Divisional order because I had been able to advance rapidly along my assigned route up to then and I was facing no strong enemy resistance. The Regiment [later] became stuck in the forest, lost much time and could only advance with difficulty.

Hansen went firm at Poteau, Recht and Kaiserbarracke. During the afternoon an American armoured infantry Battalion and part of a tank Battalion[3], both from the 7th Armored Division, advanced towards Poteau where they were engaged by Hansen's men. By last light there was stalemate – the Germans had no orders to attack and the Americans were not strong enough to do so.

(Map 8)

Meanwhile, the Leibstandarte's third KG under Rudolf Sandig had at last been able to advance. Unfortunately the route forward through Hallschlag and Losheim was clogged with vehicles and horse-drawn transport, and torn to shreds by the many tracked vehicles which had already used it. By the evening of the 18th KG Sandig had only just passed through the West Wall.

(Map 11)

What of the LAH's Fast Group? It will be recalled that Knittel had been given the option of switching routes and so, hearing that Hansen had been ordered to halt, he left his reinforced SS Reconnaissance Battalion to follow on and hurried to catch up with the Leibstandarte's tanks in the Stavelot area.[4]

(Map 15)

Jochen Peiper's plan for the 18th was logical, but as events turned out it was to cost him the best part of two companies of tanks. He knew that even after capturing the Amblève bridge in Stavelot, he would still face the problem of crossing the Amblève and Salm bridges in Trois Ponts. He decided therefore on a two-part plan designed to put his KG on the Werbomont road to the west of Trois Ponts by midday. Part One would see the area to the south of the Stavelot bridge secured, after which his Panthers would drive straight across the bridge and through the town, leaving his SS Panzer-Grenadiers to clear up any resistance. The tactics were normal for the Waffen-SS – a direct assault based on shock action. In most Allied armies this type of attack would have been considered madness – following a heavy artillery barrage, infantry would have been expected to capture most of the town before any tanks were committed in the built-up area – but that was not the way of the Waffen-SS.

Part Two of Peiper's plan was to be more or less coincidental, with his two Mk IV Panzer Companies, a Company of SS Pioneers and some paratroopers advancing via Wanne and Aisomont (Map 11), with the aim of securing Trois Ponts from the east and in particular, the Salm river bridge in the centre of the town.

It will be remembered that an American armoured infantry Company and a TD Platoon with four 3-inch guns[5] had been ordered to Stavelot (Map 13) during the early hours of the 18th to join the engineer Company[6] already there. On arrival, about four hours before first light, they found the bridge unprepared apart from some mines laid on the southern approach, and no one with any real idea about their potential enemy; and to compound matters even further, they had never set foot in the town before. Nevertheless, the Company was a very strong one and had the TF commander[7] decided to deploy his 250 men in the buildings on the northern bank of the river, supported by his four 3-inch TDs, three 57mm anti-tank guns, twenty heavy machine-guns, and eighteen bazookas, he would have presented Peiper with a major problem. But that was not the American way. Ever since the days of the Civil War the idea of taking the fight to the enemy had dominated American military thinking and, since the enemy was known to be south of the river, that was the place to be. Therefore, at about 0600 hours, the mines were removed from the bridge and two platoons of armoured infantrymen and two towed TDs were sent across with orders to secure the hill on the southern side, including the heights where the engineer roadblock had been established the night before.[8] Inevitably this force ran into Peiper's troops and was badly shot up. The 11th SS Panzer-Grenadier Company then stormed the bridge but was in turn forced to withdraw in the face of overwhelming fire from the American platoon holding the north bank. Amongst the casualties were Heinz Tomhardt, the Company commander, wounded, and one of his platoon commanders, killed.

Peiper's main attack on Stavelot began at first light with a short mortar and artillery barrage, following which his Panthers raced down the hill and 'bounced' the bridge; his Panzer-Grenadiers followed. Just after crossing the bridge the leading Panther was hit and damaged by a shot from a 57mm anti-tank gun and two others were disabled by TD fire as they made their approach. One was later repaired. The commander of the 1st SS Panzer Company leading the attack, SS Lieutenant Kremser, was wounded. The commander of the point Panther later described his part in the attack:

> The whole crew was given a very precise briefing; 'immediately after the bend there's an anti-tank gun [this was one of the American TDs which had been lost after it crossed to the south side of the bridge] – you'd better go in fifth gear. There's one of our officers lying in the middle of the bridge. Don't know if he's dead or wounded. The bridge is secure. Watch out for that officer!' Slowly it got light. We ran our engines to warm them. . . . We met no resistance. The anti-tank gun was standing there – we rammed it out of the way. On to the bridge! No officer. No sooner were we over the bridge than we were hit. . . . We drove over the trail of the anti-tank gun . . . great fire from all sides. Gradually it decreased and we were through.[9]

By 1000 hours the first battle of Stavelot was over – the engineer Company[10] had played no part in the fighting and the Americans had been routed – Peiper's tanks were on their way to Trois Ponts. For the loss of two tanks and a few officers and men, KG Peiper had overcome a major obstacle on its route.

Some of the American defenders withdrew up the Francorchamps road and took up a position covering the huge fuel dump 4km to the north of the town. The Belgian guards were ordered to set fire to the petrol to prevent the Germans capturing it. Much has been made of this incident and it featured prominently in the Hollywood film, 'The Battle of the Bulge', in which Peiper's tanks are seen being repelled by a wall of fire. In reality nothing of the kind happened and Peiper's tanks went nowhere near the fuel dump.[11]

The extra engineer Company[12] which had been called to Trois Ponts (Map 14) during the night had quickly prepared both the Amblève and Salm river bridges for demolition and, as Peiper's leading Panther approached the railway viaducts at the eastern entrance to the town, just after 1130 hours, the Amblève bridge was blown. The flimsy US defence force withdrew in the face of the German tanks after losing a 57mm anti-tank gun and its crew.[13]

With his route through Trois Ponts blocked, Peiper had no option but to turn his tanks north and follow the winding road through La Gleize and Cheneux which would eventually bring him back on to his assigned route to Werbomont and the Meuse. But what of his other tank force which had taken the eastern route to Trois Ponts, via Wanne? They set off at 0800 hours and at about noon the leading three Mk IVs reached Noupré on the high ground about a kilometre east of the town; there they ran into a platoon with two bazookas which the engineer Company commander[14] had had the foresight to place on this approach. Although the engineers failed to inflict any casualties or damage before they withdrew, their action provided some delay and gave time for the Salm bridge to be blown. This happened at 1300 hours, effectively blocking all routes through Trois Ponts.

Unfortunately for SS Captain Oskar Klingelhöfer, the commander of the force at Noupré, his tanks were now out of fuel; nevertheless, he sent some of the SS Pioneers who had accompanied his Mk IVs to Noupré, to seize another bridge over the Salm, some 2km to the south of Trois Ponts. As they approached the bridge it was blown in their faces.[15] Despite the fact that Peiper's main column would soon be to the west of them, the American engineers in Trois Ponts had been ordered to remain there[16] and prevent any German attempts to capture the third bridge or repair the others.[17]

At about 1300 hours an infantry Battalion of the 30th US Infantry Division[18] began to arrive in the area of the fuel dump just to the north of Stavelot. It had been redirected to Stavelot from Malmédy after the Divisional commander[19] learned that the town was now in German hands. Finding the road barred by burning fuel, the commanding officer[20] ordered the fire put out and his men to advance on foot. This delay allowed a major part of Knittel's Fast Group, which it will be recalled had switched from Hansen's to Peiper's route, to get through Stavelot. Knittel himself had gone on ahead, but the commander of his 2nd SS Reconnaissance Company, Manfred Coblenz, led his own SPW Company on their feet, across the bridge and then through the western part of the town. They were followed by his SPWs, the main Battalion Headquarter's vehicles, some Schwimmwagens of the 3rd Company, parts of the 4th Company including the three 150mms of the Infantry Gun Platoon, and five of the six 105mm guns of the 5th SS Artillery Battery.

During a visit to Stavelot with the author in 1986, Coblenz insisted that he and his men were fired on by civilians as they moved through the town – a claim strongly denied by the local people. Whatever the truth, it was a wise precaution not to drive through a built-up area in open-topped SPWs.

When Peiper learned that all three Trois Ponts bridges had been blown he ordered his Mk IV Panzer Companies, now stuck in the Aisomont area, to rejoin his main column as soon as possible by going back through Stavelot. Shortage of fuel however, meant that even after draining tanks, there was only enough petrol for six Mk IVs and the two SPW mounted Pioneer platoons to follow him. As they set off at about 1400 hours, Peiper's Panzer Spitze was approaching the village of Cheneux and the tail of his KG was some 25km to the rear in the region of Beaumont. Twenty-five Panthers, at least seven Tigers, Diefenthal's 3rd SS (SPW mounted) Panzer-Grenadier Battalion with his six 150mm heavy infantry guns, the 9th SS Pioneer and most of the 10th SS Flak Companies, and at least fourteen Luftwaffe Flak vehicles were already through Stavelot; but the whole of Kalischko's 1st SS Artillery Battalion, the majority of von Westernhagen's Tigers and all the KG's support elements still had to cross the Amblève bridge. It was therefore only a slight exaggeration for the American infantrymen approaching Stavelot from the north to report, at 1416 hours, 'hundreds' of enemy vehicles south of the river.

It was at about this time that the skies cleared enough for two American F-6 reconnaissance aircraft to spot Peiper's column and call in fighter-bombers. During the next two hours KG Peiper was straffed by a total of thirty-four P-47s and two RAF Typhoons.[21] Casualties were not heavy – Peiper later admitted to the loss of five to seven vehicles and the Leibstandarte history mentions three Panthers and five SPWs being hit. But casualties were not important; it was the delay that mattered – delay caused by a knocked out Panther just beyond the Cheneux bridge which completely blocked the narrow road, and by the column taking cover to avoid casualties. This delay was to prove disastrous, for it allowed more US engineers[22] to reach and prepare the vital bridge over the Lienne river which the KG still had to cross to reach Werbomont. These engineers had been ordered forward[23] as soon as Peiper's tanks were observed turning north at Trois Ponts.

It was during the air strikes that Gustav Knittel, the commander of the Fast Group, and the KG signals platoon and radio officer caught up with Peiper who had taken cover in an old wartime bunker just beyond the Cheneux bridge. For the first time in several hours he was able to communicate with his Divisional Headquarters.

Meanwhile, the two leading US infantry companies had entered the northern sector of Stavelot by 1520 hours and reported contact with twelve German tanks. These were the six Mk IVs returning from Aisomont with the two SS Pioneer Platoons in their SPWs, and some Tigers of the 1st Company of the 501st led by SS Lieutenant Jurgen Wessel. These troops were not trying to attack the Americans but merely catch up with Peiper.

The Mk IVs, SPWs and three of the Tigers made it across the bridge but the next Tiger was damaged during one of the air strikes and blocked the way. One of the Tigers which had already crossed the bridge was later immobilised in a narrow street in the town, but the tank blocking the bridge eventually managed to cross, and it and a damaged Panther remained throughout the night in Stavelot before moving off to the west the following morning.

Not surprisingly the American infantry remained in the northern outskirts of Stavelot until the air strikes were over; but between dusk and 1800 hours they were reinforced by three Shermans and three M-10 TDs[24] and they then advanced as far as the market square. During the early evening they reported having trouble with German tanks – these were of course the two Tigers and Panther already mentioned. To the south of the river there were still parts of the 3rd and 4th Companies of Knittel's 1st SS Reconnaissance Battalion, the guns of the 1st SS Artillery Battalion, some twenty-two Mk IVs awaiting fuel near Wanne and at least nine Panthers and twenty-seven Tigers in various states of repair and mobility spread out between Beaumont and the West Wall. The problem for most of the tank units was that they were without their commanders. Von Westernhagen, the commander of the Tiger Battalion, was forward with Peiper, and the commanders of the 6th and 7th SS Panzer Companies, Junker and Klingelhöfer, were in two of the six Mk IVs which had managed to get through the town in the late afternoon. They were anxious to catch up with their commanding officer, Werner Poetschke. In the same way, the commanders of the 2nd and 3rd Tiger Companies had accompanied their commanding officer when he had gone forward that morning. All four Panzer company commanders expected their subordinates to make sure that the tanks caught up once they had been refuelled and, if necessary, repaired.

(Map 15)

The air attacks on the forward part of Peiper's column ended just after 1500 hours and after clearing away the knocked out Panther near the Cheneux bridge and the other damaged vehicles, the advance continued at about 1530 hours. There was still over an hour of daylight left and, provided there was no trouble at the bridge over the Lienne river at Neufmoulin, Peiper could reasonably expect to reach Werbomont by last light. But even then his problems would by no means be over. It has often been suggested that since the ground to the west of Werbomont is more open and suitable for tanks, it would have been a comparatively simple matter for Peiper to drive through to the Meuse that same night. Whilst it is true that the country is more open after Werbomont, this suggestion ignores the fact that the largest obstacle on Peiper's route still lay across his path – the Ourthe river (Map 6); moreover, he would have known that by this time the chances of securing an intact bridge were extremely remote. Lying as it does at the bottom of a deep, heavily forested valley, the Ourthe would be a major problem for any armoured force – even with today's modern obstacle-crossing equipment.

It was about 1645 hours when the leading Panther rounded the bend 100m from the Lienne river bridge at Neufmoulin, only to see it blown sky-high. The small group of American engineers[25] had arrived just in time to make the necessary preparations.

Today it is difficult to imagine the Lienne as a serious obstacle but in the severe winter of 1944 it was in full flood and the water meadows on either side were impassable to tanks. Peiper ordered Grenadiers to investigate two other bridges to the north and within 3km of Neufmoulin, but although intact, they were found to be incapable of taking tanks. Nevertheless, two Panzer-Grenadier Companies crossed to the west bank in their SPWs. By this time most of the US engineers had withdrawn from the Neufmoulin bridge site but a Battalion of the 30th Infantry Division, backed by three 57mm anti-tank guns and four M-10 TDs[26] had been sent to cover the impending arrival of the 82nd Airborne Division at Werbomont. Part of this force reached the Oufni area, just to the north-west of the Neufmoulin bridge, shortly after dark and whilst setting up a road block, Georg Preuss's 10th SS Panzer-Grenadier Company ran straight into it. There was a brief, confused clash in which the Germans lost four SPWs and fifteen men. One Grenadier was captured and for the first time the 1st SS Panzer Division was identified on this front.

The other Panzer-Grenadier Company, the 11th, after heading south in the dark to get on to the Werbomont road at Neufmoulin, lost its lead SPW on a daisy-chain of mines pulled across the road by one of the American engineers from the Neufmoulin bridge group; it then over-shot the main turning to Werbomont and continued south instead of west.

On learning of the events on the west side of the Lienne and the state of the bridges, Peiper recalled both Companies and ordered the whole column to turn round and withdraw behind the Amblève at Cheneux. He had decided to reorganise and advance again at first light along the N-33 through Stoumont.[27]

The withdrawal began at 2100 hours. The Germans continued to hold the Neufmoulin area until midnight but then they were gone; the Belgians in Rahier counted 125 armoured vehicles moving east through their village that night, including thirty tanks.

Lack of fuel was now a critical problem and although Peiper still planned to advance west with as many tanks as possible, he decided to leave the surviving Panthers of the 1st SS Panzer Company, which had led all the way from Ligneuville, in La Gleize as a firm base.

The Hitlerjugend Front
(Maps 8 & 9)

Thirty-five kilometres to the east of La Gleize as the crow flies, and twice that distance by road, the situation in the Hitlerjugend sector was the same for both sides – confused and unsatisfactory.

The two most difficult problems facing Hermann Priess at this time were the appalling state of all the routes forward and the mis-location of the bulk of the HJ Division. The latter meant that in order to bring forward the main HJ KGs – Kuhlmann and Krause – Kraas had to move them either via Hellenthal and Hollerath and then down the main Reichsstrasse towards Losheimergraben, or via Hallschlag and Losheim. Both routes were circuitous and difficult.

During the night 17–18 December Priess gave his orders. The attack on the Twin Villages was to be continued at first light with the aim of breaking through to Elsenborn. The 25th SS Panzer-Grenadier Regiment and the 12th SS Panzerjäger Battalion would again be used, with support from the 990th Volks-Grenadiers, but this time Arnold Jürgensen's 1st SS Panzer Battalion would play a major role in the assault. At the same time the 12th VGD was to seize Hünningen and Mürringen and advance towards Büllingen, Bütgenbach and Wirtzfeld. Bremer's Fast Group was to support the attack on Krinkelt from the south and the reduced, but still very powerful, KG Kuhlmann, followed by KG Krause, was to advance along Route C through Büllingen and Bütgenbach as soon as Hünningen and Mürringen had been cleared. This decision – to split the Division and send one thrust through the Twin Villages and on to Elsenborn on the northern side of the Bütgenbach lake and the other through Büllingen and Bütgenbach[28] to the south – is difficult to understand; and the decision to weaken KG Kuhlmann and place the bulk of the HJ's armour in the northern thrust was to prove a major error.

During the early hours of the 18th the Americans[29] fought their way out of Hünningen against men of Engel's 27th Fusilier Regiment, whilst his 48th Grenadier Regiment occupied the abandoned village of Mürringen. A 12th VGD KG, consisting of assault guns, a Fusilier company and some Pioneers, then moved forward and occupied Büllingen.[30]

The way to Bütgenbach along Route C seemed to be open at last, but despite his success Major General Engel was reluctant to continue his advance. He was worried that any further move to the west would expose his right flank to the Americans in the Twin Villages and Wirtzfeld and he called a halt. Indeed, the Americans had nine infantry Battalions on that flank, supported by tanks, TDs and substantial artillery resources, but whether any of these forces, other than artillery, could have interfered effectively with movement along the N-32 through Büllingen is very doubtful; and although fresh American troops[31] had arrived in the Dom B sector, their supporting artillery Battalions would not be within range for several more hours.

But where was the German exploitation force anyway? What had happened to KGs Kuhlmann and Krause? The answer is simple – Urabl's SPW mounted 3rd SS Panzer-Grenadiers, the forty-two Jagdpanzers of the 560th Heavy Panzerjäger Battalion, the other two Battalions of Krause's 26th Regiment, the 12th SS Pioneer and Flak Battalions and part of the HJ artillery Regiment were still behind the West Wall! The route they were taking, through Marmegen, Dahlem and Hallschlag, had been turned into a river of mud through over-use and they did not even begin to arrive in Büllingen until well after last light.[32] By then the tanks of Jürgensen's 1st SS Panzer Battalion had been involved in the costly and wasteful fight for the Twin Villages for over twelve hours, and the folly of committing them in the north had been exposed by the ease with which Engel's troops had reached Büllingen.

In the northern sector of the HJ front we left Helmut Zeiner with four Jagdpanzers, a platoon of SS Panzer-Grenadiers and some eighty American prisoners in the middle of Rocherath. Knowing that he was extremely vulnerable in a built-up area he decided at about 0600 hours on the 18th to withdraw to a position just outside the village to the east of the church. He described later what happened:

We had barely arrived there when a thick hail of enemy shells set in. But another sensation was also in the making. Watching the edge of the forest, we saw Panzer after Panzer leaving it in wide formation. They were German Panzers. We waved pieces of cloth so as not to be fired on by our own, forgetting to watch out for the phosphorous shells exploding next to us. Our prisoners crawled under the Jagdpanzers for cover. Our infantry did the same.[33]

The Panzers were those of Jürgensen's 1st SS Panzer Battalion. The 1st Company of Panthers under SS Lieutenant Bormuth led the way, followed by the 3rd Panther Company and then the Mk IVs of the 5th and 6th Companies. They had already endured an appalling journey in fog and darkness, via Hellenthal and Hollerath and the Rocherath forest. After linking up with Schulze's 2nd SS Panzer-Grenadiers of the 25th Regiment, the tanks approached the American Battalion[34] defending the track junction some 2km to the north-east of Rocherath, whilst the other two Panzer-Grenadier Battalions of Müller's Regiment advanced on their left flank directly towards the Twin Villages.

The sight of the nine smouldering Jagdpanzers knocked out during the previous day and night could have done little for the morale of the Panzer crews, and the heavy fire they met, especially from artillery, added to their misery and caused heavy casualties. Nevertheless, by 0800 hours the forward American companies had been overrun – only one officer and twenty-two men escaped. A platoon of four Shermans[35] covering the withdrawal claimed three Panthers and the infantrymen said they knocked out another two; but despite these losses the Panzer spearheads were soon entering the village of Rocherath. Later in the morning they penetrated into Krinkelt and reached the road leading to Wirtzfeld at its southern exit, but the Americans would not give up and the Twin Villages became a disputed and bloody battlefield.

Peiper had gambled at Stavelot by leading his attack with tanks. Not surprisingly, with only a platoon of infantry and five anti-tank guns to oppose him, he had succeeded. For the Hitlerjugend it would be different – the best part of three infantry Battalions, supported by tanks, TDs[36] and artillery would ensure that the main street of Rocherath became a Panzer graveyard – especially since the intense artillery fire precluded the SS Panzer-Grenadiers accompanying the tanks closely into the built-up areas. Just one American Field Artillery Battalion fired more than 5,000 rounds on the 18th.[37]

The fighting in the Twin Villages was bitter and confused and there is no point in trying to detail it in this book – many distinguished authors have already done so. For readers interested in individual actions, *Against the Panzers* by Vannoy and Karamales, is particularly recommended. This author will confine himself to just two vignettes. SS Second Lieutenant Willi Engel, a Panther platoon commander remembered:

After a rapid drive we reached the village of Rocherath. . . . I sensed disaster since I was expected to act against the elementary rules of armoured combat – that a built-up area, without the security of accompanying infantry, should be bypassed if at all possible. . . . Directly in front of us lay the main street along which the Company had attacked and we had avoided. . . . I spotted our Battalion Command Post. . . . His face [the commanding officer, Arnold Jürgensen's] mirrored dejection and resignation. The failed attack and painful losses, particularly of the 1st and 3rd [Panther] Companies, obviously depressed him severely. . . . I could survey the main street. The knocked out Panzers offered a distressing picture. At that moment, a single Panzer approached the Command Post. Suddenly, only about 100m away, it turned into a flaming torch. . . . It was later determined that an immobile but otherwise serviceable and manned Sherman had scored the hit. . . . The fighting in Krinkelt flared up time and again. Both sides fought with bitter determination.[38]

Another platoon commander, Willi Fischer, confirmed the Twin Villages as 'a perfect Panzer graveyard':

> When I reached the vicinity of the church, a gruesome picture was waiting for me. Beutelhauser was knocked out. . . . His loader was killed by rifle fire as he bailed out. . . . Brödel's tank stood next to me, burning lightly. He sat lifeless in the turret. In front of me, farther along the street, more Panzers had been put out of action and were still burning. However, one was still moving; I believe it was Freier's. Under my covering fire he was able to move back.[39]

This incident is worthy of comment, for it raises moral aspects of close quarter fighting which always worry soldiers. The shooting of crews bailing out from knocked out tanks can be equated to shooting at pilots who have bailed out of crippled aircraft and, just as the Allies complained about the latter, so the Germans obviously resented the former and considered it unreasonable. Another moral aspect worth considering concerns a specific incident quoted in *Against the Panzers*:

> As they re-entered house number 65, the men of Adams's 2nd Platoon realised that they had left their two wounded German prisoners there during the tank battle. One . . . was still there since his leg was too badly injured to walk on; but the other, who also had a leg wound but a less severe one, was gone. Thinking the man could not have gotten too far, Adams ran out to look for the escaped man. He spotted the man 'wobbling down the road toward another house on the corner'. Since he was too far away and too exposed for Adams to recapture, Adams shot him.[40]

The reader will have to make up his own mind on these questions of morality.

The Hitlerjugend paid dearly for its decision to commit tanks in the battle for the Twin Villages. Precise casualties are impossible to assess. The Germans have no firm figures and American claims are certainly exaggerated. The Chief of Staff of the HJ, Hubert Meyer, states:

> The attack cost high losses in Panzer crews, Panzers and Grenadiers. [Müller's] 1st and 2nd [SS Panzer-Grenadiers] carried the main load of the fighting.[41]

The Americans claimed that their tank Battalion[42] in the area of the Twin Villages knocked out an 'estimated' twenty-seven German tanks for the loss of eleven Shermans, and that their TD Battalion[43] destroyed seventeen tanks, disabled three more and knocked out two assault guns. Claims that five Tigers were destroyed[44] are certainly in error – there were no Tigers operating in this area. In the same way suggestions that the 560th Heavy Panzerjäger Battalion took part in the actions on the 18th are wrong.

After a careful study of all the After Action Reports and unit histories, this author believes that a maximum of eighteen German tanks or Jagdpanzers were lost in this fighting on 18 December – others were certainly damaged but would soon be made operational again. It is impossible to categorise the losses into types since American tank recognition was notoriously inaccurate – many Jagdpanzers were, perhaps not unreasonably, thought to be tanks. It seems likely that the majority of the casualties were Panthers since they led the attack. There is certainly photographic evidence of fifteen Panthers, one Mk IV and two Jagdpanzers abandoned in or near the Twin Villages.

American losses on the 18th were also severe – but they had won the day. Just as Rocherath and Krinkelt had been denied to the HJ, so the 990th Volks-Grenadiers had been unable to push the Americans to the west of the Rocherath-Wahlerscheid road. Although V US Corps had decided to abandon the Twin Villages and Wirtzfeld salient by the night of the 18th, the field of battle belonged to the Americans.

This failure to break through along Route C forced Sixth Panzer Army to think again. It was now imperative to secure the Leibstandarte's right flank and resupply KG Peiper by advancing through Malmédy in the direction of Spa (Map 10). Accordingly, orders were issued for the HJ attack on the Twin Villages to be called off and for the 3rd Panzer-Grenadier Division (3rd PGD) to take over in that sector on the 19th. In the specific case of the Hitlerjugend, KGs Kuhlmann and Krause and Fast Group Bremer were ordered to move into the Büllingen area as soon as possible and then to advance to Bütgenbach with all speed, whilst KG Müller and Jürgensen's mauled 1st SS Panzer Battalion were to follow on once they had been extracted from the Twin Villages.

After the war the Chief of Staff of the Sixth Panzer Army, Fritz Kraemer, claimed that I SS Panzer Corps was told to bypass the Bütgenbach sector to the south and to advance on the axis 'Möderscheid, Faymonville to Waimes'; however, the Corps:

informed Army in the night that it was not possible for the 12th SS Panzer Division to start the attack south of Bütgenbach because the road Büllingen, Möderscheid, Schoppen was for the most part impassable because of the mire. Also the entire road network in the Losheim sector was impassable and it would take the Division a day to bring up its vehicles. The Corps asked for permission to attack once more with the 12th SS Panzer Division and the 12th VGD in order to clear the road to Bütgenbach. This was approved.[45]

Whilst there is no doubt that the roads immediately to the south of the main Büllingen-Malmédy highway were in a terrible state at this time (KG Peiper had torn them to shreds on the 17th), the whole idea of the HJ advancing on any route on the 19th was academic anyway – it would take most of the next twenty-four hours for the Division simply to assemble in the Büllingen area. We shall return to the subject of an alternative route for the advance in a later chapter.

It was during this same night, the 18th-19th, that Sixth Panzer Army, very sensibly, changed the command structure of its attacking forces. Priess's I SS Panzer Corps could no longer be expected to control the LAH west of Stavelot and at the same time to fight a breakthrough battle just beyond the West Wall. Thus, Bittrich's II SS Panzer Corps was given responsibility for all the Divisions operating between Büllingen and Elsenborn in the direction of Malmédy and Spa; these were the 3rd PGD, 3rd FSD, 12th and 277th VGDs and, most importantly from our point of view, the Hitlerjugend. To replace the HJ in I SS Panzer Corps, Priess was given, as we have seen, the 9th SS Panzer Division Hohenstaufen. 2nd SS Panzer Division Das Reich left Bittrich's command and became part of the Army reserve.

NOTES

1. C/32nd Sqn & C, E, & F/18th Sqn & A/820th.
2. Tiemann, *Die Leibstandarte* IV/2, p. 111.
3. 48th Armd Inf & 40th Tk Bns.
4. Knittel, statement at Landsberg/Lech, 15 Mar 48.
5. A/526th & A/825th.
6. C/202nd.
7. Major Paul Solis.
8. A squad from C/291st.
9. Tiemann, op. cit., pp. 81–2.
10. C/202nd.
11. LAH veterans to author, loc. cit., 7 Jun 91, Holt Giles, *The Damned Engineers*, p. 233, and Pergrin, *First Across the Rhine*, p. 120.
12. C/51st.
13. B/526th Armd Inf Bn.
14. Capt Sam Scheuber, C/51st.
15. By a squad of A/291st.
16. By Col Wallis Anderson, 1111th Engr Gp.
17. Under the command of Maj Robert 'Bull' Yates, the XO of the 51st Engrs.
18. 1/117th.
19. Maj Gen Leland Hobbs.
20. LTC Robert Frankland.
21. Details of US sorties are to be found in the Office of Air Force History, Bolling Air Force Base and RAF sorties in the PRO Kew, London.

22. Squad of A/291st.
23. By Col Wallis Anderson.
24. B/743rd Tk & C/823rd TD.
25. Squad of A/291st.
26. 2/119th Inf & A/823rd TD.
27. ETHINT 10.
28. Meyer, *The History of the 12th SS Panzer Division Hitlerjugend*, p. 251.
29. 1/23rd.
30. Meyer, op. cit., p. 253.
31. 2 & 3/26th Inf.
32. Meyer, op. cit., p. 257.
33. Ibid., p. 251.
34. 1/9th.
35. A/741st.
36. 38th Inf Regt, 741st Tk Bn, 644th & parts of 612th & 801st TD Bns.
37. Cole, *The Ardennes; Battle of the Bulge*, p. 125.
38. Meyer, op. cit., pp. 252–3.
39. Ibid., p. 252.
40. Vannoy & Karamales, *Against the Panzers*, p. 262.
41. Meyer, op. cit., p. 253.
42. 741st.
43. 644th.
44. Cole, op. cit., p. 125.
45. ETHINT 21.

CHAPTER XI

AUTUMN MIST: 19 December

The Hitlerjugend Front

(Map 9)

The 19th was an uncomfortable day for both Germans and Americans in the Twin Villages. The former had no idea that the Americans were about to pull out and the latter could never have imagined that the Germans were about to carry out one of the most difficult of all military operations – a relief in the line whilst in close contact.

The Americans were amazed to see new crews delivered to some of the immobilised German tanks so that they could still be fought as static pill-boxes. Some idea of those final hours and the lengths to which the Panzer crews went in order to salvage their damaged tanks is given in the following reminiscences:

Under the threat of a court martial, Jürgensen delegated to me the task of defending my Panzer, another 1st Company Panzer and an unmanned Mk IV. . . . The Americans were in one half of the village and the eight of us in the other with three inoperable Panzers. Luckily the Americans had no idea of that.[1]

We took a direct hit in the front of the turret. . . . The explosion virtually ripped our driver Karl-Heinz . . . to pieces. Our radio operator Gottfried Opitz lost his left arm. . . . The legs of Hannes Simon ended up full of shrapnel. I was sitting in the cupola, my legs pulled up, so I got away with just a fright. I was able to get Hannes and Gottfried on to an SPW which was on its way to a dressing station. Then our Panzer was towed to the repair company at Losheimergraben. There we buried Karl-Heinz.[2]

We were relieved during the night of 19 to 20 December. . . . We carried as many wounded as possible in each Panzer. The creek crossing was under constant harassing fire. Our Panzer had a broken brake belt; in order to steer we had to always use the reverse gear. The repair squad organised another brake belt for us the same night from a knocked out Mk IV in Krinkelt and installed it right away.[3]

In order to extract KG Müller and Jürgensen's 1st SS Panzer Battalion from the Twin Villages, the 3rd PGD, supported by an assault gun Battalion, moved into Krinkelt from the south and south-east in the afternoon. At the same time the 89th Regiment of the 12th VGD advanced towards Wirtzfeld and the 277th VGD moved forward to the north of Rocherath. It was perhaps ironic that on the day of the HJ withdrawal, Siegfried Müller was awarded the Knight's Cross for his KG's abortive efforts to open up Route A.

American artillery kept up an intense barrage to mask the withdrawal of their 2nd and 99th Infantry Divisions to the dominating ground just to the east of Elsenborn. This began at 1730 hours and a short time later the 3rd PGD completed its occupation of the Twin Villages, allowing the last elements of the Hitlerjugend to pull back into the cover of the forests. At 0200 hours on the 20th, the last Shermans left Wirtzfeld and the American withdrawal was also complete. The 'green' 99th Infantry Division had received a terrible 'baptism of fire', suffering some 1,200 casualties, but it had played a crucial part in frustrating the German plan. It is also clear that the presence of the veteran 2nd Infantry Division in the attack zone saved the day for the Americans. Its withdrawal *into* the area through which the Germans were making their main effort prevented an almost inevitable breakthrough. The 2nd Division also lost some 1,200 men in the fighting in the Wahlerscheid salient and the Twin Villages.

During the course of the night of the 18th-19th SS Captain Georg Urabl's 3rd SPW Panzer-Grenadier Battalion arrived in Büllingen where it joined the 3rd Battalion of Müller's 25th Regiment, Fast Group Bremer and some elements of the 12th VGD. It was followed throughout the rest of the night and the next day by the remainder of KG Kuhlmann which formed up in the general area astride the Losheimergraben-Büllingen road and, as Jürgensen's tanks gradually returned from the north during the following night (19th-20th), they were reintegrated into the KG. Despite its losses the 1st SS Panzer Battalion was still a very formidable fighting force with some sixty operational Panthers and Mk IVs. KG Krause also arrived in the area to the south-east of Büllingen during the 19th. The final units of the HJ to rejoin the mass of the Division were Müller's depleted 1st and 2nd SS Panzer-Grenadiers and Brockschmidt's dozen or so Jagdpanzers. None of the units returning from the Twin Villages area was able to use the direct route from Krinkelt to Büllingen since it was still well covered by American fire and the state of the forest tracks inevitably delayed the whole operation. The bulk of the HJ artillery, together with the 12th SS Werfer and 12th SS Flak Battalions, set up in the area bounded by Büllingen, Hünningen and Mürringen.

By first light on the 19th the 26th Regiment of the US 1st Infantry Division was well established in the Dom B and Bütgenbach areas, with its 2nd Battalion defending Dom B itself, the 3rd on a feature lying 1,500m to its east which dominated the N-32 from Büllingen to Bütgenbach – known as the Schwarzenbüchel – and the 1st Battalion in reserve in Bütgenbach. Mines had been put out and the four artillery Battalions of the 1st Division had arrived to provide what was to prove battle-winning support.

In 1944 Dom B was a large stone manor house with surrounding outbuildings and barns. It lay just to the south of the N-32, with Hill 600 half a kilometre to its north; a kilometre to the south were Point 613, a dense coniferous forest and the Morschheck crossroads. This latter area was occupied by the 3rd FSD. From Dom B itself it was only possible to see some 700m to the east and south. A smaller house has been built on the site of the original Dom B, the roads are much improved and there is a light industrial estate in the area to the north – but the ground is little changed today.

Owing to the fact that the Hitlerjugend was still assembling for its new mission throughout the 19th, there was little offensive action that day. Claims that serious attacks were made against Dom B and the Schwarzenbüchel position have to be questioned, particularly since the Divisional commander, Hugo Kraas, spent the day 12km away near Hollerath, 'directing the units in action at Rocherath-Krinkelt'.[4] This would indicate that his emphasis at this time was the extraction of the bulk of the HJ's armour from the area of the Twin Villages for use on the main axis, and not on launching weak and premature attacks against a strong enemy. Quite why the 3rd FSD was not used to attack and secure Dom B during the time the HJ was reassembling remains a mystery – at least two Battalions of its 9th Regiment had arrived in the Morschheck area as early as the night of 17-18 December. The responsibility for wasting these substantial resources must lie with SS General Bittrich and his Corps staff.

Reconnaissances were carried out during the early hours of the day towards Dom B and the Schwarzenbüchel – one German veteran even claimed to have penetrated along the track leading from Büllingen to Bütgenbach on the south side of the lake and to have found it unprotected. In his History of the HJ Division, Hubert Meyer attributes these reconnaissances to Urabl's 3rd SS Panzer-Grenadiers and says two SPWs were lost to enemy fire north of the Büllingen road.[5] On the other hand there are a number of American accounts of these probes in the early hours of the 19th. One says that at 0225 hours there was a major reconnaissance in force towards Dom B from the south-east by twelve Jagdpanzers and up to 300 Panzer-Grenadiers. It claims three Jagdpanzers knocked out and some 100 Germans killed. This report has to be queried – first, because it is most unlikely that any Jagdpanzers had arrived in the Büllingen area by that time; second, even if some had, why would experienced German commanders use such totally unsuitable vehicles for reconnaissance, particularly at night?; and third, because the After Action Report (AAR) of the 26th Infantry Regiment has a different account. It says that at 0225 hours a probing attack was made against one of its Companies by 'twenty truckloads of infantry and some tanks'; it goes on to claim three tanks knocked out and the infantry being dispersed by artillery fire. It seems much more likely therefore that, following an unsuccessful reconnaissance towards Dom B in daylight on the 18th, these probes were carried out by Urabl's Panzer-Grenadiers in SPWs and/or Bremer's 12th SS Reconnaissance Battalion using armoured cars and SPWs.

There are no German reports of any further actions in the Dom B sector on the 19th, but we have two American versions of another attempted incursion at 1010 hours. One claims Dom B was attacked in *thick fog* by at least a company, led by an eight-wheeled armoured car and another armoured vehicle, probably a Jagdpanzer, from the Morschheck direction. It goes on to say that twenty minutes later a second force, estimated as 'at least a company and perhaps a Battalion', attacked from the east, led by between four and eight Jagdpanzers. Both attacks are said to have been repulsed with heavy losses, including the armoured car and two Jagdpanzers. If this report is correct the mention of an eight-wheeled armoured car would again indicate that Bremer's 12th SS Reconnaissance Battalion was involved. For its part the AAR of the 26th Infantry merely says:

> two tanks and one company of enemy infantry were spotted south of the 2nd Battalion positions. One tank was halted by anti-tank gun fire and the anti-tank gun in turn was taken under enemy rocket-gun fire which destroyed the gun.

In view of the fact that one of these actions took place in the dark and the others in thick fog, it is not surprising that there was confused reporting. In any event it was all over by 1100 hours and both sides then reverted to heavy shelling.

The Leibstandarte KGs
(Map 11)

KG Hansen was forced to waste the whole of the 19th waiting at Recht for the arrival of the 9th SS Panzer Division. Fuel problems and traffic congestion delayed its move and it was last light before Hansen's men could begin their extremely difficult advance along the forest trails towards Wanne. Today, even in daylight and using modern maps, it is difficult enough to find one's way – in 1944, in the dark and in appalling weather conditions, it must have been a nightmare. It was first light on Wednesday the 20th before the Spitze reached Logbiermé.

(Maps 11 & 13)

The second battle of Stavelot began soon after first light on the 19th. No doubt spurred on by their Divisional commander, Wilhelm Mohnke, five Mk IV tanks from the now refueled 6th and 7th SS Panzer Companies at Wanne, supported by paratroopers and SS Pioneers, approached the Stavelot bridge, followed by Schwimmwagens from the 1st SS Reconnaissance Battalion, trying to catch up with the rest of their Battalion. This attempt was soon seen off by the Americans[6], who used intense artillery fire and managed to close to the river by 1000 hours. Four M-10 TDs[7] were then sited to cover the southern approaches. However, orders to blow the bridge were impossible to implement with German tanks and machine-guns sitting just across the river. A report by a Mk IV tank commander of the 7th Company describes this first German attempt on the 19th to force the bridge:

> We launched an attack on Stavelot together with the remaining Panzers of the 6th Company. We were also supported by a company of paratroopers who fought as infantry. As we approached with our Panzers we came upon the eastern [south-eastern] sector of the town. . . . No enemy activity was noticed. The portion of the town on the other side of the river, however, was occupied by strong enemy forces. . . . We were immediately engaged by heavy anti-tank and mortar fire, and infantry fire as well. It proved impossible to gain a bridge crossing despite numerous attempts.

A second, larger German attack was launched at 1300 hours by a mixture

93

of ten Tigers and Mk IVs, again supported by paratroopers, Pioneers and Knittel's men. It came to a halt when a Tiger was immobilised at the entrance to the bridge. A graphic description is given by Tom Raney, an American officer present at the time:

> We saw the long tube of the Tiger 88mm gun emerge from behind the last building. The M-10 gunner must have been tracking the tank with his telescopic sight, for as the Tiger cleared the building, the M-10 fired one round of armor piercing shot which penetrated the armor on the right side above the track, about 14-inches under the turret. . . . The Tiger stopped in its tracks.

Suggestions that the infantry supporting this attack were from KG Sandig can be discounted. Due to the stubborn US defence in the Büllingen area, Sandig had been forced to take the extremely difficult route via Heppenbach, Amel, Montenau and Ligneuville – a route congested in the early stages by the 9th SS Panzer Division on its way to relieve Hansen. This route, like those being used by the Hitlerjugend KGs as they moved up to Büllingen, had been virtually destroyed by tracked vehicles – in extreme cases tanks were moving through mud which came up to their decks.

Sandig's leading, truck-mounted, 1st Battalion finally reached Vaulx Richard at about midday and his 2nd Battalion halted behind it at Lodômé. Peiper's 1st SS Artillery Battalion, which had been unable to cross the river, was deployed near La Bergerie and in a position to give support, so Mohnke ordered Sandig to attack as soon as possible using all available tanks and any other 'left-overs' he could find.

The attack went in at 1500 hours and coincided with another on the western side of the town by Knittel's main force, which had been ordered by Peiper to return from the La Gleize area and secure his lines of communication. It was supported by the two Tigers which had moved west from Stavelot shortly after first light.

Sandig's attack on the bridge was rushed, uncoordinated and a failure. The SS Panzer-Grenadier Company commander involved, SS Second Lieutenant Friedrich Pfeifer, described it as follows:

> We arrived during the afternoon and I suspected a trap; my suspicion was confirmed because we found two dead comrades and an abandoned Tiger immediately in front of the bridge. . . . Colonel Sandig appeared suddenly on a motor-cycle. He said things were going too slowly. I told him I needed fire support from the heavy weapons of the 4th Company; however, it had been delayed. . . . When half of us reached the north side of the bridge we were shot to pieces.[8]

Meanwhile, Knittel launched his attack from the west using Coblenz's 2nd Company down the main Trois Ponts-Stavelot road, supported by two Tigers and his three 150mm heavy infantry guns and 120mm mortar platoon firing from the Petit Spai area. SS Lieutenant Heinz Goltz's Headquarter Company, which comprised large Bicycle, Pioneer and Signals platoons, was held in reserve – the Pioneer Platoon alone was over sixty strong. Coblenz told the author[9] that the two Tigers, which had been on their way to join Peiper when they were commandeered by Knittel, never fired a shot during the whole attack, but the commander of one wrote later that he had been unable to help because the entrance to Stavelot was mined.[10]

Despite heavy casualties from intense US artillery fire, Coblenz's men reached the western edge of the town by 1800 hours; there they were held by artillery, infantry and tank fire and despite the commitment of Goltz's Company on the northern flank into Parfondruy, no further progress could be made.

At 1930 hours, under the cover of an artillery barrage, a small American engineer party[11] managed to blow the north span of the Amblève bridge – a gap of some 8m – and the way through Stavelot was blocked.

At 2200 hours Sandig's 1st and 2nd SS Panzer-Grenadier Battalions launched a night attack near the Challes footbridge in Stavelot; but the steepness of the ground and state of the river proved too difficult and at around midnight the 2nd Battalion was told to cross via the Petit Spai bridge, 4km to the west, and reinforce Knittel, whilst the 1st was to consolidate on the south bank. Sandig's idea was to take the town the following day from the west and thus enable Pioneers to repair the bridge without direct interference.

And so ended another day in the terrible battle of Stavelot. The few defenders[12] had done remarkably well to withstand the numerous German assaults and in particular, the attempted night infiltrations. It is doubtful whether they could have done so without the support of the 30th Division artillery. One Battalion[13] alone fired over 3,000 rounds into an area of one square kilometre near the bridge.

For the citizens of Stavelot it had been an horrific day. At least sixty-five civilians had died, most of them at the hands of the Leibstandarte; nearly half were women and children and all were found in the areas occupied or fought over by Knittel's men. In the garden of the Legaye house on the N-23, two men, eleven women and ten children lay dead, butchered in cold blood. Whether these barbaric acts had anything to do with the partisan attacks on the Hitlerjugend in the same general area during the withdrawal the previous September will never be known, but Stavelot was known to the Germans as a centre for partisan activity and it is clear that once again the *furor Germanicus* had been visited upon the local people.

(Map 15)

The hilltop village of La Gleize was a hive of activity during the night of the 18th-19th. In the woods just to the west of the village, Peiper's men were preparing to attack the village of Stoumont and so continue their advance along the Amblève river valley. In the village itself the Panthers of the 1st SS Panzer Company were joined by the six Mk IVs which had managed to get through Stavelot, five Tigers – plus another immobilised on the hill just to the east of the village – and Manfred Coblenz with a sizeable proportion of Knittel's Fast Group. This gave Peiper a total tank strength of six Tigers, nineteen Panthers and six Mk IVs. Four more Tigers had crossed the Amblève but would see action with Knittel between Trois Ponts and Stavelot rather than with Peiper. Knittel's Fast Group was allowed to rest before returning on the morning of the 19th to attack Stavelot from the west – but not before the five 105mm guns of its 5th SS Artillery Battery had been commandeered to replace Peiper's missing 1st SS Artillery Battalion.

The German plan for attacking Stoumont was dictated by the ground. The main road towards the village, the N-33, leaves the woods where the tanks and Grenadiers of the KG had assembled, north of the massive Château Froidcour, and runs for 800m due west before it bends right round a slight hill and then almost at once enters Stoumont. On the left of the road the ground slopes very steeply down to cliffs above the Amblève and it is impossible to deploy vehicles on this flank for the first 500m. On the right of the road there is a gently sloping hill which hides the village until the very last moment.

We have already heard about the dense fog on the Tuesday morning. It shrouded the whole of the Amblève valley and was to be a great ally in Peiper's attack. The tactics he chose were simple and typically Waffen-SS – seven Panthers of the 2nd Company, together with a few Mk IVs, would drive straight down the road, while Jupp Diefenthal's Panzer-Grenadiers, Rumpf's 9th Pioneers and the remaining paratroopers would hook round to the south of the village on foot. If the tanks ran into trouble they were instructed to deploy off to the right of the main road. One of Diefenthal's Companies would remain in its SPWs as a reserve.

Peiper had no idea what he was up against. In fact an American infantry Battalion, supported by eight TDs, and a single 90mm AA gun[14] deployed in a ground role, had taken up positions in Stoumont during the night, and just before dawn ten Shermans arrived in the village.[15] Another Battalion of the same Infantry Regiment[16] had deployed just to the west of Stoumont station at the same time.

The battle of Stoumont began shortly after 0800 hours and was all over in two hours. The American TDs, sited on the south side of Stoumont to cover the road, were overrun by Peiper's infantry in the fog before they could fire a shot – they were abandoned by the infantry Company meant to protect them. Similarly the Company at the east end of the village and the Shermans soon withdrew, leaving the third Company isolated on the northern flank and with little option other than to withdraw into the woods north of the village. The only real opposition was provided by the single 90mm AA gun which knocked out the lead Panther at point blank range from its position beside the church. A second tank was damaged by bazooka fire but could still move, and while three Panthers manoeuvred round to the right flank, the Company commander, SS Lieutenant Christ, and another tank followed up on the road. US losses were harrowing – 315 men, including 284 taken prisoner, eight TDs, three 57mms and the 90mm AA gun – a second 90mm was also lost after becoming mired on its way into the village earlier that morning.

When the American Regimental commander[17] heard of the impending disaster at Stoumont he despatched a Company from his reserve Battalion[18] to help. When it reached Targnon, it met the ten Shermans carrying back the sad survivors of the Stoumont garrison and it too turned back.

Peiper's victory at Stoumont was complete but it was hollow – he had almost no fuel left for any exploitation. He therefore sent out two reconnaissances to the north – one from Stoumont and one from La Gleize. Neither was successful. At the same time he ordered his Mk IVs and Rumpf's 9th SS Pioneer Company back to La Gleize, and most of Diefenthal's Grenadiers and the paratroopers to take up defensive positions in Stoumont. This left seven Panthers, two anti-aircraft vehicles, the SPW mounted 11th SS Panzer-Grenadier Company and a platoon of Siever's 3rd SS Pioneers, also in SPWs, to continue the advance.

At about midday Peiper ordered his last probe to the west to begin. If he had known what was in front of him he might well have reconsidered this order. The reserve US infantry Battalion just to the west of Stoumont was occupying an extremely strong position where the Amblève river, railway and N-33 all run side by side in a valley only some 300m wide. The American right flank rested on the river and on the left the ground was forested and rose steeply from the road. In addition to the infantry Battalion, twelve Shermans and four TDs[19] had taken up positions in this narrow valley. And there was even more – a single 90mm AA gun[20], which had been unable to reach Stoumont in time, had taken up an isolated position in front of the main defence line, just by the station.

The road from Stoumont to its station is steep, twisting and runs through thick woods – there is no chance to deploy vehicles off it. Not surprisingly, Christ's Panthers advanced slowly. After about forty minutes, as they emerged from the protection of Targnon village, they were engaged by US artillery; they withdrew into the cover of the houses, only to be ordered on again by the commander of the 1st SS Panzer Battalion, Werner Poetschke. A short time later the leading tank rounded the bend some 200m short of the station and was immediately knocked out by the 90mm AA gun. SS Panzer-Grenadiers debussed and advanced between the river and the road, causing the crew of the 90mm to destroy their gun and withdraw.

The remaining five Panthers – another had been damaged and returned directly to La Gleize – followed by the Grenadiers, continued the advance; but as the Panthers rounded the bend beyond the station at about 1500 hours, the first two were knocked out and a third immobilised, either by being hit or getting stuck as it deployed to the left of the road. They had run into a classic tank ambush – the Panther crewmen claimed they never had time to return fire. In a letter from one of the American infantry Company commanders present at this action we read:

When the Panther tanks came round the curve in sight of us our tanks cut loose at them. . . . These young inexperienced tankers of ours fired four shells and knocked out three Panther tanks.[21]

US artillery then hit the whole German column, causing some fifty to seventy casualties, mainly to the Panzer-Grenadiers in their open-topped SPWs. The acting commander of the 11th SS Panzer-Grenadier Company, SS Senior Sergeant Rayer, described his part in the action at the station:

Our leading tank was knocked out by an anti-tank gun by the station. I was ordered to take the station on foot. We did this after light resistance. . . . We were ordered to take out enemy tanks and anti-tank guns on the right of the road. We failed in close combat and only extracted with great difficulty and losses.[22]

It was a hopeless situation and Poetschke, who was present at the station, gave the very necessary order to withdraw back to Stoumont, with Siever's 3rd SS Pioneers setting up a series of hasty minefields as they went. It is said the Peiper himself was in the vicinity of the station at the time and approved the order.

The battle of Stoumont station was over. Jochen Peiper would advance no farther. He had covered over 100km in seventy-two hours in appalling conditions. Forty-six years later, using the very latest technology and equipment, it took the British 1st Armoured Division only two hours less to cover the same distance in the 1991 Gulf War against Saddam Hussein.

NOTES

1. Meyer, *The History of the 12th SS Panzer Division Hitlerjugend*, p. 254, SS Second Lieutenant Engel, 3rd SS Pz Coy.
2. Ibid., Max Sölner, 6th SS Pz Coy.
3. Ibid., Heinz Nussbaumer, 6th SS Pz Coy.
4. Ibid., p. 257.
5. Ibid.
6. 1/117th.
7. C/823rd.
8. Pfeifer to author, loc. cit., 2 Oct 85.
9. Coblenz to author, loc. cit., 22 Jun 86.
10. Letter from Werner Wendt dated 22 Sep 91.
11. A/105th.
12. 1/117th Inf; Mortar, Aslt Gun Pls/526th Armd Inf, 3rd Pl, A/526th Armd Inf; 1st Pl, C/823rd TD; 3rd Pl, B/743rd Tk; 1st Pl, A/105th Engrs.
13. 118th.
14. 3/119th Inf, A/823rd TD, & C/143rd AAA.
15. C/743rd.
16. 1/119th.
17. Col Edwin Sutherland.
18. 1/119th.
19. C/743rd Tk & A/823rd TD.
20. C/143rd AAA.
21. Letter from Bud Strand, 1/119th Inf, to author 1982.
22. Rayer, statement at Dachau, 26 Apr 47.

CHAPTER XII

The Other Side of the Hill: 19 – 20 December

(Map 15)

It was mid morning on 19 December before the 82nd Airborne Division was complete at Werbomont, and after the gruelling and freezing journey from France with many of the men in open-topped trucks and trailers, there was much sorting out to be done. It is interesting to speculate on what might have happened if the bridge at Neufmoulin had not been blown the previous evening and Peiper's Panzers and SS Grenadiers had been at Werbomont to greet the paratroopers – but that is one of the 'ifs' of history!

Despite the difficult move, the first Regiment of the 82nd crossed the Lienne river at 1900 hours and by 0500 hours on the 20th its Battalions were dug in at Rahier[1] and Froidville.[2] They were expecting to be attacked by the Germans at any moment and had no idea that

99

Peiper had gone on to the defensive at Cheneux, Stoumont and La Gleize.

Another Regiment[3] of the 82nd Airborne reached Haute Bodeux and Basse Bodeux by last light on the 19th and moved forward to the Salm river on the 20th, where one Battalion[4] took up positions in Trois Ponts at 1300 hours alongside the brave band of engineers who had been holding on there for over forty-eight hours, while the other two were directed farther south to the Rochelinval area.

During the night of the 19th the Americans at Stoumont station prepared for the difficult advance towards Stoumont, which they planned to start soon after first light. With the village standing high above the Amblève, the river and cliffs on the right of the road and steep, forested ground on the left, it was going to be a difficult task.

In the same way that Sixth Panzer Army had reorganised its I and II SS Panzer Corps on the 19th, so the Americans decided to make some important changes in their command structure at this time. The 30th Infantry Division was transferred from V Corps to XVIII Airborne Corps and CCB of the 3rd Armored Division was attached to the 30th Division. It was hoped that this would provide the armoured punch needed to deal with Peiper. V Corps in the meantime would be able to concentrate on defending what had become known as the North Shoulder – the ridge running from Elsenborn, through Bütgenbach and Waimes to Malmédy, and then on to Stavelot.

CCB of the 3rd Armored Division was initially organised as two TFs and by midnight on the 19th TF Lovelady[5] had arrived from the Aachen area in Spa and TF McGeorge in La Reid. During the night TF McGeorge[6] was reorganised to form a third group called TF Jordan[7]. Each TF was named after its commanding officer.

The orders issued by the commander of XVIII Airborne Corps, Major General Matt Ridgway, for dealing with KG Peiper were simple: the group at Stoumont station, now known as the 119th Regimental Combat Team (119 RCT)[8], and TF Jordan from the La Reid area, were to secure the north bank of the Amblève from inclusive Stoumont to inclusive La Gleize. The first phase of the operation was to secure Stoumont. At the same time, TF Lovelady was to clear all Germans from the east and north banks of the Amblève between La Gleize and Stavelot, and Major General Jim Gavin's 82nd Airborne Division was to secure the south and west banks from Cheneux to Rochelinval.

NOTES

1. 1 & 2/504th.
2. 3/504th.
3. 505th.

4. 2/505th.
5. LTC Bill Lovelady – 2/33rd Armd Regt, with two Sherman coys, a lt tk coy, an armd inf coy, recce and engr pls, four aslt guns & an arty bty.
6. Maj Kenneth McGeorge – 1/33rd Armd Regt with a Sherman coy, an aslt gun pl, a mortar pl, an armd inf pl, an engr squad & an arty bty.
7. Capt John Jordan – 1/33rd Armd Regt with a Sherman coy, two lt tk pls, an armd inf coy, mortar & aslt gun pls & an arty bty.
8. Col Edwin Sutherland – 119th Inf Regt – 740th Tk Bn & four M-10s, A/823rd TD.

CHAPTER XIII

AUTUMN MIST: 20 December

The Leibstandarte KGs

The Stoumont Sector

(Map 15)

Despite the topographical difficulties, the advance of the 119 RCT towards Stoumont on the 20th went surprisingly well. The commander of the armoured Battalion[1] described the day as follows:

> The tank part of the job was to spearhead the attack and as soon as the village of Targnon was captured, to place two or more tank platoons on its high ground to support the attack on Stoumont. . . . The attack jumped off . . . as planned and Targnon was captured by noon [it was undefended]. Lt Tompkin's tank hit a minefield about 1000 yards east of Targnon which blew both tracks off. One enemy halftrack, one Panther and one enemy held Sherman were engaged and destroyed during the day. The attack proceeded slowly from Targnon and by dark had failed to reach Stoumont by about 500 yards. . . . During the afternoon the enemy launched three heavy, fanatical, counter-attacks which drove our infantry back several hundred yards, but each time they were driven back they quickly regained the ground.[2]

The German defence of Stoumont, under the command of Werner Poetschke, was well organised and based on a large, fortress-like structure at the west end of the village known as the St Edouard Preventorium. It was a home for some 200 deprived and needy children who had taken shelter in the cellars with the nuns and priests who looked after them. The building itself and the north-west sector of Stoumont was defended by Siever's 3rd SS Pioneers, whilst the 9th and 12th SS Panzer-Grenadier

Companies had positions in the main parts of the village. Five Panthers covered all the western approaches and Georg Preuss's weak 10th SS Panzer-Grenadier Company was in reserve near the Château Froidcour.

The American infantry[3] claimed they crossed five minor minefields before reaching the western edge of Stoumont at about 1720 hours. It was there that they ran into the problem of the Preventorium.

In the meantime TF Jordan had advanced on Stoumont from La Reid. The leading Sherman was lost to mines a kilometre short of the village at about midday and an hour later another tank was lost to direct fire as it rounded the bend immediately above Stoumont. With a sheer drop on the right of the road and thick forest on the left, deployment was impossible – Jordan withdrew the way he had come.

The Americans managed to capture the Preventorium after vicious hand to hand fighting by about 2000 hours, but three hours later a violent counter-attack by SS Panzer-Grenadiers retook it. At midnight Stoumont was still firmly in German hands:

> This building [the Preventorium] changed hands at least three times during the day and night. . . . Jerry retook all but one room of it. This room was held by infantrymen of the 1st Battalion who had decided to fight it out there. The fact that we had men in the building, and our line was within 200 yards of it, precluded bringing Divisional artillery on it. We managed to hold our ground during the night and started planning for the next day's attack.[4]

During the night of the 20th Major General Hobbs placed his Deputy, Brigadier Walter Harrison, in charge of both the 119 RCT and TF Jordan in a force known as TF Harrison. In addition Harrison was given an infantry Battalion[5] from the 30th Divisional reserve located at Lorcé.

Cheneux

At 0300 hours on the morning of the 20th Mohnke cancelled the order for Sandig's 2nd SS Panzer-Grenadier Battalion to reinforce Knittel and directed it instead to join Peiper in La Gleize. This was achieved by 1000 hours and Peiper immediately sent its 6th Company on to Cheneux where he had established another stronghold with Major von Sacken's Luftwaffe Flak detachment and Diefenthal's 11th SS Panzer-Grenadier Company. The latter had been moved there after the unsuccessful Stoumont station battle. In, and to the east of Cheneux, five 105mm guns of SS Lieutenant Butschek's 5th SS Artillery Battery were in position to support the defenders of Stoumont, Cheneux and if necessary, La Gleize.

The American advance from Rahier towards Cheneux began just after midday. It was undertaken by just two Companies of paratroopers[6] and, not surprisingly, it was stopped without difficulty. The German positions were well sited on reverse slopes and the ground over which the Americans had to advance was criss-crossed by barbed wire cattle fences.

A night attack by the same Companies was ordered for 1930 hours – the only planned assistance being a ten-minute artillery barrage, which never materialised, and two M-36 TDs[7] which failed initially to advance with the paratroopers. By 2300 hours the airborne soldiers had, as the US Official History describes it, achieved a 'slight toehold' in Cheneux, but only at a cost of 225 casualties.

The Trois Ponts Sector
(Map 14)

We left KG Hansen struggling along muddy forest trails towards Wanne. The move continued all day on the 20th and it was well after last light before reconnaissance patrols could be sent out towards Trois Ponts.

Recall that another US Parachute Regiment had been ordered to secure the line of the Salm river and that one of its Battalions[8] had joined the engineers[9] in Trois Ponts by 1300 hours. After repairing the bridge in the centre of the town, a single Parachute Company[10], with two 57mm anti-tank guns, crossed the river and took up a position on the high ground near Noupré. Hansen's patrols discovered these Americans on the east side of the Salm and as the rest of his KG assembled in the Wanne area during the night, he made plans to evict them.

The Cauldron
(Map 15)

Jochen Peiper had established his KG Headquarters in the farm of the Château Froidcour during the night of 19 December. German and American wounded were looked after by makeshift medical teams, without anaesthetics or proper equipment, in the cellars of the Château and US prisoners from the Stoumont battle were housed in the attics. With the three main defended localities of Stoumont, Cheneux and La Gleize forming a triangle around him, Peiper was thus in the centre of what became known to the SS men as 'The Cauldron'.

The La Gleize Sector
(Map 16)

It will be remembered that La Gleize was already defended by Panthers, Mk IVs and Tigers – dug in up to their tracks or concealed amongst the buildings. There was, however, an urgent need to supplement Rumpf's few 9th SS Pioneers, and the arrival of Schnelle's 2nd SS Panzer-Grenadier Battalion during the morning of the 20th provided a very welcome injection of infantry.

Soon after first light TF McGeorge began its advance from Spa. McGeorge's orders were to capture La Gleize, and for this task he was given an additional infantry Company and two more Sherman platoons[11] from the 30th Infantry Division. These he picked up at Cour, before advancing in thick fog to Bourgomont, 2km north-east of La Gleize. Leaving the 30th Division tanks there, a further advance began at 1400 hours but within an hour TF McGeorge had lost a Sherman to direct fire and run into a strong German road block near the Nabonruy stream. A second Sherman was soon in flames and the advance ground to a halt with the infantry taking up positions on the north-east side of the stream. Sometime later under cover of darkness, an attempt was made to capture the vital ground at Hassoumont, but a counter-attack by Rumpf's SS Pioneers cut off this probe and only a further attack by Shermans and more infantry enabled the Americans to withdraw successfully. By 2115 hours TF McGeorge was back in Bourgomont and Hobbs made it part of TF Harrison – the Americans knew they needed a better plan for the capture of La Gleize.

The Stavelot Sector
(Maps 16 & 17)

The mission of the most powerful of the CCB TFs, Lovelady, was to advance from Spa, through Ruy and Roanne, clear any German forces on the east bank of the Amblève down as far as Trois Ponts and then move on the north bank as far as Stavelot. The route chosen was totally unsuitable for armour and, like Peiper, Lovelady was forced to advance on a one tank front.

Starting at first light, Lovelady moved through Andrimont and Ruy to join the N-33 just to the south of the Moulin Maréchal. This mill was Knittel's Main Headquarters and, since it controlled the only approach from Trois Ponts to La Gleize, it was strongly held by a Tiger, a Mk IV, three Puma armoured cars and a few Panzer-Grenadiers. Fortunately for Lovelady it was a very foggy day and as the mill was below the level of the Roanne road and obscured by trees, his tanks were able to continue on their way without interference.

During the advance the Americans ran into two convoys taking supplies and reinforcements to Peiper and these were knocked out or captured – they included anti-tank and artillery guns, five ammunition trucks and an indeterminate number of infantry.

By late afternoon TF Lovelady's leading Shermans[12] were approaching the Trois Ponts railway viaducts. Unfortunately for them, just to the east of the viaducts Knittel had positioned a Tiger and two 75mm anti-tank guns so that within minutes of turning east the first four Shermans were destroyed and the point Company commander killed.[13] There was no possibility of getting off the road and with over fifty tanks in a single file from Roanne-Coo station to the viaducts, Lovelady's men were highly vulnerable – particularly as night was approaching and it was foggy. Fortunately for the Americans, there were no Germans capable of taking offensive action against them at this time. Nevertheless, from the Leibstandarte's point of view the insertion of TF Lovelady between KG Peiper and the rest of the Division, was a disaster – it ensured that no further supplies or reinforcements would reach 'The Cauldron'.

Stavelot
(Map 13)

The main action in the battle of Stavelot on the 20th was again on the western flank. With infantry, tanks and TDs[14] covering the Amblève bridge area, backed by plentiful artillery, there was no possibility of SS Major Karl Richter's 1st SS Panzer-Grenadier Battalion forcing a crossing. Friedrich Pfeifer's Company, which had managed to get across the previous afternoon, was withdrawn early in the morning. The men had to swim or wade back:

> We maintained our position on the other river bank for about eighteen hours but only had one machine-gun left and very little ammunition. . . . When dawn came we began our retreat across the Amblève, downstream from the bridge under heavy fire. I recollect the undertaking cost twenty-three men their lives.[15]

Following Knittel's orders, Manfred Coblenz's 2nd SS Reconnaissance Company, reinforced with some sixty Pioneers and backed by two Tigers, renewed its attack on the town from the area of the Château Lambert soon after first light. By mid-morning the Americans[16] had been forced back to the line of the railway station and Goltz's Company was threatening the town from the north-west. However, intense artillery fire and the commitment of a reserve Company[17] saved the day for the Americans and by early afternoon they had reoccupied their original positions. Coblenz's men were holding the houses at the western end of the town and the Château Lambert, and Goltz's Company was firm in Parfondruy and Renardmont, but the Germans were simply not strong enough to capture the town. The second battle of Stavelot was over.

The Hitlerjugend Front
(Map 9)

By last light on the 19th Bittrich had concluded that it would take a major effort by at least three Divisions to open up Route C through Bütgenbach to Malmédy and he ordered the 12th VGD to attack towards Elsenborn through Wirtzfeld, the 3rd FSD towards Weywertz from the Möderscheid area and the Hitlerjugend through Dom B to Bütgenbach. Hugo Kraas had no option therefore but to order KG Kuhlmann to attack before his main offensive arm – the 1st SS Panzer Battalion – was ready. Remember that during the night of 19-20 December Jürgensen's tanks were still struggling to reach the HJ assembly area in and to the east of Büllingen. Kuhlmann, in turn, had no choice other than to use Major Streger's totally unsuitable 560th Heavy Panzerjäger Battalion in a night attack against Dom B – unsuitable because the crews of the fourteen Jagdpanzer Vs and twenty-eight IV/48s were untrained in attack tactics and their vehicles, mounting a gun with only a very restricted traverse, were at a great disadvantage in this role and in the dark. Then the fact that neither the commander nor gunner could see in the dark without sticking their heads out of the vehicle put them at yet another disadvantage; and finally, when one adds to all this the foggy conditions, one can imagine that morale in this unit at midnight on the 19th was not particularly high.

There are conflicting versions of what happened when the HJ attacked Dom B and the Schwarzenbüchel feature that night – even the number of attacks is disputed.

According to the American Official History:

About 0600 twenty German tanks and a rifle Battalion converged on Dom Bütgenbach in the early morning fog and mist [first light was not before 0730] from south and east. The front lit up as the American mortars and artillery shot illuminating shell over the roads leading to the village. Concentration after concentration then plunged down, three Battalions of field artillery and a 90mm battery of AA artillery firing as fast as the pieces could be worked. The enemy infantry, punished by this fire and the stream of bullets from the American foxhole line, wavered, but a handful of tanks rolled off the road and into Dom B. . . . Here, in the dark, Battalion anti-tank guns placed to defend the 2d Battalion command post went to work firing point-blank at the exhaust flashes as the German vehicles passed. Two enemy tanks were holed and the rest fled the village, although the anti-tank gun crews suffered at the hands of the German bazooka teams that had infiltrated in with the tanks. A second try came just before dawn, this time straight down the road from Büllingen. Ten German tanks in single file were sighted as they came over a slight ridge to the front of Company F. Two TDs and three anti-tank guns drove off or at least caused them to turn west in search of a weaker spot in the 2d Battalion defences. In the next thrust a platoon of Company G was badly cut up before friendly artillery finally checked the attack. Fifteen minutes later, apparently still seeking a hole, the Germans hit Company E, next in line to the west. The 60mm mortars illuminated the ground in front of the company at just the right moment and two of three tanks heading the assault were knocked out by bazooka and 57mm fire from the flank. The third tank commander stuck his head out of the escape hatch to take a look around and was promptly pistoled by an American corporal. By this time shellfire had scattered the German infantry. Nor did the enemy make another try until dusk, and then only with combat patrols.[18]

The AAR[19] of the 26th Infantry Regiment has another version of events:

At 0330 hours about twenty tanks and a Battalion of infantry hit the 2nd Battalion positions . . . maximum artillery fire was called for by LTC Daniel. . . . Tanks succeeded in overrunning the lines between Companies 'E' and 'F' but the infantry remained in their places, trusting to the TDs and anti-tank guns behind them to dispose of this threat to their rear. . . . The enemy infantry seeking to follow through was unable to penetrate the lines that held under the most intense pressure ever experienced by the companies. The mist and smoke . . . made the fighting a matter of close range firing. Anti-tank guns waited· until the tanks were within pointblank range. . . . Five German tanks had pushed up to 100 yards of the Battalion CP. . . . Two were knocked out, the other three withdrew some distance. A lull occurred about 0530 hours. . . . Mines and TDs were requested by the 2nd Battalion commander. Three more anti-tank guns were sent up at 1000 hours. . . . [The mines] did not arrive until late in the afternoon. Heavy enemy fire still pounded the 2nd Battalion positions after the enemy tanks and infantry withdrew. The withdrawals were only temporary and throughout the morning and late afternoon the enemy launched three separate attacks. . . . All these efforts were frustrated in large part due to the artillery's tremendously effective fire. Following a heavy attack launched by six tanks and two companies of infantry which pressed close to the Battalion CP once more before it was beaten off, the enemy stopped his attacks for the night.

Against the Panzers by Vannoy and Karamales[20], provides additional details from a wealth of unit AARs and Combat Interviews. It says a force comprising SS Panzer-Grenadiers of Krause's 1st Battalion and

Jagdpanzers of the 560th, started its attack at 2310 hours on the 19th but got lost and ended up south of Dom B at Morschheck at about 0150 on the 20th. There it was hit by an intense US artillery barrage and lost two Jagdpanzers; after turning back and starting again, it was 0330 hours before it approached the eastern American perimeter. The authors go on to say that the German attack was then mounted in three columns. The first, consisting of Streger's Jagdpanzer V Company and some SS Panzer-Grenadiers of the 3rd Battalion of Krause's 26th Regiment, attacked the US Battalion[21] on the Schwarzenbüchel feature and managed to take the southern part of the hill. The attack then faltered but the fighting went on for several hours.

The centre group is said to have comprised an indeterminate number of Jagdpanzers and SS Panzer-Grenadiers of the same Regiment. Apparently the commander of the leading Jagdpanzer was shot in the head and his reversing vehicle collided with the one behind. Despite the confusion this caused, the attackers are said to have pressed on and heavy fighting ensued with the US Company sited 500m south-east of Dom B.

The most successful attack, according to Vannoy and Karamales, was carried out by the 1st Jagdpanzer IV Company and infantry of Krause's 1st Battalion on the left flank. Although half the Jagdpanzers got stuck in the soft ground, five of them broke through and made it to the area of the manor house itself. Their accompanying SS Panzer-Grenadiers were, however, held by the American infantry and although they were able to use their Panzerfausts effectively against some of the anti-tank guns, they were unable to keep up with their armour. As a result, two Jagdpanzers were knocked out near the house and then two more as they withdrew.

Meanwhile, the battle on the southern slopes of the Schwarzenbüchel continued with American armour 'pounding away at the German vehicles until they were either destroyed or retreated'. The Americans lost two Shermans and an M-10 TD and the German attacks 'petered out by 0530 hours'.

According to Vannoy and Karamales[22], a further German attack was mounted within thirty minutes – before 0600 hours and again in the dark. Ten *tanks* are said to have attacked out of Büllingen and eight Jagdpanzers due north from Morschheck. All ten *tanks*, advancing in single file, are said to have been knocked out, one by one by three 57mms and two TDs, after which the accompanying Panzer-Grenadiers were pinned down by artillery and the attack broken off. This version contrasts strongly with that already quoted in Cole's Official History and would appear to be physically unlikely.

The attack from due south of Dom B by the eight Jagdpanzers fared no better. Artillery 'deflected the advance of the Jagdpanzers' and six were said to have been knocked out or immobilised, after which 'voluminous fire' from four artillery Battalions caused the German infantry to retreat.

By 0800 hours it was all over, although 'the Germans continued to launch smaller infantry attacks every four or five hours until nightfall'.

There are no detailed German reports on the fighting in this area on the 20th. In his History of the HJ, the Chief of Staff of the Division merely says that KG Kuhlmann 'presumably' started its attack at about 2200 hours on the 19th. Since the Schwarzenbüchel feature threatened the right flank of the advance, it had to be dealt with and he agrees that the southern portion of the hill was captured. Meyer then goes on to say that one Jagdpanzer V company with men of Krause's 1st Battalion broke into the American positions at Dom B; however, after the second Jagdpanzer V company on the right flank pulled back in the fog, the attack could not be sustained and the Division ordered it suspended.

From these differing accounts the reader will have to make up his own mind about what really happened on the night of the 19th-20th. In doing so, the following points should be taken into account. First, the fact that the main attacks took place in the dark and in fog must inevitably lead to confused reports of the fighting. Second, whilst it is certainly possible that the Jagdpanzers got lost in the darkness and fog, it is difficult to understand how they could have been observed 500m away in the Morschheck area under such conditions and how artillery could have been directed against them with such accuracy. Third, Hubert Meyer is wrong to say there were two Jagdpanzer V companies in the 560th Battalion – there was only one. Fourth, since we have firm casualty figures for personnel in the 560th Heavy Panzerjäger Battalion on this day[23] – two killed, twenty-two wounded, including three officers, and two missing – the statement[24] that only three Jagdpanzer Vs and ten Jagdpanzer IVs were left operational at the end of the day must be open to doubt. This would mean that a total of twenty-nine were disabled during the fighting; this author believes a figure of ten would be more sustainable. And fifth, in the final analysis the exact details of this fighting are irrelevant – the only important point is that the 12th SS Panzer Division failed in its attempt to capture Dom B and open up Route C.

NOTES

1. LTC George Rubel of the 740th Tk Bn.
2. Rubel, *Daredevil Tankers*, Chapter IX.
3. 1/119th.
4. Rubel, op. cit.
5. 2/119th.
6. B & C/504th.
7. B/703rd.
8. 2/505th.
9. C/51st & A/291st under Maj Yates.
10. E/505th

11. K/117th & A/743rd.
12. E/33rd.
13. Lt Hope.
14. B/1/117th Inf, B/743rd Tk & C/823rd TD.
15. Pfeifer to author, loc. cit., 2 Oct 85.
16. A & D/1/117th Inf, B/743rd Tk, C/823rd TD.
17. C/1/117th.
18. Cole, *The Ardennes: Battle of the Bulge*, pp. 130–1.
19. Whilst in no way wishing to detract from this particular AAR, unit AARs and War Diaries in general have to be treated with caution. They are usually written by someone who did not witness the events described and, human nature being what it is, mistakes and events which show up the unit in a bad light are usually omitted.
20. Vannoy & Karamales, *Against the Panzers*, pp. 288–91.
21. 3/26th.
22. Vannoy & Karamales, op. cit., pp. 291–3.
23. Meyer, op. cit., p. 259.
24. Vannoy & Karamales, op. cit., p. 293.

CHAPTER XIV

AUTUMN MIST: 21 December

The Hitlerjugend Front

(Maps 9 & 11)

The revised II SS Panzer Corps plan for opening up the routes to the west and resupplying KG Peiper involved a number of more or less simultaneous attacks along the entire length of the North Shoulder. Whilst it was theoretically sound, the plan was grossly over-optimistic in terms of preparation time and the forces available. In essence it involved the HJ capturing Bütgenbach, Skorzeny's 150th 'Panzer' Brigade clearing a way through Malmédy, and parts of KGs Sandig and Hansen and Fast Group Knittel securing Stavelot; diversionary attacks by 3rd FSD and the 12th and 277th VGDs towards Weywertz and Elsenborn respectively were designed to stretch American resources, particularly artillery.

The Hitlerjugend's part in the overall plan meant, according to the HJ Chief of Staff, making a new attack 'from another direction and with stronger forces'. Accordingly, the forces employed on the 21st were the strongest and most balanced so far employed by the 12th SS Panzer Division in the Ardennes campaign, and the American soldiers in the Dom B sector, who had already experienced more action in twenty-four hours than many Allied soldiers saw in the whole war, were about to suffer a terrible extension of that experience.

Despite the strength of the planned HJ attack, the direction chosen was militarily unsound and gave the soldiers involved little or no chance of success. The plan saw the Dom B area being bypassed and an assault made on Bütgenbach through Point 575. Dom B was to be secured in a later phase. Implementation involved dividing the Division into three strong groups which were to form up in the woods to the south of the Morschheck crossroads and Point 613. SS Captain Hauschild's 2nd SS Panzer-Grenadier Battalion of the 26th Regiment and Brockschmidt's depleted 12th SS Panzerjäger Battalion were to form the right hand group and advance on the right of the route described, while the main force under SS Major Kuhlmann would advance on the left. This main group was to be led by SS Captain Brückner's 3rd SS Panzer-Grenadier Battalion of the 25th Regiment, followed by Jürgensen's 1st SS Panzer Battalion and Streger's 560th Heavy Panzerjäger Battalion, less one company. Also included in this group was SS Captain Urabl's SPW mounted 3rd SS Panzer-Grenadier Battalion, which would provide close infantry support for the 1st SS Panzer Battalion once the breakthrough was achieved. In reserve was SS Captain Hein's 1st SS Panzer-Grenadier Battalion of the 26th Regiment with a company of Jagdpanzers from the 560th. The 12th SS Artillery Regiment and 12th SS Werfer Battalion were to support the attack, which was timed for 0340 hours, from positions near Hünningen, Büllingen and Honsfeld. It is the author's estimate that nearly 100 tanks and Jagdpanzers were available for this attack – over 70% of the HJ's original armoured force.

The reason for launching the attack in the dark was the very real fear that the attacking forces would be 'decimated by fire from the flank' – from the Dom B positions – if it were carried out in daylight. This was certainly true because tanks, Jagdpanzers and SPWs were prevented from deploying into any sort of attack formation until they were well past the thick woods directly to the south of American positions at Dom B. Even under the cover of darkness, the plan was asking for trouble, and it is not at all surprising that it started to go wrong long before H-Hour.

Hubert Meyer's excuses that 'numerous marshy sections and extensive forests' prevented armoured vehicles from attacking Bütgenbach directly from the south, and that it would be too difficult to form up in the 'attack sector of 3rd FSD', are not credible. The HJ had already formed up and attacked through other Divisions' sectors on both 18 and 19 December and, in the event, it chose to attack Bütgenbach with tanks from that direction the following day.

It is not clear who was responsible for this plan but Hugo Kraas must bear a large part of the responsibility – it was, after all, his Division; but it is difficult to understand why neither Sixth Panzer Army nor II SS Panzer Corps intervened to insist on the attack being launched well to the west – in the Faymonville-Waimes or Ondenval-Baugnez areas. This would have bypassed the whole Bütgenbach sector – as suggested by Sixth Panzer Army on the night of the 18th-19th. The 3rd FSD, whose potential had been largely wasted up to this time, could have provided both security for the forming up area and assistance, and the attack could have been coordinated with the adjacent one on Malmédy. Overcast skies precluded any threat to movement from Allied aircraft and a covered approach was available from just south of Büllingen, via the Morschheck crossroads, to Möderscheid and Schoppen. After the war von Manteuffel severely criticised his running mate's tactics in Richardson and Freidin's fascinating study, *The Fatal Decisions*:

> Sixth Panzer Army, completely forgetting its primary mission, committed strong forces against the Americans there [Elsenborn-Krinkelt-Rocherath]. Violent fighting, entailing heavy casualties, developed. . . . The proper course to have followed, once the toughness of the enemy's resistance had been recognised, would have been to have thrown a defensive ring around the enemy's positions sufficiently strong to cover the drive westwards which should have been continued with the maximum forces available.

There can be little doubt that the appearance of some 100 armoured vehicles close to Malmédy, and near the vulnerable boundary between the 1st and 30th Infantry Divisions, would have struck panic into many an American heart! The only possible objections to this plan could have been the state of the roads and tracks and the extra time it would have taken to assemble the attack force farther to the west. However, the HJ used the route through Morschheck and Möderscheid to Schoppen the following day, thus proving the feasibility of such a plan, and a twelve-hour delay might therefore have been well worthwhile. An attack in the Waimes-Baugnez area would have had the added advantage of taking place beyond the range of much of the American artillery.

Having criticised the plan, it is also necessary to query its implementation. Hubert Meyer tells us that with one exception the whole force reached its assembly area on time. The exception was SS Captain Hauschild's 2nd SS Panzer-Grenadier Battalion which, with the 12th SS Jagdpanzers, was due to lead the attack on the right flank. When at H-Hour Hauschild's Battalion had still not appeared, Kraas, located at the Morschheck crossroads, postponed the whole attack for one hour. Worse was to follow – by 0430 hours Hauschild's Battalion had still not appeared and Kraas, instead of ordering his reserve Battalion to take over the 2nd Battalion's role, changed the complete plan and ordered that Dom B be attacked first from the south and east. Only after Dom B had been neutralised was the advance on Bütgenbach to be continued. This astonishing decision ignored the threat from the Schwarzenbüchel feature and removed what little chance of success had previously existed.

Hauschild's SS Grenadiers eventually reached the assembly area at 0600 hours and at 0645 the preparatory barrage commenced. Hugh M. Cole describes it:

> This fire continued unremittingly until the first light in the east [about 0800], inflicting many casualties, destroying weapons by direct hits and tearing large gaps in the main line of resistance. . . . Now, as the Germans crossed the fields in assault formation [in daylight], the American forward observers called for a defensive barrage to box their own front lines. At least ten field artillery Battalions ultimately joined the fight (for this batteries of the 2d and 99th Divisions were tied into the 1st Division fire control system) and succeeded in discouraging the German infantry.[1]

'Discouraging' is an understatement! SS Senior Sergeant Karl Leitner, of the 2nd SS Panzer-Grenadier Battalion remembered the agony:

> Only the NCOs had any front experience. . . . Suddenly, a barrage set in. . . . My Sergeant and I jumped into a ditch. . . . After approximately ten minutes a shell hit to the right of us, probably in a tree. We were hit by shrapnel in our ditch. My Sergeant must have been badly wounded in the lung, he only gasped and died after a short time. I had taken a piece of shrapnel in my right hip. Then a shell exploded in a tree behind me. A piece of shrapnel hit me in my left ankle and pierced it. Other fragments slashed my right foot and ankle. I pushed myself half under my dead comrade. Soon after, fragments from another shell hit me in the left upper arm. That was at about 9 o'clock in the morning. In the afternoon an SPW ambulance arrived and collected us while the barrage was still going on. All my three Sergeants and I were taken out of battle.[2]

The deployment and problems of the advancing tanks and Jagdpanzers is well described by a member of the 3rd Panther Company:

> Our attack objective [Dom B] lay in that dead ground. . . . Instinctively, as if by order, all turrets swung toward the row of trees on our right flank. . . . We fired a few salvos from our turret machine-guns between those trees, opening the battle against an imagined enemy, in the knowledge that he was hiding somewhere, well camouflaged, his eye pressed to the sight of his anti-tank gun. . . . The point Panzer was commanded by SS Second Lieutenant Schnittenhelm, followed by Captain Hils, SS Second Lieutenant Engel, an SS sergeant of the staff company, behind

113

him the Mk IVs of the 5th and 6th Companies, then the Jagdpanzers and SP infantry guns. Schnittenhelm had just reached a protrusion of the forest when a flash of flame . . . shot up from the rear of his Panzer. . . . Hils issued orders to take up positions facing 3 o'clock. . . . He fired a signal flare to mark the final direction of attack. It died away on the ground sloping down to the estate [manor house]. We awaited the order, 'Marsch! Marsch!'. . . Nothing happened, I looked towards his Panzer. The turret was burning!. . . Abruptly, an almost indescribably devastating fire from the American artillery set in. The pasture turned into a ploughed field, a number of Panzers took direct hits. . . . Engel was also knocked out.[3]

A member of the 5th Mk IV Company, which attacked on the left of the road leading north from Point 613, remembered:

The Grenadiers were stalled and unable to keep pace with us because of the heavy artillery fire. . . . We were knocked out close to the first houses of the estate. . . . Since we were without Grenadiers, the order came to pull back.[4]

Another member of the same Company said later:

The previously white, snow-covered pasture had turned black. . . . When there was a break in the fire, I ran over to the closest Panzer IV, to ask it to pull mine back [onto its track]. Regrettably, it had been knocked out. The other Panzer IVs and the SP gun had suffered the same fate; most were knocked out by artillery and heavy mortar hits.[5]

According to the US Official History, the 1st, 2nd and 99th Divisional artillery units fired over 10,000 rounds in eight hours in support of the Dom B defenders on 21 December.[6] At about midday Kraas recognised failure and the attack was called off.

In 1990, shortly before his death, Hugo Kraas described 21 December as the darkest day of his military life. Exact losses cannot be confirmed. The 26th Infantry Regiment claimed eleven tanks destroyed[7] but reports such as that of a single M-10 TD knocking out seven tanks in rapid succession[8] are probably exaggerated. Nevertheless, German losses were grievous and certainly amounted to at least another company's worth of armour and many SS Panzer-Grenadiers, including Hauschild, the commander of the 2nd Battalion, who was wounded during the fighting. American losses were minor in comparison – two Shermans, one M-10, three 57mm anti-tank guns and an unknown but significant number of infantrymen.[9] In conclusion it has to be said that the achievement on this day of the 1st Infantry Division in general, and the 26th Infantry

Regiment in particular, must go down as one of the greatest in the whole campaign.

The Malmédy Sector
(Map 18)

The 150th 'Panzer' Brigade's part in the German operations on 21 December was just as disastrous as the Hitlerjugend's. Readers will recall that Skorzeny had been unable to launch his Brigade as originally planned and Dietrich had accepted his recommendation that it be employed as a conventional force. It was decided therefore to use it for an attack through the Malmédy area with the aim of linking up with the Leibstandarte at Stavelot.

Only two of Skorzeny's three KGs had managed to assemble in the Ligneuville area the day before the attack – Lieutenant Wolf's KG Z, consisting of two infantry companies and a support company but no armour, had still not arrived and therefore had to be earmarked as a potential reserve. SS Captain von Foelkersam's KG X, which was the strongest of the three, and Captain Scherff's KG Y were woefully inadequate for their mission.

Skorzeny's plan was to draw the American reserves by attacking the east side of Malmédy with KG Y during the hours of darkness and then to launch his main attack with KG X to seize the road junction just to the west of the Warche river bridge on the west side of the town. Possession of this junction was vital for opening up the N-32 to Francorchamps (Route C) and the N-23 to Stavelot and Peiper.

Although one of his own patrols had penetrated into Malmédy on the 17th and had found a few engineers[10] manning roadblocks on all the approach roads, Skorzeny had no real idea of what he was up against on the 21st. The Americans had certainly used the intervening period wisely. By last light on the 20th there were over three Battalions of infantry, two TD Companies and most of an engineer Battalion defending the town[11], with six field artillery Battalions within range to provide support. And if Skorzeny was lacking information about the Americans, the reverse was certainly not true. During the afternoon of the 20th, one of his men was captured and revealed, under interrogation, that the town was to be attacked at 0330 hours the following morning – before midnight all American units had been warned!

Scherff's KG Y, with six camouflaged StuGs, two infantry companies of about 150 men each and a heavy company with two Panzer-Grenadier and heavy mortar, Pioneer, Signals and anti-tank platoons, passed through the Baugnez crossroads junction at 0300 hours and ran into an American infantry Company[12] dug in at Mon Bijou at the east end of Malmédy a short time later. The US Company commander, Captain Murray Pulver, described what happened in his book, *Longest Year*:

> An American half-track came down the road followed by a column of tanks and other vehicles. The half-track hit a mine and lost its front wheels. . . . A group of German soldiers moved forward and yelled, 'Hey! We're American soldiers – don't shoot!'. . . The road was narrow with a high bank on the right and a gully on the other side making it impossible for the German tanks to advance. . . . I think every gun in the 230th Artillery fired in our support . . . things remained pretty hot until daylight.

This was one of the first occasions when American artillery used the new and highly secret 'Pozit' fuse, which caused a shell to burst above, rather than on contact with, the ground, thereby showering fragments over a much wider area. This had a devastating effect on Scherff's infantry and, following the loss of two StuGs, the KG withdrew.

The main attack on Malmédy was launched at 0650 hours by von Foelkersam's KG X, which had the same strength as Scherff's, but with a Sherman and five camouflaged Panthers instead of StuGs. Skorzeny watched it from the high ground near La Falize.

Whilst a small part of KG X moved towards the railway underpass near the main viaduct, the strongest group headed for the Warche river bridge. Its mission was to secure the road complex just to its north-west. This took the Americans by surprise and by midday part of their defences had been pushed back towards the Burninville area. But there was never any real question of Skorzeny's men achieving their mission. They lacked both the power and the numbers to overcome well sited defences, backed by highly effective artillery fire[13], and by mid-afternoon it was clear to Skorzeny that his attack had failed. Only one Panther had managed to cross the Warche bridge and none of his men had breached the railway embankment running along the south side of the town. When they withdrew from the field of battle they left behind four Panthers and some 150 killed, wounded and missing comrades. Skorzeny himself was wounded by artillery fire as he arrived back in Ligneuville that evening.

The Leibstandarte KGs
The Stavelot Sector
(Map 17)

Wilhelm Mohnke's orders to Max Hansen for 21 December were to secure the east bank of the Salm river between Trois Ponts and

Grand Halleux with two Battalions and to reinforce Knittel on the north bank of the Amblève with his Jagdpanzers and remaining Battalion of Panzer-Grenadiers. It was Mohnke's intention that Knittel, having been thus reinforced, should launch a strong attack on Stavelot from the west, whilst Sandig's remaining 1st SS Panzer-Grenadier Battalion should attack once again across the Amblève from the south.

Accordingly, early on the Thursday morning SS Major Emil Karst's 1st SS Panzer-Grenadier Battalion crossed the Petit Spai bridge, 1000m to the east of Trois Ponts, climbed the 200m cliff north of the railway line and swung east towards Stavelot. Hansen ordered Karl Rettlinger's Jagdpanzers to follow, but as soon as the first twenty-five-ton vehicle drove on to the bridge it collapsed.

In the meantime, Karl Richter's 1st SS Panzer-Grenadiers prepared to wade and swim the Amblève in a forlorn attempt to support the planned attack from the west. The eighteen 150mm and six 210mm mortars of SS Major Klaus Besch's 1st SS Werfer Battalion opened fire, but then came the surprising order that the attack was cancelled. Richter's men were unaware of it, but during the morning the whole situation in the Stavelot area was changing, and changing dramatically – instead of attacking the town the Germans were being forced on to the defensive.

The collapse of the Petit Spai bridge had immediate and serious consequences for Mohnke's men north of the river – they were deprived of essential armoured and heavy weapon support. The first attempt to bridge the river was swept away by the strong current and the second by American artillery which soon zeroed in on the site. Although further attempts were made to build a vehicle bridge across the Amblève throughout the next twenty-four hours, none was successful and shell-fire caused appalling casualties to the SS Pioneers and others ordered to help.

The second event which changed the situation in the Stavelot area on the 21st was the advance of further American troops from the west and north-west. TF Lovelady's tanks could not advance along the N-23 from the Trois Ponts viaducts due to Knittel's Tigers and anti-tank guns; but this did not prevent them moving directly east from the Coo valley towards Stavelot via Parfondruy, and nine Shermans and an armoured infantry group soon advanced on that axis. At the same time two companies of infantry[14] from the 30th Division moved from Roanne towards the hamlets of Renardmont and Ster.

Furious and very confused fighting went on throughout the day in the villages to the north-west of Stavelot and in the western outskirts of the town. Coblenz's and Goltz's Companies were reinforced during the battle by Karst's 1st SS Panzer-Grenadiers but by then the Americans had already secured Ster and Renardmont. Although the Germans were still holding Parfondruy and the houses at the west end of the town at last light, they were very much on the defensive. In 1948 a member of Coblenz's Company described some of the fighting:

In the afternoon we had a severe attack supported by tanks. . . . The enemy succeeded in carrying forward this attack up to about 50-80m of our positions. . . . In our platoon there were only a few men and as we had neither eaten nor slept for several days . . . we were totally exhausted. . . . In the evening of the 21st we had to dig out two or three men of a machine-gun crew who had been wounded and buried through tank shells. . . . From the voices in the adjoining cellar we could tell it was full of civilians. . . . After each detonation we could hear the cries and moans.[15]

Gustav Knittel also made a statement in 1948:

The clear orders of the Division and comradeship with KG Peiper forced me to hold my hopeless position. . . . On 21st the situation of those parts of my Battalion employed in the bridgehead became even more desperate . . . there was not a single man in reserve.[16]

By midnight on the 21st, it was clear to Mohnke, Hansen, Sandig and Knittel that the third and final battle for Stavelot had been lost.

The Trois Ponts Sector
(Map 14)

The reader will recall that Hansen's patrols had discovered the Americans at Noupré, to the east of Trois Ponts, soon after dark on the 20th. It is unclear who gave the crazy order for a single airborne Company[17] with two 57mm anti-tank guns to cross the Salm, but whoever it was offered the men as hostages to fortune.

Early on the 21st Max Hansen told SS Captain Böttcher's 3rd SS Panzer-Grenadier Battalion, supported by at least four Mk IVs from the combined 6th and 7th SS Panzer Companies in the Wanne area, to evict the Americans. Not surprisingly the paratrooper's situation soon became untenable and although a second airborne Company[18] was very unwisely sent to assist, it was not long before both Companies had been routed. By 1630 hours they were back across the river and the temporary bridge blown behind them.

American pride was hurt at Trois Ponts and the casualties incurred were unnecessary, but at the end of the day the west bank of the Salm was secure and that was all that mattered. No Germans would ever cross the river in this sector to support Peiper. The only consolation for Mohnke and Hansen was that no Americans would cross either whilst they were responsible for the Trois Ponts front.

Cheneux
(Map 15)

We left other American paratroopers[19] clinging to their 'toehold' in Cheneux after their brave but misguided attempt to capture the village during the early part of the night of the 20th. A German counter-attack by SS Panzer-Grenadiers early on the 21st failed with considerable loss. The village remained fairly quiet for the rest of the day, but by 1530 hours another Battalion[20] of paratroopers had outflanked Cheneux on its southern flank and the American commander gave orders for a joint attack at 1750 to clear the village and close up to the Amblève. The attack proved unnecessary – Peiper's men withdrew back to La Gleize as soon as darkness fell and the Americans were on the river by 2300 hours with minimal casualties. They found fourteen Flak wagons, five 105mm guns, two 75mm anti-tank guns, six SPWs and four trucks in Cheneux – they were all out of petrol. The fighting in the village was later described by some of those who took part as the most vicious in the entire Ardennes campaign; a former member of the 6th SS Panzer-Grenadier Company confirmed to the author that it had certainly been 'a good fight'! But one man who saw the survivors of the US Battalion which had borne the brunt of the fighting later recorded his impressions:

> The shattered remnants of the 1st Bn came straggling listlessly down the road, a terrible contrast to the happy Battalion which had only two days before gone up the same road wisecracking and full of fight. They were bearded, red eyed, covered with mud from head to foot, and staring blank-facedly straight to the front. No one spoke. . . . They carried their rifles any way that seemed comfortable, some in Daniel Boone fashion. They had written a page in history which few would ever know about. . . . In the swirling holocaust of fire and fury which had descended on the peaceful valley of the Amblève river in Belgium, it might not even be mentioned in the newspapers, such was the confusion of places, units and deeds being churned around in the Witch's Brew which was the present battle of the Ardennes.[21]

The Stoumont Sector
(Map 15)

At 0300 hours on the Thursday morning, Brigadier General Harrison issued new orders for the capture of Stoumont. One infantry Battalion[22], with TF Jordan under command, was to attack again from the north and secure the east end of the village, 119 RCT was to take the Preventorium and west end, and another infantry Battalion[23] was to circle round through the woods to the north of Stoumont and cut the N-33 near the Château Froidcour.

The best laid plans go wrong and Harrison's suffered major disruption when, at 0500 hours, a violent SS counter-attack hit the 119 RCT and knocked out four Shermans just to the west of the Preventorium. This counter-attack inevitably affected the attack from the north as well – as one of the Company commanders recalled:

An attack order was finally issued at 0530 hours. We moved out at 0630. It was very foggy. By 0800 we were in position above the town. It was so foggy we couldn't see over 25 feet. . . . We were in the edge of the woods. The jump off time was changed again and finally set for 1245 hours.[24]

Both American attacks failed. The knocked out Shermans blocked the western approach for armour and the infantry assault stalled in the face of withering machine-gun and small arms fire; by 1535 hours the western group was back where it started. TF Jordan's tanks, in the face of fire from five Panthers, could get no farther than they had the previous day and their accompanying infantry became separated and disorganised in the foggy conditions. At 1515 hours this force too was ordered back to its start positions. The intensity of the struggle is again described by the infantry Company commander:

It was so foggy that one of our men found himself ten yards from a German machine-gun before he knew it. . . . Everyone had been pushed about as far as he could be. Nerves were being broken on men whom one would have thought would never weaken. Finally we got word to hold up for the night. We organised with the light tanks and dug in.

The only successful part of Harrison's attack was the move to cut the main N-33 road behind Stoumont. This was achieved at 1400 hours but a quick counter-attack by Georg Preuss's under-strength 10th SS Panzer-Grenadier Company from the area of the Château Froidcour soon forced the Americans to pull back – their commanding officer[25] being captured in the process. Preuss was later awarded the Knight's Cross for his Company's performance during AUTUMN MIST.

It had not been a good day for the Americans. The casualty rate was reaching unsustainable levels, with just one of the infantry Battalions losing 116 men killed and wounded and another eighty-one missing in a single day. At 1600 hours Harrison reported:

> The real picture is that two of these Battalions are in pretty bad shape. . . . We can stop them [the Germans] alright. . . . [But] I don't think the troops we have now, without some improvement, can take the thing [Stoumont].

The only 'improvement' readily available was air power and artillery and Harrison, unaware that Peiper had already decided to evacuate Stoumont that night, resolved to use both in liberal quantities the following day.

Two things caused Peiper to pull out of the village. First, the vulnerability of his long northern flank had been demonstrated when the Americans cut the N-33, and second, during the day he had received a message from Mohnke telling him that part of Hansen's KG had been ordered to advance via Coo to join him. These factors, coupled with the impending loss of Cheneux, brought Peiper to the inevitable conclusion that it was time to concentrate his remaining forces in the more easily defended hill-top village of La Gleize, where he already had a strong, firm base. He moved there himself at 1600 hours after giving orders for the withdrawals from Stoumont and Cheneux to begin soon after last light.

The La Gleize Sector
(Map 16)

The basic structure of Jochen Peiper's defence of La Gleize was already in place before the withdrawals from Cheneux and Stoumont began. The village lies on a 'saddle' of land running for about 1000m in a north-south direction and Peiper had ordered strongpoints to be established at the four corners of this 'saddle' – Les Montis, Hassoumont, the Werimont farm and the Dinheid feature. As extra troops and tanks arrived in the village, these strongpoints were built up. Minefields were laid and tanks sited to cover all approaches.

TF McGeorge advanced again soon after dawn, straight down the road from Bourgomont. It did not get far – as soon as the leading Shermans and infantry reached the outskirts of Hassoumont they were halted by Rumpf's SS Pioneers, backed by four Mk IVs, a Tiger and a Panther. A second attempt, at about 1330 hours, to make a left flanking attack was stopped in its tracks by the small force at the Moulin Maréchal. McGeorge resolved to try again the next day from a different direction and he spent the next few hours moving his whole TF back the way it had come, and then via Roanne to the area of the Minières.

He planned to advance on the 22nd using the N-33 as his axis of attack.

(Map 6)

The men of the Leibstandarte and Hitlerjugend Divisions had fought bravely on 21 December, but the failures at Dom B, Malmédy and Stavelot ended forever any hope they might have had of fulfilling their mission in the Ardennes offensive.

As this fatal day ended, the Divisional and KG commanders of the two Divisions were unaware that Hitler had already moved the focus of his offensive to von Manteuffel's Fifth Panzer Army front. They had no way of knowing that St Vith had just fallen and that although Bastogne was holding out, two Panzer Divisions and a Volks-Grenadier Division[26] had pushed well past the town and were already within 40km of the Meuse. The men who wore Hitler's name on their cuff bands would never bask in the glory their Führer had intended for them.

NOTES

1. Cole, *The Ardennes: Battle of the Bulge*, p. 131.
2. Meyer, *The History of the 12th SS Panzer Division Hitlerjugend*, p. 261.
3. Ibid., p. 260.
4. Ibid.
5. Ibid., p. 261.
6. Cole, op. cit., p. 132.
7. 26th Inf Regt AAR, 21 Dec 44.
8. 634th TD Bn AAR.
9. Casualty figures for the 26th Inf Regt are only available for the whole period of the Dom B fighting: 13 officers and 487 men killed, wounded and captured.
10. Pergrin's 291st.
11. 1 & 3/120th Inf, 99th (Separate) Inf, HQ & B/526 Armd Inf, B/823rd (-) & A/825th TD, 291st Engrs (-).
12. B/120th.
13. 30th Div artillery fired 3,000 rounds during the battle.
14. I & L/117th.
15. Makamul, statement at Freiburg 31 Aug 48.
16. Knittel, statement at Landsberg/Lech 15 Mar 48.
17. E/505th.
18. F/505th.
19. B & C/504th & G/504th.
20. H & I/504th.
21. Graves, *Blood and Snow – the Ardennes*.
22. 3/119th.
23. 2/119th.
24. Lt David Knox, L/119th, letter to author Oct 84.
25. Maj Hal McCown.
26. 2nd & 116th Pz and 560th VGD.

CHAPTER XV
AUTUMN MIST: 22 December
The Leibstandarte KGs
Stoumont
(Map 15)

The German withdrawal from Stoumont was completed without difficulty during the night of the 21st. A few snipers and machine-gunners
were left behind to deceive the Americans and only walking wounded
and fit American prisoners were taken back to La Gleize. Some eighty
badly wounded Germans and a few Americans were left in the care of
two American medics and a single German medical NCO in the Château
Froidcour.

Brigadier General Harrison had no idea that Stoumont had been
abandoned and when bad visibility prevented air support for his attack,
he determined on a lavish use of artillery in order to keep casualties
to a minimum. The barrage started at 0900 hours and continued until
1400 hours. By then, of 150 houses in Stoumont, 100 were uninhabitable,
thirty-five completely destroyed and five burned. The Americans moved
in without resistance and by evening the village and the Château.were
firmly in their hands. Amazingly, all the children and their carers in the
Preventorium survived and only four civilians died in the four days'
fighting. According to some Belgian sources one Tiger, eighteen Panthers
and one Mk IV were found abandoned or destroyed between Stoumont
station and the Château. This count is undoubtedly exaggerated.

The Stavelot Sector
(Map 17)

During the Thursday/Friday night SS Major Scheler's 1st SS Panzer
Pioneers managed to construct a light infantry bridge across the Amblève
near Petit Spai and Mohnke, having finally accepted that he was not
going to capture Stavelot, ordered Hansen to attempt a breakthrough to
La Gleize.

This was a desperate measure which had little hope of success. Hansen
had no armour or heavy weapons north of the river and only two
Battalions available for the task – the 1st which was firmly locked in

123

battle on the north-western side of Stavelot and the 3rd covering the Trois Ponts sector.

Friday morning, which dawned misty with sleet showers, saw both sides in the Stavelot area preparing to attack – the Americans to capture Parfondruy and the western houses of the town, and the Germans to move north-west through Ster and Biester towards La Gleize.

The Americans struck first – against Coblenz's men in the western houses. After severe fighting, in which Coblenz was wounded and captured and many others killed and wounded, the Germans were left holding the Château Lambert but little else; however, they still controlled the road between the Château and Trois Ponts.

Reports of atrocities against civilians in the areas freed soon reached the American officer[1] in command of the sector north of the river between La Gleize and Stavelot. TF Lovelady's medical officer, A. Eaton Roberts, wrote in his book, *Five Stars to Victory* in 1949:

When D Company with infantry liberated the tiny village [Parfondruy] they found only a few living civilians, huddled in dark corners of cellars, too terrified, too overcome by grief, to move or welcome American troops with their usual hearty greetings. For, strewn about the houses were the corpses of whole families from babies to parents and grandparents. . . . Compassion for the victims and burning hate for the foe welled up simultaneously in the hearts of the soldiers who witnessed these gruesome scenes. . . . With redoubled efforts, TF Lovelady suddenly became a wild beast, stampeding enemy positions with increased ruthlessness and ferocity.

Knittel and Coblenz were sentenced to life imprisonment at the 1946 Dachau War Crimes Trials, and Goltz, by the Belgians in July 1948, to fifteen years, for atrocities committed by German troops in the Stavelot area during December 1944.[2] In order however, to keep some sort of balance, it has to be pointed out that house to house fighting is one of the most savage of all military operations and the following account of an incident in Stavelot by an American officer is pertinent:

A new man who had only been with the Company a couple of weeks heard a noise in a cellar. He called 'Heraus' but panicked when there was no reply. He pulled the pin and rolled a grenade down the steps. The cellar was jammed with civilians. After the wounded were carried from the basement, our aidmen went to work. The rest of the men walked away, unable to watch.

The intended advance by Karst's 1st SS Panzer-Grenadiers was a total failure – Karst himself was killed by shrapnel before it even started.

The Americans between Renardmont and Ster[3] were far too strong for their assailants and at the end of the day the Germans found themselves blocked on a line from Point de Vue de Ster to a point just south of the tiny village itself.

The most successful part of the day for the Germans was the advance by Böttcher's 3rd SS Panzer-Grenadiers through the Coreu forest. After crossing the Amblève they reached the high ground above Biester at about 1600 hours and then swept down to cut TF Lovelady into two parts. This bold and aggressive action caused panic in the southern half of the column where there was even talk of surrender. But both sides were now in crisis for, although the Germans had achieved much, it had been at great cost – Böttcher had been wounded and the Belgians later reported more than 160 corpses in the fields around Biester. Faced with these losses and with his other Battalion halted south of Ster, Hansen knew he would never break through to La Gleize. He told his men to go firm where they were and informed Mohnke accordingly. The incessant artillery fire was causing despair to Germans and Americans alike – the former with twenty-four Werfers, twenty-two 150mm, four 100mm and twenty-four 105mm guns and howitzers available, and the Americans with twenty-four 75mm, ninety 105mm and forty 155mm guns within range.

La Gleize

(Map 16)

Jochen Peiper's last remaining outpost, at the Moulin Maréchal, joined the rest of his KG in La Gleize during the night of 21-22 December. His total strength was now about 1,500 men and within his defended perimeter there were six Tiger IIs, thirteen Panthers, six Mk IV tanks, three Pumas, forty-six SPWs, four 20mm Flak wagons, twelve other vehicles, four 120mm mortars and six 150mm infantry guns.[4] The tanks were spread throughout La Gleize, with eight in the northern half of the village and seventeen in the southern half where the fields of fire were much better.

The Americans had hoped for air support on the Friday morning but, as previously mentioned, poor visibility again prevented flying in the Amblève valley area and the ground forces had to operate alone. Apart from artillery fire, the western approaches to La Gleize were quiet all day – TF Harrison was fully occupied, first of all bombarding, and then securing Stoumont. On the eastern side of La Gleize it was a different story.

The first action of the day involved Peiper sending a strong force of three tanks, including one Tiger, and infantry from the Hassoumont area to Les

Tscheous. The reason for this move is unclear but he was presumably worried about this north-east flank with its covered approaches. Whatever the reason, the result was a disaster. American artillery, which was to play an increasingly important part in the battle, forced the infantry to withdraw in the early afternoon and knocked out all three tanks.

Shortly after this, at about 1400 hours and following a thirty-minute artillery barrage, TF McGeorge began its advance from the Minières area up the N-33. An hour later the leading Shermans reached the first major bend in the road below the village and ran onto mines. At about the same time the two rear tanks were immobilised by fire from at least five Panzers covering this approach and the whole column then came under concentrated fire from a variety of weapons. TF McGeorge fell back in disorder to the line of the Roannay stream. The only success on this flank was the disablement of two Tigers at the Werimont farm by artillery fire.

Any elation which Peiper might have felt in defeating McGeorge's attack soon evaporated with the news, received at 1700 hours, that Hansen's attempts to break through to him had failed. After discussions with his senior commanders – von Westernhagen, Poetschke and Diefenthal – Peiper sent a message to Mohnke at his Headquarters in Wanne, demanding permission to break out. This was refused. Despite the highly unfavourable situation Hermann Priess still entertained hopes of relieving KG Peiper and he submitted a request to Sixth Panzer Army for the 9th SS Panzer Division, now approaching Grand Halleux only 8km to the south, to be diverted to Stavelot. This request was also refused.

At about 2000 hours on the Friday night, three JU 52 transport aircraft attempted to drop desperately needed fuel and other supplies to the KG. Only 10% fell within Peiper's very limited perimeter and in the first clear and moonlit night of the offensive, his men had to watch with dismay as the rest fell behind US lines. The clear night also brought with it the dreaded prospect of US air strikes in the morning.

The Hitlerjugend Front
(Map 9)

During the Thursday night Hugo Kraas was told to make one 'last effort' to capture Bütgenbach on the 22nd, but that he could use only his 'armoured group'. The rest of his Division was to be withdrawn as soon as possible for use farther south and the 'armoured group' would catch up later. The Bütgenbach attack was to be made in cooperation with Major General Engel's 12th VGD which was to take on Dom B.

In order to gain surprise the HJ assault began an hour before dawn at 0630 hours. Despite Hubert Meyer's remarks that the ground was unsuitable, it was mounted from the Schoppen area[5] by, according to the Americans[6], some twenty tanks and Jagdpanzers, under the command of SS Major Arnold Jürgensen, supported by Urabl's SPW mounted 3rd SS Panzer-Grenadiers and the similarly mounted 1st Company of SS Captain Taubert's 12th SS Panzer Pioneers, commanded by SS Second Lieutenant Betz.

By 0900 hours the German armour and SS Panzer-Grenadiers had penetrated into Bütgenbach. Tanks overran one American Company[7] and broke through another[8], but Shermans, TDs and bazookas were taking their toll and claims that five 'Panzers' were knocked out do not seem unreasonable. Certainly Jürgensen's own Panther was hit and set ablaze about one kilometre south of Bütgenbach church and both he and Urabl, who was riding in the same tank, were badly burned.[9] This undoubtedly had a major effect on the battle and, following a spirited counter-attack shortly after midday, things began to go the way of the Americans. Three hundred artillery fire missions were laid on in support of the defenders. The failure of the 12th VGD to take Dom B inevitably affected events. Engel reported later:

Both attacks initially advanced well. The Panzers of the HJ pushed into Bütgenbach and took the village [this was an obvious overstatement], but it was impossible to clear the village of enemy. . . . In the evening hours the remaining Panzers were back in their starting positions. The attack on the Bütgenbach estate [Dom B] also stalled before reaching the objective.[10]

By last light it was all over – the Germans would never take Bütgenbach or its estate.

The extraction of other elements of the Hitlerjugend was carried out successfully during this day and by the evening most of the 12th SS Reconnaissance and Panzerjäger Battalions and Müller's 25th SS Panzer-Grenadier Regiment were on their way to a new assembly area between Möderscheid and Born (Map 10).

NOTES

1. Col Walter Johnson, commander 117th Inf Regt; TF Lovelady was placed under his command late on 21 Dec.
2. 142 Belgians died during the fighting in the Stavelot area and seven more died later as a result of injuries received. Full details were provided to the author in Apr 94 by Joseph Dejardin, Secretary for Social Services for the territory of Stavelot, 1941–1984.
3. I & L/117th Inf, D/33rd & B/743rd Armd.

4. Pictures of most of this equipment exist and one of the villagers, Monsieur Gérard Grégoire, recorded the positions of most pieces when he returned to La Gleize on 9 Jan 45.
5. Karl-Heinz Heck, a resident of Bütgenbach and an expert with a metal detector, has found many items of equipment, etc. over a period of many years which prove that the Jürgensen 'armoured group' used the Morschheck, Möderscheid, Schoppen route to launch this attack.
6. Cole, *The Ardennes: Battle of the Bulge*, p. 133.
7. A/26th.
8. G/18th.
9. Jürgensen died the following day.
10. Meyer, *The History of the 12th SS Panzer Division Hitlerjugend*, p. 263.

CHAPTER XVI

AUTUMN MIST: 23 – 27 December

The Hitlerjugend

(Map 19)

Bittrich's II SS Panzer Corps reassumed command of the 2nd Das Reich and 9th Hohenstaufen SS Panzer Divisions on 23 December and, in accordance with Hitler's revised plan, they were ordered to advance on the left flank of the Sixth Panzer Army. By that evening 2nd Panzer Division's Reconnaissance Battalion had already bypassed Marche-en-Famenne and was within 10km of the Meuse, whilst Das Reich had captured the important road junction at Baraque de Fraiture and Hohenstaufen was preparing to attack in the Salm river sector near Grand Halleux and advance towards Lierneux. It was Bittrich's intention that as soon as the Hitlerjugend could be reorganised and resupplied, it would support this renewed thrust. The biggest problem was a shortage of fuel – Allied air attacks were having a detrimental effect on the amount reaching the forward units and, because the leading formations of von Manteuffel's Fifth Panzer Army were nearing the Meuse, their demands had a higher priority.

The Hitlerjugend Division, with its Headquarters in Eibertingen near Amel, spent Saturday the 23rd trying to reassemble its units in the Möderscheid-Born area (Map 10), where it could lick its wounds and prepare for its next mission. The biggest task was the recovery and repair of the armoured vehicles which littered the area over which the Division had moved and fought. Many had been destroyed, but others were merely immobilized due to the terrain or enemy action. The three armoured units had, of course, suffered badly in the previous few days –

the 1st SS Panzer Battalion had lost its commander and the senior officer left was SS Lieutenant Bormuth; the 560th Heavy Panzerjäger Battalion had suffered one company commander killed and another wounded, and a further company commander in the 12th SS Panzerjäger Battalion had been wounded. Vehicle casualties are impossible to estimate with any real accuracy, but at least 40% of the Division's 142 tanks and Jagdpanzers had been knocked out or immobilized by the time the HJ was withdrawn on 23 December. The claim in the AAR of the 26th Infantry Regiment that on that day patrols from its 2nd Battalion 'established that thirty tanks had been knocked out in their area alone' would seem to be well founded.

On 24 December the Panzer Lehr Division captured Rochefort, the 2nd SS Das Reich Division attacked north-west from Baraque de Fraiture, the 116th Panzer Division through Marche-en-Famenne, and the HJ began its move to the south-west – but not until after dark. By next morning the Headquarters and Divisional Escort Company, the 12th SS Reconnaissance and Flak Battalions and the 25th SS Panzer-Grenadier and 12th SS Artillery Regiments had completed their move to the Beho area – not much more than 20km! However, when one considers the general state of the roads and the need to negotiate the devastated town of St Vith, this is not altogether surprising.

The move continued during the following night, and by early on the 26th Kraas's Headquarters, the Artillery Headquarters, the Divisional Escort Company and parts of the 12th SS Reconnaissance Battalion were established in Samrée. Müller's 25th SS Panzer-Grenadier Regiment, the 3rd SPW Battalion of Krause's 26th Regiment – now commanded by SS Lieutenant Brinkmann – the three artillery, Flak and Werfer Battalions all took twenty-four hours longer and were not complete in the Samrée area until midday on the 27th. The trucks carrying the other two Battalions of Krause's Regiment ran out of fuel near Beho and the men had to march the remaining 35km, delaying them even longer.

Readers will no doubt be wondering what had happened to the HJ's armour – it was still refitting in the Losheimergraben-Amel area.

The Leibstandarte KGs
The Stavelot Sector
(Map 17)

The American plan for eliminating the Germans north of the Amblève river on 23 December involved holding firm in the villages to the north-west of Stavelot and advancing on two separate axes – south on the N-33 to link up with the forward elements of TF Lovelady at the Trois Ponts viaducts[1], and south through the Point de Vue de Ster to the

Trois Ponts-Stavelot railway line and then east towards Stavelot.[2] At the same time the group in Stavelot itself[3] was to push strong patrols west along the N-23. Standing in the way were the two under-strength Battalions of Hansen's 1st SS Panzer-Grenadier Regiment – the 3rd, now under SS Lieutenant Haft, at Biester and the 1st, under SS Captain Rink, in the area of the Point de Vue de Ster and the Farm Masures. Although the Americans hoped to interdict the German artillery with air strikes, the forces they committed were hardly adequate for the task.

The advance began at 0830 hours and, despite the commitment of an additional infantry Company[4], it took until 1600 hours before Haft's SS Grenadiers were evicted from the Biester area. German casualties were heavy, with US artillery taking a steady toll – the 12th Company had almost ceased to exist by last light and the commander of the 11th Company, Knight's Cross holder Frank Hasse, was dead. It has been said that he was murdered by Belgian partisans near Petit Coo[5], but since resistance fighters rarely operated in the vicinity of a battle, this has to be questioned.

Shortly after dark the remnants of Hansen's Battalions were still holding the area known as the Six Moines in the Coreu forest, but the Americans had finally captured the Château Lambert on the western edge of Stavelot. The few remaining members of Knittel's 1st SS Reconnaissance Battalion had withdrawn to the vicinity of his Command Post at the Farm Antoine on the N-23 where there were still four Tigers of von Westernhagen's Battalion.

Sunday 24 December saw the survivors of Hansen's two Battalions withdraw successfully across the Amblève to the hills known as Les Sept Montagnes. Despite the deployment of more than two Battalions of infantry[6] with tank support, the Americans were only half way to the railway line by the end of the day; but at least contact had been re-established with TF Lovelady's vanguard at the Trois Ponts viaducts where it had been cut off for four days. Incredibly, the few survivors of Knittel's Battalion and two of von Westernhagen's four Tigers were still holding a small bridgehead north of the river around Petit Spai at last light.

That evening Gustav Knittel told his last few men and the crews of the Tigers to withdraw before first light on Christmas day. Most crossed the river at about 0400 hours using the remains of the infantry bridge and, while one of the Tigers managed to wade across, the second was blown up by its crew.

At 0900 hours on Christmas Day, TF Harrison, supported by the infantry, tanks and TDs[7] which had defended Stavelot so valiantly for nearly a week, advanced once more towards the Amblève. They met no resistance and as the men looked down from the railway line they saw the Germans had gone. The battle of Stavelot and its environs was over at last – it had cost Hansen over five hundred men, Knittel some 280 and the Americans 302 killed, wounded and missing. A good proportion of the 57,275 artillery rounds fired by the 30th Division during the previous six days had fallen in the Stavelot area.

During the 27th and 28th Mohnke's men were relieved of their responsibilities south of the Amblève and east of the Salm by elements of the 18th and 62nd VGDs. Sepp Dietrich and Hermann Priess had a new task for them – in the Bastogne area.

La Gleize

(Map 16)

Despite the Americans' overwhelming superiority, particularly in artillery, none of their actions against KG Peiper on 23 December was successful. One hundred 155mm and 105mm guns and thirty medium mortars[8] were now within range of the village to support the attacks of more than three infantry Battalions and four tank companies. Brigadier General Harrison's plan was for the 119 RCT to attack along the axes of the N-33 and Cheneux roads on the west side of La Gleize, while TF McGeorge advanced up the N-33 on the east side.

One of the US commanding officers described the western attack:

We resumed the attack at daybreak on the 23rd but it soon fizzled out and no gain was made. The enemy was covering our attack with all types of fire. Most of it came from La Gleize but the thing that stopped us was the flanking fire from the high ground north-west of the town [Les Montis and Hassoumont].[9]

The After Action Report of the 119 RCT describes the attack by the southern group on that flank:

The 1st Battalion [with a Company of Shermans[10]] attacked east at 0830 and advanced to the crossroads [north-east of the station] before meeting any resistance. At this point an enemy minefield covered by anti-tank fire was encountered. One tank burned and another disabled by the anti-tank fire before it was knocked out by our tanks. The minefield was removed and the Battalion advanced approximately 300 yards, where it was held up by automatic and direct fire weapons on the high ground in and south of La Gleize. The remainder of the day was spent in reconnaissance and directing fire on enemy positions.

The attack on the east side of the village fared no better. McGeorge started at 0900 hours with an advance by infantry from the Bourgomont direction, whilst his Shermans moved forward using the N-33 as their axis. By 1530 hours his infantry had failed to get beyond Les Tscheous and his tanks, although they managed to get quite close to the Werimont Farm position, were pinned down by tank fire from Hassoumont and the east side of La Gleize.

Peiper's request for permission to break out had been initially refused by Sixth Panzer Army, but authority was eventually delegated to Divisional level and Mohnke agreed at 1400 hours on the Saturday. Stories that Peiper was ordered to bring out all his wounded, vehicles and weapons are nonsense – it was clearly out of the question; indeed, his tanks had been virtually without fuel for over two days.

There was only one possible escape route and that was to the south, over the Amblève, south again and then east to join the rest of the Division on the Wanne heights. Peiper and his senior commanders agreed that all lightly wounded would accompany the marching column and as many weapons as possible would be carried. All others were to be rendered useless, but vehicles and tanks were not to be blown up or immobilized except during artillery fire for fear of warning the Americans that a withdrawal was imminent. The badly wounded would, of course, have to be left and those slightly less serious given the task of sabotaging as many tanks and heavy weapons as possible after the main body had departed. Assembly for the march out was planned for 0200 hours the following morning – Christmas Eve.

Before describing the escape from La Gleize, it is interesting to consider the state of morale of Peiper and his men after a week of fighting – a week which had seen the KG reduced to a quarter of its original strength and fail in its mission. The American commanding officer who had been taken prisoner near the Château Froidcour, Major Hal McCown, gave his views soon after the battle, based on his own observations and on impressions gained during six hours of conversation with Peiper himself during the night of the 21st-22nd:

Morale was high throughout the entire period I was with them despite the extremely trying conditions. The discipline was very good. . . . The physical condition of all personnel was good, except for a lack of proper food. . . . All the men wore practically new boots and had adequate clothing. . . . The relationship between officers and men, particularly the commanding officer, Col Peiper, was closer and more friendly than I would have expected. On several occasions Col Peiper visited his wounded, and many times, as we were climbing the steep hills [during the breakout from La Gleize] I saw him speak a couple of cheering words and give a slap of encouragement on the back of heavily loaded men.

He and I talked . . . our subject being mainly his defence of Nazism and why Germany was fighting. I have met few men who impressed me in as short a space of time as did this officer. . . . He was completely confident of Germany's ability to whip the Allies. He spoke of Himmler's new reserve army at quite some length, saying that it contained so many new divisions, both armored and otherwise, that our G-2s would wonder where they all came from. He . . . told me that more secret weapons like those [V-1 and V-2] would be unloosed.[11]

Escape
(Map 15)

Sometime after 0200 hours on Sunday the 24th, Peiper's column of some 800 men set out up the path known as La Coulée, passed over the Dinheid feature and made its way down to the Amblève. It was a clear, bitterly cold night and there was snow on the ground. Two Belgian guides[12] were forced to lead the way through the forest from La Venne to the summit of Mont St Victor. Hal McCown, whom Peiper took with him as a type of hostage[13], described the early part of the march:

We crossed the Amblève river near La Gleize on a small highway bridge immediately underneath the railroad bridge and moved generally south, climbing higher and higher on the ridge line. At 0500 we heard the first tank blow up and inside thirty minutes the entire area formerly occupied by Col Peiper's command was a sea of fiercely burning vehicles, the work of the small detachment he had left behind to complete the destruction of all his equipment.

Peiper's intention had been to link up with Hansen's men on the east side of the Amblève by crossing the cascade bridge at Coo; however, on reaching the heights of Mont St Victor soon after first light, he could see the bridge was blown. His only remaining option was to move much farther south in the hope of crossing the Salm below Trois Ponts.

Soon after first light on the 24th the Americans advanced on La Gleize from three sides and, apart from some brief skirmishes with the stay-behind parties and a few Germans who had not received the order to withdraw, they met little resistance. As they took between 100 and 300 prisoners, many of them badly wounded, and released 170 American GIs, they were amazed to find the bulk of the Germans had escaped. There was only one way they could have gone and spotter planes were sent up to try to find their erstwhile enemy.

Peiper decided to lie up in the woods during daylight on the 24th and resume the march after dark. The column then bypassed Brume, which was occupied by US paratroopers, and headed for the N-23 near Henri Moulin. McCown again:

We pushed down into the valley in single column with a heavily armed point out ahead. The noise made by the entire 800-man group was so little that I believe we could have passed within 200 yards of an outpost without detection. As the point neared the base of the hill I could hear quite clearly an American voice call out 'Halt! Who is there?' The challenge was repeated three times, then the American sentry fired three shots. A moment later the order came along the column to turn round and move back up the hill. The entire column was half-way back up the hillside in a very few minutes. . . . The point moved along the side of the hill for a distance of half a mile, then turned again down into the valley, and this time passed undetected through the valley and the paved road which ran along the base. The entire 800 men were closed into the trees on the other side of the valley in an amazingly short period of time.

The two Belgian guides managed to escape during this minor incident. Meanwhile the SS men moved on past Mont de Fosse and up to the heights of Bergeval where, near St Jacques, they again ran into the enemy. By an amazing coincidence the Americans were also withdrawing to new positions. This controversial move was caused by the serious German threat which had developed to the south of Werbomont on the 24th, and had led the commander of the XVIII Airborne Corps[14] to order the 82nd Airborne Division to pull back to a more defensible line running from Trois Ponts to Manhay (Map 19). It was these paratroopers of the 82nd Airborne who clashed twice with Peiper's column during the early hours of Christmas Day. The final clash, almost certainly between Bergeval and Rochelinval, is again described by McCown:

Firing broke out not very far from where I was standing. My guards and I hit the ground, tracer bullets flashed all around us and we could hear the machine-gun bullets cutting the trees very close over us. The American unit which I later found out was a company[15], drove forward again to clear what it obviously thought was a stray patrol. . . . The mortar fire fell all around the German position. . . . Shrapnel cut the trees. . . . I could hear commands being shouted in German and English. . . . There was considerable movement around me in the darkness. I lay still for some time waiting for my guards to give me a command. After a time I arose cautiously and began to move at right angles from the direction of the American attack, watching carefully to see if anyone was covering or following me. . . . After moving approximately 100 yards I turned and moved directly toward the direction from which the American attack had come. I can remember that I whistled some American tune. . . . I had not gone over 200 yards before I was challenged by an American outpost of the 82nd Airborne Division.

The final obstacle for Peiper's exhausted men was the Salm river. It was crossed using small fords and with the tallest soldiers standing up to their chests in the freezing water to assist their shorter and weaker comrades. On Christmas morning 770 survivors of KG Peiper reached the sanctuary of the east bank. They had covered roughly 20km in almost exactly thirty-six hours and only thirty men had been lost on the way. As far as the author can establish every officer under Peiper's command who crossed to the north bank of the Amblève survived to reach Wanne.

After reporting to his Divisional commander, Jochen Peiper set up his own Headquarters in a small château at Blanche Fontaine, one kilometre east of Petit-Thier (Map 11). We shall not hear of him again until 14 February 1945 when he reappears as the commander of a 'Panzer-Gruppe' in Hungary. The only mention of him before that date is a press release on 6 February saying that he had received Swords to his Knight's Cross from the Führer on 4 February for his achievements during the Ardennes offensive. An allegation at the Dachau War Crimes Trial that Peiper gave an order on 10 January 1945 at Petit-Thier for a stray and exhausted US soldier to be shot, can be discounted. This order was allegedly given in the presence of Hein von Westernhagen and the senior medical officer of the Leibstandarte, SS Major Doctor Sickel. By 10 January the LAH had already been engaged in the Bastogne area for nearly two weeks and it is inconceivable that Mohnke would have left behind his Panzer Regimental commander, senior medical officer and the commander of his Tiger Battalion when his Division moved to that area.

It is the unsubstantiated opinion of this author that as a result of the strain of command between 16 and 24 December and particularly the trauma of the march out from La Gleize on the 24th and 25th, Peiper suffered a mental, and perhaps even physical breakdown at the end of December. His name appears on no staff list in I SS Panzer Corps for January 1945 and all command appointments are shown being filled by other officers. On 30 January 1945 Doctor Sickel signed a document, which still exists, showing Peiper suffered a 'commotio cerebri' in 1945, i.e., during January 1945. Commotio cerebri is a medical term for concussion or, in serious cases, mental breakdown. It seems more than likely that Peiper was evacuated to Germany for convalescence during the period 27 December 1944 to 14 February 1945.

During the night 27-28 December the men and wheeled vehicles of the

Leibstandarte moved to a new assembly area in the vast forests to the east of Vielsalm; by then the tracked elements were already concentrated in a separate area just to the west of St Vith.

NOTES

1. B/33rd Armd & 36th Armd Inf.
2. L/117th.
3. 1/117th.
4. F/120th.
5. Schneider, *Their Honor was Loyalty*, p. 152.
6. 1/117th, 2/120th & L/117th Inf.
7. 1/117th Inf, B/743rd Tks & C/823rd TD.
8. Ten 155mm and fifteen 105mm batteries and five 81mm mortar pls.
9. Rubel, *Daredevil Tankers*.
10. C/740th.
11. McCown's statement in *Annexe I to Part C of Intelligence Notes No 43* dated 6 Jan 45, HQ US Forces, European Theater.
12. Yvan Hakin & Laurant Gason.
13. Peiper, having left his American prisoners in Stoumont and La Gleize, tried to arrange an agreement with McCown that, as a quid pro quo, his wounded would be released by the Americans at some future date and he would then release McCown. The latter signed the document but said his signature was worthless since it was a matter for higher authorities.
14. Major General Matthew Ridgway.
15. I/505th.

CHAPTER XVII

The Big Picture: 27 – 29 December

(Map 19)

By last light on 27 December the situation in the Ardennes had changed radically – in favour of the Americans. The Germans had been forced on to the defensive everywhere. The 'extended index finger', as it was called, of the 2nd Panzer Division had been cut off and destroyed within 10km of the Meuse near Dinant. This was to be the western limit of the German advance. As Chester Wilmot put it in his brilliant book, *The Struggle for Europe*, 'the spearhead of Manteuffel's Fifth Panzer Army lay broken in the snow. The Germans had looked upon the Meuse for the last time.'[1]

Hitler had directed that the Marche-en-Famenne plateau should be secured as a base for a concerted drive to the Meuse in support of von Manteuffel's leading elements, but the resulting attack over Christmas by the rest of the 2nd Panzer Division, supported by Panzer Lehr and the 9th and 116th Panzer Divisions on the right flank had come to nothing.

Taking the German front on the evening of the 27th from west to east – the severely weakened 2nd Panzer Division was back at Rochefort, 9th Panzer south-east of Buissonville, the crippled 116th Panzer south-east of a line drawn from Marche to Hotton, and the 560th VGD south of a line from Hotton to near Amonines; Bittrich's II SS Panzer Corps, now on the right flank of the Fifth Panzer Army, had 2nd SS Panzer Division Das Reich to the south-east of Manhay and a depleted 9th SS Panzer Division Hohenstaufen in defence to the south of the Bra to Basse Bodeux road. Panzer Lehr had been pulled back and made responsible for defending the southern flank of the Fifth Panzer Army from Rochefort to Bastogne.

But still Hitler would not give up his offensive. Bittrich was ordered to attack again across the Ourthe astride Durbuy with the Das Reich, Hohenstaufen and Hitlerjugend SS Panzer Divisions, and then to continue on to the Meuse between Namur and Huy. The Leibstandarte, which was now reforming in the Vielsalm-St Vith area, was to join in this new thrust as soon as possible, at which point the HJ would rejoin Priess's I SS Panzer Corps.

This revised plan had no chance of success and most of the senior German commanders knew it. The forests, cliffs and built-up areas made it impossible to cross the Meuse anywhere other than at existing bridge sites and these were now strongly held by the Americans and British. To make matters worse, Allied aircraft were crowding the skies, making the daylight movement of vehicles almost impossible – 15,000 sorties were flown in the period 25-28 December.[2] And finally, substantial Allied reserves were beginning to arrive in theatre which would soon enable the Americans to go over to the offensive – a situation similar to that pertaining at Falaise and between the Dives and Somme rivers was returning to haunt the German commanders.

On 24 December Hitler had refused a joint request by von Rundstedt and Model for the offensive be curtailed. He firmly rejected their recommendation that a firm western flank should be established on the Meuse, followed by a drive north-east to eliminate the Allied salient at Aachen (Map 2). However, three days later Hitler and his senior commanders were at least agreed on one subject – Bastogne. The capture of this major road centre in the first few days of the offensive would have given von Manteuffel's armour a clear run to the Meuse, but it was still in American hands[3] and it was becoming the centre of gravity of the 'Battle of the Bulge'. When troops of Patton's Third Army raised the siege of Bastogne on the 26th they created a salient in the side of the Fifth Panzer Army which posed a major threat to any further advance to the north-west – an advance which the Führer was still demanding.

On 28 December Hitler addressed von Rundstedt and the commanders responsible for launching Operation NORDWIND – the attack into Alsace – which had always been designed to take advantage of any weakening of the southern part of the American front brought about by AUTUMN MIST. In order to provide assistance for this offensive Hitler now ordered a major attack against the Bastogne salient (Map 20) – an attack which would tie down Patton's Third Army and prevent it from interfering with the Alsace operation. The fact that the Americans had already been forced 'to withdraw something like 50% of the forces from their other fronts' (Hitler's words)[4] had convinced the Führer that his overall plan was working and that the Alsace offensive would succeed.

Von Rundstedt immediately contacted Model and that afternoon he sent the following confirmatory message to Headquarters Army Group 'B':

1. It is of *decisive importance* that the enemy attack wedge towards Bastogne . . . be destroyed as soon as possible. . . .
2. For this I agree that 1st SS Panzer Division LAH be moved expeditiously into the Bastogne area in order to give the concentrated attack of the 3rd PG and 167th VGDs against the exposed flank [of the American salient] the required emphasis. . . . The attack should take place on 29.12 at the latest in order to prevent further enemy reinforcements.[5]

Hitler's authorisation for a major attack on Bastogne clearly suited Model. That evening he wrote his recommendations for the next phase in the offensive. It included the phrase, 'clench into a fist the hand which has till now been spread open'. He went on:

The final target of Antwerp must be abandoned for the time being. The task which now presents itself is to strike at the enemy with annihilating force to the east of the Meuse and in the Aachen area. . . . The attacking arrowhead should be . . . pushed forwards in a northerly direction . . . in order to capture Liège and Maastrict and thus cut off the enemy units in the Aachen area. . . . After the successful conclusion of this partial attack . . . it should be possible to develop the operation against Antwerp.

This recommendation was in fact little more than a repetition of the 'Small Solution' which he had proposed the previous November as an alternative to Hitler's master plan; though this time Hitler went along with it since he believed NORDWIND would succeed and Model's clever inclusion of Antwerp as a final objective inevitably struck a responsive chord.

The 28th of December was also a day of decision for the Allies, for it was on this day that Eisenhower allotted the SHAEF reserve of three divisions to Patton's Third Army so that pressure could be intensified against the German southern flank, particularly in the Bastogne sector. In furtherance of this aim he gave the go-ahead for a thrust from the Bastogne salient towards Houffalize. Patton acted immediately and that evening gave orders for VIII Corps to attack on the west side of Bastogne in that direction on the 30th and for III Corps to follow up towards St Vith on the 31st.

On the 29th von Manteuffel held a conference with his senior commanders and set out his aims.[6] They were as follows: to close the ring around Bastogne, push the Americans back to the south and then capture the town. To this end XXXIX Corps, which would include the Leibstandarte, was to attack the American corridor south of Bastogne from the east on 30 December, whilst XLVII Corps, comprising the Führer Begleit Brigade (FBB) and 3rd PGD was, at the same time, to attack from the west. At the same conference Hermann Priess was promised that his I SS Panzer Corps would be reformed by bringing over the HJ to rejoin the LAH as soon as conditions allowed.

The decisions to renew the attack towards the Meuse on the 27th and begin the elimination of the Bastogne salient on the 30th were to have severe consequences for the designated Divisions of I SS Panzer Corps.

NOTES

1. Wilmot, *The Struggle for Europe*, p. 602.
2. Ibid., p. 603.
3. The US forces defending Bastogne were the 101st Airborne Div, CCB/10th Armd Div and CCR (37th Bn) 4th Armd Div.
4. Wilmot, op. cit., p. 606.
5. Meyer, *The History of the 12th SS Panzer Division Hitlerjugend*, p. 270.
6. In Jun 76, the author spent two days with von Manteuffel and other former German and US officers, including Bruce Clarke and William Desobry, touring the Bastogne battlefields and discussing the events of Dec 44 – Jan 45.

CHAPTER XVIII
A New Hitlerjugend Front: 27 – 30 December

(Maps 19 & 21)

By early on 27 December a substantial part of the 12th SS Panzer Division had managed to concentrate in the Samrée-Dochamps area. It comprised Siegfried Müller's 25th SS Panzer-Grenadier Regiment, the 3rd SPW

Battalion of Krause's 26th Regiment, the Divisional Escort Company, the 12th SS Werfer and Flak Battalions and most of the 12th SS Artillery Regiment. The 1st SS Panzer and 12th SS Panzerjäger Battalions and the 560th Heavy Panzerjäger Battalion had still not rejoined, but as the ground over which the Division was due to move in the first phase of the forthcoming operation was unsuitable for armour, this was not critical.

Recall that the other two Panzer-Grenadier Battalions of Krause's 26th Regiment had been forced to march the final 35km to Samrée with the result that they were unavailable for the new operation which SS General Bittrich, in accordance with the Sixth Panzer Army plan, ordered for 1930 hours that evening. This involved the seizure of the ridge-line running from Hotton to Grandmenil. Whilst the Hitlerjugend was tasked with capturing the Sadzot and Briscol part of the ridge, the 560th VGD was to take the Hotton to Erezée sector and the 2nd SS Panzer Division Das Reich was to advance north-west through Grandmenil. A firm base would thus be provided from which the HJ, Das Reich and Hohenstaufen SS Panzer Divisions could launch their major thrust through Durbuy to the Meuse. It was foreseen that the HJ's armour would rejoin in time for this advance.

Sixth Panzer Army had planned to relieve significant parts of the 2nd SS Panzer Division with 9th SS Panzer in order to reinforce the Hitlerjugend for the first part of the operation. In the event the slow arrival of the 9th SS Panzer Division and an unfavourable situation in the Grandmenil sector prevented Das Reich from providing more than a single KG. It was commanded by SS Major Ernst Krag and consisted of the 2nd SS Reconnaissance Battalion, the 9th SPW Company of the Der Führer Regiment, an assault company and the 3rd Battalion of the Das Reich Artillery Regiment. It was given the mission of advancing on the HJ's left flank along the Dochamps-Amonines road. Bremer's 12th SS HJ Reconnaissance Battalion replaced the Das Reich Reconnaissance Battalion in the Manhay sector.

The region between Dochamps and Briscol is hilly and densely wooded and Kraas had no option but to use Siegfried Müller's reduced 25th SS Panzer-Grenadier Regiment for the attack. The Chief of Staff of the Hitlerjugend claimed later that Kraas complained to II SS Panzer Corps about the whole operation:

> Because of the aerial situation, the attack would have to be carried out through broken, forested terrain at night. . . . Panzers, SPWs and wheeled vehicles could not be taken along or brought up later. On leaving the forest [in the area of the objectives], at the best, only medium mortars and Panzerfausts would be available to fight off tanks. Effective artillery support would be close to impossible due to uncertain communications in the hilly terrain.[1]

Despite these accepted difficulties Sixth Panzer Army insisted that the attack go ahead as planned, and soon after dark Müller's three Battalions were lifted in trucks to Dochamps. From there they marched to the road junction 3km north of the village where a track led through the forest to Sadzot. Fortunately scouts had discovered a gap in the US defences at this point and it was decided to mount a night infiltration operation. The batteries of the 12th SS Artillery Regiment were deployed to provide support but in the interests of surprise, no ranging was allowed.

Facing the Germans on the Erezée-Amonines-la Fosse-Grandmenil front were elements of CCA of the 3rd Armored Division. TF Orr, with six tanks and two infantry companies, was located at Amonines where it had already held off a strong attack by a Battalion of the 560th VGD Division on Christmas Eve; and a parachute infantry Battalion[2] and a small armoured group, known as TF Richardson[3], were to be found just to the west of Erezée. The largest group, however, was a Combat Team (CT), based on the 289th Infantry Regiment, comprising its own three infantry Battalions, a field artillery Battalion and tank, TD, engineer and chemical Companies[4]. This CT had been ordered to defend the line of the Aisne river from inclusive Erezée to inclusive Grandmenil. This was potentially a very strong position but much too large for a single infantry regiment.

The 289th Infantry Regiment had never been in action before it arrived in the Ardennes on 22 December, but on the 26th its 3rd Battalion supported a successful assault on Grandmenil by TF McGeorge of the 3rd Armored Division.[5] After the withdrawal of this TF at 1115 hours on the 27th[6], the 3rd Battalion remained in position with the tank Company and most of the TD Company assigned to the CT. The weight of the 289th CT was therefore on the eastern flank of its front at Grandmenil. Meanwhile the 1st and 2nd Battalions of the Regiment had moved forward to secure the line of the Aisne river between Amonines and la Fosse. On the western flank the 1st Battalion did so without difficulty, but the 2nd Battalion became disorganised in the forest to the west of la Fosse and it was 1400 hours on the 26th before it reached the Aisne river line to the south-west of that hamlet. Even then it had no contact with the 1st Battalion on its right flank and the resulting 1000m gap between the two Battalions was the one which Müller's men were about to exploit.

The Headquarters of the 289th Infantry CT was located in Briscol and the attached chemical Company and a platoon of TDs were to be found in Sadzot, together with the forward elements of an armoured field artillery Battalion[7], the guns of which were in place to the north of the hamlet.

The 25th SS Panzer-Grenadier Regiment's infiltration began on time at 1930 hours with SS Lieutenant Colonel Richard Schulze's 2nd Battalion leading, followed by SS Captain Werner Damsch's 1st Battalion and then SS Captain Wilhelm Dehne's 3rd Battalion; three 75mm anti-tank guns at the rear had to be man-handled forward by their crews.

The summit of the hill to be climbed was 120m above the starting point but there was a full moon which helped orientation in the forest and snow deadened the sound of the men as they struggled upwards under the weight of their weapons and ammunition. It was bitterly cold.

Once across the river there was nothing to stop Müller's men and at about midnight the leading elements of the 2nd Battalion emerged from the forest near Sadzot. After a short rest Schulze's Grenadiers penetrated into the village whilst Damsch's 1st Battalion bypassed it to the east and followed a stream towards Briscol. The 3rd Battalion remained in reserve on the northern edge of the forest.

The Americans, most of whom were asleep in the houses of Sadzot, were completely surprised by the appearance of enemy troops in the middle of the night – after all, as far as they were concerned they were well behind the front line. Headquarters 289th Infantry CT was equally surprised when at 0200 hours it received a message from its TD Company reporting rifle and machine-gun fire in Sadzot, to be followed twenty minutes later by another from its chemical Company based in the hamlet which read, 'Location attacked by small enemy force. Completely disorganised.'[8] Shortly afterwards another message read, 'Enemy infiltrating positions. Request help.'[9]

These messages were relayed back to the Headquarters of CCA, 3rd Armored Division, where its commander, Brigadier General Doyle Hickey, immediately ordered the parachute infantry Battalion and TF Richardson near Erezée to advance to the rescue. A statement in the US Official History[10] that the paratroopers became involved with KG Krag during their move east is unconfirmed on the German side and has to be questioned since Krag's men did not even reach Amonines that night.

Schulze's SS Grenadiers did not take long to clear Sadzot and they took a substantial number of prisoners in the process; but they were extremely vulnerable, having only Panzerfausts and the three 75mm anti-tank guns with which to resist any counter-attack by tanks. The guns were sited with the 3rd Battalion in the edge of the forest.

The arrival of American paratroopers in the dark at Sadzot led inevitably to very confused close-quarter fighting in which everybody fired at anything which moved; both sides suffered heavy casualties. One American report, written after the battle, describes thirty-five to forty SS dead found lying in the snow outside a burnt building which had obviously been used as an aid-station.

Daylight saw the arrival of TF Richardson's light tanks on the Erezée-Briscol road in support of the paratroopers and a significant increase in American artillery fire. At 1115 hours Headquarters 289th CT, which had moved from Briscol to Erezée at 1025 after coming under heavy German artillery fire[11], reported:

509 Parachute Battalion captured Sadzot, took 32 prisoners and 64 wounded. 3 TDs and one platoon light tanks with them. Mediums [Shermans] coming up.[12]

Rather than risk encirclement Schulze had pulled his men back to the 3rd Battalion's lines in the forest edge and the appearance of tanks similarly forced Damsch's 1st Battalion to pull back from the road near Briscol and take cover in the woods; a single anti-tank gun fought off the pursuing light tanks. Despite a significant gap between the 1st and 2nd Battalions, all three units then adopted a defensive posture. Of major concern was the lack of artillery support caused by the predicted disruption in communications. In fact the situation was one of stalemate – the Germans, although outnumbering the Americans, could not advance against tanks and intensive artillery fire, and the American tanks dared not advance into woods full of infantrymen with anti-tank weapons. The exact strength of Müller's Battalions is unknown. The 289th Regiment's AAR reported that 'an enemy force estimated to be one Battalion infiltrated . . . and attacked Sadzot'. The Germans had of course suffered badly in the fighting in the Twin Villages and around Bütgenbach and the American estimate (800–1,000) may well be near the mark, but the fact that none of the Battalions had been amalgamated would indicate that they were still viable and therefore probably at about half their authorised strength – for a total of roughly 1,000 to 1,500.

Meanwhile the associated advance by KG Krag along the Dochamps-Amonines road had come to nothing. The start had been delayed until midnight and then, according to the Chief of Staff of the HJ, contact within the various elements of the KG soon broke down and the advance stalled.

As far as the Americans were concerned, the main task now that the German advance had been halted was to close the gap on the Aisne river and prevent the Germans in the woods south of Sadzot escaping or being reinforced. Accordingly, at 1255 hours on the 28th an additional infantry Battalion[13] was attached to the 289th CT and given the task of filling the gap.

From the German point of view there was no question of Müller's men pulling out and escaping to the south – quite the contrary. Bernhard Krause's 26th Regiment was ordered to advance on Müller's left flank during the night of the 28th-29th and secure the villages of Hazeille and Erpigny, and then, despite the previously stated difficulties, both SS Panzer-Grenadier Regiments were to advance and secure the Erezée to Briscol stretch of road. Why this operation had not taken place the night before remains a mystery. Although two of Krause's Battalions had not arrived in time for the attack, the 3rd SPW Battalion was available and it could have advanced in concert, or in tandem, with the 25th

Regiment along the track leading to Hazeille and Erpigny which were never occupied by the Americans. The appearance of Germans just to the south of Erezée as well as at Sadzot and Briscol would have given the Americans a major problem – not least in the case of TF Orr at Amonines.

In a complementary operation on the night of the 28th-29th, KG Krag, now returned to the command of the 2nd SS Panzer Division, was to advance again along the Amonines road and seize the road junction to the west of Erezée.

Beginning at 2230 hours KG Krag began its advance up the Amonines road and it was followed by SS Lieutenant Brinkmann's 3rd SPW SS Panzer-Grenadier Battalion, part of Bernhard Krause's 26th Regiment. The other two Battalions were again, for some inexplicable reason, held in reserve.

Krag's KG managed to reach Amonines but then ground to a halt. SS Sergeant Günther Burdack later described what happened to Brinkmann's Battalion:

The SPWs were left behind in a ravine south of Samrée. The crews . . . marched via Dochamps. . . . The road was totally clogged by abandoned and destroyed enemy vehicles, mostly artillery, and was under constant heavy enemy shelling. After approximately 6km [in Amonines] the Battalion was directed by a liaison officer of the Der Führer Regiment [2nd SS Panzer Division] to leave the road and advance in a northerly direction along a track toward the twin villages of Hazeille-Erpigny. After some 1.5km we reached the designated position at the edge of the forest. The villages could not be observed from the edge of the forest as they were at a higher location than our own position. . . . The deeply frozen ground did not allow us to dig in. The Battalion did not have any heavy weapons with it, only rifles and light machine-guns. Harassing fire covered the whole area.[14]

Why the other two Battalions of Krause's Regiment remained in reserve and were not deployed in support is a mystery, particularly since the only troops who could have resisted them were, as we shall see, fully engaged against the 25th Regiment. At the very least they could have been used to evict TF Orr from Amonines which would have helped to unhinge the US defence. The only explanation can be the intense artillery fire which came with the advent of daylight; certainly Brinkmann's men were pulled back during the morning and the whole attack abandoned.

Meanwhile the Americans were still trying to fill the gap through which Müller's men had infiltrated on the first night; however, the Battalion which had been given the task lost its way in the forest and by 1800 hours on the 29th, far from plugging the gap, its leading elements were 'in Sadzot and their line extending generally north and south . . . instead of east and west'.[15]

Unaware that the gap on the Aisne was still open, Brigadier General Hickey ordered the light tanks of TF Richardson and the paratroopers in Sadzot to advance south against Müller's Panzer-Grenadiers during the early daylight hours of the 29th. The attack was not a success – it collided with Müller's men who were also advancing in accordance with the new plan. At 1250 hours the log of the 289th CT records a message from the parachute Battalion reading, '509 Parachute Battalion being pushed back near Sadzot'. Three of the six Stuart light tanks supporting this attack were knocked out and the parachute Battalion's casualties now totalled 120 men.[16]

Despite the failure of the American attack, by midday on the 29th it was obvious to the German commanders that the attempt to seize the Hotton to Grandmenil ridge had failed. In any case, by this time a decision had been taken at the highest level that the Hitlerjugend and parts of the 9th SS Panzer Division were to be withdrawn for use in another sector.

Details of exactly how Müller's 25th Regiment withdrew successfully from the Sadzot area are not recorded but it can only have come out the way it went in – through the gap between the two Battalions of the 289th CT on the Aisne river. The Battalion trying to plug the hole did not do so until 0700 hours on the 30th[17] and by then the SS Grenadiers were long gone.

Later on the 30th Kraas was ordered to assemble his Division near La Roche. As we have heard, Priess had been promised by von Manteuffel that the Hitlerjugend would be returned to its parent formation as soon as conditions allowed, and the 560th VGD began relieving the HJ in the Samrée sector on the same day. Having already failed twice and suffered grievously in the Ardennes offensive, it was to be given yet another chance to enhance its reputation – this time in the Bastogne area.

NOTES

1. Meyer, *The History of the 12th SS Panzer Division Hitlerjugend*, p. 266.
2. 509th Para Inf.
3. Five Shermans, eighteen Stuarts and two inf pls.
4. 730th Fd Arty, A/750th Tk, A/629th TD, A/275th Engr & B/87th Chemical. The latter was a 4.2 inch mortar unit equipped to fire high explosive, white phosphorus & smoke rounds.
5. This was the same TF which had fought KG Peiper in La Gleize only two days previously.
6. AAR 289th Inf.
7. 54th Armd Fd Arty.
8. AAR 289th Inf, S-3 log 27–28 Dec 44.
9. Ibid.
10. Cole, *The Ardennes: Battle of the Bulge*, p. 602.

11. AAR 289th Inf.
12. AAR 289th Inf, S-3 log 27–28 Dec 44.
13. 2/112th Inf of the 28th Inf Div.
14. Meyer, op. cit., p. 268.
15. AAR 289th Inf.
16. Cole, op. cit., p. 601.
17. AAR 289th Inf, S-3 log, 29–30 Dec 44.

CHAPTER XIX

The Leibstandarte at Bastogne: 28 December – 12 January

Background

(Map 19)

The details of the fighting in the Bastogne area before 29 December 1944 are irrelevant to the story of I SS Panzer Corps. Readers who are particularly interested in this part of the campaign are recommended to read S. L. A. Marshall's *Bastogne – The First Eight Days*. No – the story of the Leibstandarte and the Hitlerjugend Divisions at Bastogne does not begin until *after* the first eight days and *after* the famous siege of the town had been raised.

Recall that by 26 December the Bastogne salient posed such a significant threat to the flank and rear of Army Group 'B' that it could no longer be ignored. As a consequence, the designated Divisions of the I SS Panzer Corps, despite their heavy losses, found themselves moved suddenly to this new battlefield. The fighting in which they were about to take part was some of the most bitter and costly of the entire campaign and it will probably come as a surprise to many readers to learn that American casualties in the second half of the 'Battle of the Bulge' (30 December to 12 January) were nearly one third higher than in the first half.[1]

(Maps 19, 20 & 22)

Late on 28 December the Leibstandarte was transferred to XXXIX Panzer Corps in von Manteuffel's Fifth Panzer Army and began its move towards the Bastogne area via St Vith and Trois-Vierges. Headquarters Army Group 'B' reported that night:

Kampfgruppe 1st SS Panzer Division, with its Panzer Regiment,

146

Panzerjäger Battalion, 1st Panzer-Grenadier Regiment, Artillery Regiment, Pioneer Company and Armoured Reconnaissance Platoon, left the Vielsalm area at 1625 hours and moved into the . . . Longvilly area.[2]

In fact, owing to fuel shortages, some elements of the LAH were unable to start their move until midday on the 29th, by which time the Division had become part of Army Group Lüttwitz, a new unified command comprising both the XXXIX and XLVII Corps. General von Lüttwitz had been given the task of eliminating the Bastogne salient.

In setting the scene for the actions of the Leibstandarte it is important to understand the configuration of Patton's III Corps in the period immediately after Christmas. Following the relief of Bastogne by the 4th Armored Division on 26 December, it was vital for the Americans to fill the 10km gap between that Division and the 26th Infantry Division to its south-east. In particular it was important to push the Germans away to the east from the Bastogne-Arlon road – the main open artery into the Bastogne pocket. To this end, the 35th Infantry Division was ordered to advance into the gap and given the Bastogne-Longvilly road as its ultimate objective. By the evening of the 29th it was lying directly in the path of the eastern prong of the German counter-attack designed to cut the III Corps' corridor into Bastogne.

During the night 29th-30th the LAH moved farther south to the Tarchamps-Lutremange area, from where it was to launch its attack on the eastern flank of the American corridor. This part of the Duchy of Luxembourg was hilly and heavily forested, with a very restricted road network. It was bitterly cold, the roads were icy and a blanket of snow covered everything. The Divisional CP set up in Bras.

The Leibstandarte's attack was to be supported on its northern flank by Lieutenant General Hoecker's 167th VGD and a KG of Panzer Lehr's 901st Regiment, which included some Mk IV tanks. The latter was already in sector but worn down and under-strength. Hoeckner's Division had arrived from Hungary on 24 December and then, after detraining on the east bank of the Rhine, had experienced great difficulty in reaching the Bastogne sector. To add to its problems, the Division had no heavy weapons and although a third of its men were veterans of the Russian Front, many others were recently joined Luftwaffe personnel.

On the LAH's southern flank a Regiment of the 5th FSD, already in the line and resisting the advance of the US 35th Division, had also been ordered to support the attack but it too was tired and seriously under-strength.

For its new mission Wilhelm Mohnke divided his Division into two KGs. The northern KG, under the command of Werner Poetschke, comprised all the available tanks, two weak Battalions of Panzer-Grenadiers

147

and a Pioneer Company. It was tasked with capturing Lutrebois and then advancing to the Bastogne-Arlon road in the vicinity of Remonfosse (now spelt Remoifosse). At the same time the southern KG, under Max Hansen, was to capture Villers-la-Bonne-Eau and reach the Bastogne-Arlon road via Losange. It consisted of the 1st SS Panzerjäger Battalion, all the remaining Panzer-Grenadiers, an SS Reconnaissance Platoon and a Pioneer Company. After reaching the Bastogne-Arlon road, both KGs were to continue their advance west to link up with the FBB and 3rd PGD in the area between Assenois and Hompré. H-Hour was set for 0600 hours on the 30th.

How strong was the LAH at this time? There is very little firm information from German sources but it is still possible to determine the strength of the Division with reasonable accuracy. Taking armour first, it is clear that the 1st SS Panzer Battalion still had a theoretical strength of sixteen Panthers and twenty-six Mk IVs. Karl Rettlinger's 1st SS Panzerjäger Battalion had suffered little and should have had about eighteen Jagdpanzer IVs and the Corps' 501st SS Heavy Battalion still counted thirty-three Tiger IIs on strength although it is unlikely that more than fifteen were operational. How many of these tanks and Jagdpanzers actually reached the Bastogne area remains a matter of conjecture and, out of a total of ninety-three, it is unlikely that more than fifty saw action there. In the case of artillery, the 1st SS Artillery Regiment and Werfer Battalion were largely operational but fuel shortages and Allied air interdiction meant there was a serious shortage of ammunition. The 88mm guns of the LAH Flak Battalion remained in the Ligneuville sector[3] (Map 10) – almost certainly to give cover to the workshops still working on damaged vehicles.

With regard to infantry, Hansen's 2nd and Sandig's 1st SS Panzer-Grenadier Battalions were allocated to KG Poetschke and reinforced with the few Grenadiers who had escaped from the La Gleize pocket, while Hansen was left with the remnants of his 1st and 3rd Battalions under the command of SS Lieutenant Haft. Overall it seems probable that each Leibstandarte KG had the equivalent of about one Panzer-Grenadier Battalion.

The relevant front line on 30 December ran south from Neffe, through the woods to the east of Marvie, then along the line of the woods and the Lutrebois-Lutremange road to Villers-la-Bonne-Eau and Livarchamps, and finally away to the east below Harlange.

As previously mentioned, the American 35th Infantry Division lay directly in the path of the German attack. One of its Regiments[4] had captured 'most of' Lutrebois in the early evening of 29 December and another[5] had taken Sainlez and Livarchamps from the 5th FSD and, during the night 29th–30th, penetrated into Villers-la-Bonne-Eau with two companies. According to the Divisional History, 'They couldn't completely dislodge a company of German Pioneers and ended up sharing the village with them for the rest of the night.'

The third Regiment[6] of the 35th Division was at this time 'engaged in bitter battle' with elements of 5th FSD around a farm and in the woods 1000m south-east of Harlange.[7] The Division had suffered 148 battle casualties in three days' fighting to reach this line.

The artillery fire-plan heralding the LAH attack was 'weak and had little effect because the ammunition available was only a fraction of the amount needed'.[8] Nevertheless, the leading tanks of KG Poetschke moved forward from Lutremange on parallel roads at 0625 hours. Suggestions in the US Official History that some of the infantry accompanying the KG were Volks-Grenadiers from the 167th Division and/or the 5th FSD can be discounted. Elements of both Divisions did attack on the 30th but in their own sectors. All the infantry with the LAH KGs were members of the Leibstandarte.

Fortunately for Mohnke's men the morning of the 30th dawned cloudy, with poor visibility. Although this kept the Allied fighter bombers away for the first few hours of the attack, it also prevented the assistance which had been promised by the Luftwaffe.

Poetschke's tanks met no resistance other than from artillery fire as they approached Lutrebois, which was held by a Battalion[9] of the 35th Division, with another Battalion[10] deployed in the wood-line on the ridge dominating the valley to its south. Artillery fire delayed the advance but Panzer-Grenadiers soon infiltrated the American lines south of Lutrebois, others 'engulfed' the village and seven tanks hooked round to the north. American TDs[11] claimed four of them and two were said to have been knocked out by artillery fire, while one was immobilized on a mine[12].

News of the German attack reached the Headquarters of CCA of the 4th Armored Division at 0635 hours. This Combat Command was located just to the east of the Bastogne-Arlon road and behind the northern Regiment of the 35th Division. It was basically facing north with its advanced elements at Remonfosse. The American commander[13] wasted no time and ordered his units to turn east in support of the 35th Infantry Division. According to CCA's AAR:

A counter-attack of at least infantry Battalion strength supported with SP guns and 20 to 30 tanks drove 3/134 out of Lutrebois and enemy infantry infiltrated through the woods to within 400 yards of the highway [Bastogne-Arlon road] seriously threatening our position.[14]

With the northern Regiment of the 35th Division being forced to withdraw south through the woods towards Losange, the 6th SS Panzer Company's Mk IVs nearing Point 535, from where they could see Remonfosse and some 3–4km of the Bastogne-Arlon road, and the 7th Panzer Company heading for Saiwet, CCA's situation was indeed becoming serious. Urgent action was needed and, as well as deploying an armoured infantry Battalion with two tank Companies in support into the woods to the west of Lutrebois[15], the Americans brought ground-attack aircraft and all available artillery into play. The weather had improved as the day progressed and the LAH tank Companies, now that they were out in the open, were extremely vulnerable. CCA's AAR goes on:

At about 1100 hours B Company (strength six tanks) engaged thirteen enemy tanks advancing NW out of Lutrebois, destroying eleven of them without loss. With clear weather and good visibility air and artillery support was excellent, the air getting seven confirmed tank kills and the artillery breaking up several troop concentrations.

Hugh M. Cole's Official History of the US Army adds more information about the air support:

The main body of the 1st SS Panzer Kampfgruppe appeared an hour or so before noon moving along the Lutremange-Lutrebois road; some twenty-five tanks were counted in all. It took two hours to bring the fighter-bombers into the fray, but they arrived just in time to cripple or destroy seven tanks and turn back the bulk of the Panzers.

Further details are to be found in the AAR of the CCA tank Battalion involved in this action:

Thirteen German tanks . . . reached the woods south-east of Lutrebois, but a 4th Armd Div artillery spotter in a Cub plane spotted them and dropped a message to Co B of the 35th Tank Bn. . . . six Sherman tanks and a platoon from the 701st TD Bn formed an ambush near a slight ridge that provided hull defilade and waited. The leading German company (or platoon) which had six Panzers, happened to see Co A of the 35th and as the fog briefly lifted, turned, with flank exposed, in that direction. The first shot . . . put away the German commander's tank and the other tanks milled about until all had been knocked out. Six more German tanks came along and all were destroyed or disabled. In the meantime the American TDs took on some accompanying assault guns, shot up three of them, and dispersed the neighbouring Grenadiers.

These reports equate reasonably well with the few German accounts we have of events on the 30th, although they claim many more tanks knocked out. A member of the 7th SS Panzer Company, Manfred Thorn, remembered:

At about 0930 hours we reached the Lutrebois hills. . . . American infantry were scattered through the left portion of the forest, right along the road. The forest lined the road for only a hundred metres, then the first houses of Lutrebois could be seen. . . . At the end of the forest a Panther stood on the right. . . . On the horizon to the west I saw the last Panzers of the 6th Company disappearing behind a hill. They were driving in the direction of Remonfosse. . . . The Company then drove in a wide wedge formation towards the hills 4km south of Bastogne [north of Remonfosse]. On our right were the woods, to our left open ground, behind us Lutrebois. . . . At 1515 hours we noted several Panzers behind us already hit and burning. Within ten minutes six of our Company's Panzers were knocked out.[16]

Whether the Panther referred to was that of Werner Poetschke we shall never know, but his command Panther was certainly put out of action and he and his Adjutant, Rolf Reiser, were given a lift back to their CP later in the day in a 7th Company Mk IV.[17] Thorn's Mk IV withdrew into the forest after last light and eventually reached Bras.

Another member of the 7th Company, Rolf Ehrhardt, described how:

We bypassed the centre of the village [Lutrebois], leaving it on our left and . . . headed north-west. . . . Suddenly we saw movement near the 6th Company. The Panzers angled to the left and one fired its main armament. . . . The artillery fire became stronger. Then there was a new tone in the explosions – a harder, drier whipcrack. . . . The fire was coming from due west [from a dominating wooded, ridge which runs for some 3km along the west side of the Bastogne-Arlon road]. . . . The Amis must have set up anti-tank guns farther to the left of the 6th Company. Two shells exploded in front of our tank. . . . A tank was knocked out in front of us. . . . It was almost a relief when we were hit ourselves. . . . When the smoke cleared I saw that my hatch was gone. What I did not see was that the hit had torn our cannon right away from the turret.[18]

Yet another member of the same Company told later how he and his tank commander drove forward again that night to search for damaged tanks. They found six, all from their own Company and still burning, in a row in an open field.[19] Amazingly, only two crewmen had been killed during the day; SS Captain Oskar Klingelhöfer had suffered burns but would soon return to command what was left of the Company.

In the southern sector of the LAH's front, KG Hansen's advance progressed well despite an appalling route which twisted its way through woods and up and down deep valleys. By mid-morning Haft's Panzer-Grenadiers, with support from at least seven Jagdpanzers, had relieved the few German Pioneers who had shared Villers-la-Bonne-Eau with the Americans the previous night. The AAR of the 35th Division describes what happened:

Companies K and L of the 3/137th Inf came under attack by seven tanks [Jagdpanzers] heavily supported by infantry. The Panzers moved in close, blasting the stone houses and setting the village ablaze. At 0845 a radio message reached the CP of the 137th Inf asking for the artillery to lay down a barrage of smoke and high explosive, but before the gunners could get a sensing the radio went dead. Only one of the 169 men inside the village got out.

The US infantry Regiment involved gives more details:

At 0645 the 3rd Bn held four buildings in Villers-la-Bonne-Eau and by 0900 the enemy activity and resistance in the town increased considerably. Enemy assault guns [Jagdpanzers] and SS troops moved into the town in the morning to reinforce the enemy garrison [Pioneers] and the armored guns moved in and around the town shooting into the houses occupied by elements of the 3rd Bn. Two of these guns were knocked out by bazooka fire and the rest withdrew out of bazooka range and shelled the houses with direct fire. . . . Companies K and L were cut off from the rest of the Battalion.[20]

At 1445 hours the German advance continued and the Château Losange was captured by 1600. But this was to be the high-water mark of Hansen's advance, for as the leading elements of his KG reached the main Bastogne-Arlon road, just to the west of the Château, they came under intense artillery fire and direct tank and anti-tank fire from parts of CCA and the 137th Infantry Regiment – the attack was halted and Hansen gave orders for his men to dig in.

By last light on 30 December the Leibstandarte was holding Point 535, Lutrebois, the Château Losange area and Villers-la-Bonne-Eau, and the 35th Division had been forced back to a line running from Remonfosse to Sainlez to Livarchamps. But the German counter-attack had failed in its mission of crossing the Bastogne-Arlon road and reaching the Assenois area, and the cost had been heavy – at least twenty tanks and Jagdpanzers lost and many Panzer-Grenadiers killed and wounded. The AAR of the 134th Infantry Regiment (Lutrebois sector) claims sixteen enemy tanks (all types) destroyed in the period ending 31 December.

Nevertheless, the attack had driven a wedge 3km wide and 3km deep into the flank of the American corridor and, as the US Official History says:

It had achieved an important secondary effect, becoming, as it did, a true spoiling attack that put the 35th [Division] out of the running from 31 December on.[21]

The concurrent attack by the 167th VGD along the axis of the Bras-Bastogne road met with some initial success and reached the first houses of Bastogne itself; however, in the face of intense artillery fire, attacks by fighter-bombers and finally a counter-attack by armoured elements of CCA, the Division ended the day at the western edge of Marvie.

The 5th FSD held its ground on the 30th against limited attacks by the 35th Division but was too weak to join in the overall German assault on the Bastogne corridor.

According to Ralf Tiemann's History of the Leibstandarte[22], several KGs of the XXXIX Panzer Corps were withdrawn at last light into their departure positions in order to be reorganised for a resumption of the attack on the 31st; he does not specify which KGs.

There are no detailed reports of the fighting on the eastern side of the Bastogne corridor on 31 December from either the Americans or Germans. Clear weather produced plenty of air activity – the Germans claiming 3,550 Allied aircraft operating against 550 of their own.[23]

Tiemann's History says the fighting continued with 'undiminished ferocity' on the 31st, with both LAH KGs reaching the Bastogne-Arlon road at about midday before being pushed back again to their start points by 'massive artillery fire and counter-attacks' during the afternoon by the 4th Armored and 35th Infantry Divisions. Neither of the US Divisional AARs makes any mention of this. CCA of the 4th Armored merely says, 'positions taken up late on 30 Dec were improved and strengthened. . . . one enemy tank lurking in edge of woods was destroyed'[24]; the 35th Division's AAR says:

> The Division was ordered to attack to the north-east, supported by tanks from the 4th Armd Div, to capture the two 510m high hills north-east of Lutrebois, but no progress was made.

The battle casualties recorded by the 35th Division for 30-31 December total 580, including 305 captured or missing – this obviously includes the two Companies lost at Villers-la-Bonne-Eau on the 30th.

CinC West's War Diary has the following entry for the 31st:

> A report from Army Group B at 1215 hours again described the ferocity of the fighting around Bastogne. The western attack group [3rd PGD and FBB] cannot advance any farther without the support of the eastern

group [LAH and 167th VGD]. The eastern group has indeed resumed the attack, but can only gain a little ground. The deployment of artillery will bring some relief. In spite of this, the forces committed so far appear to be insufficient to achieve the assigned objective.[25]

Despite the serious threat posed by the German counter-attacks on the Bastogne corridor on 30 December, General Patton was determined to press ahead with the strike towards St Vith by III Corps, and that night the 6th Armored Division was ordered to move into the Bastogne perimeter in readiness for an attack north and north-east on the 31st. CCA, using the secondary road through Assenois (only 2km from the Leibstandarte's positions around Point 535!), reached Bastogne but CCB became entangled with another armoured Division[26] and was forced to halt 6km to the south; this meant it would be unable to attack until New Year's Day. Since the the actions of CCA on the 31st are irrelevant to events in the Lutrebois-Losange sector but important to the overall situation, they will be described in the next Chapter.

The 1st and 2nd of January 1945 saw only limited activity on the Leibstandarte's front. The Americans claim to have cleared Hansen's men from Losange and the woods to the west of Villers-la-Bonne-Eau, but KG Poetschke still controlled the area of Point 535 and Lutrebois.

Field Marshal Model had now come to the conclusion that there was little or no chance of cutting the Bastogne corridor and that a direct attack against the town was more likely to bring success. This decision was to bring the LAH's sister Division into action in the Bastogne sector.

On 3 January elements of the 35th Infantry[28] managed to infiltrate into Lutrebois, and on the 4th KG Poetschke launched a local counter-attack with armour to recover the village. Although initially successful the attack failed and by last light the Americans were in control with the German tanks back in Lutremange; even so the Germans continued to hold the woods to the south and east of Lutrebois and although Hansen's men had lost the road junction just to the north-west of the village, they were still firmly in control of Villers-la-Bonne-Eau.

Farther east, the AAR of the 35th Division mentions German counter-attacks by *tanks* as well as infantry after the 137th Infantry had captured four houses in the village of Harlange, and so it seems likely that part of Hansen's KG assisted the 5th FSD in resisting American attacks in that area too – the so-called *tanks* probably being Jagdpanzers.

The American AARs for 5 and 6 January speak only of heavy resistance to all their attempts to advance against the LAH and make no mention of the following account of events in the History of the Leibstandarte:

On 5 and 6 January the attack [against the Bastogne-Arlon road] was continued in the 167th VGD and 1st SS Panzer Division sectors. The advance of the 3rd SS Panzer-Grenadier Battalion of the 1st Regiment, which contained only eighty men, together with the remaining assault guns, out of Villers-la-Bonne-Eau against Losange stalled right from the start under concentrated blocking fire from the artillery of the 35th Infantry and 4th and 6th Armored Divisions.

The attack by the 2nd SS Panzer-Grenadier Battalion of the 1st Regiment out of the forest west of Tarchamps to regain Lutrebois with approximately 100 men supported by the remnants of the 6th SS Panzer Company and several combat groups from the 1st SS Panzer Regiment consisting of Panthers, made it to the enemy positions on the edge of the town, where it was repulsed by the concentrated commitment of all infantry weapons and heavy anti-tank gun fire.[28]

Although the Leibstandarte continued to hold its positions throughout 7 January, the overall situation facing the Germans at this time was becoming so serious that there was a distinct possibility of another 'Falaise Pocket' type disaster. The following day Hitler authorised Model to give up the area west of Houffalize and south of Bastogne. The withdrawal of the LAH was scheduled for the 10th – in the meantime current positions were to be held.

On 9 January the US III Corps launched a coordinated attack to eliminate the mini 'Bulge' south-east of Bastogne. The AAR of the 35th Division is succinct in its report of the day's events:

The Division was ordered to resume attacking to the north-east. The 320th Inf, with elements of the 6th Armd Div in support, advanced 800m. The 134th Inf gained a kilometer.

According to the History of the LAH:

The Americans attacked . . . along with strong armoured support and continuous artillery fire, from the direction of Losange and Livarchamps against the 3rd SS Panzer-Grenadier Battalion's positions on the western edge of Villers-la-Bonne-Eau. During the evening a single penetration was achieved into the centre of the village. It was blocked by the Battalion and SS Pioneers committed with the support of assault guns. The Battalion prepared to counter-attack . . . during the night.[29]

There are no reports of similar actions on other parts of the front.

On 10 January the 5th FSD and 167th VGD began to fall back to the line Bizory-Wardin-Bras. Early that morning the LAH also began its withdrawal to an area east of St Vith where it was to return to the command of I SS Panzer Corps. By that date the US 35th Division had suffered 1,432 battle casualties[30] – its only consolation being that it had inflicted grievous harm on its major adversary.

A member of Hansen's 2nd SS Panzer-Grenadier Battalion described part of the withdrawal:

In the early morning of 10 January we received orders to evacuate the Lutremange – Villers-la-Bonne-Eau corridor and assemble to the east. It was nearly light when we reached the hilltop on the road to Harlange [Tarchamps]. There [at the boundary with the Duchy of Luxembourg] we again came under fire from American tanks and suffered bloody losses. We reached Doncols, east of Bastogne in the afternoon.[31]

The US Regiment tasked with the capture of the same area described events as follows:

Supported by tanks and TDs[32], the 137th Infantry pushed ahead against the enemy on January 10, making a slight gain and capturing the much sought and fought for town of Villers-la-Bonne-Eau, a target of the Regiment for the past thirteen days. The Regiment attacked at 0915 . . . and by 1400 had two buildings on the edge of the battered town. Later in the afternoon, the entire village was cleared. . . .

At 1400 the road leading from Lutremange was choked with enemy vehicles and an air strike and artillery pounded the column. . . . The Regiment suffered heavy casualties today.[33]

Villers-la-Bonne-Eau had only fifteen houses before it became engulfed by war, so it is hardly surprising that by 10 January it had almost ceased to exist. The Americans estimated that 6,000 artillery rounds fell on it in just one day's fighting.

During the following four days a few minor but costly actions were carried out by small armoured elements of the Leibstandarte to cover the withdrawal, but to all intents and purposes the LAH's commitment in Hitler's last great offensive in the West was over. After three weeks of intense combat it was a mere shadow of the Division which had entered battle on 16 December. We have no firm figures for the Panzer-Grenadier Battalions but it would appear that they totalled no more than a few hundred men. In the case of armour we can be more precise because we have official strength returns for the LAH and the Corps 501st SS Heavy Panzer Battalion dated 15 January 1945. Somewhat surprisingly, they show sixty-two tanks and fifteen Jagdpanzers or assault guns still on strength – nineteen IVs, twelve Panthers, eleven Jagdpanzer IVs, four StuGs and thirty-one Tiger IIs; of these, three Mk IVs, one Panther, both StuGs and thirteen Tigers were under repair. From these figures it is possible to make a reasonable estimate of the losses suffered during the fighting in the Bastogne area – seven Mk IVs, four Panthers, seven Jagdpanzers and two Tigers. Coincidentally, US Army personnel photographed two of the Panthers and the two Tigers soon after the battle[34] – one of the Tigers was allegedly near Villers-la-Bonne-Eau and the other in the Wardin area.

Readers may be surprised that the losses in armour quoted above are much lower than those claimed by the Americans; but it has to be appreciated that the nature of the ground in the Lutrebois-Losange area precluded the deployment of large numbers of armoured vehicles and, as the US Official History states:

> Two or three units would claim to have destroyed what on later examination proves to have been the same enemy tank detachment and a cumulative listing of these claims – some fifty-odd German tanks destroyed – probably gives more Panzers put out of action than 1st SS Panzer brought into the field.[35]

Readers may also find it strange that there has been no mention by either side of Tigers being involved in the Lutrebois-Lutremange fighting. This would seem to indicate that very few reached that area and the fact that we have a photograph of one allegedly knocked out on 8 January in the First US Army sector[36], would tend to confirm this. There is however, a report by an American tank Company[37] which claims that two Tigers knocked out four of its tanks in the Mageret area in the late afternoon of 4 January (details are given in the next Chapter), and the 'Summary of Operations' for January 1945 by the Battalion of which that Company was a part has the following entry for 5 January: 'Destroyed 2 Tiger tanks.'[38] These reports tend to confirm statements that a KG Möbius, comprising some fourteen to sixteen Tigers of the 501st SS Heavy Panzer Battalion, operated in the general area to the east of Bastogne during the period 28 December to 10 January[39]; nevertheless, no reliable details of this KG's actions are provided.

When the Leibstandarte reached its assembly area to the south-west of St Vith, it found the Hitlerjugend Division already in the same general area and in the process of refitting after its part in the Bastogne fighting. Once more the twin Divisions were side by side and Hermann Priess's I SS Panzer Corps, reconstituted as originally planned, was again part of Sepp Dietrich's Sixth Panzer Army. The 15 January 1945 strength returns show eighteen Mk IVs, twenty-nine Panthers, two Jagdpanzer IVs and six Tigers on their way through the resupply system to the Leibstandarte and Corps Tiger Battalion, and it will come as no surprise to readers to learn that a new task had already been planned for Hitler's 'Fire Brigade'.

NOTES

1. Total US casualties 16 to 29 Dec – 63,557; 30 Dec to 12 Jan – 109, 563.
2. Tiemann, *Die Leibstandarte* IV/2, p. 162.
3. Ibid., p. 167.
4. 134th.
5. 137th.
6. 320th.
7. AAR 35th Inf Div dated 4 Feb 45.
8. Tiemann, op. cit., p. 168.
9. 3/134th.
10. 2/134th.
11. 654th TD Bn.
12. Cole, *The Ardennes; Battle of the Bulge*, p. 626.
13. Brigadier General Earnest.
14. AAR CCA/4th Armd Div dated 18 Jan 45.
15. 51st Armd Inf Bn and B & D/35th Tk Bn.
16. Tiemann, op. cit., pp. 168–70.
17. Ibid., p. 175.
18. Ibid., pp. 171–3.
19. Ibid., p. 175.
20. AAR 137th Inf Regt dated 1 Jan 45.
21. Cole, op. cit., p. 634.
22. Tiemann, op. cit., p. 179.
23. Ibid.
24. AAR CCA/4th Armd Div dated 18 Jan 45.
25. Tiemann, op. cit., p. 180.
26. 11th.
27. 134th.
28. Tiemann, op. cit., p. 189.
29. Ibid., p. 192.
30. The 101st Airborne Div and its attached units suffered 2,048 casualties in the period 18–27 Dec 44.
31. Tiemann, op. cit., pp.194–5.
32. C/735th Tk Bn and pl/C/654th TD Bn.
33. AAR 137th Inf Regt dated 1 Feb 45.
34. Pallud, *The Battle of the Bulge, Then and Now*, pp. 401, 407–8 and 410.
35. Cole, op. cit., p. 625.
36. Pallud, op. cit., p. 317.
37. B/69th Tk Bn.
38. HQ 69th Tk Bn dated 1 Feb 45.
39. Schneider, *Tigers in Combat II*, p. 265.

CHAPTER XX

The Hitlerjugend at Bastogne:
30 December – 10 January

(Maps 19, 20 & 23)

The clash between the American VIII and German XLVII Corps on the west side of Bastogne on 30 December caused both sides to re-think the situation. From von Manteuffel's point of view the failure of the German counter-attack was bad enough, but it was the threat posed by the American attack which caused him more concern. As a consequence, the following day he ordered Priess's I SS Panzer Corps to take over that sector with the Hitlerjugend, Panzer Lehr and FBB and to attack again as soon as possible – preferably on New Year's Day.

As far as the Americans were concerned, and George Patton[1] in particular, the failure of the VIII Corps attack on the 30th was disappointing and the German counter-attack against the eastern flank of the Bastogne corridor by the Leibstandarte and 167th VGD was still presenting serious problems, but neither event was seen as a reason to delay the planned attack by III Corps towards St Vith scheduled for the 31st. This thrust was designed to link up with another by Hodges' First US Army in the north and to cut off at least those German forces still west of a line drawn from Bastogne to Manhay. Montgomery, who remained concerned about the situation in the First US Army sector, finally gave his agreement on the 31st that the northern thrust could begin on 3 January.

In accordance with Patton's plan the newly arrived 6th Armored Division was ordered to strike east and north-east out of the Bastogne salient on the 31st against the 26th VGD with two Combat Commands abreast and the 35th Infantry Division in support on its right flank. In fact, as described in the last Chapter, the delayed arrival of one of the Combat Commands, due to poor planning and road congestion, and the inability of the 35th Division to support the attack, meant it went off 'at half cock'. It was finally launched at noon by a single Combat Command of two TFs.[2] By nightfall, just as the first elements of the HJ left the Samrée area, Neffe had been captured but no further gains could be made.

The HJ continued its move throughout the night using three different routes and shortly after first light on New Year's Day it was more or less complete in an assembly area 12km to the north-west of Bastogne.

By then the 6th Armored Division attack, this time with two full Combat Commands[3], had been resumed and by the time darkness fell CCB had captured Bizory, Hill 510 and Mageret, and had briefly penetrated into Arloncourt. Nevertheless, it could not clear the woods north of Bizory and was forced to withdraw from both the woods and Arloncourt. CCB had in fact been expecting elements of the 101st Airborne Division to clear the woods but, unknown to the commander of the 6th Armored Division[4], the order to the 101st had been cancelled.[5] CCA reached a line from Neffe to Wardin but was then stopped by a German counter-attack and was unable to clear the woods between the villages.

The American attacks, although not fully successful, caused a crisis in the German command. Von Manteuffel considered the threat against the two weakened and over-stretched Regiments of the 26th VGD to be now so serious that at 1800 hours he ordered Priess to cancel his planned attack in the west and take over the 26th VGD sector with effect from 1200 hours the following day. He was to take the Hitlerjugend with him to bolster the 26th VGD and be given another VGD, the 340th, currently on its way down from the Aachen area.

In fact the situation was not as serious as von Manteuffel perceived it. The Leibstandarte's counter-attack had ended any hope of the 35th Infantry Division advancing in support of the 6th Armored Division, and that evening the 6th Armored was forced to extend its front to the south to include Wardin – this meant that it too was over-stretched.

As a consequence of the changed situation the Hitlerjugend received new orders on the afternoon of New Year's Day – it was to rejoin I SS Panzer Corps on 2 January, take over responsibility for the area north and north-east of Bastogne and, together with the 26th and 340th VGDs, push the Americans back into their Bastogne perimeter.

The HJ Divisional Escort Company began its move to a new concentration area at Bourcy at 1600 hours on the same day, and as soon as it arrived it took up positions along the railway line to the south of the village. Within a few hours it was joined by eleven Mk IVs and Panthers of 1st SS Panzer Battalion which had moved south via Houffalize and Noville. Following the death of Arnold Jürgensen this Battalion was now commanded by SS Lieutenant Rudolf von Ribbentrop, a veteran of the Russian and Normandy campaigns and holder of the Knight's Cross. The arrival of the rest of the Division was greatly delayed by the serious situation to the west and north-west of Bastogne where American VIII Corps spearheads were threatening to break through and cut the roads from Bastogne to St Hubert and Marche-en-Famenne (Map 19). This necessitated the deployment, at 1600 hours on the 1st, of most of the 2nd SS Panzer-Grenadier Battalion of Krause's 26th Regiment into blocking positions astride the Marche-en-Famenne road. Despite these complications the 3rd SPW Battalion, carrying the 7th Company of the

2nd Battalion on its vehicles, managed to reach Noville that night, and during the early hours of the 2nd it took up positions in the forest 1500m south of the Noville-Bourcy road.

During the night of 1 January the US 6th Armored Division was reorganised for further action on the 2nd, and at 0925 hours CCA, reinforced with two fresh Battalions[6], attacked south of the railway line Bastogne-Benonchamps, and CCB, now with three TFs[7], to the north. The attack by CCA was costly[8] and unsuccessful and need not concern us.

In the case of CCB, TF Wall met little resistance in Oubourcy and the village was secured by 1100 hours; but then the Americans came under concentrated artillery and mortar fire and the advance came to a halt. Despite this TF Wall, supported by massive artillery fire, made further progress, and by 1500 hours had penetrated into Michamps. It was at this moment that elements of the Hitlerjugend Division intervened in the battle. Rudolf von Ribbentrop's eleven Mk IVs and Panthers, supported by the Divisional Escort Company under SS Second Lieutenant Erwin Stier, who had only returned from hospital that morning, counter-attacked from the line of the railway north of the village. By 1930 hours TF Wall was back where it started and the Germans were again in possession of Michamps and Oubourcy.

The American attack against Arloncourt was even less successful. Beginning at 1300 hours:

> TF Davall advanced towards Arloncourt, but as the leading elements reached the outskirts they were subjected to intense direct fire from enemy tanks and anti-tank guns (which were well camouflaged with white paint) as well as small arms fire from enemy infantry. . . . These leading elements took severe punishment and although supporting artillery put heavy concentrations on the town [a very small village], they were unable to secure a foothold and were forced to withdraw [at 1640 hours] to the high ground to the west.[9]

The Americans lost eight Shermans in this attack and, although the German 'tanks' referred to may well have been StuGs of the 26th VGD, it is more than likely that von Ribbentrop's tanks joined in, firing from Oubourcy.

The only successful action of the day was carried out by TF Kennedy which 'cleaned out the large woods east of Mageret without much difficulty'[10] by 1230 hours.

But where was the rest of the Hitlerjugend Division? The balance of the 2nd SS Panzer-Grenadier Battalion reached Vaux at about midnight on the 2nd and then marched to Rachamps where it made camp. But the other units, including Müller's 25th Regiment and the balance of the armour, were not expected before first light on the 3rd, and even then some of the artillery units would still be missing. A similar situation pertained with the 340th VGD but a request by Priess for a postponement of the planned counter-attack until the 4th was refused[11]. However, as some sort of recompense, Field Marshal Model told Priess he was placing parts of the 9th SS Panzer Division Hohenstaufen under his command for the operation.

3 January

The commanders of the Hitlerjugend and Hohenstaufen SS Panzer Divisions and the 340th VGD spent the morning of 3 January trying to assemble their units for the major counter-attack ordered by Field Marshal Model. The 9th SS Panzer Division, with thirty tanks and one SS Panzer-Grenadier Regiment, was to advance at 1300 hours through the Compogne area with the objective of Longchamps. Its second SS Panzer-Grenadier Regiment had yet to catch up. Two Regiments of the 340th VGD moved into an assembly area in the northern part of the Bois Jacques during the morning in preparation for their attack on the east side of the Noville-Bastogne road. They too were scheduled to attack at 1300 hours.

The Hitlerjugend axis of attack lay between the Bois Jacques and the Michamps-Arloncourt-Mageret road but, due to the delayed arrival of his units, Kraas was unable to conform to the same timetable and was forced to postpone his attack until 1400 hours.

How strong was the HJ on 3 January? Various commentators have estimated the strength of its Panzer-Grenadier Battalions at about 120 men each – from an establishment figure of nearly 1,000. Hubert Meyer, the Chief of Staff, gives no figures except when quoting a senior sergeant in the 2nd SS Panzer-Grenadier Battalion of Krause's 26th Regiment:

As I recall, the losses of the 7th Company in the period from 3 to 7 January 1945 amounted to 23 killed, about 50 wounded and 21 missing.[12]

Since we know that this Company certainly had a few men left on 7 January, it is clear that it had a strength of about 100 before the 3 January attack and this would indicate a Battalion strength of some 400 to 500 men. This is however, a risky assumption since the strength of each company would have varied, and indeed, the same can be said of each of the six Panzer-Grenadier Battalions in the Division. The best estimate that can be made is that the Battalions had strengths of between 100 and 500. The fact that none of the Battalions had been amalgamated, despite the heavy losses in officers and NCOs, would indicate a higher rather than the lower figure.

In the case of armour we can be more precise because we can refer to a report sent to the General Inspector of Panzer Troops by 12th SS dated 31 December 1944.[13] This shows that the Hitlerjugend had a total strength of twenty-nine Mk IVs, twenty-three Panthers, and nineteen Jagdpanzer IVs on that date, but that only thirteen Mk IVs, seven Panthers and fifteen Jagdpanzers were 'combat-ready' – the remainder being under short- or long-term repair. Even more surprising are the figures for the 560th Heavy Panzerjäger Battalion. It had twenty-eight Jagdpanzer IVs and thirteen Jagdpanzer Vs and they were all 'combat-ready' except for one Jagdpanzer IV. As a matter of further interest the Division had 141 operational SPWs at that time.

These figures may come as a surprise to some readers; but it has to be remembered that the German recovery and repair companies, renowned for their efficiency, had nine days in which to work between the last armoured action in the Bütgenbach area and the date of this report, and that some replacement vehicles were issued in the same period. For example, it is known that three Jagdpanzer IVs and seven Jagdpanzer Vs were 'in supply' to the 560th in the period 15-31 December. The total number of 'combat-ready' tanks and Jagdpanzers in the 12th SS Panzer Division on 31 December would appear therefore to have been seventy-five but, as will become evident later, we cannot be certain that more than about forty of them reached the Bourcy area by 3 January.

The HJ units formed up for the counter-attack with Krause's 26th SS Panzer-Grenadier Regiment on the right; its three Battalions, supported by a maximum of fifteen Jagdpanzer IVs of Brockschmidt's 12th SS Panzerjäger Battalion, assembled in a wooded area just to the south of the Noville-Bourcy road. To their left the three SS Panzer-Grenadier Battalions of Müller's 25th Regiment and part of the 12th SS Panzer Regiment were to be found behind a ridge just to the south of Bourcy and north of the railway line, while von Ribbentrop's eleven tanks and the Divisional Escort Company were still in the villages of Oubourcy and Michamps. The positioning of the bulk of the armour on the left flank was dictated by the open ground on that side of the axis of attack. The HJ artillery Battalions moved into positions to the north of Bourcy as they arrived in sector and the 12th SS Flak Battalion, which was still en route from Samrée, was ordered to support the attack with its 88mm batteries as soon as possible after arrival, leaving the 37mm battery to provide air cover. A Volks artillery Corps was in position to support both the HJ and 340th VGD attacks. Kraas located his Tactical Headquarters in Bourcy, alongside that of his artillery commander, SS Lieutenant Colonel Drexler, whilst the Main Divisional Headquarters was at Hardigny. By 1400 hours the troops were ready.

US armoured divisions were not structured to hold ground and, as previously mentioned, by last light on 2 January the 6th Armored Division was over-stretched, with no depth to its positions and only two companies in reserve. Nevertheless, with 168 Shermans, thirty-six TDs and the potential backing of nearly 200 artillery pieces[14] within the Bastogne salient, it had tremendous firepower. CCB had ninety-five Shermans and twelve TDs – TF Wall, with seventeen tanks and four TDs, was located to the west of Oubourcy but it had been forced to extend its frontage into the Bois Jacques for reasons which will be explained. TF Davall, with thirty-nine Shermans and four TDs, was to the south of TF Wall on the high ground to the west of Arloncourt, and TF Kennedy, with another thirty-nine tanks and four TDs, was in and to the south-east of Mageret. The boundary with CCA[15] was the Bastogne-Benonchamps railway line. It will not have escaped the reader's notice that TFs Wall and Davall were lying directly in the path of the Hitlerjugend attack.

The only offensive action planned by the US III Corps for 3 January was a limited advance through the Bois Jacques by two Battalions of a Regiment[16] of the 101st Airborne Division to secure the line of the Foy-Michamps track. The Map Book which forms part of Hubert Meyer's History of the 12th SS Panzer Division incorrectly shows these US Battalions already north of this track before the attack started.

It was to free the parachute Battalions for this operation that TF Wall had been required to extend its frontage into the forest. The attack was scheduled for 1200 hours and would put the Americans on a collision course with the 340th VGD.

With a few exceptions the American AARs for 3 January give no impression of the severity or seriousness of the fighting on that day. Two examples will suffice:

> 501st Parachute Infantry attacked in Bois Jacques at noon but later withdrew . . . in order to strengthen their position and establish contact with the 6th Armored Division on the right.[17]

> In accordance with the Commanding General's plan, units [of CCB 6th Armored Division] . . . spent the day consolidating their positions and organising their defenses. About 1600 enemy artillery increased to a large degree. TF Wall was subjected to Nebelwerfer fire. At the same time the 501st Parachute Regiment was subjected to a counter-attack which drove in their right flank and caused Co A 50th Armd Inf Bn to withdraw. The counter-attack was beaten off and Co A restored its original positions.[18]

Such reports give a distorted view of the real situation.

The clash on the HJ's right flank between the two Battalions of the

501st Parachute Infantry Regiment and the two weak Regiments of the 340th VGD developed soon after 1200 hours. The Paratroopers caught the Volks-Grenadiers in their assembly area and only a quick counter-attack by the Divisional Pioneer Battalion saved the day.[19] According to the Americans:

Enemy positions were developed [encountered] in the thickly wooded terrain 200 yards past the line of departure and bitter fighting ensued resulting in heavy casualties on both sides. Visibility was limited to 50 yards. Armor and artillery support was therefore impractical. The objective, an unimproved east-west road running from Foy to Michamps, was attained by some elements of both Battalions. The rest of the units were within 200 yards of it when an armor and infantry counter-attack developed in the right flank and rear. This was particularly confusing since the right flank was supposedly secured by friendly armored-infantry units [TFs Wall and Davall]. Artillery, rocket and tank fire was devastating. Headquarters and E companies bore the brunt of the fighting, knocking out armored vehicles [SPWs] right in our own positions. Casualties were very heavy and the evacuation of wounded difficult.

At 1730 the attacking Bns were ordered to withdraw. During the night the last elements disengaged and the Regiment assumed new positions on the unimproved road running SE to NW through Mageret [to Foy].[20]

The 'armor and infantry counter-attack' was of course that carried out by the Hitlerjugend. At 1400 hours the 3rd SS Panzer-Grenadiers of Krause's 26th Regiment moved forward in their SPWs and soon reached the area where the railway crosses the Foy-Michamps track. The 2nd Battalion, following on its feet, caught up at 1450 hours. As the Germans advanced farther to the south-west so the American fire increased, particularly from the Bois Jacques, and although some 3rd Battalion Grenadiers were diverted into the forest (as described in the 501st AAR quoted above) this fire could not be eliminated. Not surprisingly, several SPWs were lost in close range exchanges in the forest – six in the 9th Company alone. By 1600 hours the 2nd Battalion too was encountering stiff resistance from TF Wall just to the north of the Azette wood, including fire from Sherman tanks. According to Hubert Meyer two of them were knocked out by Panzerfausts and another by Jagdpanzers.[21] But despite this limited success, the Grenadiers in the snow-covered open fields suffered heavy losses and were unable to continue the advance. An idea of the fighting in the 2nd Battalion sector is given by SS Senior Sergeant Ewald Rien:

Any movement was answered by heavy fire from the right flank [Bois

Jacques] as well as from the hills in front of the Company. . . . The Chief of the 7th Company was among the many men already killed or wounded. However, they could not be rescued or cared for because of the heavy fire. . . . After it had turned dark, we collected our wounded as best we could and pulled our forward line back by about 300–400 metres. Orders arrived from Battalion to dig in there. Of the 4th Platoon, led by Senior Sergeant Müller, which had remained behind at the corner of the woods, no one was found again. . . . At approximately 2000 hours, the 2nd Battalion was only about sixty NCOs and men strong.[22]

The TF Wall account of this fighting, although more flamboyant, adds to the picture:

This was a battle between ground forces; it was exclusively men and tanks, as the planes of both sides were grounded and artillery observation was steadily becoming more difficult due to bad weather conditions. With visibility almost nil, the German played his trump card; he sent in his reserves who exerted such pressure that the greatly weakened Battalion[23] was required to withdraw to the original line west [should read east] of the Bois Jacques to avoid encirclement. . . . desperate measures were called for since the Battalion had been cut to pieces. To meet the critical situation all available troops were rushed to the front lines regardless of their regular assignments. . . . The following hours became a horrid night-marish blur. . . . The intense cold, the extremely low visibility and lack of communications and organisation aided an already numerically superior enemy.[24]

The concurrent attack by the 12th SS Panzer Regiment and Müller's 25th SS Panzer-Grenadier Regiment, with two Battalions abreast and one in reserve, also met heavy resistance. Nevertheless, Panthers and Mk IVs of the 1st SS Panzer Battalion advanced from Michamps to Arloncourt, while the 560th Battalion's Jagdpanzers moved south through Oubourcy. The 6th Armored Divisional Intelligence Report for this day mentions nine German tanks near Oubourcy at 1538 hours and fifteen German tanks and estimated company of infantry moving south from Bourcy at 1630 hours; it claims three German tanks knocked out during the day. This armoured thrust certainly forced TF Davall to the south-west but not before it caused heavy losses amongst Müller's Grenadiers, bringing their advance to a halt between the Azette wood and Arloncourt.

By midnight on 3 January the Hitlerjugend had advanced 3km to the south-west and George Patton is said to have commented to his staff, 'They are colder, hungrier and weaker than we, to be sure. But they are still doing a great piece of fighting'.

The new American line ran along the track coming south-east out of Foy, through the Azette wood, and thence south-east to Hill 510 and Mageret where TF Kennedy was still in position.

The associated advance on the western flank by the 9th SS Panzer Division was less successful. In the face of intense US artillery fire, the attack stalled short of its objectives and it was decided to delay any further attempts until after dark. If it had done nothing else though, the Hohenstaufen attack had disrupted the American VIII Corps' plan for another thrust towards Noville and Houffalize.

4 January

Shortly after midnight the 340th VGD resumed its advance through the Bois Jacques with the aim of reaching the Foy-Bizory track, and at 0400 hours the Hitlerjugend followed suit with Bizory and Mageret as its objectives. Since there was no direct contact with the 340th Volks-Grenadiers, Krause's 3rd SPW Battalion was ordered to move on foot west of the railway line as right flank protection, whilst his 2nd Battalion was to advance on the east side and then turn due south to seize Bizory. The 1st Battalion was to move behind the 2nd as a reserve. The Jagdpanzers of the 12th SS Panzerjäger Battalion and Regimental heavy infantry guns were to move east of the forest and fire into the Azette wood and Bois Jacques ahead of the advancing Grenadiers. At the same time the Division's Panzer and 25th Regiments were to attack in the open ground to capture Mageret and Hill 510. This combined advance was to be preceded by a surprise artillery and Nebelwerfer barrage. It is important to understand that Bizory and Mageret were extremely difficult objectives for the HJ, lying as they did in dead ground to the axis of advance.

On the right flank the Hitlerjugend advance went well and by 0700 hours Krause's 2nd and 3rd SS Grenadiers had reached the line of the Foy-Mageret track against little opposition. Beyond that line American resistance stiffened with every metre being contested throughout the day. By 1100 hours the 340th VGD had also reached the Foy-Mageret line on Krause's right flank but then, rather than attempt to advance farther, it spent the rest of the day clearing up the opposition it had bypassed in the Bois Jacques.

The AAR of the 101st Airborne Division and staff reports of the 501st Parachute Regiment have remarkably little to say about the fighting in the area between Foy and the Azette wood on this day, and what they do say is misleading. The Division erroneously reports, 'During the morning a light enemy tank attack was repulsed by the 501st Parachute Infantry'; perhaps even more surprising is a report by the 2nd Battalion of that Regiment which says, 'no contact with the enemy' – this despite the fact that it reports its positions as east of the Foy-Bizory track![25] Meanwhile the 3rd Battalion recorded that it, 'maintained screening position until rest of regiment withdrew behind it', and that by 2000 hours it was in reserve near Lahez.[26]

The AARs of CCB of the 6th Armored Division and TF Wall are more explicit – first that of CCB:

At about 0730 the Germans counter-attacked with an estimated two companies of infantry, supported by six tanks [Jagdpanzers] . . . astride the railroad and hit our lines at a point where they tied in with the 101st Airborne Division. . . . After a slight withdrawal the enemy returned with an estimated Battalion of infantry supported by eight tanks [again Jagdpanzers] and continued to exert strong pressure at the same point. The brunt of this attack was borne by the 501st Parachute Regiment. The enemy subjected the front line troops, especially those of TF Wall to heavy time [artillery] and Nebelwerfer fire. It was decided, due to the depleting strength of the front line troops, to shorten our front lines by falling back slightly to a better and more secure position. The 101st Airborne Division agreed to this and the line agreed upon ran generally from Foy, south-east to the railroad, then just east of Bizory and along the high ground west of Mageret, thence south to tie in with CCA. Elements of the 101st Airborne Division assisted in covering the withdrawal of the infantry elements of TF Wall while tank elements, also assisting, completed their withdrawal at dusk. This placed our front lines generally in the same area as when we jumped off [on 2 January].[27]

And now TF Wall:

Throughout the night 3rd and all day the 4th attack followed attack on our positions. . . . The loss of Lt Col Wall, Battalion and TF commander, who was evacuated suffering from concussion as a result of a nearby shell burst, was a serious blow. . . . On the night of 4 January so many key officers and NCOs had become casualties that the Battalion was faced with complete disorganisation. A further withdrawal was effected to a line running from the railroad tracks north-east of Lahez to the road junction north-west of Bizory where a composite company was formed of the remaining infantry elements.[28]

In an attempt to relieve the pressure on the paratroopers, and more particularly on TF Wall which was rapidly disintegrating, and to plug the widening gap between the two groups, the 501st committed part of its reserve in the early evening. Team O'Hara, a mixed force of tanks and armoured infantry, clashed with Krause's Grenadiers and Brockschmidt's

Jagdpanzers along the line of the railway; but still the gap could not be closed nor the Germans forced back – hence the American withdrawal to the line described.

But the German success on the western flank was not matched in the east where there was little or no cover once the darkness lifted. Massive American artillery fire, including the use of phosphorus shells, soon brought the advance of Müller's Grenadiers to a halt to the south-east of the Azette wood. Hubert Meyer said later that losses in the 1st and 2nd Battalions were so severe that the survivors had to be consolidated into one unit under SS Captain Werner Damsch.

The HJ armour played its part by forcing TF Davall to pull back to Bizory but its attack towards Mageret, lacking infantry support, was a failure. The Americans claimed five Mk IV or Panther tanks knocked out during the day's fighting.[29]

By dusk Krause's 26th Regiment was also exhausted. His Battalions had suffered grievously, particularly from American artillery fire – in the case of his 2nd Battalion, the three rifle companies totalled only one NCO and twenty-eight men.[30] Without support on either flank, Krause called a halt; his men had gained another 2km and were only 3km from Bastogne.

On the right flank of the 6th Armored Division the decision to 'shorten the line and fall back to better and more secure positions' resulted in chaos. Just as the withdrawal began in the late afternoon, pressure by a Regiment of the 340th VGD caused panic in one of CCA's TFs; men broke and fled all the way back to Bastogne, giving rise to reports that some units had been cut off and destroyed. The unit AAR described this incident as follows:

Early in the afternoon enemy forces hurled another attack at our troops and after one hour of fierce battling succeeded in surrounding Company B's forward CP. The surrounded men quickly fought their way through the enemy and managed to escape with only a few men slightly wounded. An order was issued to both companies to fall back to a new position . . . enemy artillery accounted for extremely heavy casualties on our part.[31]

Although the HJ's armour had failed to capture Mageret, at 1500 hours TF Kennedy was forced to conform to the movements of TF Davall and CCA and pull out of the village:

1630 – Heavy enemy counter-attack of SP guns, tanks and infantry
1700 – Attack repulsed but due to threat of counter-attack, Task Force withdrawn in good order to defensive position east of Bizory.
1800 – Positions secured. TF Command Post withdrawn to Bastogne.[32]

The three tank Companies and single armoured infantry Company of TF Kennedy took up new positions to the west of Mageret, occupying Hill 510 and the ground to the south of it as far as the railway line.[33] The History of the 69th Tank Battalion records:

> [It] was the first time we had to retreat because of enemy pressure. It was a bitter pill to swallow, to give up terrain for which we had fought so doggedly, but it had to be.

There have been suggestions that Tigers and Panthers of the Leibstandarte took part in this action and that, 'the 1st SS Panzer Division attacked into the middle of our [the 6th Armored Division's] retreat'[34]. The log of an American tank Company involved certainly has the following entry:

> At 1500 the Germans counter-attacked and surrounded one infantry company's CP. . . . As our tanks were preparing to leave they were fired on by two Tiger tanks, knocking out four of our tanks.[35]

This would seem to confirm that some of the LAH's tanks were indeed involved alongside those of the HJ at this time and that if the latter had pressed its attack towards Mageret the American withdrawal might well have turned into a rout. Why it did not do so is unclear but the question of casualties must have been a major factor and this question will be addressed shortly.

5 – 10 January

Hermann Priess ordered the sad remnants of the 12th SS Panzer Division and the 340th VGD to attack again late on 5 January. The Volks-Grenadiers were to advance on the west side of the Bastogne-Bourcy railway line, Krause's 26th SS Panzer-Grenadier Regiment on the east side, with the railway station as its initial objective, and the HJ armoured force was given the task of breaking through in the Mageret and Bizory sector.

The 340th VGD reached a line just short of the Foy-Bizory track before encountering serious opposition. It was then unable to advance farther since the well fortified positions of the 501st Parachute Regiment, backed by powerful artillery resources, were too much for the exhausted Volks-Grenadiers.

Reconnaissances carried out during the night 4-5 January showed that the Americans had abandoned the Azette forest and that the way was clear as far as the railway station north-west of Bizory. Krause's men wasted no time reaching this point but the associated advance in the open ground on the east side of the woods soon ran into trouble. The Americans described what happened:

> Enemy infantry estimated to be approximately a Battalion accompanied by tanks were observed coming through the woods . . . turning south . . . and thence along our front lines. TF Kennedy's tanks fired direct at the enemy column, knocked out two tanks and inflicted severe casualties which caused the enemy to withdraw. Later a PW stated this attack was made by the 3rd Bn, 26th PG Regt, 12 SS Div.[36]

More details are provided by the US tank Battalion involved:

> The TF was attacked by approximately one Battalion of infantry and tanks. After a heavy engagement the attack was beaten off. TF casualties were eight wounded but no vehicles lost. Destroyed: two Tiger tanks, one assault gun and 100 enemy killed. Wounded were evacuated by the enemy. Attack lasted three hours. Our force was supported by artillery.[37]

On the eastern flank elements of the 12th SS Panzer Regiment, supported by Müller's Grenadiers and, according to the Americans, SPW mounted infantry, occupied the abandoned village of Mageret and, for a short time, Hill 510. But tank fire from TF Wall in Bizory and intense artillery fire soon forced the Germans to give up their exposed positions on the hill. The American AAR completes the picture:

> Another enemy column of tanks, half tracks (approximately two companies) were observed moving on the west side of Mageret going south-west along our front. Tanks took them under fire and artillery concentrations were placed on the column. Heavy casualties were inflicted, several vehicles were set on fire and the enemy forced to withdraw to the east. . . . At 1950 the situation was well in hand and other than enemy patrols and artillery activity the sector was reasonably quiet.[38]

At 2330 hours on 5 January the 26th SS Panzer-Grenadier Regiment HJ received orders that it was to be relieved that same night by the 340th VGD. Events elsewhere were dictating that the Hitlerjugend's participation in the battle of Bastogne was coming to an end – and not before time, for the Division was incapable of any further major offensive action. It was therefore to be withdrawn into Corps and Fifth Panzer Army reserve. The relief began in earnest during the early hours of 7 January, but some elements of the 1st SS Panzer and 12th SS Panzerjäger Battalions remained in the Michamps area until as late as the 10th to act as a mobile reserve for the 340th VGD and I SS Panzer Corps, and casualties were still being suffered up to that date.[39]

We left the attack by the 9th SS Panzer Division Hohenstaufen on 3 January stalled in front of Longchamps. Although the Division managed to enter the village on the 4th it was unable to secure it and the following day it too was ordered to hand over its sector to a Volks-Grenadier Division (the 26th). Two days previously the US First Army had launched its counter-attack against the northern flank of the 'Bulge' and there was now an urgent need to reinforce Dietrich's Sixth Panzer Army with armour.

Recall that on 8 January, faced with the realisation that his remaining armour was in danger of being trapped, Hitler authorised Model to give up the area to the west of Houffalize (Map 19). With one exception the attacks of the SS Panzer Divisions on the Bastogne salient were at an end – that exception was the Hitlerjugend which was required to launch one final attack at first light on the same day!

In accordance with a direct order, allegedly given by Field Marshal Model, Hill 510 was to be secured so that observed artillery fire could be directed against the town of Bastogne. The fact that it was quite impossible to see *into* Bastogne from Hill 510 was unknown to the staffs of Army Group 'B'; but Hugo Kraas and his Chief of Staff knew this, and moreover knew that the chances of anyone remaining alive for long on the featureless hill in broad daylight in the face of the available American fire power were minimal. Nevertheless, their objections were overruled and at 0700 hours on 8 January some eighty men of the 2nd Company of the 12th SS Pioneer Battalion, assisted by the Divisional Escort Company, went into the attack. Under the command of SS Captain Johannes Taubert, the Pioneer Battalion commanding officer, they were supported by tanks of von Ribbentrop's Battalion, the whole of the HJ Divisional artillery, including the 88mm guns of the 12th SS Flak Battalion and the Nebelwerfers of the 12th SS Werfer Battalion, and the Corps 501st Artillery Battalion. Against all expectations the assault was successful. In close-quarter fighting a number of dug-in tanks were knocked out with explosives and flame-throwers and by 0940 hours the hill had been taken – but the success was to be short-lived. Heavy casualties and a lack of anti-tank weapons, coupled with a delay in the arrival of reinforcements from the 340th VGD, spelt disaster for Taubert's men. A counter-attack by an American tank company, backed by overwhelming artillery fire, forced them back to Mageret by 1100 hours. Over fifty men were lost. An American account gives further details:

On 8 January the enemy again mounted a joint attack by tanks and infantry against our right flank and along the Bizory-Mageret road.

Six tanks of A Company were knocked out like clay pigeons. . . . The enemy then concentrated on the hill [Hill 510]. In the end, before he could inflict major damage, Jerry was driven off by our TDs [tanks?] and artillery.[40]

The last offensive action of the HJ on the Western Front was over and during the following forty-eight hours the mauled units of the Division gradually withdrew to an assembly area in the Beho area, south west of St Vith (Map 19).

How badly had the HJ suffered during the recent fighting? There are no surviving records of personnel casualties but they had obviously reached catastrophic proportions. In the case of armoured vehicles we can be more precise. A return dated 15 January for the 12th SS Panzer Regiment shows twenty-two Mk IVs and seventeen Panthers on strength on that date and another dated 1 February for the 12th SS Panzerjäger Battalion shows thirteen Jagdpanzer IVs. In the case of the 560th Heavy Panzerjäger Battalion, a return dated 1 February shows seventeen Jagdpanzer IVs and six Jagdpanzer Vs on strength. By comparing these figures with those reported for 31 December, and taking into account that the HJ was out of action from 9 to 31 January, we can deduce that thirty-seven armoured vehicles – seven Mk IVs, six Panthers, seventeen Jagdpanzer IVs, seven Jagdpanzer Vs – were lost during the fighting in the Bastogne area. Eighteen SPWs were also lost.

And so ended the part played by the designated Divisions of Hitler's Bodyguard Corps in the Ardennes campaign. Once again they had given their all and been reduced to mere spectres of the Leibstandarte which had participated in the campaign in Russia in 1943 and the Hitlerjugend in Normandy in 1944. In summary, it can be said that they had been ordered to fight through unsuitable terrain, starved of essential supplies and denied the air support this type of offensive demanded. But it also has to be said that, due to failures by German intelligence staffs, the men of the LAH and HJ had often been surprised by the situations in which they found themselves – for example, by the presence of the 2nd US Infantry Division in the northern attack area – and by the speed of the American reaction to their attacks, e.g., the rapid movement of the 1st and 30th US Infantry Divisions and CCB of the 3rd Armored to the threatened areas. But there was one more thing which spelled disaster for Hitler's last offensive in the West – the bravery and tenacity of the American front-line soldier. This came as a shock to the Germans who, like their Führer, had a poor opinion of the US Army – and it may also have come as a surprise to many readers. Hopefully this narrative will have helped to correct the widely held misconception that the Americans were routed in the Ardennes and that the majority of the 'GIs' ran away – as the Waffen-SS found to its cost, nothing could be further from the truth.

*   *   *

The first personnel replacements arrived in the Hitlerjugend assembly area south-west of St Vith on 12 January – the day Stalin launched 180 divisions from Poland and East Prussia in what was to be the greatest Soviet offensive of the war. This offensive would result in the final destruction of I SS Panzer Corps, for on 16 January, as the pincers of the American First and Third Armies closed at Houffalize, Adolf Hitler ordered von Rundstedt to withdraw his four Waffen-SS Panzer Divisions[41] behind the West Wall for refitting and transportation to Hungary. Armageddon awaited them.

NOTES

1. Commander Third US Army.
2. CCA with TFs Kennedy & Brown.
3. CCA (TFs Kennedy & Brown) comprised the 69th Tk Bn & 44th Armd Inf Bn; CCB consisted of TF Wall with the 50th Armd Inf Bn (less a coy) & M/68th Tk Bn and TF Davall with the 68th Tk Bn (less a coy) & B/50th Armd Inf Bn; all were supported by the 603rd TD Bn, 25th Armd Engr Bn and the Div arty Bns.
4. Maj Gen Robert Grow.
5. Cole, *The Ardennes: Battle of the Bulge*, pp. 629–30.
6. 15th Tk Bn & 9th Armd Inf Bn.
7. TFs Wall & Davall as before but in addition, TF Kennedy with the 69th Tk Bn (less a coy) & A/44th Armd Inf Bn.
8. Cole, op. cit., p. 633: the 15th Tk Bn lost seven Shermans and the 9th Armd Inf Bn a quarter of its strength.
9. AAR CCB/6th Armd Div dated 1 Feb 45.
10. Ibid.
11. Meyer, *The History of the 12th SS Panzer Division Hitlerjugend*, p. 272. In his Report MS # A-877 dated Mar 46, Hermann Priess is mistaken when he says his request for a delay until the 4th was agreed; this makes the timings in the rest of his report incorrect by 24 hours.
12. Ibid., p. 276.
13. Anl. zu 12. SS-Pz.Div. HJ/ Ia Tgb. Nr. 1518/44 vom 31.12.44; this, and all othe German strength returns quoted, can be seen in the Bundesarchiv, Germany.
14. Five armd fd arty bns, two 155mm, four fd arty bns, three lt how bns and one 105mm how bn.
15. TFs Brown, Lagrew & Britton.
16. 2 & 3/501st.
17. AAR 101st Airborne Div for Jan 45.
18. AAR CCB/6th Armd Div dated 1 Feb 45.
19. Meyer, op. cit., p. 273.
20. AAR 501st Para Inf Regt dated 15 Mar 45.
21. Meyer, op. cit., p. 273.
22. Ibid., pp. 273–4.
23. 50th Armd Inf.
24. AAR 50th Armd Inf Bn dated 31 May 45.

25. 501st Prcht Inf S-3 Report for 4 Jan 45.
26. Ibid.
27. AAR CCB/6th Armd Div dated 1 Feb 45.
28. AAR 50th Armd Inf Bn dated 31 May 45.
29. AARs CCB/6th Armd Div dated 1 Feb 45 & 603rd TD Bn dated 15 Feb 45.
30. Meyer, op. cit., p. 274.
31. AAR 44th Armd Inf Bn dated 1 Feb 45.
32. S-2-3 Journal TF Kennedy.
33. AAR 69th Tk Bn dated 1 Feb 45.
34. Tiemann, *Die Leibstandarte* IV/2, p. 189.
35. History of Co B 69th Tk Bn dated 1 Feb 45.
36. AAR CCB/6th Armd Div dated 1 Feb 45.
37. AAR 69th Tk Bn dated 1 Feb 45.
38. AAR CCB/6th Armd Div dated 1 Feb 45.
39. Meyer, op. cit., p. 278.
40. *68th Tk Bn in Combat*, p. 30.
41. Leibstandarte, Das Reich, Hohenstaufen and Hitlerjugend.

CHAPTER XXI

The Situation in early 1945

(Maps 2 & 24)

Hitler's intention of delivering a devastating blow on the Western Front in order to buy the time and resources needed to deal with the deepening crisis in the East had come to nothing. Although the Ardennes offensive seemed to have bought him a short respite, it had in fact frittered away many of the men and much of the equipment needed to throw back and destroy the Soviet armies now threatening the Third Reich. As von Manteuffel said later:

> The rapid advance by the Red Army [in January 1945] nullified the possible effects of the Ardennes offensive. It made a speedy end to the war inevitable. Time gained on the Western Front was thereby rendered illusory.[1]

Hungary

By the end of 1944 the Second and Third Ukrainian Fronts[2] of the Red Army had surrounded Budapest and established strong defensive positions running from Esztergom on the Danube to Lake Balaton. On the last day of the year the provisional government set up by the Soviets

175

in those parts of Hungary occupied by the Red Army, threw in its lot with the Allies and declared war on Germany. The last of Hitler's partners in his European Axis had deserted him – but not the Hungarian Army. In order to protect the country from the Bolsheviks, whom they feared and hated, what was left of the Hungarian Army continued to fight alongside the Germans.[3]

On New Year's Day 1945 the only sizeable German reserves on the Eastern Front launched an offensive, code-named KONRAD, to relieve Budapest and secure the southern Hungarian oil reserves. By 6 January the Totenkopf and Wiking SS Panzer Divisions of General Gille's IV SS Panzer Corps had come to within 25km of the Hungarian capital but then, in the face of rapidly re-deployed Soviet units, the attack stalled. On the same day the Russians launched an attack across the Gran river, north of the Danube, with the equivalent of two tank divisions and four infantry divisions[4], designed to disrupt the German offensive; it was successful and by the 8th they had advanced some 50km. German counter-measures succeeded in halting the attack and by the 14th the Russians had lost half their gains and some 200 tanks; nevertheless, they still held a sizeable bridgehead west of the Gran river (Map 25).

In the meantime Gille's IV SS Panzer Corps had renewed its attack on 10 January and, after taking the Soviets completely by surprise, had advanced to within 21km of Budapest by the 13th. Then, despite Herbert Gille's assurance that he was on the point of a breakthrough, Headquarters Army Group South inexplicably called a halt. SS Lieutenant Colonel Fritz Darges, commanding the Wiking's SS Panzer Regiment said later:

The head of our assault unit could see the panorama of the city in their binoculars. We were disappointed and we could not believe the attack was stopped. Our morale was excellent and we knew we could free our comrades the next day.

Be that as it may, Hitler and the OKW had other plans. On 16 January von Rundstedt, more than 1000km away on the Western Front, received the following order:

CinC West is to withdraw the following formations from operations immediately and refit them:
I SS Panzer Corps with 1st SS Panzer Division LAH and 12th SS Panzer Division HJ;
II SS Panzer Corps with 2nd SS Panzer Division DR and 9th SS Panzer Division H.
Last day of refitting is 30 January. Reinforcements will be provided under the authority of the SS Supreme Operations Office.[5]

I SS Panzer Corps had been returned to Dietrich's command two days earlier and was already concentrating to the south and west of Cologne. But, as we learned in the last two Chapters, both the Leibstandarte and Hitlerjugend Divisions were in a wretched state and in urgent need of rest, reinforcements and new equipment. Nevertheless, at this time Hitler sent his personal adjutant, SS Major Otto Günsche, to Sepp Dietrich to warn him that he was sending the Sixth Panzer Army to the Eastern Front in order to launch a new offensive, code-named SPRING AWAKENING (FRÜHLINGSERWACHEN), designed to secure the vital oil deposits in southern Hungary and perhaps even regain the oil of Rumania. The refitting and move of Dietrich's Army was to be completed in less than a month! Both Dietrich and General Heinz Guderian, the Chief of Staff of the OKH, had wanted the Sixth Panzer Army deployed behind the Oder in order to protect Berlin and northern Germany, but Hitler would have none of it. The only natural oil deposits in German controlled-territory were those around Nagykanizsa in southern Hungary and, with Allied air attacks disrupting and often neutralising the synthetic gasoline production sites for long periods, it was essential to protect them. Without this crude oil the battle could not be continued – Dietrich and the trusted Divisions of the Waffen-SS were to be given responsibility for SPRING AWAKENING.

The decision to send the Sixth Panzer Army to Hungary meant that six of the seven SS Panzer Divisions were to be located in the Danube valley in the southern part of the Eastern Front and well away from Berlin. When American intelligence became aware of this, it added to the suspicion that Hitler and his Nazi regime were planning to withdraw into some sort of mountain stronghold around Berchtesgaden:

> The main trend of German defence policy does seem directed primarily to the safeguarding of the Alpine Zone. This area is, by the very nature of the terrain, practically impenetrable. . . . The evidence indicates that considerable numbers of SS and specially chosen units are being systematically withdrawn to Austria . . . and that some of the most important ministries . . . are already established in the Redoubt area.[6]

Although the idea of a National Redoubt turned out in the end to be mythical, it was realistic enough at the time to lead Eisenhower to conclude that the southern part of the European theatre was of greater significance than Berlin; this led in turn to acrimony between the Allies and to thirty-one American divisions being directed south-east towards the Danube valley and the so-called National Redoubt, leaving only eight on the direct route to Berlin. But we are getting ahead of ourselves and away from our main theme!

In view of the time needed to refit and move the Sixth Panzer Army to the Eastern Front, and in order to secure the ground west of the Danube for the new offensive, Hitler ordered a third attack in Hungary on 18 January using much larger forces.[7] This was designed primarily to cut off and destroy all Soviet troops north of a line drawn from Lake Balaton, through Székesfehérvar, to Budapest, and secondly to liberate that city – the Pest garrison had in fact withdrawn across the Danube to the hills of Buda the night before. Since the Russians had weakened their defences in this area to meet the previous German attacks in the north, the new offensive was initially very successful. Within three days a large section of the west bank of the Danube had been secured 35km south of Budapest and the Germans then turned north and north-west, threatening to link up with other forces attacking in the north and to cut off an entire Soviet Front. By the 26th, however, with their forces in the south only 20km from Buda and in the north half that distance, the Germans were exhausted, and this was the moment when Marshal Malinovsky went over to the attack. Although Székesfehérvar and the ground between it and Lake Balaton was held, by 3 February the Germans were more or less back to their original positions – KONRAD had failed. Buda fell finally on 14 February – the siege had lasted fifty-one days and had cost the Axis over 70,000 men.

Meanwhile, Zhukov's and Konev's offensives in the north had advanced over 150km; Warsaw, Lodz and Cracow had fallen and a Soviet Army had entered East Prussia. The Red Army was now a mere 200km from Prague and, worst of all for the German people, it had crossed the river Oder and was only 70km from Berlin.

This then was the crisis situation into which I SS Panzer Corps was about to be launched.

Move to the East

Extraordinary measures were taken to conceal the fact that the Sixth Panzer Army was being moved to the Eastern Front – all ranks were ordered to remove their sleeve bands and special codenames were given to all components. Thus, I SS Panzer Corps became 'SS Sector Staff South', the LAH 'The Death's Head Replacement Team' and the HJ 'The Viking Replacement Team'. Even Regiments were redesignated as 'Construction Teams'.

Other deception measures included unloading part of the Sixth Panzer Army Staff near Berlin and making it known that their final destination was in the Frankfurt-am-Oder area and, despite the air threat, actually sending the Tiger IIs of the 501st SS Heavy Panzer Battalion via the Berlin area before routing them through Vienna to Hungary.[8]

The move of I SS Panzer Corps to the new assembly area around Györ, some 100km to the south-east of Vienna and the same distance

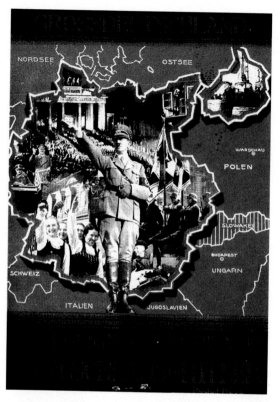

1 'Hitler is Germany, Germany is Hitler'. Postcard printed for the union with Austria, 1938. (Courtesy: Ferdinand Pachler)

2 Sepp Dietrich after receiving Diamonds to his Knight's Cross from Hitler, August 1944. (Author's collection)

3 Hermann Priess, commander I SS Panzer Corps in the Ardennes
and Hungary. (Author's collection)

4 Wilhelm Mohnke, commander 1st SS
Panzer Division LAH in the Ardennes.
(Author's collection)

5 Otto Kumm, commander 1st SS
Panzer Division LAH from mid-
February 1945. (Author's collection)

6 Hugo Kraas, commander 12th
Panzer Division HJ in the Ardennes
and Hungary. (Author's collection)

7 Mk IV tank, workhorse of the Panzer corps.   (Author's collection)

8 Leibstandarte SPW/9, mounting a 75mm gun, abandoned in the Market Square, Stavelot, 18 December 1944.   (Courtesy: Gérard Grégoire)

9 Leibstandarte Tiger II, number 105, immobilized in Stavelot, 18 December 1944.   (Courtesy: Gérard Grégoire)

10 Leibstandarte Panther abandoned in La Gleize, December 1944. (Courtesy: Gérard Grégoire)

11 Jochen Peiper, commander 1st SS Panzer Regiment LAH in the Ardennes and Hungary. (Author's collection)

12 SS Lieutenant Herbert Kuhlmann in 1940. As an SS major he commanded KG Kuhlmann in the Ardennes. (Courtesy: Bill Warnock)

13 Max Hansen, commander
1st SS Panzer-Grenadier Regiment
LAH in the Ardennes
and Hungary.
(Author's collection)

14 Rudolf Sandig, commander
2nd SS Panzer-Grenadier Regiment
LAH in the Ardennes.
(Author's collection)

15 Sherman M4A1s of the 35th Tank Battalion near Bastogne. (Author's collection)

16 US M36, mounting a 90mm gun, in the Ardennes. (Imperial War Museum)

17 Waffen-SS 75mm anti-tank gun in ambush position.
(Author's collection)

18 Waffen-SS 'Wespe' 105mm self-propelled gun.
(Author's collection)

19 Siegfried Müller as a young SS lieutenant. As an SS major, he commanded the 25th SS Panzer-Grenadier Regiment HJ in the Ardennes and Hungary. (Courtesy: Bill Warnock)

20 Bernhard (Papa) Krause, commander 26th SS Panzer-Grenadier Regiment HJ in the Ardennes and Hungary. (Author's collection)

21 Gerd Bremer on promotion to SS major, 30 January 1944. He commanded the 12th SS Reconnaissance Battalion HJ in the Ardennes and Hungary. (Courtesy: Bill Warnock)

22 Werner Poetschke, commanding officer 1st SS Panzer Battalion LAH in the Ardennes and Hungary. (Author's collection)

23 Arnold Jürgensen, commanding officer 1st SS Panzer Battalion HJ in the Ardennes.
(Courtesy: Bill Warnock)

24 Rudolf von Ribbentrop as a young SS lieutenant. He commanded the (Panzer-less!) 1st SS Panzer Battalion HJ in Hungary.
(Author's collection)

25 Hans Siegel, commanding officer 2nd SS Panzer Battalion HJ in Hungary.
(Author's collection)

26 Jupp Diefenthal, commanding officer 3rd SS (SPW) Battalion LAH in the Ardennes and Hungary.
(Author's collection)

27 Ralf Tiemann as a young SS captain. He was Chief of Staff, 1st SS Panzer Division LAH from 18 December 1944 to February 1945. (Courtesy: Ralf Tiemann)

28 Hubert Meyer in 1943. He was Chief of Staff, 12th SS Panzer Division HJ in the Ardennes and Hungary.
(Courtesy: Hubert Meyer)

29 Major General Leland Hobbs, commander 30th US Infantry Division, is congratulated by the 12th Army Group commander, Lieutenant General Omar Bradley. (Imperial War Museum)

30 Lieutenant Colonel Dave Pergrin, commanding officer 291st Engineer Combat Battalion in the Ardennes. (Courtesy: Dave Pergrin)

31 Werner Sternebeck in the uniform of a lieutenant colonel in the post-war West German Army. (Courtesy: Gerd Cuppens)

32 Soviet T-34s in the assault.
(Courtesy: Library of Frunze Military Academy)

33 Hitlerjugend Panther on the move in Hungary.
(Author's collection)

34 Martin Gross (right), commander 12ᵗʰ SS Panzer Regiment HJ in Hungary with Jochen Peiper, commander 1ˢᵗ SS Panzer Regiment LAH.
(Author's collection)

35 The Leibstandarte drives into captivity, 8 May 1945.
(Author's collection)

36 Dietrich (11), Kraemer (33), Priess (45) and Peiper (42).
The Dachau Trial, 1946. (Author's collection)

37 Sepp Dietrich as a
prisoner of war, 1945.
(Author's collection)

from Budapest, was carried out by rail and in the case of some units took nearly two weeks.

Refitting

Needless to say it proved impossible to refit fully the LAH and HJ for offensive operations by 30 January, and both personnel and material replacements continued to arrive during loading, during the move and even after arrival at Györ. Hubert Meyer gives two examples: the 2nd SS Panzer-Grenadier Battalion of Bernhard Krause's 26th Regiment received two officers and 157 men one hour after it began loading vehicles at its entraining station near Cologne, and NCOs and Luftwaffe technical personnel joined the 3rd Battalion as it passed through Dresden.[9]

In view of the massive, and by now almost continuous, Allied air onslaught, the general state of the German war economy and, not least, the appalling casualty rate sustained in five and a half years of war by the German Armed Forces, it is astounding that Dietrich's Army was made ready for action in less than one month. More men were drafted in from the Luftwaffe and Navy, lightly wounded and sick returned to their parent formations and vehicles and tanks delivered direct from factories. As appropriate in a specialised History, details will only be provided for I SS Panzer Corps.

Readers will probably be surprised to learn that by the time these Divisions were committed to battle on 17 February, the LAH was some 500 men *over* and the HJ only 1,700 men under the authorised strength of a Waffen-SS Panzer Division – approximately 18,500 all ranks.[10] Nevertheless, these figures do not reveal the severe shortfall in both officers and NCOs – roughly 30% and 50% respectively. Another important weakness was the fact that many of the reinforcements had received little or very limited military training and no field experience with their units. As Hugo Kraas wrote of the Hitlerjugend at this time:

> The combat strength of the Panzer-Grenadier Regiments is not very high since the positions of Battalion and company commanders are, in the main, filled by new officers, and because unit exercises are not possible.[11]

The equipment state of both Divisions was also surprisingly high. By 17 February the LAH had thirty-seven Mk IVs, forty-one Panthers, twenty-one Jagdpanzer IVs, three StuGs and 175 SPWs on strength and the 501st SS Heavy Panzer Battalion, still attached to the Division, thirty-six Tiger IIs. Lower figures are quoted in the Leibstandarte History[12] but these are for a week earlier and do not take into account further vehicles in the delivery system.

The HJ Division was even better off, with the following armoured vehicles shown on strength on 10 February: thirty-eight Mk IVs, forty-four Panthers, twenty-one Jagdpanzer IVs and 165 SPWs. The 560th Heavy Panzerjäger Battalion, still officially attached to the Division, is shown with thirty-one Jagdpanzer IVs and sixteen Jagdpanzer Vs.

The question of how many of these armoured vehicles were combat-ready on 17 February is, as we shall see, a different matter. Figures varied from day to day and even hour to hour. For example, the 501st SS Heavy Panzer Battalion is said to have had nineteen Tiger IIs operational on 31 January, twenty-three on 1 February, fifteen on 8 February and nineteen again on the 17th when it went into action in Hungary.[13]

The method used to ensure that sufficient crews were trained and available to man this impressive number of vehicles is of interest. During the Ardennes offensive personnel (new, wounded and sick returned to duty) of the 2nd and 4th Panther Companies and 7th and 8th Mk IV Companies of the HJ received up-to-date instruction and practical experience at the armoured training grounds in Fallingbostel, northern Germany. Then during January 1945, before the move to Hungary, they took over the replacement tanks. At the same time the surviving crews of the 1st and 3rd Panther Companies and 5th and 6th Mk IV Companies were returned to Fallingbostel for refitting.

With regard to artillery pieces both Divisions were more or less up to strength. In the wheeled transport sector however, there were serious problems – a 30% shortfall in the truck strength of the LAH and 78% in the case of the HJ. Nevertheless, by early February Kraas was able to report of the Hitlerjugend, 'The Division is conditionally ready for offensive action tasks'; no doubt the Leibstandarte was also judged fit for operations, even if there were some provisos.

Personalities

Wilhelm Mohnke was promoted to the rank of SS Major General on 13 January and left the Leibstandarte for duties in Berlin. He was not immediately replaced and the refitting of the Division and move to Hungary were overseen by the Regimental commanders. On 15 February, just two days before the Division went into action, SS Major General Otto Kumm assumed command. He had joined the SS in 1934 and fought in the French and Russian campaigns with the Der Führer Regiment of the 2nd SS Division Das Reich, winning the Iron Cross 1st and 2nd Class, German Cross in Gold and Knight's Cross with Oakleaves. He came to the LAH from commanding the 7th SS Mountain Division Prinz Eugen in Serbia and

Croatia, where he added Swords to his Knight's Cross. He was 35 years old.

February and Hungary saw the return of Jochen Peiper to the LAH – fit and well after an absence of some six weeks. His 1st SS Panzer Regiment still consisted of a mixed Battalion of two Panther and two Mk IV Companies under the command of Werner Poetschke and von Westernhagen's 501st SS Heavy Panzer Battalion.

The senior commanders in Max Hansen's 1st SS Panzer-Grenadier Regiment were unchanged except for his 2nd Battalion – SS Captain Unterkofler had been killed in the Ardennes and the name of his replacement is not recorded.

Rudolf Sandig had suffered some sort of mental breakdown after, it is said, a series of furious arguments with his superior, Wilhelm Mohnke, concerning the recent campaign. His place as commander of the 2nd SS Panzer-Grenadier Regiment was taken by SS Lieutenant Colonel Bernhard Siebken who was transferred across from the HJ. Siebken had commanded a Battalion of that Division in Normandy but had not taken part in the Ardennes offensive. The commanders of his 1st and 2nd Battalions were newly appointed – SS Majors Möllhof and Max Junge respectively – but Jupp Diefenthal, who had been awarded the Knight's Cross for his part in the Ardennes offensive, was still in command of the 3rd SPW Battalion.

Gustav Knittel had been wounded on the last day of December in the Bastogne sector and his place as commander of the LAH Reconnaissance Battalion had been taken by SS Captain Emil Wawrzinek.

Except in the case of the Panzer-Grenadier Battalion commanders who, not surprisingly after the Ardennes fighting, were all new, there were only two personnel changes amongst the senior ranks of the Hitlerjugend. SS Major Hans Siegel, a Normandy Knight's Cross winner and former platoon commander of Michael Wittmann, replaced von Ribbentrop's mixed 1st SS Panzer Battalion with his mixed 2nd SS Panzer Battalion, and SS Captain Ziesenitz took over the 12th SS Werfer Battalion from Willi Müller.

Morale

The remarkable esprit de corps which the Leibstandarte achieved in its early days has already been described. This intense sense of comradeship grew even stronger as the war progressed and was easily instilled in the Hitlerjugend Division by its first leaders, the majority of whom, it will be remembered, came from the LAH. The fact that the non-volunteers and replacements from the Navy and Air Force who joined the twin Divisions after the Ardennes offensive were soon imbued with this great sense of 'family' seems all the more remarkable when one considers the parlous state of the Third Reich at this late stage of the war.

By February 1945 the soldiers of I SS Panzer Corps knew their country had no chance of winning WWII, but they were determined not to surrender 'unconditionally', as the Allies had demanded. Above all they were determined to try to safeguard their Homeland from the Red Army whose members, they had been taught – and believed – were little more than sub-human. They, like their leader, still harboured forlorn hopes that if Germany could just hold out long enough, the Western Allies would recognise the Bolsheviks as their real enemy and join Germany in a common crusade. This motivation, however flawed, explains, at least to some degree, the astonishing performance of these men in the final weeks of the war.

Another factor determining the performance of I SS Panzer Corps in these last months was that most of their leaders had fought together for over five years; they therefore knew each other's strong and weak points and, above all, they trusted each other. The vast majority of the officers we have mentioned – men like Kraas, Peiper, Hansen, Siebken, Poetschke, Hubert Meyer, Junge, Diefenthal, von Westernhagen, Siegel, Krause, Rettlinger, the Müllers, Drexler, Bremer, Taubert, Möbius and so on – had fought together in the harshest conditions year after year. They were not about to give up at this stage, when the most feared and hated enemy of all was at the very gates of their beloved Heimat.

NOTES

1. Von Manteuffel, *The Fatal Decisions, The Ardennes*, p. 253.
2. A Front was the equivalent of a British or American Army Group.
3. The Third Hungarian Army was to play an important part in the forthcoming fighting.
4. IX Gds Mech Corps & V Gds Tk Corps of the Sixth Gds Tk Army & four Rifle Divs of the XXV Gds Rifle Corps; however, neither of these Mech & Tk Corps equated to more than a Waffen-SS Pz Div. The whole subject of Soviet organisations and strengths will be discussed in the next Chapter.
5. Meyer, *The History of the 12th SS Panzer Division Hitlerjugend*, p. 283.
6. SHAEF Int Summary dated 11 Mar 45.
7. IV SS Pz Corps, III Pz Corps, I Cavalry Corps & VIII Hungarian Army Corps.
8. Schneider, *Tigers in Combat* II, p. 265.
9. Meyer, op. cit., p. 284.
10. Tiemann, *Die Leibstandarte* IV/2, p. 234 and Meyer, op. cit., p. 284.
11. Meyer, op. cit., pp. 284.
12. Tiemann, op. cit., p. 234.
13. Schneider, op. cit., p. 265.

CHAPTER XXII

The Soviet Side of the Hill

The contrast between the Eastern and Western Fronts cannot be over-emphasised. The scale of the fighting, the topography, and in particular the enemy and his tactics, all differed greatly from those found in Normandy and the Ardennes. Moreover, because the majority of the officers and senior NCOs of I SS Panzer Corps had considerable experience of operations against the Red Army, none relished a return to that Front. As already mentioned, there was a terrible fear of being captured and for those who had yet to serve in the East and who knew the vulnerability of the Third Reich at this stage of the war, the prospect was little short of terrifying – particularly for soldiers who wore SS runes on their collars.

The way the Germans viewed their Soviet enemies and the Eastern Front was described after the war by Lieutenant General Günther Blumentritt; in January 1945 he was the commander of the German Twenty-Fifth Army:

Eastern man is very different from his Western counterpart. He has a much greater capacity for enduring hardship, and this passivity induces a high degree of equanimity towards life and death. . . . Eastern man does not possess much initiative; he is accustomed to taking orders, to being led. . . . [The Russians] attach little importance to what they eat or wear. It is surprising how long they can survive on what to a Western man would be a starvation diet. . . . Close contact with nature enables these people to move freely by night or in fog, through woods and across swamps. They are not afraid of the dark, nor of their endless forests, nor of the cold. They are accustomed to winters in which the thermometer frequently falls to 45 degrees of frost Centigrade.

The Siberian, who is partially or completely an Asiatic, is even tougher and has greater powers of resistance than his European compatriot. . . .

Distances in the East seem endless . . . which inevitably affects the European with a sensation akin to awe. This is reinforced by the melancholy and monotonous nature of the . . . landscape, which is particularly oppressive during the gloomy days of autumn and the interminable winter darkness. The Russian is much influenced by the country in which he lives, and it is my belief that the landscape is largely responsible for his passivity and monotony.

The psychological effect of the country on the ordinary German soldier was considerable. He felt small and lost in that endless space. . . . A man who has survived the Russian enemy and the Russian climate has little more to learn about war.[1]

Organisation

As mentioned in a footnote to the last Chapter, a Soviet *Front* was the equivalent of an Allied Army Group; it comprised usually three or more *Combined Arms Armies* and sometimes one or two *Tank Armies* or mechanized groups. The former were made up basically of infantry, with formidable artillery support, and were used for defensive and breakthrough operations; independent *tank brigades and regiments* were assigned to provide extra punch during assault operations but training in the infantry support role meant that such units rarely performed well in tank versus tank engagements. *Tank* armies were normally employed in counter-penetration tasks, to complete a breakthrough and in the pursuit.

Combined Arms armies consisted of two to five *rifle corps*, usually three, and sometimes had *tank or mechanized corps* placed in support for operations requiring tactical mobility. *Tank* armies on the other hand had two to three *tank or mechanized corps* under command but, as will be seen from Appendix VI, *a tank and mechanized corps*, even at full strength, was in practice the equivalent of no more than a Waffen-SS Panzer *division*.

Rifle corps comprised two or three, and occasionally four, *rifle divisions*. The organisation of a rifle division is shown at Appendix VII.

Readers should also note that Soviet formations and units which had distinguished themselves in action were given the title 'Guards'.

The terminology used in describing Red Army formations and units differed greatly from Western practice and has led to many misunderstandings about the size of the Soviet forces involved in various battles. Perhaps the best example of this is the Soviet *tank or mechanized corps* which, as just mentioned, was only the equivalent of a Waffen-SS Panzer *division*. In the same way Soviet tank *brigades* amounted to no more than Allied armoured *Battalions* and Soviet tank *Battalions* were only slightly larger than Allied or German tank *companies*; Soviet artillery *regiments*, like their British counterparts, were the size of American or German artillery *Battalions*.

In order to avoid confusion and to assist the reader, the equivalent German organisation will therefore be shown in brackets after the Soviet title in certain instances in this and subsequent Chapters.

Finally, on the subject of Soviet organisations, it is important to remember that the Red Army had been advancing since August 1944 and had suffered appalling casualties by this stage of the war – many of its formations, particularly the rifle divisions, were as much as 50% below strength. The scale of Soviet military casualties in WWII is difficult to comprehend: over five million deaths in action on land, sea and in the air, over one million died of wounds and nearly four and a half million missing.[2]

Tactics

By 1945 Soviet military thinking also differed considerably from that of both the Western Allies and the Germans. As far as the Soviets were concerned it mattered not at all that their enemy, even to the end, demonstrated a *tactical* supremacy on the battlefield; all that mattered to them was success in a series of inter-related operations, each of which was a step towards their ultimate *strategic* goal. Defeat or a reversal in one limited area could be sustained provided it enabled overwhelming forces to be concentrated in what the Soviets considered to be the main axis or area of operations. It was at this *operational* level of warfare that the Soviets generals were, by January 1945, outclassing their invaders.

For the purposes of this book there is no point in discussing Soviet offensive operations; for although the Red Army had seized the strategic initiative by January 1945 and was becoming increasingly confident and competent in breakthrough operations, it was Dietrich's Sixth Panzer Army – and in our case I SS Panzer Corps in particular – which was about to go over to the attack in Hungary. It is therefore the Soviet system of defence which concerns us at this particular time.

A typical Soviet army consisted, as we have said, of any number of corps from two to five. A three-corps army in defence usually had a depth of some 12 to 20km and relied on manoeuvre as the basis of that defence. A system of mutually supporting anti-tank strongpoints, each based on an anti-tank Battalion or regiment protected by infantry and minefields, was created in a checkerboard manner, with ambushes placed on the most important axes. Such an army usually deployed in a single echelon, but with anti-tank reserves and obstacle-creating and mine-laying detachments available for counter-penetration tasks. There was usually a reserve of one or two tank brigades (sixty-five tanks each) or a tank or mechanized corps (Panzer division) to deliver attacks into the flanks and rear of any breakthrough; and once the main enemy thrusts had been identified, units of any size would be stripped from quiet sectors to meet them. This ability to move forces quickly to meet changing combat requirements had been, and would continue to be, a major problem for the Germans. The redeployment of rifle corps between armies, rifle divisions between corps and even armies, and the constant movement of tank and mechanized corps (Panzer divisions) to meet rapidly changing situations, was often a source of wonder to those who had invented and practised Blitzkrieg. And to further complicate the situation for any attacker, behind the first echelon army or armies another army would provide the overall commander with Front second echelon forces.

At the tactical level Soviet armoured units were hampered by a desperate shortage of radios – normally only one per platoon – and inadequate crew training which sometimes amounted to as little as seventy-two hours; this led to poor use of ground and rigid geometric attack formations.

By January 1945 Soviet close air support was well developed and plentiful and was consistently used on targets beyond artillery range.

Equipment

The most famous item of Soviet equipment was of course the T-34 which became the most widely used tank of all time. When it first appeared on the battlefield in July 1941 it came as a complete surprise and instantly outclassed all German tanks then in service in fire-power, armour and performance.

Although the original T-34/76 was an impressive tank, it did in fact suffer from some serious failings. The most serious was a small, two-man, ergonomically inefficient turret which demanded that the commander had to observe the ground, co-ordinate his tank with that of his unit and load the main armament and coaxial machine-gun. In addition, the turret did not allow 360° vision and, when the German Tigers and Panthers began to appear in late 1942 and 1943, its 76.2mm gun was found to be inadequate. These drawbacks led, in the Spring of 1944, to the introduction of the splendid T-34/85 which had an 85mm gun, better armour and a three-man turret with all round vision; this was to be the main adversary of I SS Panzer Corps in 1945.

Other effective weapon systems in the Soviet armoury were the SU-76: a 76mm self-propelled gun capable of firing up to twenty rounds a minute; the SU-122 and SU-152, which provided self-propelled 122mm and 152mm close fire support for tank and mechanized corps; and the SU-100 which was a self-propelled 100mm tank destroyer. All these SUs, like the T-34/76s and T-34/85s, were produced in vast numbers and, with the exception of the SU-76, had the same armoured protection as the tanks.

Soviet tanks and self-propelled guns, unlike their Allied and German counterparts, used diesel fuel rather than gasoline.

A further point of interest relates to artillery. Readers will have noticed from Appendices VI and VII that, apart from a mere twenty 122mm guns, rifle divisions had no artillery pieces larger than 76mm, and even tank and mechanized corps were restricted to only twenty-one 85mm and twenty-one 122mm weapons – all self-propelled. Heavy guns and howitzers in the calibres of 122mm, 152mm and 203mm were formed into artillery brigades and divisions and usually controlled at Army and Front levels.

NOTES

1. Blumentritt, *The Fatal Decisions*, pp. 37–8.
2. According to figures published in Moscow in 1993.

CHAPTER XXIII

The Gran Bridgehead: 12 – 24 February

(Maps 24 & 25)

Author's Note: For the benefit of readers who may visit the 1945 Slovakian and Hungarian battlefields, current place names are shown on Maps 24 to 30 and in the text, rather than those used in 1945. The only exception to this is the Gran river which is now called the Hron.

Readers will recall that by mid-February 1945 the Red Army had succeeded, except in the Székesfehérvar area, in pushing the Germans back to their 1 January positions, and in retaining a considerable bridgehead across the Gran river north of Esztergom. This bridgehead was seen by the Germans as a potential assembly area for a major thrust towards Vienna and as such it had to be eliminated before they could launch their own Operation SPRING AWAKENING – the offensive to clear all Soviet forces from the area west of the Danube and north of the Drava rivers and to secure the Nagykanizsa oil deposits. This preliminary operation was given the code-name SOUTH WIND (SÜDWIND).

On 13 February Headquarters Army Group South ordered the commander of the German Eighth Army:

To attack, concentrating all available infantry and armoured forces, and accepting the consequent weakening of other front sectors, with the newly arrived I SS Panzer Corps. . . . After a short artillery preparation, to thrust from the north, to destroy the enemy in the Gran bridgehead.[1]

Although the bridgehead had existed for over a month, the Germans had no detailed intelligence of Soviet strengths or dispositions within it. The 13 February Operation Order merely stated that aerial photography and ground observation indicated that the Soviets were in a defensive posture and that as well as a Mechanized Corps[2] (Panzer Division) in the centre of the bridgehead, a Guards Mechanized Corps (Panzer Division) and a Guards Tank Corps (Panzer Division) 'with the attached Sixth Guards Tank Army [Panzer Corps] are probably located in the refitting area east of the Gran'. These units could be expected to reinforce the bridgehead if necessary. It added that there were known to be anti-tank blocking positions, supported by mortars, to the west of Bruty, a continuous 'fighting trench' running from Obid in the south, through Muzla and Gbelce, to just south of Bruty, that the Parizs canal formed a considerable obstacle due to flooding, and that although the roads and tracks were beginning to thaw out, they were not yet soft. Single bridges across the Gran existed at Bina and Kamenin and there were two more near Nana.

In fact the Soviets were much stronger than the Germans realised. As well as the Guards Mechanized Corps[3] (Panzer Division) already mentioned, which provided a centrally located mobile reserve, there were two Guards Rifle Corps in the bridgehead with a total of seven Rifle Divisions[4]. Five of the Rifle Divisions were in perimeter defence, while the other two provided second echelon defence in depth. Even if these Divisions were below strength, as suggested in the last Chapter, this would still mean that the Germans were up against well over 60,000 men with between 100 and 230 tanks and SUs, over 100 anti-tank guns, some 200 heavy mortars and over 200 guns and howitzers.

Containing the Soviet bridgehead before the opening of the German offensive were three German infantry Divisions, together with one Hungarian infantry Division and parts of another, supported by elements of a German Panzer Division.[5]

The Germans were correct in their appreciation that the Soviet forces were in a defensive posture. Although a new offensive was being planned, this would not take place until mid-March and in the meantime the troops west of the Gran were clearly vulnerable. The bridgehead was only 20km deep and 20km wide and, with a 30–40m wide river behind them, it was clearly going to be difficult to reinforce them or, in the worst case, withdraw them.

From the German point of view too, the forthcoming battle was not without its problems. Mounting the main attack from the south across the Danube was obviously out of the question and an attack from the west would run against the grain of the country. The Germans therefore chose to attack from the north. But even this had its difficulties: the Parizs canal (today narrow and silted up) was a major obstacle due to the early thawing of the winter snows, and in the final stages of the advance the assault force would be compressed into a narrow corridor, less than 10km wide, by a ridge to the south of Luba and the Danube river.

Operation SOUTH WIND was to be led by Panzer Corps Feldherrnhalle ('F').[6] This Corps consisted of three infantry Divisions[7] and an armoured group of some twenty-five tanks. Its initial task was to seize the high ground, particularly Point 190, to the south of Svodin, but the villages of Svodin and Bruty were to be taken from the rear and any fighting there was not to be allowed to interfere with the general advance south. I SS Panzer Corps was to follow closely behind Panzer Corps 'F' and, after crossing the Parizs canal, was to capture the ridge running east from Gbelce, before pushing on towards the Danube at Sturovo. A reinforced regimental group[8] from the Sixth Army south of the Danube, known as Regimental Group Hupe, was to establish a bridgehead across the river near Obid in the early phases of the offensive and cooperate with Priess's men attacking from the north.

The Luftwaffe was tasked with supporting SOUTH WIND by attacking known anti-tank defences south of Svodin and Bruty and in the Muzla-Luba sector, as well as delaying and destroying any Soviet reinforcements attempting to cross the Gran river.

12 – 16 February

During the period 12 to 15 February I SS Panzer Corps moved to a staging area around Nové-Zamky (Map 24). Tracked vehicles moved by rail and wheels by road. A platoon commander in the 9th SS Panzer Pioneer Company recalled:

> Rations were excellent. We learned from the civilian population the various uses of paprika. The people were very friendly. They recounted to us the good old days – Germany, Austria, Hungary. During the evenings we drove to see films in Nové-Zamky.[9]

Then, on the night of the 16th, the LAH and HJ moved again into a final assembly area behind Panzer Corps 'F'; the latter's infantry Divisions were located in and around the villages of Ruban, Dubnik, Velké and Kvetna, and the armoured group near Farna. This was an ideal forming up place – with rolling hills and plenty of cover – reminiscent of the part of Normandy lying north-west of the infamous Hill 112.

In readiness for the attack, SS Major General Otto Kumm, who readers will recall had only assumed command of the LAH on 15 February, divided the available parts of his Division into a Panzer-Grenadier Group under the command of Max Hansen and a Panzer Group under Jochen Peiper. The former consisted of parts of both the 1st and 2nd

SS Panzer-Grenadier Regiments, a detachment from the 1st SS Reconnaissance Battalion, SS Captain Otto Holst's 1st Company of the 1st SS Panzerjäger Battalion, and two 37mm Flak batteries. KG Peiper was made up of twenty-five Panthers and twenty-one Mk IVs in one Panzer Battalion under Werner Poetschke, nineteen Tiger IIs of Hein von Westernhagen's 501st SS Heavy Panzer Battalion, Jupp Diefenthal's 3rd SS (SPW) Panzer-Grenadier Battalion and part of the 1st SS Panzer Artillery Battalion under SS Captain Kalischko. According to Ralf Tiemann's *Die Leibstandarte* IV/2, the rest of the Division was still in transit to the new battle area when the offensive began.

In contrast, we get the impression from Hubert Meyer's History of the Hitlerjugend, that the 12th SS Panzer Division was more or less complete for SOUTH WIND and fought in its conventional groupings; he claims thirty-eight Mk IVs, forty-four Panthers and thirteen Jagdpanzer IVs were operational just before the attack. The only combat unit not mentioned in his account of the Gran bridgehead fighting is the 560th Heavy Panzerjäger Battalion.[10] If therefore we exclude this latter unit, we have a figure of 160 operational tanks and Jagdpanzers in I SS Panzer Corps at the beginning of Operation SOUTH WIND. This figure contrasts starkly with the 102 quoted by Army Group South[11] but lower figures were sometimes used by higher headquarters in the hope of obtaining further reinforcements.

17 – 21 February

Despite the widespread flooding and poor road conditions caused by the early thaw, Operation SOUTH WIND began at 0500 hours on 17 February. Leaving high ground on their right flank and with the Gran river on their left, the Germans attacked across open, rolling, agricultural land with few villages and no serious obstacles.

The artillery of I SS Panzer Corps joined in an opening barrage by the guns of Panzer Corps 'F' and in the most critical area of the attack – the centre – the Russians were taken by surprise. By 0900 hours the leading elements of the 46th Infantry Division were near Point 190, having penetrated the Soviet defences between Svodin and Bruty, but there they ran into an anti-tank screen and a few individual T-34/85s. After calling for support from the LAH, a successful attack was launched at 1140 hours and by 1700 hours elements of both the LAH and 46th Infantry Divisions had reached the Parizs canal in the area of Sarkan, only to find the bridges there destroyed. A loader in one of Peiper's tanks later remembered:

Peiper ordered five King Tigers to drive over the hill. What a sight!

As on a silver platter, they appeared on the hill and immediately began taking fire from the Russian anti-tank guns. We saw the shells bounce off the front of the Tigers. That must have been a shock for the Russians, especially since the Tigers destroyed one anti-tank gun after another. . . . Peiper immediately gave the order: 'Panzers – march!' A hurricane of fire was released as the KG drove over the hill in formation. . . . The tanks and SPWs drove at full speed, firing all barrels. . . . There was only one thing for the Russians to do – clear out. . . . KG Peiper suffered no losses.[12]

During the early part of the night a small infantry bridgehead was established by KG Hansen but no vehicles could cross. Nevertheless, it had been a good day for the LAH and its associated 46th Infantry Division – they had broken through the Soviet defences and advanced nearly 10km.

On the left flank things did not go nearly so well and the 211th Infantry Division of Panzer Corps 'F' was stopped in front of Bruty by the 72nd Guards Rifle Division in fortified positions, supported by anti-tank guns, mortars and artillery.

Similarly on the right flank, the 44th Infantry Division of Panzer Corps 'F' ran into strong opposition from the 6th Guards Airborne Division between Strekov and Svodin and it was only after tanks joined in the attack that further progress could be made. By 1700 hours Svodin had been captured and the advance continued towards the canal and Vieska.

What of the Hitlerjugend Division? It had followed on behind the LAH and during the afternoon the 26th SS Panzer-Grenadier Regiment was committed on the right flank of its sister Division to secure a crossing of the Parizs canal. The 1st Battalion of 'Papa' Krause's 26th Regiment, under the command of SS Major Kostenbader, managed to make a crossing just to the north of the large village of Gbelce by about 2100 hours and the 2nd Battalion, now under SS Captain Ott, followed into the shallow bridge-head. Soon after midnight Ott's Battalion had reached the road junction 1500m north-east of Gbelce and both Battalions then consolidated. A small canal crossing, capable of taking wheeled vehicles, was discovered in the same area. During the night the Russians counter-attacked with a Battalion of infantry and at least two T-34/85s but were beaten off, it is said with heavy casualties.

The commander of Army Group South, General Wöhler, was anxious that the Soviets should not be allowed to recover their balance and build up a second defensive line to the south of the canal; to this end and to cause a major distraction, the Hupe Regimental Group from south of the Danube was ordered to cross the river that same night. Despite the alleged presence of elements of the 93rd Guards Rifle Division in the Obid area, this was achieved without opposition.

In the early hours of the 18th KG Hansen expanded its small bridgehead and Leibstandarte Pioneers were able to bridge the Parizs canal. Four T-34s were claimed by Hansen's 6th SS Panzer-Grenadier Company during this fighting. Mines caused some further delay but soon after midday the first of Poetschke's Mk IVs and Panthers crossed the canal and, despite an air attack by Soviet fighter-bombers, by early evening KG Peiper had reached the Gbelce-Nana railway line, 3km north of Muzla.

Meanwhile, to the west of the LAH, Panzer Corps 'F''s 44th Infantry Division had forced a passage over the Parizs canal near Vieska and in the early afternoon its tanks too were able cross. Then, in conjunction with Krause's 26th SS Panzer-Grenadier Regiment, a joint attack was launched on Gbelce. The Feldherrnhalle Group was joined by SS Major Hermann Brand's 3rd SS SPW mounted Panzer-Grenadier Battalion and they took the western part of the town, whilst Kostenbader's 1st Battalion captured the eastern sector and Ott's 2nd Battalion went on to secure the high ground 2km farther east. By evening infantry and armour of Panzer Corps 'F' were in possession of Point 129, 3km south of Gbelce, and in contact with the Leibstandarte.

Readers will have noticed that the only part of the Hitlerjugend so far mentioned as a participant in the fighting has been Krause's 26th SS Panzer-Grenadier Regiment. It is possible therefore that, despite previous comments, the rest of the Division did not arrive in time to take part in the actions on 17 and 18 February.

On the 19th the weather improved, with sunshine and temperatures of +6° Celsius, and at 0530 hours I SS Panzer Corps resumed its attack. KG Hansen of the Leibstandarte was given the task of clearing the enemy from the vine-covered ridge south of Point 250, while KG Peiper resumed its advance on the north side of the Gbelce-Nana railway. It was by no means an easy advance – as SS Lieutenant Rolf Reiser later described:

In the early morning our assembly was considerably delayed by a Russian fighter-bomber attack; we suffered the loss of several tanks and wounded. . . . We set out astride the road with seven tanks of the 1st Company. I advanced . . . between the road and railway line with the three Panthers of my Platoon. . . . Ivan attacked our open right flank at short range with tanks from behind the cover of the railway embankment. One of the Panthers . . . was hit and stalled. . . . SS Senior Sergeant Strelow, the 3rd Platoon leader, set up to the right of me. Then there was a detonation a short distance away and his tank was ablaze. I drove behind a shed and slowly probed the other side until I had the T-34 broad-side in front of me – no more than 50m away. . . . He burst into flames on the first shot, the turret flew off after the second! Then the Tigers and Panthers of the 2nd Company caught up and joined in the armoured battle. Two more enemy tanks were destroyed.[13]

Farther to the west, SS Captain Hans Siegel's 2nd SS Panzer Battalion of the Hitlerjugend, with Brand's SPW mounted 3rd SS Panzer-Grenadier Battalion attached, had formed up during the night to the south of Gbelce, protected by the 25th and 26th SS Panzer-Grenadier Regiments. They too advanced at 0530 hours, with Grenadiers leading the way on both sides of the Sturovo road in case of mines and the tanks on the road itself. Shortly before daybreak KG Siegel came under artillery and anti-tank gun fire from Muzla but a quick attack, led by SS Lieutenant Helmut Gaede's 1st SS Panzer Company, took the village and the surrounding area was soon cleared by the 1st and 2nd Battalions of the 26th Regiment.

Whilst the HJ was preparing to resume its advance on Sturovo on the south side of the Muzla-Sturovo road by way of Obid, the Division suffered a serious loss. SS Lieutenant Colonel Bernhard 'Papa' Krause was killed in a surprise rocket attack. He had been a stalwart of the HJ since its foundation and was revered by all its members. SS Major Kostenbader immediately took over the 26th Regiment and SS Captain Schmidt assumed command of its 1st Battalion.

The advance began again soon after midday, with the HJ moving on Sturovo from the south-west and KG Peiper of the Leibstandarte from the north-west.

At about 1300 hours, when they were some 3km short of Sturovo, the infantry element of KG Peiper – Diefenthal's 3rd SS SPW mounted Panzer-Grenadier Battalion – swung north-east to attack Nana, while Poetschke's Mk IVs and Panthers and von Westernhagen's Tiger IIs were joined by twenty StuGs and infantry of the Hupe Regimental Group from the Obid area for the assault on Sturovo. In his citation for Poetschke's Oakleaves, Peiper wrote:

Rushing headlong and firing wildly, his tanks overran the anti-tank nests in front of Muzla and Sturovo, and after making contact with the Southern Group [Hupe], which had been ferried over the Danube in assault boats, . . . pushed through to Esztergom.[14]

At the same time an assault group from an infantry Division[15] holding Esztergom, crossed the Danube[16] and joined in the attack. The Russians had no chance in this vulnerable corner of their bridgehead and before last light the men of I SS Panzer Corps were gazing at Esztergom cathedral, standing like a sentinel above the far bank of the mighty Danube. They knew they had completed the hardest part of their task – Nana and Sturovo were in the hands of the Leibstandarte and Hitlerjugend. In passing, it has to be said that the coordination of such an attack, involving troops from four different Divisions, could not have been without its problems.

In other relevant actions on 19 February, Batorove Kosihy and Buc were occupied by a KG of Army Group South following their evacuation by the Russians and the 44th Infantry Division of Panzer Corps 'F' captured Kravany on the Danube and the forest to its east. In the eastern part of the bridgehead the 46th Infantry Division, with armoured support, had cleared the wooded, hilly area just to the west of Kamenny Most but, north of the Parizs canal, other elements of the Division were repulsed by a Soviet counter-attack 2km short of Kamenin. In the north, Bruty remained firmly in Russian hands.

From the outset of Operation SOUTH WIND the Germans had been worried that the Soviets would attempt to reinforce their bridgehead. They had correctly identified parts of the IV Guards Mechanized Corps (Panzer Division) in the northern part of the bridgehead but they were particularly worried about the whereabouts of the Sixth Guards Tank Army, and when aerial reconnaissance reported 3,000 vehicles moving north from the Budapest area, they became alarmed. Orders were issued for immediate night attacks on Kamenny Most and Kamenin. Leaving the bulk of the LAH armoured group in Sturovo to replenish, the Mk IVs of KG Peiper, with part of the 46th Division, therefore attacked from Nana along the Kamenny Most road, whilst another part of the 46th Division advanced north of the Parizs canal on Kamenin. Both attacks failed and Soviet air superiority and artillery fire from the east back of the Gran precluded any further attempts during daylight on the 20th.

A two-phase operation was then ordered. In the first phase, the LAH and 46th Infantry Division were to take Kamenny Most in the south of the remaining bridgehead, whilst the HJ, with support from the 211th VGD, was to secure Bruty in the north. In a second and final phase, the twin Divisions of I SS Panzer Corps would clear Kamenin and Bina respectively.

Parts of KGs Peiper and Hansen, with support from the 46th Division, successfully entered Kamenny Most during the night of the 21st but soon after dawn they were forced on to the defensive by Soviet artillery fire and continuous air attacks. In Poetschke's citation for Oakleaves, Peiper wrote:

> In the battle for the rest of the bridgehead, Poetschke and his tank unit engaged in bitter night fighting on 21 February at Kamenny Most.

And Rolf Reiser recalled:

> Peiper had decided upon a night attack because we were covered by massive fire during the daytime from enemy artillery positions on the raised eastern bank of the Gran. . . . We rapidly crossed the softly rolling terrain directly under the chain of hills that ran west of the

road and railway line. . . . We turned east . . . in order to penetrate frontally. Then massive Russian artillery fire was initiated. A curtain of iron and fire hung before us. Flares and tracers illuminated the night and showed us the way to the enemy positions. . . . We rattled across the railway – then there was a crack and flash of light. We were hit! . . . We caught fire immediately. . . . my gunner followed me as the last one out of the turret. We landed in a trench with Ivan, who was as surprised as we were. Armed only with pistols and bare fists, we defended ourselves . . . we finished off the Soviets in the cover of the burning tank and the exploding ammunition.[17]

Meanwhile, during the 20th and 21st, the Hitlerjugend was relieved by the 44th Infantry Division and moved to a new assembly south-east of Farna in readiness for its assault on Bruty. I SS Panzer Corps was thus poised for its final battles west of the Gran river. With aerial reconnaissance and other intelligence sources confirming that the IV Guards Mechanized Corps (Panzer Division) had withdrawn across the Gran and other troop movements towards the river apparently halted, Hermann Priess and his men had every reason to be confident of success. Headquarters Army Group South concluded that the Soviets must be expecting a German assault across the Gran and were therefore preparing defensive positions on the east bank with all available reinforcements. In fact Hitler had forbidden any such assault and demanded that his Leibstandarte Corps be freed as soon as possible for his new offensive, SPRING AWAKENING, in the Lake Balaton area.

22 February

In preparation for his attack on Bruty, Hugo Kraas had to rely mainly on aerial reconnaissance and on information provided by the 211th VGD which had already failed to take the village. This revealed that the area was heavily fortified, with minefields backed by large numbers of machine-guns, mortars and anti-tank guns in considerable depth. Since the ground was completely open, Kraas decided on a night operation.

The preliminary phases of the attack were marred by a number of unfortunate incidents. Müller's 25th SS Panzer-Grenadier Regiment, on the right flank, failed to reach its start-line in time for the assault and, in the darkness, some of Siegel's tanks failed to recognise Kostenbader's Grenadiers who were leading the attack on the left and opened fire on them; five men were killed, including a company commander, and another eight wounded. This second disaster alerted the Russians who opened fire with machine-guns and mortars.

Despite these problems, Siegel's tanks began their attack at about 0445 hours in the wake of a bombardment by artillery, mortars and Werfers. Within minutes however, the leading tanks ran into a minefield and several, including Siegel's, were immobilized. These were repaired under fire and the tanks then withdrew behind a reverse slope from where they supported the attack of the 9th SPW mounted Panzer-Grenadier Company, led by SS Lieutenant Dieter Schmidt; this Company was on the left flank of the attack and outside the minefield. Although some of its SPWs floundered in the soft ground of a stream bed, the rest managed to break through the defenders and reach the southern edge of the village.

In the meantime, Müller's 25th Regiment had joined in the attack and together with the other two Battalions of Kostenbader's 26th Regiment, the western and lower sector of the village was taken.

SS Sergeant Burdack of the SPW Battalion later described the scene:

> The village was choked with enemy vehicles. . . . Several T-34s and T-43s [light tanks], still inside the village, forced the SPWs to take cover. . . . The Russian tanks, without the protection of infantry, left . . . in the direction of Bina.[18]

And SS Lieutenant Ross, who was in Brand's SPW, remembered:

> Fire from our heavy weapons had badly damaged most of the buildings. Roofs had been stripped off, walls had crumbled. During the pitched battle, civilians came out of the ruins of their houses . . . unconcerned with what was going on around them. . . . They were obviously happy beyond measure to be liberated again from their 'liberators'.[19]

Bruty was finally cleared by Müller's Regiment later that morning in conjunction with troops of the 211th VGD who had advanced on the right flank of the HJ and entered the village from the south. Eighty prisoners were taken and a large number of anti-tank guns and mortars, two undamaged T-34s and six large calibre howitzers were found in the area. Bruty was in German hands but the cost had been high – particularly in the 25th Regiment.

In the meantime, in preparation for the assault on Kamenin, elements of KG Peiper had secured the road junction immediately north of Kamenny Most.

23 – 24 February

I SS Panzer Corps spent 23 February preparing for its final assaults on Kamenin and Bina. The Leibstandarte, with elements of the 46th

Infantry Division, was to attack the former and the Hitlerjugend, still with support from the 211th VGD, was to secure Bina and its bridge across the Gran. Intelligence sources indicated that there were elements of two motorized brigades still in the bridgehead. H-Hour was set for 0200 hours on the 24th.

In the HJ sector the most bitter fighting occurred in the area of the railway line which runs north-south just to the west of Bina. This had been heavily fortified, as had some of the flood dykes, but by using the main Kvetna-Bina road as their axis and taking advantage of the gently sloping ground, which dropped some 30m down to the village, the tanks and SS Panzer-Grenadiers soon overcame all resistance and by 0830 hours the village had fallen. The last Russians blew the Gran bridge as they withdrew.

In the southern part of the bridgehead, elements of the 46th Infantry Division moved on Kamenin from the west, while the LAH attacked from due south. The Mk IVs, Panthers and Tigers of KG Peiper used the main road as their axis and soon encountered a screen of thirty-seven anti-tank guns sited on the dominating ground to the south of the village. Nevertheless, the attack was pressed home without regard to possible casualties and the sheer power of the armoured assault was too much for the Russians who abandoned their guns and fled. Hansen's Grenadiers followed up and after some bitter house-to-house fighting the defence was broken. By late afternoon the Gran bridgehead had been eliminated.

The Germans claimed seventy-one tanks, 179 guns, howitzers and anti-tank guns, 537 prisoners and 2,069 Russian dead in the fighting up to 22 February.[20] Of these, Peiper credits Werner Poetschke's mixed SS Panzer Battalion with twenty-three T-34s destroyed, thirty Hungarian, Italian, British and German built tanks captured and 280 enemy killed.[21] According to a return signed by Fritz Kraemer, the Chief of Staff of the Sixth Panzer Army, I SS Panzer Corps suffered 2,989 casualties, including 413 killed in the same period and, rather surprisingly, only three Mk IVs, six Panthers and two Tigers lost or in need of long-term repair. Figures quoted in the Histories of the LAH and HJ would indicate that this is a major understatement.

Operation SOUTH WIND was, without doubt, a brilliant success. In eight days I SS Panzer Corps, admittedly with valuable assistance from Panzer Corps Feldherrnhalle, had recaptured over 400 square kilometres of territory, inflicted 8,800 casualties on the Red Army[22] and cleared seven infantry Divisions and a Guards Mechanized Corps (Panzer Division) from west of the Gran. It is remarkable that such an effective fighting machine could have been produced within a month of the Ardennes disaster – the more so when one takes into account that many of the men involved had received only minimal training. As Otto Kumm described the Leibstandarte:

The Division was in miserable shape, only a shadow of its former self. After the heavy losses in Normandy and during the Ardennes offensive, it had only recently been refitted with personnel who were poorly trained former members of the Army, Navy, Air Force, labour service and police.[23]

The performance of both the LAH and the HJ in SOUTH WIND can be explained only by superb leadership, high morale and fighting spirit and a brilliant reinforcement and replacement system.

That said, the question arises as to whether this elite SS Panzer Corps should have been used in this operation at all. Despite all the measures taken to disguise the arrival of the Sixth Panzer Army on the Hungarian front, units of I SS Panzer Corps were soon detected in the Gran bridgehead operation. Its commitment there, rather than in the northern part of the Eastern Front, and the knowledge that a second SS Panzer Corps had arrived in Hungary, immediately alerted the Soviets to the possibility of a German offensive. It is also obvious that the premature use of the Corps interrupted the proper refitting of the two SS Panzer Divisions and indeed, actually ensured that their effectiveness in SPRING AWAKENING would be reduced. Taken together, these facts indicate that the use of I SS Panzer Corps in Operation SOUTH WIND was a serious mistake. The Chief Operations Officer of the Sixth Panzer Army, SS Lieutenant Colonel Georg Maier, expressed similar thoughts in his book *Drama Between Budapest and Vienna*, published in 1975.

NOTES

1. Meyer, *The History of the 12th SS Panzer Division Hitlerjugend*, p. 286.
2. IV Gds Mech Corps.
3. IV Gds Mech Corps.
4. XXIV Gds Rifle Corps with the 6th Gds Airborne, 72nd and 81st Gds Rifle Divs and XXV Gds Rifle Corps with the 63rd, 375th & 409th Rifle Divs and the 93rd Gds Rifle Div.
5. The 44th Reichsgrenadier Div 'Hoch und Deutschmeister', the 46th Inf & 211th VG Divs, the 20th and parts of the 23rd Hungarian Inf Divs and elements of 13th Pz Div.
6. The original Feldherrnhalle Div was destroyed at Stalingrad in 1943. Reformed as a Pz-Gren Div, the bulk of the Div was trapped in Budapest at the end of 1944 but some of its armour escaped and gave Pz Corps 'F' its title.
7. 44th Reichsgrenadier Div, 46th Inf Div & 211th VGD.
8. From the 96th Inf Div.
9. Tiemann, *Die Leibstandarte* IV/2, p. 231. In 1945 the area immediately north of the Danube was part of Hungary (see Map 24); today it is part of Slovakia.

10. This Bn was not formally part of the HJ but had of course fought with it in the Ardennes and would do so again the following month.
11. Meyer, op. cit., p. 291.
12. Tiemann, op. cit., p. 237.
13. Ibid., pp. 241–2.
14. Citation signed by Peiper on 26 Feb 45; recommendation supported by Otto Kumm and Oakleaves awarded 15 Mar 45.
15. 711th Inf Div.
16. The remains of the old bridge across the Danube at Esztergom are still visible but today there is no bridge between Slovakia and Hungary at this point.
17. Tiemann, op. cit., pp. 245–6.
18. Meyer, op. cit., p. 290.
19. Ibid.
20. Army Group South War Diary.
21. As Note 14.
22. Soviet figure.
23. Tiemann, op. cit., p. 250.

CHAPTER XXIV
SPRING AWAKENING
The Setting
(Maps 26 & 27)

Hitler's aims for Operation SPRING AWAKENING were as wildly ambitious as those he had laid down for AUTUMN MIST in the Ardennes three months previously. They were: to destroy the Soviet forces in the region bounded by Lake Balaton and the Danube and Drava rivers, secure the Hungarian oil deposits, and establish bridgeheads over the Danube with a view to further offensive operations.

The attack was to be carried out between Lakes Balaton and Valencei in the north by Sepp Dietrich's Sixth Panzer Army[1] and the III Panzer Corps[2] of Balck's Sixth Army, and in the south, between the Drava river and the south-west corner of Lake Balaton, by the Second Panzer Army[3] (part of Army Group South-East and a 'Panzer' Army in name only).

Serious concerns were expressed by Sepp Dietrich and his senior staff officers that as the Sixth Panzer Army and III Panzer Corps moved south-east, they would become increasingly vulnerable to any counter offensive launched by the Soviet forces already located north of Székesfehérvar and west of the Danube. These comprised a Soviet Army of three Rifle Corps, backed by a Guards Mechanized Corps (Panzer Division).[4] Since, as will become evident, Balck's Sixth Army defences in this area[5] were woefully inadequate, these concerns were fully justified. Nevertheless, a proposal that these Soviet forces should be dealt first, or at least engaged, was rejected by Hitler and the date of the offensive confirmed as 6 March.

For its premier role in this final German offensive in WWII, Dietrich's Sixth Panzer Army was reinforced to a strength of six Divisions: I SS Panzer Corps with the Leibstandarte and Hitlerjugend; II SS Panzer Corps with the 2nd SS Das Reich and 9th SS Hohenstaufen Panzer Divisions; and I Cavalry Corps with the 3rd and 4th Cavalry Divisions.[6] The latter were genuine mounted troops and were a considerable asset in the conditions of the Eastern Front where the horse sometimes had advantages over motorized transport.

Whilst the Germans were preparing SPRING AWAKENING, the Soviets were planning their own offensive which was due to start on 15 March. It was designed to capture Vienna and was to be launched by the Second and Third Ukrainian Fronts (Army Groups) with four Armies.[7] However, during the Gran bridgehead fighting the Soviets learned of the impending German offensive and were able to change their posture to meet it. Even so STAVKA, the Supreme Soviet Headquarters, decreed that two of the Armies[8] due to take part in the Vienna offensive were to continue their preparations and were not to be included in any defensive planning.

Since the main German threat was known to be in the Third Ukrainian Front sector, the Soviets concentrated the bulk of their forces between Lake Balaton and a point some 20km to the north of Székesfehérvar. Here Marshal Tolbukhin massed three Armies, together with two Tank Corps (Panzer Divisions) and a Guards Mechanized Corps (Panzer Division).[9] According to the Soviet Official History[10], his forces totalled 407,000 men, 6,890 guns and mortars, 407 tanks and self propelled guns and 965 aircraft, but it is likely that many of his formations were much weaker than these figures indicate.

The Third Ukrainian Front commander reasoned that if and when the Germans attacked, they would be sufficiently weakened by the depth of his defences for him to be able to launch his own offensive as originally planned, using the STAVKA reserve Armies and any forces unaffected by the fighting.

German intelligence of the Soviet defences was good. Although it failed to identify the correct designation and exact positioning of every formation, it estimated the number of Armies, Corps and Divisions in the attack area with remarkable accuracy. Its only serious errors were in not detecting a Guards Mechanized Corps (Panzer Division) and a Guards Cavalry Corps[11] in the path of the Sixth Panzer Army, and the positions of two of the three Corps of Tolbukhin's second echelon Army astride the Danube.[12]

To the north of the Third Ukrainian Front, Marshal Malinowski's Second

Ukrainian Front numbered some half a million men and another 600 tanks, but over 400 of these were in STAVKA reserve for the forthcoming offensive.

The part of the SPRING AWAKENING offensive[13] in which we are interested can be narrowed down to the area between Lakes Balaton and Valencei. There, as already mentioned, the attack involved Sepp Dietrich's Sixth Panzer Army and the III Panzer Corps of the Sixth Army, with some 300 tanks and assault guns. These forces were opposed by over 1,200 guns and mortars[14] and in theory, but in the event not in practice, by some 300 Russian tanks and SUs.

I SS Panzer Corps: 25 February – 5 March

We have heard how the Leibstandarte and Hitlerjugend Divisions suffered nearly 3,000 casualties during SOUTH WIND. However, in the nine days available before the opening of SPRING AWAKENING, the refitting and replacement system did its best to bring the Divisions back up to strength. We know that the LAH had a combat strength of 12,461 two days after the offensive started and that there were 'three strong, one medium strength and three average Battalions available for the attack'[15]; doubtless it received a similar number of reinforcements to the HJ – 1,123 including twenty-three officers and sixty NCOs.[16] Many of them were from the Navy and Luftwaffe:

> We received replacements, more than fifty NCOs and men per company, formerly of the Luftwaffe but they already wore our uniforms. None of them had any infantry experience.[17]

And some men arrived in the forward assembly areas only twenty-four hours before H-Hour:

> More replacements reached us. . . . This time they were exclusively Schwabians . . ., aged from seventeen to thirty-five. Over sixty infantrymen. All of them 'young' soldiers that had left their homes for the first time and were correspondingly depressed. . . . Could the young sons of farmers find a new home with us?[18]

The wheeled transport situation remained a problem, with a 28% shortfall in the LAH and 50% in the HJ, and in terms of armoured vehicles the picture was far from satisfactory. Although the tank and Jagdpanzer units appeared reasonably strong on paper, the number of operational vehicles was depressingly low. The LAH numbered only fourteen Mk IVs, twenty-six Panthers, fifteen Jagdpanzers and StuGs operational on 6 March, and the 501st SS Heavy Panzer Battalion was down to just four

Tiger IIs. In the case of the HJ, only twelve of the thirty-four Mk IVs, nine of the thirty Panthers and thirteen of the thirty-one Jagdpanzer IVs were combat-ready when the attack started. Its attached 560th Heavy Panzerjäger Battalion had fourteen Jagdpanzer IVs and Vs. In total strength I SS Panzer Corps had just over 100 tanks and Jagdpanzers and thirty-three heavy towed anti-tank guns ready for action on 6 March.

The only significant personnel changes were in the Hitlerjugend, where SS Lieutenant Colonel Martin Gross had arrived to take change of the 12th SS Panzer Regiment and a Major Goldammer was now commanding the attached 560th Heavy Panzerjäger Battalion.

In preparation for the attack, the Divisions of I SS Panzer Corps moved initially to a general holding area some 40km to the south of Györ (Map 24), thence between 3 and 4 March to staging areas in the forested areas north of Polgardi and finally, on the 4th and 5th, to their forward assembly areas 10km farther to the south-east. Due to the appalling ground conditions, most of the Panzer-Grenadiers had to march the last 10km.

The state of the ground caused great anxiety. At the end of February the weather had become unexpectedly warm, +11° Celsius by day, and as the ground thawed all movement became difficult and cross-country movement, even by tracked vehicles, virtually impossible. The onset of what is called 'razputitza', a three- to four-week period of almost complete immobility in spring and autumn due to muddy conditions, did not augur well for Hitler's last offensive, particularly in the HJ sector where there were no suitable roads and few tracks. Dietrich's Chief Operations Officer reported:

In the constricted area between Lakes Balaton and Valencei the mud became alarming. The closer one came to the . . . assembly area, the more widespread the land that was under water – impassable for all kinds of vehicles. It looked the same . . . in the enemy area, as far as the terrain permitted observation.

He added the comment:

A Panzer attack in open terrain under these conditions is out of the question.[19]

As a result of this report a request was made to Headquarters Army Group South that the attack should be postponed for at least two days and Dietrich himself asked General Guderian at OKH to support the proposal – to no avail.

Despite all the problems, the LAH had assembled on the left of the Corps, just to the north-west of Soponya, by the night of 5-6 March, and the

HJ was on its right near Kislang. The Bozot river was the inter-Divisional boundary, giving each Division an attack frontage of about 7km. To the left of Priess's Corps, II SS Panzer Corps formed up to the north of Aba. Its Das Reich and Hohenstaufen Divisions, which had not of course participated in the Gran bridgehead fighting, had 131 tanks and Jagdpanzers and seventy-one heavy towed anti-tank guns between them. The Sarviz canal, which together with the adjacent 15m wide Sarviz river formed a major obstacle, was the inter-Corps boundary. On the right of I SS Panzer Corps, the I Cavalry Corps was to be found north of Enying. Units of Balck's Sixth Army were manning the forward defences in front of these assault forces.[20]

The initial objective of the I Cavalry and I SS Panzer Corps was the Sio canal between Szabadhidvég and Simontornya, 15km and 25km away respectively.

The ground to the south-east of Polgardi rises, almost imperceptibly, from a shallow basin to a high plain and, as well the Sarviz canal and river, two other rivers run south-east (in the general direction of the attack); both are obstacles in themselves and are fed by numerous streams. The whole area is virtually flat and featureless, with few reference points. Visibility from the height of a tank turret is some 2km but a man on his feet can see no more than 100m.[21]

There were only two hard-surface roads in the area of the attack and even these had been turned into rivers of mud by the thaw. One, fortunately for the LAH, ran almost directly from Szabadbattyan via Soponya to Simontornya. The other, which cut diagonally across the HJ's axis of advance, also ran to Simontornya, but from Balatonkenese in the I Cavalry Corps sector, via Enying.

The Soviet Defence

The Soviet defences between Lakes Balaton and Valencei were in great depth – on average some 30km. Six Rifle Divisions were in the first echelon between the Lakes – two opposite II SS Panzer Corps, two facing I SS Panzer Corps and two to the east of Lake Balaton in front of I Cavalry Corps. The equivalent of another division[22] was opposing III Panzer Corps just to the south of Lake Valencei. Between Sarbogard, Mezökomarom and the south-east edge of Lake Balaton, four more Rifle Divisions, two of which were in the path of I SS Panzer Corps, provided second echelon defence. A Tank Corps (Panzer Division) provided a mobile reserve. Six more Rifle Divisions were to be found in a third defensive belt on the west bank of the Danube, less than 20km east of Seregélyes in the north of the zone, and a Guards Mechanized Corps (Panzer Division), Guards Cavalry Corps of three Divisions and a further Rifle Division were positioned farther south. The Sixth Panzer Army had indeed been given a formidable task.

Looking at I SS Panzer Corps' front in more detail, we find the 68th Guards Rifle Division[23] and part of the 233rd Rifle Division[24] entrenched in front of the LAH and the rest of the same Rifle Division opposing the HJ. Behind them the 236th Rifle Division, which arrived only the day before the attack, took up a position between Dég and the Sio canal; this gave an overall depth of some 20 to 25km. XVIII Tank Corps (Panzer Division), with a minimum of seventy-five tanks and SUs, provided a mobile reserve 15km to the east of Aba.

We are fortunate in having the benefit of a very detailed Russian Study[25] on the Lake Balaton offensive which gives the strength and dispositions of the 233rd Rifle Division opposing the Hitlerjugend and part of the Leibstandarte. Although the Study is written in the 'heroic' style and perhaps, for understandable reasons, quotes the *total* rather than the *operational* number of German tanks engaged in the forthcoming battle, it gives a fascinating picture of the Soviet defences opposite I SS Panzer Corps.

The Study says the 233rd Rifle Division had, between 18 February and 5 March, dug 27km of trenches, 130 gun and mortar positions, 113 dugouts, seventy command posts and observation points and laid 4,249 anti-tank and 5,058 anti-personnel mines – all this on a frontage of 5km! It goes on to quote a figure of 114 guns and mortars, including six 122mm howitzers and thirty-three 120mm mortars for the Division, giving an average of twenty-two guns and mortars per kilometre of front, with up to sixty-seven being able to fire on the most important axes. Although there were no tanks in this defensive zone, there was an average of seventeen anti-tank guns per kilometre, forming twenty-three tank 'killing grounds'.

The Division was deployed with two Regiments forward – one directly opposing the HJ and the other in the path of the right flank of the LAH. The third Regiment was sited on the western flank in greater depth and was given counter-attack tasks into what the Divisional commander, Colonel Cidorenko, considered to be the three areas of vital ground. This Regiment would also find itself opposing the HJ.

In terms of strength the Study claims that on 6 March Cidorenko's Division was 70% below its authorised strength and that its Regiments, with an average strength of only 665 men each, had therefore been reduced to two instead of three Battalions. This may well be true, but just as we have seen the Germans exaggerate their losses so that the actions of the survivors appear more heroic, so it is more than likely that the real Divisional strength was in fact higher – at least in the region of 40% of authorised establishment, or in other words nearer 5,000 than the 3,500 quoted.

The defences which the HJ was required to penetrate were made up of three zones. The first, 1 to 1½km deep, consisted of two continuous trench lines and parts of a third. Some 1½ to 2km farther back there was another position comprising one continuous and one intermittent trench and then, 3 to 5km from the front line, lay a final trench line and strongpoint. We can assume that the 68th Guards Rifle Division opposite the Leibstandarte was deployed in the same way.

NOTES

1. The Sixth Panzer Army is usually described as the Sixth *SS* Panzer Army to distinguish it from the Sixth Army, but this was not its correct title.
2. 1st and 3rd Pz Divs and the 356th Inf Div.
3. LXVIII Army Corps and XXII Mountain Corps with the 16th SS Pz-Gren & 13th SS Mountain Divs and three inf divs.
4. The Forty-Sixth Army with three Rifle Corps and II Gds Mech Corps (Pz Div).
5. Astride and north of Székesfehérvar, Army Gp Balck comprised the Third Hungarian Army with two Corps and Gille's depleted IV SS Pz Corps. The 6th Pz Div was also part of Balck's Army Gp, but Hubert Meyer claims that only the 'armoured elements' of the Div were present.
6. Each div comprised two regts, each of two bns, supported by partly motorized units including recce and anti-tank bns, an arty regt and an engr coy.
7. Fourth & Ninth Gds Armies, Forty-Sixth Army and the Sixth Gds Tk Army.
8. Sixth Gds Tk Army with V Gds Tk Corps (Pz Div) & IX Gds Mech Corps (Pz Div) and Ninth Gds Army with nine Rifle Divs.
9. Twenty-Sixth Army with CIV, CXXXV & XXX Rifle Corps and XVIII Tk Corps (Pz Div); Fourth Gds Army with XXI, XX & XXXI Gds Rifle Corps and XXIII Tk Corps (Pz Div); Twenty-Seventh Army with XXXIII, XXXV & XXXVII Rifle Corps; I Gds Mech Corps (Pz Div) in reserve.
10. IVOVSS, Vol 5, Pt 1, p. 195. But, as an example of reduced strengths, A. I. Radzievskiy in his *Army Operations* claims the XVIII Tk Corps (Pz Div) numbered only seventy-five tanks & SUs; the official establishments of the XVIII and XXIII Tk Corps and I Gds Mech Corps totalled 604 tanks and 166 SUs.
11. Three divisions, each with an official strength of about 5,000 men and including SU, anti-tank, mortar and AA Battalions.
12. Twenty-Seventh Army.
13. Known to the Germans as the Plattensee Offensive.
14. Radzievskiy, *Army Operations*, p. 204.
15. Tiemann, *Die Leibstandarte IV/2*, p. 262.
16. Meyer, *The History of the 12th SS Panzer Division Hitlerjugend*, p. 292.
17. Tiemann, op. cit., pp. 258–9.
18. Ibid., p. 261.
19. Ibid., p. 259.
20. 23rd Pz Div with approximately thirty tanks and assault guns and the 44th (German) Inf & 25th (Hungarian) Inf Divs.
21. The area south-west of Soponya and Kaloz and south of Kislang, known as the Mezöföld, is today a very poor area and difficult to enter – even in a

four-wheel drive vehicle; there is little to see there other than rundown or abandoned farmsteads.

22. 1st Gds Fortified Region; about the same size as a Rifle div but stronger in MGs and arty.
23. Part of XXX Rifle Corps.
24. Part of CXXXV Rifle Corps.
25. Appendix 21 of the Soviet Frunze Military Academy Study on the Lake Balaton Offensive by Lt Col V F Yashin.

CHAPTER XXV

The Balaton Offensive: 6 – 18 March

(Maps 26 & 27)

6 March

On the day of the German offensive snow was falling from low cloud and the temperature hovered on either side of 0° Celsius. Tracks were soft and although the ground was frozen near the surface, men and vehicles sank into thick mud the moment they moved off the few roads available. Conditions were very similar to those experienced in the Ardennes only three months previously.

In the Leibstandarte sector the attack against the 68th Guards Rifle Division began with an artillery barrage at 0430 hours. SS Lieutenant Colonel Siebken's 2nd SS Panzer-Grenadier Regiment, after crossing a substantial minefield, succeeded in taking Point 149, 5km to the north-east of Kislang, soon after midday; but when Werner Poetschke's 1st SS Panzer Battalion and SPWs of Jupp Diefenthal's SS Panzer-Grenadier Battalion (some eighty armoured vehicles according to the Russians) attempted to move past the west side of Point 149, they ran into a well prepared Regiment[1] of the 233rd Rifle Division and after only 2km the advance stalled in soft terrain. The Rifle Division claimed four tanks and three SPWs knocked out in the day's fighting and the LAH commander, Otto Kumm, admitted losing a number of tanks in the minefields.

On the left (eastern) flank of the Corps sector, the 2nd and 3rd Battalions of Max Hansen's 1st SS Panzer-Grenadier Regiment managed to penetrate into the western part of Soponya after hand-to-hand fighting against part of the 68th Guards Division. A member of the 6th Company reported:

> When we reached the Russian trench system we found directly in front of it a long row of dug in flame-throwers which could be set off electrically . . . our Panzer-Grenadiers ran into a wall of flame.[2]

SS Captain Otto Holst of the 1st SS Panzerjäger Battalion said later:

The 2nd Company had the mission of supporting the infantry attack against Soponya along the Kaloz road. The 3rd Company was to support the 3rd Battalion on the right. . . . The frozen ground turned bottomless. Of the seven operational Jagdpanzers of the 3rd Company, six quickly became hopelessly stuck. They sank up to their track guards. . . . the infantry companies continued without our support.[3]

According to the Russians[4], the German artillery barrage in the Hitlerjugend sector did not start until 0520 hours and it was 0600 before the first enemy appeared in front of their forward defences. Müller's 25th SS Panzer-Grenadier Regiment advanced on the right flank, with the 1st SS Pioneer Company attached, whilst Kostenbader's 26th Regiment, less its SPW Battalion but with the 2nd SS Pioneer Company under command, moved forward from the Kislang assembly area. Their immediate objectives[5] were some 4km and 2½km south-east of their start-lines. SS Captain Brockschmidt's 12th SS Panzerjäger Battalion with its thirteen Jagdpanzers was due to follow up soon after dawn when the crews would have enough light to detect and engage enemy anti-tank guns and strongholds. Hans Siegel's Mk IVs and Panthers, supported by Brand's SPW Battalion, waited for the Grenadiers to make a breakthrough. Once this was achieved their task was to penetrate the rear areas as rapidly as possible and reach the Sio canal around Ozora.

Despite the shock of finding the Russians well prepared for their attack, the 25th Regiment's Grenadiers broke through the forward Russian positions but were brought to a halt by artillery and mortar fire as soon as it became light. Casualties were heavy and with the ground in the area too soft to take the weight of the Jagdpanzers, close armoured support was impossible. In order to restart the attack Brand's SPW Battalion was brought forward and after bitter fighting the lighter vehicles were able to over-run the second Russian trenchline. Further progress proved impossible in the face of overwhelming artillery and mortar fire. The deepest penetration in this sector was therefore only about 4km and there was no question of a breakthrough for the armoured group to exploit.

We have differing reports on what happened on the left flank where, whether by accident or design is unclear, Kostenbader's 26th SS Panzer-Grenadiers attacked on the boundary between the 233rd Rifle Division's two forward Regiments. According to Hubert Meyer's History, the Germans found themselves fighting through well-fortified trench systems and after forty-five minutes they were still 500m short of their first objective. Like their comrades in the 25th Regiment, they too came under heavy artillery and mortar fire as soon as it became daylight and the attack wavered. At 1330 hours, however, support from two Jagdpanzer IVs led by

SS Lieutenant Hurdelbrink, a returned Normandy veteran and Knight's Cross holder, enabled the 2nd Company to drive the defenders out of their trenches – they fled, allegedly abandoning their heavy weapons. Nevertheless, a further attack at 1745 hours was again brought to a halt in front of the farmstead objective by rocket and mortar fire. SS Second Lieutenant Deutsch, commanding the 5th Company was killed. In view of the high losses, Kostenbader called off the attack and began planning a new assault with tank support for the following morning.

The Russian Study on the attack against the 233rd Rifle Division would have us believe that at 0730 hours a Panzer-Grenadier Battalion of the 26th Regiment advanced, supported by forty armoured vehicles, including tanks, assault guns and SPWs. Two Grenadier companies and twenty-five armoured vehicles attacked the right flank Regiment but after one hour the tanks were halted by artillery fire and the Grenadiers forced to withdraw to their start-lines. A later attack by twenty-seven tanks and fourteen SPWs into the left forward Regiment was also beaten off.

The Soviet Study also claims that the 233rd Rifle Division launched a counter-attack at 2300 hours against the penetration made by the LAH, but after some initial success this had to be halted due to a German attack in the same area by the HJ's 26th Regiment, supported by thirty tanks. There is no mention of the German attack in Meyer's History of the HJ, but the LAH's SS Captain Holst confirmed that a Soviet counter-attack forced his crews to abandon their mired Jagdpanzers during the night – but not before they had removed the vital firing pins and main armament telescopes.

Whatever the truth about the fighting on 6 March, it was certainly not a good day for the Germans – they had failed to surprise their enemy and their gains were depressing small. In the case of I SS Panzer Corps the deepest penetration was a mere 4km.

On the western flank of Dietrich's Panzer Army, the 3rd and 4th Cavalry Divisions had been forced back to their start-lines by Soviet counter-attacks and on the left flank, II SS Panzer Corps had failed to reach its assembly areas on time and did not even begin its attack until after last light. In the III Panzer Corps sector, the 1st Panzer Division advanced some 4km, south of Lake Valencei, and penetrated into Seregélyes.

The Soviet reaction to the German offensive was swift. Lieutenant General Gagyen, the Twenty-Sixth Army commander, immediately ordered his reserve Rifle Division[6] to move to the threatened axis south of Lake Valencei on the east side of the Sarviz canal and Marshal Tolbukhin simultaneously reinforced Gagyen with two tank brigades (Panzer Battalions) from his reserve XVIII Tank Corps (Panzer Division) and three anti-tank regiments. At the same time a tank regiment (Panzer Battalion) of I Guards Mechanized Corps (Panzer Division) took up positions near Sarkeresztur.[7]

Tolbukhin also ordered two Divisions from his reserve Army to take up positions in a second defensive line immediately to the south of Lake Valencei and, more significantly from our point of view, a complete Rifle Corps[8] from east of the Danube to move to a new position to the south of Simontornya. This would place it in the path of I SS Panzer Corps.

7 – 8 March

The German attack was renewed in rain mixed with light snow before first light on the 7th. Little progress was made on the right flank by the Hitlerjugend's 25th SS Panzer-Grenadier Regiment but on the left, after Pioneers had cleared a way through a minefield, the 2nd Battalion of Kostenbader's 26th Regiment, supported by some SPWs from the 3rd Battalion and a company of tanks, penetrated 4km into the Soviet defences. Despite heavy counter-attacks from the right flank, the ground gained during the day was consolidated.

The Leibstandarte, after regrouping during the night, launched its main effort from the area of Point 149 soon after dawn. Hansen's 3rd SS Panzer-Grenadier Battalion was left to hold the northern part of Soponya, whilst his 2nd Battalion and the whole of Siebken's 2nd SS Panzer-Grenadier Regiment advanced south-east towards the Kaloz-Simontornya road. On reaching the road, just to the south of Kaloz, Siebken's Grenadiers took up positions facing south, whilst Hansen's men turned north towards the village. At the same time tanks of KG Peiper advanced from the west. SS Lieutenant Werner Sternebeck said later:

> The 3rd SS Panzer Company attacked as part of the Panzer Group over Point 149 against Kaloz. After the destruction of the anti-tank defence, the momentum of the initial attack threw the enemy back . . . . West of Kaloz we had to use a valley with a soft muddy bottom so that we could approach our objective only slowly. . . . We suffered only a few losses. Several Panzers stuck in the deep mud and could only be extracted with great difficulty.[9]

By midday Kaloz had been secured and the tanks, with infantry support, continued north to clear Soponya. They soon linked up with Hansen's 3rd Battalion, moving south to meet them, and the Russian defenders were forced to flee across the Sarviz river. A member of the 12th SS Panzer-Grenadier Company recalled:

> We reached . . . without any losses to speak of, the first houses. . . . There was heavy infantry fire, which we believed came from the withdrawing enemy forces, but it was ineffective. After combing the

houses which lay astride the long street, we ran into our Panzer group at the far end of the village.[10]

In an interesting footnote to the day's events, Otto Holst later recorded that the crews of the 3rd SS Panzerjäger Company recaptured the Jagdpanzers they had been forced to abandon in the mud the previous day. 'They were almost undamaged' and made operational 'within a short period of time'.

The wider Soviet Study of the Balaton offensive[11] confirms that by 2000 hours on the 7th, the LAH attack had breached the second line defences of the 68th Guards Division on a 5km front. This caused the Corps commander, Major General Lazko, to order the Division to withdraw behind the Sarviz canal where the Army's reserve Rifle Division[12] had already taken up defensive positions. This move began at 0100 hours on the 8th and, according to the Study, despite the efforts of the LAH to disrupt the withdrawal, the Division was dug in on the east bank by first light. A statement that the Germans attempted a crossing of the canal can be discounted – the axis of advance in the I SS Panzer Corps sector was south-east, not east.

During 7 March the leading elements of the Rifle Corps[13] which Marshal Tolbukhin had ordered forward from the east side of the Danube reached the river at a point 30km east of Simontornya, and on the same day the reserve Soviet Cavalry Corps[14] was ordered to take up temporary positions behind the Sio canal from where it could deploy farther forward if necessary.

On 8 March the I SS Panzer Corps attack began to gain momentum.

Whilst Max Hansen's Grenadiers mopped up around Soponya and Kaloz, Siebken's 2nd SS Panzer-Grenadier Regimental group, which included the LAH's Jagdpanzers, advanced south-east and by evening had secured Nagy against minimal opposition. KG Peiper followed up and replenished in the woods just to the north of the village.

In the 12th SS Panzer Division's sector, simultaneous attacks by both SS Panzer-Grenadier Regiments also made progress. Müller's 25th Regiment, with Siegel's tanks and Brand's SPW Battalion in the lead, soon broke through the Russian defences and by last light had reached the Enying-Dég road about 3km west of Dég, which was now the main HJ objective. On the left flank, the 26th Regiment kept pace and seized a group of farms 4km to the north-east of the village, but during the attack SS Major Kostenbader was killed by fire from Soviet ground attack aircraft. His place, as commander of the Regiment, was taken by SS Lieutenant Colonel Braun.

The only obstacle to the final assault on Dég, planned for the following day, was a Russian strongpoint, including several anti-tank guns, still holding out on Point 125 between the two SS Panzer-Grenadier

Regiments. In any other army the task of eliminating such a position at night would almost certainly have been given to infantry on their feet, with support from artillery and mortars – particularly since in WWII there were none of the night-vision aids to be found in today's armoured vehicles. But that was not the way with the Waffen-SS and, in an extraordinary decision, Hugo Kraas ordered Siegel to attack Point 125 during the night of the 8th using fourteen Jagdpanzer IVs and Vs of the 560th Heavy Panzerjäger Battalion, some Mk IVs of his own Battalion, several Flakpanzers and some unspecified parts of Gerd Bremer's 12th SS Reconnaissance Battalion – a total of about forty armoured vehicles in all. Even Hubert Meyer, in his History of the Hitlerjugend, called it an 'unconventional' attack! Siegel later reported:

> During the deployment of the unit into a wide wedge formation, our own artillery shelled the blocking position – mostly dug-in anti-tank guns. The concentrated force of the fire and movement, added to which the din of motors and the rattle of the tracked vehicles firing tracers in front of them, explosions from grenades hurled from SPWs on the move – all that happening during otherwise total darkness, probably discouraged even the most hardened Red Army man. . . . We overran the anti-tank barrier and the fortified positions without loss.[15]

The failure of II SS Panzer Corps to make progress on the east side of the Sarviz canal was causing deep concern in Headquarters Army Group South and this led, on the night of the 8th, to the re-allocation of the 23rd Panzer Division to Dietrich. The Division, with some fifty tanks, Jagdpanzers and assault guns, was then ordered to follow behind the LAH and to be prepared to cross the Sarviz canal and attack the Soviet forces in the rear of the II SS Panzer Corps in the Sarkeresztur area.

Strength returns show the LAH with thirty-four, and the HJ thirty, operational tanks and Jagdpanzers on 8 March – a total of forty-three less than when they began the attack, though of course not all these would have been destroyed. Readers will have noted that no Russian tanks have been mentioned in the fighting up to this time.

9 – 11 March

On 9 March the situation began to change dramatically. The Leibstandarte advanced south in two groups, towards Saregres on the Sarviz river and Simontornya 5km to the south-west. The left-hand group, under Hansen, comprised his own Regiment and the Divisional Reconnaissance and Panzerjäger Battalions. It overcame well defended positions covering the Nagy-Saregres road to the north of Saregres, before being brought to a halt by an anti-tank screen immediately north of the village. This rather bland description of the day's events gives no impression of what it was like for the Grenadiers involved, but Diether Kuhlmann gives a brief glimpse:

On 9 March we marched farther to the south. . . . The roads were deep and mushy and there were large puddles in the fields. Dead Red Army soldiers and pieces of equipment lay all around. . . . Suddenly we heard a roaring overhead and all hell broke loose. We were caught in a barrage of heavy Soviet mortar fire. There were screams and curses, and then a breathless stillness. . . . The stunned survivors picked themselves off the ground. . . . In a barn we laid the wounded down and examined them. Herbert called faintly for me. On each side of his chest he had a hole the size of a pigeon's egg. A thin stream of blood ran out of the corner of his mouth. He had closed his eyes.[16]

In spite of the unfavourable ground conditions, KG Peiper, with additional infantry support from Siebken's Regiment, advanced on the right in what Tiemann's History describes as 'a spirited attack' towards Simontornya. It reached the high ground 2½km north of the town before being halted by dug-in anti-tank guns and heavy artillery fire from positions south of the Sio canal. Nevertheless, it had been a good day for the LAH with advances of over 15km.

In the HJ sector things also went reasonably well – particularly when one considers that there were no roads and few negotiable tracks in the area. The HJ attacked Dég early in the morning using parts of both Panzer-Grenadier Regiments and the armoured group. Siegel again describes the action in dramatic terms:

I stood in the turret of the Jagdpanther and followed, through binoculars, the progress which was almost like a drill. Everything went well – then, just outside the village, an explosion. One Panzer stopped. Anti-tank gun or mine? . . . My gunner had already taken aim at the target and was waiting only for the order to fire. An explosion – a hit on our own Jagdpanther's front plate! The scissor telescope was gone, rivet heads popped off, ricocheting – criss-cross – through the fighting compartment. 'Back into cover!' Right away, a second hit on the right drive sprocket. The Panzer swung its front to the left and rolled into a hole. Luckily it was not burning. Out! My own Panzers were inside the village – out of sight – and without leadership! 'Motorcycle, over here!' . . . Into the village at full speed, following in a Panzer track so as not to be blown up by mines! . . . My Panzers had their hot moments behind them already. They had encountered 100mm Russian assault guns – about a dozen of them. The Soviets were surprised, some of them were knocked out, others were able to escape.[17]

After the clearance of extensive minefields, the advance continued and by evening Müller's 25th Grenadiers with Brand's SPW Battalion were to the north-west of Mezöszilas, while two Battalions of Braun's 26th Regiment with Jagdpanzers from the HJ's 12th SS Panzerjäger Battalion, were immediately north of the village. SS Lieutenant Gaede's Panther Company caught up towards evening after getting stuck in marshy ground whilst chasing a withdrawing Russian vehicle column.

On the right flank of Priess's Corps, one Division of I Cavalry Corps exploited the gap created by the HJ and reached the main road between Enying and Mezökomarom, whilst the other attacked Enying.

The Russians viewed the events of 9 March with some alarm. As the Frunze Military Academy Study describes it:

From the morning of 9 March, the operational situation on the XXX Corps front [opposite II SS Panzer Corps] sharply deteriorated. The success of the enemy in breaking through the tactical defence zone of CXXXV Corps [on the I SS Panzer Corps front], created a serious threat to the rear of the Twenty-Sixth Army. . . . Because of this breach [by the LAH and HJ Divisions], control between the two left-hand Corps of the Army and XXX Corps became too complicated, so CinC Front [Tolbukhin] ordered XXX Corps transferred to the Twenty-Seventh Army.[18]

This transfer was part of an overall restructuring of the Third Ukrainian Front (Army Group). From the night of 9 March Tolbukhin's reserve Twenty-Seventh Army became responsible for the sector between Lake Valencei and the Sarviz canal; thus the Soviet XXX Rifle Corps, part of which had opposed the LAH, disappears from our picture. Suffice it to say though that, with other formations of that Army, it played a major part in halting the advance of II SS Panzer Corps towards the Danube on the east side of the Sarviz.

Meanwhile, General Gagyen's Twenty-Sixth Army remained responsible for halting what Tolbukhin considered to be the main threat – I SS Panzer Corps and I Cavalry Corps between the Sarviz canal and Lake Balaton. To this end Gagyen was reinforced with a tank regiment (Panzer Battalion)[19], a self-propelled artillery brigade and two anti-tank regiments, and the main weight of the Third Ukrainian Front's close air support effort was re-targeted to his sector.[20] Readers should note that the tank unit mentioned above was the only one to become involved in resisting the advance of I SS Panzer Corps.

Whilst the 9th had been a good day for Priess's men on the west side of the Sarviz canal, Dietrich and his senior commanders were acutely aware that the left flank of I SS Panzer Corps was becoming dangerously exposed. II SS Panzer Corps had still not reached Sarkeresztur and only the difficulties of crossing the Sarviz river and canal were preventing the Russians from attacking the flank of the German penetration – as called for in their basic doctrine described in an earlier Chapter. Marshal Tolbukhin, however, was not slow to recognise the operational opportunities offered by the situation and on the same day he requested the release of one reserve Army to his control and the use of another.[21] STAVKA refused, saying that these Armies were earmarked for the forthcoming general offensive and that he would have to make do with what he had. In fact STAVKA went further and, on this same day, gave both Tolbukhin and Malinovsky revised missions. The Third Ukrainian Front (Army Group) was to continue to defend south of Lake Balaton with two Armies[22], but was to be prepared to launch a major attack north of Lake Valencei with two reserve Armies[23], one of which Tolbukhin had just requested. The aim of this attack was, as Dietrich had feared, to strike the rear of the Sixth Panzer Army. Malinovsky's Second Ukrainian Front (Army Group) was to join in the attack after one or two days, with two Armies attacking westwards along the south bank of the Danube. Later on, the Armies north of the Danube and south of Lake Balaton were to join in the offensive. The initial attack by Tolbukhin was to be made as soon as the Sixth Panzer Army's offensive had been halted. This was expected to be on 15 or 16 March.

The strength of the Soviet position derived from their early knowledge of the forthcoming German offensive and their ability to formulate and develop an overall strategy to deal with it both before and during the fighting. The fact that they were facing reverses in one area did not distract them from their long-term aim and the, albeit serious, situation on the west side of the Sarviz was seen as an opportunity rather than a crisis. The similarities between the Balaton offensive, the Mortain counter-attack in Normandy and the Battle of the Bulge are obvious – the difference being that the Americans had no prior warning and had to react to events rather than pre-plan them.

The enemy situation on the I SS Panzer Corps front as darkness fell on the 9th can be summarised as follows: the 233rd Rifle Division, which had originally opposed the HJ and parts of the LAH, had been pushed to the south-west by the HJ and was now behind the Sio to the south of Enying; the 68th Guards Rifle Division, which had opposed the LAH, had been forced to withdraw east of the Sarviz; the 236th Rifle Division, which had provided second echelon defence between Dég and the Sio canal, had withdrawn behind the canal to the south of Mezőkomarom; two of the three Rifle Divisions[24] which had been ordered forward from the east side of the Danube had taken up positions astride the canal between Ozora and Simontornya, and the third[25] was east of the Sarviz near Cece. The Cavalry Corps[26] was still in reserve behind these Rifle Divisions.

*   *   *

The weather conditions on 10 March did not favour the Germans. It was raining and snowing, the ground was soft and the tracks were still ribbons of mud. Little progress was made except in the sector of I Cavalry Corps where the 3rd Cavalry Division managed to seize a bridgehead over the Sio, 5km to the west of Mezökomarom, and the 4th Division encircled Enying.

On the Hitlerjugend front the 25th SS Panzer-Grenadier Regiment continued its slow and painful progress towards Ozora whilst the reinforced 26th Regiment, after capturing Mezöszilas by 2100 hours, moved on during the night and captured Igar, 4km to the north-west of Simontornya. An interesting incident during the day was later recounted by a member of the HJ's SS Reconnaissance Battalion, SS Second Lieutenant Lochbihler:

> I remember scouting from Dég . . . we were driving along an open road up the rear slope in the direction of Mezökomarom. There we spotted, on the opposite slope, Russians in Battalion strength digging in. Suddenly, seven Russian combat aircraft were overhead. . . . In line with the Russian position they swung left and, when they were right overhead their friends, they unloaded. The Russians fired signal flares but all was in vain. After the aircraft had disappeared, two of our SPW crews fired into the disarray.[27]

On the same day, the 23rd Panzer Division, despite heavy anti-tank and artillery fire from the east side of the Sarviz canal, closed up to Saregres. By nightfall it had taken over from the LAH on that flank and this allowed Kumm's Division to concentrate for its attack on Simontornya and subsequent crossing of the Sio canal. This was to be no easy task for, it will be recalled, two fresh Russian Rifle Divisions[28] had taken up strong positions south of the canal, on the high ridge running from Simontornya to Ozora and beyond, and had placed forward outposts on the high ground on the north side of the Sio and in both towns.

Total personnel casualties in I SS Panzer Corps at this stage of the offensive are unknown. Tiemann says the LAH had lost 321 men, including fifty-seven killed[29], but in the case of the HJ, Hubert Meyer merely says that all its Panzer-Grenadier Battalions were 'weak'. He goes on to say that the Division had lost six Mk IV tanks, seven Jagdpanzer IVs and one Werfer battery. Strength returns show the HJ with twenty-six and the LAH with thirty operational tanks and Jagdpanzers on the 10th – roughly half the number available four days earlier. The LAH is said to have had another fifty-six under repair.[30]

After a stormy night, Grenadiers of the LAH spent the day of the 11th clearing the important ridge lying just to the north of Simontornya, including Point 146. At the same time some of the HJ's Jagdpanzers and elements of Braun's 26th SS Panzer-Grenadier Regiment cooperated by capturing the road junction 1500m south of Igar. This secured the jumping off positions for the final attack on Simontornya, which was to be carried out the following day by the LAH, with the 1st and 2nd Battalions of the HJ's 26th Regiment and Brockschmidt's 12th SS Panzerjäger Battalion under command. Eight Tiger IIs of Hein von Westernhagen's 501st SS Heavy Panzer Battalion were also available.[31] Otto Kumm was able to report to his Corps Headquarters:

The Division, after fierce fighting with the enemy north of the Sio, is now concentrated . . . and ready to cross. The removal of thousands of mines took time. The bridging columns have caught up. The enemy has constructed a defensive front on the south bank of the Sio with many anti-tank guns and much artillery and he is now reinforcing it with infantry. The Kaloz-Simontornya road [Divisional supply route] is being *.eavily interdicted by artillery and anti-tank fire [from the east bank].[32]

On the Corps left flank, the 23rd Panzer Division penetrated into Saregres but was unable to clear it. Army Group South's hopes of launching an attack across the Sarviz in this area, in support of II SS Panzer Corps, were proving highly optimistic.

On the right flank, Müller's 25th SS Panzer-Grenadier Regiment, reinforced by two Companies of Brand's SPW Battalion, six Mk IVs and nine Panthers from Siegel's 2nd SS Panzer Battalion and five Jagdpanzers from the 560th Heavy Panzerjäger Battalion, was given the mission of seizing the bridge across the Sio canal at Ozora and capturing the heavily wooded hills on the south side.[33] This was a major task for the canal was over 30m wide. The only thing in the Germans' favour was that, for some inexplicable reason, the bridge had not been blown by the Russians when they withdrew.

The Ozora attack was delayed while some of the armoured vehicles were refuelled and rearmed and by the late arrival of various sub-units; during this period attacks by Soviet aircraft caused casualties amongst the Jagdpanzers.

The first wave of the attack, which was preceded by an artillery barrage, was composed of the two SPW Companies and the tanks, followed by the 25th SS Panzer-Grenadiers on their feet. An SS sergeant in the SPW Battalion described what happened:

Taking advantage of depressions in the terrain and our own artillery fire, we reached a hill approximately 400m from the canal. . . . One SPW and the [six] Panzer IVs tried to reach the bridge through a ravine dropping down to the Sio canal but were prevented from doing that by heavy anti-tank fire. Now it became obvious why the enemy had withdrawn in our attack sector. On the opposite slope – south of the canal – he had set up an anti-tank position in the brush.[34] It resembled a volcano. Three Panzer IVs were knocked out immediately before the entrance to the bridge, another took a hit on the bridge, lost its track and blocked the bridge. [Shades of Stavelot in the Ardennes!] Attempts to tow it away under the cover of artificial smoke failed in the anti-tank fire. The 3rd Battalion moved into a reverse slope position on the north bank. The Grenadiers of the 25th Regiment arrived and took over securing our sector.[35]

12 – 14 March

Although the descriptions of the fighting on 12 March are very similar in both the LAH and HJ Divisional Histories, there are conflicting claims as to which units carried out the assault across the Sio canal just to the west of the Bozot river. Ralf Tiemann states that it was made by Hansen's 1st SS Panzer-Grenadier Regiment LAH and the Division's 1st SS Reconnaissance Battalion, with 'elements' of the HJ's 26th Regiment. Hubert Meyer, on the other hand, claims that the assault was carried out by the 1st and 2nd Battalions of Braun's 26th SS Panzer-Grenadier Regiment, with support from the heavy weapons of the Regiment, artillery, and some of Brockschmidt's Jagdpanzers. In the opinion of this author, Meyer is more likely to be correct, since the sector to the west of the Bozot was the responsibility of the Hitlerjugend and there was a greater need for the Leibstandarte's infantry in the attack on the built-up area of Simontornya. The description of subsequent events will therefore be based on this assumption.

The two Battalions of the HJ reached the canal at 1430 hours but then faltered in the face of withering mortar and artillery fire; heavy machine-gun fire punctured many of the rubber assault boats and anti-tank fire forced the Jagdpanzers to pull back into the cover of the buildings at Igar. Despite numerous sorties by German fighter-bombers and supporting fire from the Jagdpanzers and artillery, the Grenadiers were unable to cross until after dark. Even then they managed to secure a bridgehead of only a few hundred square metres – a bridgehead they were forced to defend against several Soviet counter-attacks during the night.

The Leibstandarte's attack on the town of Simontornya was launched from the high ground north of the Sio canal by Hansen's and Siebken's Panzer-Grenadiers, strongly supported by Poetschke's 1st SS Panzer Battalion. The use of tanks against a built-up area may surprise some readers but the ground on the west side of the Bozot river was unsuitable for armour and at least the open flat area directly north of the town allowed for a rapid advance. Werner Sternebeck, the commander of the 3rd SS Panzer Company, described what happened to his tanks:

Attacking from the reverse slope, we raced across the open plain and reached the western edge of the town without stopping to fire. From there, we attacked to the east and south through the town. The fighting was heavy and brief. . . . We lost three Panzers on the open plain and another two in the town. The enemy had no time to withdraw the anti-tank and anti-aircraft guns so we were able to destroy or capture them.[36]

Fierce house-to-house fighting continued all day but by last light Simontornya, north of the Sio, was mainly in German hands with only a few pockets of resistance remaining. A member of the 9th SS Pioneer Company recalled:

The Russians had blown the bridge across the Sio. Our Pioneers tried [unsuccessfully] to build a new one in the midst of artillery and mortar fire. . . . The Russian fighter-bombers gave us no rest.[37]

The 88mm and 37mm batteries of SS Major Ullerich's 1st SS Flak Battalion were quickly brought up and positioned in the town but the fighter-bomber attacks continued relentlessly until last light.

A slightly surprising success on the 12th came in the I Cavalry Corps sector, where the 3rd Cavalry Division managed to cross the canal and secure a 6km square bridgehead to the west of Mezökomarom, whilst the 4th Cavalry Division closed up to Balatonszabadi. Nevertheless, there was little doubt that the Sixth Panzer Army's offensive was losing its momentum.

Undetected by German intelligence, the build-up for the forthcoming Soviet offensive was proceeding rapidly on this day. The movement of the Sixth Guards Tank Army (Panzer Corps), with some 500 tanks[38], to an assembly area just west of Budapest was completed and a second attack Army[39] was in the process of moving in behind the Army[40] defending the sector immediately to the north of Lake Valencei. The scene was being set for the final destruction of I SS Panzer Corps.

During the early hours of 13 March, Max Hansen's 1st SS Panzer-Grenadier Regiment succeeded in establishing a second bridgehead across the Sio canal – within the town of Simontornya. A joint attack was then mounted, with the two Battalions of Braun's 26th Regiment already across the canal to the west, against the vine-covered ridge lying just to the south of the town. Supporting fire was provided by tanks, 20mm guns of Siebken's SPW Battalion and artillery, and by midday the most dominating feature on the ridge, Point 220, had been taken and a series of strongpoints set up in the tiny bridgehead – it was still less than three square kilometres in size. Throughout the remainder of the day the Soviets launched numerous counter-attacks, all supported by tanks and aircraft, but these were successfully repulsed.

Meanwhile, the Leibstandarte's 2nd Panzer-Grenadier Regiment had cleared the final pockets of resistance in Simontornya and advanced to the cemetery at the southern edge of the town. This allowed the Leibstandarte's Pioneers, reinforced by the HJ's 3rd Pioneer Company, to continue their attempts to bridge the 30m wide and 4m deep canal. Observed Russian artillery fire made this impossible in daylight but soon after last light the task was completed and two Jagdpanzers of Karl Rettlinger's 1st SS Panzerjäger Battalion rolled across. SS Captain Holst later described this event:

> SS Lieutenant Bröcker was the first to cross the bridge. He was followed by SS Lieutenant Piegeler whose vehicle collapsed the middle of the bridge. . . . SS Major Rettlinger and Bröcker were alone on the southern bank of the Sio.[41]

A Hitlerjugend Pioneer gave further details:

> The bridge . . . was repeatedly damaged by artillery fire and partially collapsed by a Panzer. There were considerable losses in killed and wounded in both Pioneer companies. The bridge had to be constantly maintained. The vehicles returning from the south bank of the Sio canal would not stop on instructions from the Pioneers. Perhaps they did not understand. Being under pressure from the constant fire, they drove too close together and the bridge bent. It was necessary to make constant repairs but we kept it open.[42]

Readers will have noted the first mention of Soviet tanks on this day. They were used against both I SS Panzer Corps and I Cavalry Corps. The Tank Regiment (Panzer Battalion) concerned[43] had a maximum of forty-one T-34/85s and it was some of these which were used in counter-attacks against the Panzer-Grenadiers on Point 220. Others were allegedly used against 3rd Cavalry Division's bridgehead west of Mezökomarom.

In other relevant sectors on the 13th, the Hitlerjugend group at Ozora failed again to force a crossing of the Sio but, after three attempts, and with strong Luftwaffe support, the 23rd Panzer Division finally managed to clear Saregres on the Sarviz river by the evening. A subsequent attempt to force a crossing of the canal near Cece failed in the face of tenacious resistance. This ended, at least temporarily, Army Group South's hopes of supporting II SS Panzer Corps' advance with attacks from west of the Sarviz.

During the night 13th-14th Soviet pressure on Point 220 caused Kraas to reinforce the two Battalions of Braun's 26th Regiment with his HJ Divisional Escort Company and the LAH to send four more of Rettlinger's Jagdpanzers into the slender and vulnerable bridgehead.

While the Sixth Panzer Army persisted in its efforts to implement the basic strategy of Operation SPRING AWAKENING, the Soviet preparations for their own offensive were nearing completion. In addition to the Sixth Guards Tank Army (Panzer Corps) already assembled just to the west of Budapest, another twenty-four Rifle Divisions, a Tank Corps[44] (Panzer Division) and a Guards Mechanized Corps[45] (Panzer Division) were being made ready for the strike across the rear of Sepp Dietrich's command.

The 14th of March was mainly sunny and the temperature climbed to 13° Celsius, drying the ground. The bridge in Simontornya was badly damaged by Soviet artillery fire early in the day and, although a start was made on a second bridge to the west of the town, there was little hope of moving anything across the canal in daylight. The Corps' armour and heavy weapons were forced to remain on the north bank.

During the morning the Germans south of the canal were subjected to several counter-attacks and constant artillery fire and air attack. Nevertheless, in the afternoon, Hansen's 1st SS Panzer-Grenadiers carried out a successful assault on Point 115, lying 2km to the south-east of the town, and this expanded the Simontornya bridgehead to some five square kilometres.

Meanwhile, the Soviets were attempting to establish their own bridgehead across the Sarviz canal in the Saregres sector and during the day a Leibstandarte KG, formed from Siebken's 2nd SS Panzer-Grenadier Regiment and Rettlinger's 1st SS Panzerjäger Battalion, was sent to assist the 23rd Panzer Division. Similarly at Ozora, on the Hitlerjugend front, it was the Russians rather than the Germans who were trying to cross the canal and their resulting bridgehead was contained only with great difficulty by Müller's 25th SS Panzer-Grenadier Regiment.

These Russian counter-attacks across the Sarviz and Sio canals were seen by all the senior commanders in I SS Panzer Corps as ominous signs of things to come. At Army Group and Army level, German intelligence had detected part of the Soviet build-up on the 13th, but the moves had been misinterpreted as local reinforcements and it was not until the evening of the 14th that the Army Group South War Dairy recorded:

Today's movements leave no doubt of the enemy's intentions. Based on the results from aerial observation, motorized columns of at least 3,000 vehicles are moving out of the rear area from Budapest . . . to the south-west, most of them in the direction of Zamoly [Map 28]. His objective will be to cut the rear connections of the German forces [Sixth Panzer Army and III Panzer Corps] which have advanced from the narrow passage of Székesfehérvar, by an attack in the direction of Lake Balaton.[46]

That evening Kumm ordered the armour of KG Peiper and the eight operational Tiger IIs of the 501st SS Heavy Panzer Battalion to withdraw to an assembly area near Dég.

15 – 18 March

On 15 March I SS Panzer Corps continued to hold its slender bridgehead across the Sio and Hansen's men even managed to extend it some 500m to the south. It is perfectly possible of course that, in view of their forthcoming offensive, the Soviets were not seriously trying to eliminate the Simontornya bridgehead at this time, but merely baiting the trap.

It was now clear to most German commanders on the ground that SPRING AWAKENING had failed. Sepp Dietrich recommended an immediate withdrawal to a suitable defensive line in the north of his area but this was ruled out by his superior, General Otto Wöhler, the commander of Army Group South. At 1510 hours the latter gave his assessment of the situation to OKH. He pointed out that any attempt to advance farther south in the I SS Panzer Corps area would be 'inexpedient' due to the hilly terrain and the Corps' exposed left flank. This was a major understatement. The ground to the south was not only hilly; it was broken, wooded and bounded on both sides by waterways – something which should have been foreseen when the original plan was made! Wöhler proposed therefore to leave the 23rd Panzer Division where it was in the Saregres sector and, after relieving I SS Panzer Corps on the Sio with I Cavalry Corps and a Hungarian Division, to move it north to a position behind II SS Panzer Corps and III Panzer Corps. All three Panzer Corps would then attack east, between Sarkeresztur and Gardony, towards the Danube, before turning south in accordance with the original plan. He estimated it would take four days to complete the necessary regrouping. OKH approved this plan but demanded that it be put into effect in three days, not four, and added that if the 23rd Panzer Division could secure a bridgehead across the Sarviz that night, I SS Panzer Corps was to follow across immediately.

Although this plan was considered impracticable by most of the field commanders involved, the necessary orders were issued at 2300 hours and during the same night the first units of the HJ were withdrawn from the battle area.

On 16 March the Leibstandarte, awaiting relief by the Cavalry Corps and Hungarians, was required to hold its existing positions – Hansen's Grenadiers in the bridgehead south of the canal and Siebken's on the Sio between Simontornya and the 23rd Panzer Division at Saregres. The LAH Reconnaissance Battalion had been detached to a KG of the 2nd SS Panzer Division Das Reich in the Kaloz area.

The HJ Battalions were withdrawn from the Simontornya bridgehead during the early hours of the 16th, whilst the rest of the Division continued its preparations for withdrawal. This included the reception of reinforcements! Müller's 25th SS Panzer-Grenadier Regiment spent the day trying, unsuccessfully, to eliminate the Soviet bridgehead across the Sio at Ozora.

Meanwhile, a small bridgehead, which the 23rd Panzer Division had managed to establish across the Sarviz during the night, had to be given up soon after dawn in the face of a violent counter-attack by the Soviets.

(Map 28)

At 1430 hours on 16 March two Soviet Armies[47] launched a major attack on a 20km front in the IV SS Panzer Corps sector between Székesfehérvar and the Vertes hills to the north. Behind them stood the Sixth Guards Tank Army (Panzer Corps) and on their northern flank another Army[48] waited to join in the offensive. The immediate Russian objectives were Tatabanya and Györ in the north and Varpalota and Veszprem in the south. The southern thrust was of course designed to cut off and destroy Dietrich's Sixth Panzer Army. Unbelievably, as late as 2300 hours on the same day, General Wöhler still believed he could implement his plan to attack east with his three Panzer Corps, and that same night Headquarters Sixth Panzer Army issued orders for the relief of I SS Panzer Corps and its move into an area to the north of Seregélyes during the following two nights. However, at 0120 hours on the 17th, General Guderian, Chief of Staff at OKH, recommended to Wöhler's Chief of Staff that preparations be put in hand for I SS Panzer Corps to attack north rather than east! At 0145 hours, in spite of Hitler's refusal to allow any changes to his master plan or to allow any major redeployments without his personal permission, the Chief of Staff Army Group South, Lieutenant General von Grolmann, instructed Dietrich to prepare I SS Panzer Corps for just such an attack.

Dawn on 17 March brought rain and a consequent worsening of the ground conditions. The progress of the Soviet offensive will be described in the next Chapter; suffice it to say at this stage that the overall situation was becoming critical for the Germans, not least because Hitler still refused to authorise the necessary redeployments.

In the particular case of I SS Panzer Corps, the 17th saw Müller's 25th Grenadiers clear up the Soviet bridgehead at Ozora before pulling back to join the rest of the HJ which was already on its way to an assembly area near Székesfehérvar.

The Leibstandarte had a much more difficult time. The heavy weapons supporting Hansen's Regiment were withdrawn from the Simontornya bridgehead, but a serious accident on the bridge delayed the withdrawal of the last parts of the Regiment until the following day. SS Major Karl Rettlinger described what happened:

The bridge was wrecked. A new crossing was created by the Pioneers. While the 3rd and 4th guns [Jagdpanzers] crossed, the right column of the bridge sagged. The bridge and the Panzers fell into the canal. The crews were rescued.[49]

In view of the increasingly critical situation in the north, General Wöhler, during the morning of the 17th, finally requested permission from OKH to use I SS Panzer Corps for an attack from the Varpalota area towards Zamoly – into the flank of the Soviet advance. This was followed by another request at 2145 hours for authority to withdraw II SS Panzer Corps, which was now dangerously exposed in the Aba-Sarkeresztur area, behind I SS Panzer Corps as soon as it arrived in the vicinity of Székesfehérvar. Hitler eventually gave his permission for these deployments at 0140 hours on 18 March and at 0200 hours Wöhler ordered Dietrich to move I SS Panzer Corps to the area north of Varpalota and subordinate it to Army Group Balck.

By 1800 hours on the 18th the LAH had completed its withdrawal from the Simontornya sector and was concentrated around Dég. From there it set out to join the HJ which, in the meantime, had moved to a new concentration area near Varpalota. Rolf Reiser, of KG Peiper, described the move:

During the night 18-19 March we redeployed into the assigned assembly area east of Inota. . . . The march was particularly difficult because the roads were not only being used and jammed by refugees, but also entire supply convoys had to be withdrawn. . . . The refugees swarming out of the Székesfehérvar area blocked the roads, which could only be cleared by force.[50]

So ended the last offensive action of I SS Panzer Corps. Some commentators, mainly German, making use of statements made later by important commanders like Sepp Dietrich, have claimed that the main reason for the failure of SPRING AWAKENING was the unusual weather which made the terrain totally unsuitable for armoured forces. But, as seen in this narrative, Dietrich exaggerated greatly when he said in a post-war interrogation:

When tanks were employed to exploit the initial successes, the terrain proved completely impassable. The ground, which was supposed to be frozen hard, and which General von Wöhler had maintained to be passable, was wet and marshy. For reasons of secrecy, I had been forbidden to make an early ground reconnaissance. Now 132 tanks were sunk in the mud and fifteen Royal Tigers were sunk up to their turrets, so that the attack could be continued only by infantry.[51]

Although it is certainly true that ground conditions made movement extremely difficult, I SS Panzer Corps was still able to advance 27km in six days against a prepared enemy, Siegel was still able to carry out a successful night attack with armour and the tanks of KG Peiper were still able to participate in the attack against Simontornya. No, the major reason for failure was a flawed operational concept which, in the face of a numerically superior enemy, inevitably exposed all three Panzer Corps to encirclement, and launched I SS Panzer Corps into an area bounded by two major water obstacles (the Sarviz and Sio canals) and then brought it into ground unsuitable for armour (as pointed out in Wöhler's assessment of 15 March). If the aim of SPRING AWAKENING was to cut off and destroy the Soviet forces on the west side of the Danube, it would surely have made more sense to have dealt with the Soviet forces north of Lake Valencei first and then to have concentrated all three Panzer Corps on the east side of the Sarviz canal. The fact that this did not happen and indeed, the fact that SPRING AWAKENING was launched at all, was a tragedy for the Leibstandarte and Hitlerjugend; nevertheless, Dietrich's 'boys' had every reason to be proud of their achievements between 6 and 17 March.

Personnel casualties during SPRING AWAKENING are not available for the Hitlerjugend, but were probably similar to those of the Leibstandarte – 1,435, including 211 killed.[52]

NOTES

1. 572nd Rifle Regt.
2. Tiemann, *The Leibstandarte* IV/2, pp. 209–10.
3. Ibid., p. 210.
4. Appendix 21 of the Soviet Frunze Military Academy Study on the Lake Balaton Offensive by Lt Col V F Yashin.
5. These objectives were little more than names on a map – a small farmstead or manor house at best.
6. 21st Rifle Div.
7. Radzievskiy, *Army Operations*, p. 205.
8. XXXIII Rifle Corps.
9. Tiemann, op. cit., pp. 211–12.
10. Ibid., p. 212–13.
11. *The Frunze Military Academy Study of the Defence by Formations of XXX Rifle Corps of the Twenty-Sixth Army in the Balaton Defensive Operations* by Lt Col V F Yashin.
12. 21st Rifle Div.
13. XXXIII Rifle Corps.
14. V Gds Cavalry Corps.
15. Meyer, *The History of the 12th SS Panzer Division Hitlerjugend*, p. 294.
16. Tiemann, op. cit., p. 215.
17. Meyer, op. cit., p. 295.
18. See Note 7.
19. From I Gds Mech Corps (Pz Div).
20. Radzievskiy, op. cit., p. 206. As mentioned in Chap XXIV, Tolbukhin's 17th Air Army had 965 aircraft on 6 Mar, but after the German attack he was reinforced, on orders from STAVKA, with additional aircraft from Malinovsky's 5th Air Army.
21. Ninth Gds Army and Sixth Gds Tk Army (Pz Corps).
22. Twenty-Sixth and Twenty-Seventh Armies.
23. Fourth and Ninth Gds Armies.
24. 337th and 202nd Rifle Divs from XXXIII Rifle Corps.
25. 206th Rifle Div from XXXIII Rifle Corps.
26. V Gds Cavalry Corps.
27. Meyer, op. cit., p. 295.
28. 337th and 202nd Rifle Divs.
29. Tiemann, op. cit., p. 218.
30. Ibid.
31. Schneider, *Tigers in Combat* II, p. 266.
32. Tiemann, op. cit., p. 217.
33. Ozora is today an attractive village; its ruined castle still bears the marks of the 1945 battle.
34. More likely from positions beside or in the buildings adjacent to the bridge.
35. Meyer, op. cit., p. 296.
36. Tiemann, op. cit., p. 221.
37. Ibid.
38. Glantz, *Art of War Symposium*, US Army War College, Carlisle, Pa, 1986, but

Zavizion and Kornyushin, *I na Tikhom okeane* . . ., give a figure of 406 tks and SP guns.
39. Ninth Gds Army.
40. Fourth Gds Army.
41. Tiemann, op. cit., p. 223.
42. Ibid.
43. From I Gds Mech Corps.
44. XXIII Tk Corps.
45. II Gds Mech Corps.
46. Meyer, op. cit., p. 298.
47. Fourth and Ninth Gds Armies.
48. Forty-Sixth Army.
49. Tiemann, op. cit., p. 234.
50. Ibid., p. 235.
51. US Seventh Army Interrogation Report SAIC/43 dated 11 Jun 45.
52. Tiemann, op. cit., p. 228.

CHAPTER XXVI

The Storm from the East: 16 March – 1 April

(Map 24)

The last two months of the fighting on the southern sector of the Eastern Front have, in the main, received only cursory treatment by western writers – two of our most renowned historians devote less than twenty pages to the subject between them. But since the Second and Third Ukrainian Fronts were of secondary importance to those of Marshals Rokossovsky, Zhukov and Konev in the north and centre, perhaps this superficial treatment is not altogether surprising. Nevertheless, statements such as:

> The Russians were on the move with a thundering charge of tanks, unleashed in the wake of the defeat of the German attack and overwhelming the remnants of Sixth Panzer Army in a pell-mell engagement where the few German Panthers fired into the massed ranks of Soviet heavy tanks in a fruitless attempt to hold this armoured rush.

and

> . . . the bulk of Sixth Panzer Army faced the threat of complete encirclement south of Székesfehérvar, with only a narrow corridor less than a mile wide and already swept by guns and machine-gun fire providing a hazardous route to safety.

do little for our understanding of what really happened and are presumably derived from Soviet 'heroic' accounts of the fighting. Such descriptions have unfortunately resulted in many people being left with the impression that the Germans were quickly overwhelmed in Hungary and forced into a chaotic retreat by a mass of Soviet tanks and hordes of infantry. It was not like that – not at all!

The first misconception which has to be corrected is that the Soviets vastly outnumbered the Germans. In fact, the fifty-four Soviet divisions[1], including six armoured and three cavalry, which took part in the offensive between Lake Balaton and the Danube, were opposed by twenty German and six Hungarian divisions, eleven of which were armoured[2] – nothing like the 3:1 ratio normally expected in assault operations. Readers will be aware already that, regardless of nationality, few if any of these divisions were anywhere near up to strength.

The second myth concerns the armoured aspect of the fighting in Hungary in March 1945. The 'Balaton Operation', which can be said to include both SPRING AWAKENING and the Soviet counter-offensive, has been described as one of the greatest armoured battles of WWII – comparisons have even been made with the German offensive at Kursk (Map 1) in 1943, with figures of over 1,000 Soviet and some 900 German tanks and self-propelled guns being quoted. But, as we have seen, very little Soviet armour was used to counter SPRING AWAKENING – it was basically an infantry battle on both sides – and, according to this author's investigations, by the time the Soviet counter-offensive was launched on 16 March the Germans had fewer than 400 operational tanks and assault guns. Figures showing combat-ready vehicles are available for 15 or 17 March, depending on the formation concerned; in the case of I SS Panzer Corps, they show the LAH numbered thirty-seven tanks, four Jagdpanzers or StuGs and nine Tiger IIs (some additional Tigers had been blown up by their crews south of Székesfehérvar due to a lack of recovery vehicles[3]), whilst the HJ is shown with eighteen tanks and twenty-three Jagdpanzers. The 23rd Panzer Division had another twenty-eight operational tanks, Jagdpanzers and StuGs.[4] Dietrich's other SS Panzer Corps – II and IV – and Balck's Sixth Army had just over 250 tanks and assault guns between them.[5]

The Soviet Offensive: 16 – 18 March

(Map 28)

The Red Army assault in the Lake Balaton area on 16 March was carried out, in accordance with its tactical doctrine, by two Combined Arms Armies – the Fourth and the Ninth. The Germans talk of 'approximately twenty [Russian] tanks per kilometre of attack front'[6], but in fact these

Armies had very little armour. The Ninth Guards had no mechanized or tank corps (Panzer divisions) allocated to it and most of the Tank Corps[7] (Panzer Division) in the Fourth Guards Army was already committed in the fighting to the south-east of Lake Valencei.

These two Armies which, even at half strength, numbered some 100,000 men and 4,000 guns, attacked between Székesfehérvar and the Vertes hills in the IV SS Panzer Corps sector. Their aim was to cause maximum attrition and to create a wide breach through which armour could debouch. Only after this breach had been made, and Marshal Tolbukhin was convinced that the ground conditions were suitable for armoured forces, would the massed tanks[8] of the Sixth Guards Tank Army (Panzer Corps) be released for the exploitation phase – across the rear of Dietrich's Sixth Panzer Army.

Despite all the careful and secret preparations, the attack against Gille's IV SS Panzer Corps, which included a Hungarian tank Division, was not a success. After some early reverses the Germans and Hungarians managed to hold their ground and at the end of the first day the Russians had made little or no progress.

On the following day, 17 March, a third Soviet Army[9] from Malinovsky's Second Ukrainian front opened a new attack in the sector between the Vertes hills and the Danube, with Tata, Komarom and Györ as its immediate objectives. This Army had a Guards Mechanized Corps[10] (Panzer Division) in support; at full strength, which is unlikely, it would have amounted to some 200 tanks and SUs. This attack was successful. Although the 2nd Hungarian Panzer Division and 3rd SS Panzer Division Totenkopf held their ground around Mor and Söred (Map 29) respectively on the 18th, and the 5th Wiking SS Panzer Division remained firm in and around Székesfehérvar, the single Hungarian 1st Hussar Division defending a 20km sector in the wooded Vertes hills was overwhelmed and, in the ensuing breakthrough, Dad fell to the Russians.

On the day of this breakthrough, General Wöhler, the commander Army Group South, reorganised his command and issued new orders. With effect from 1400 hours on 19 March, Balck's Sixth Army was to take responsibility for the sector between Lakes Valencei and Balaton and Sepp Dietrich's Sixth Panzer Army from the south-west tip of Lake Valencei to the Danube – Dietrich would thus become responsible for the area of the breakthrough. He was to take command of IV SS Panzer Corps covering the front from Mor to Székesfehérvar and the 6th Panzer Division and Third Hungarian Army between Mor and the Danube. He was to retain command of I SS Panzer Corps, but II SS Panzer Corps would only revert to him after it had disengaged from the fighting south-east of Székesfehérvar. The WWI sergeant-major and Hitler's former personal bodyguard was thus to become an Army Group commander! General Balck took over I Cavalry and III Panzer Corps and the Second Hungarian

Army and, as just mentioned, he was to command II SS Panzer Corps until it could disengage.

This decision – to change the command structure in the face of the Soviet offensive – seems extraordinary and ill-judged. It has been described as 'not having many parallels in military history'. After all, it meant extracting Dietrich's I and II SS Panzer Corps (four Panzer Divisions) from another commander's area of responsibility and condemning I SS Panzer Corps to the defence of the Bakony forest (Map 28) and the mountains between Varpalota and the Marcal canal – a region totally unsuitable for armour. The administrative difficulties caused by this change were no less serious; for example, the General commanding Balck's Communication Zone was required to move his Headquarters and administrative units over 60km to the south, from near Györ to the Sarvar area.[11] But a glance at the map shows why this decision was made. Between the Danube and Lake Balaton there were, and still are, only two major routes leading west – one runs through Komarom and Györ to Vienna, and the other from Székesfehérvar to Janoshaza, and then on to Körmend in a generally south-westerly direction. Since this latter route led away from southern Germany it was obviously of lesser importance. Therefore, despite the disruption and complications of switching forces in the middle of a battle, it made complete sense to Hitler to use his trusted and still relatively powerful Waffen-SS Panzer Divisions on the route leading directly to Vienna, Linz and München.

I SS Panzer Corps

Author's Note: In the last few chaotic weeks of the war it was inevitable that many unit records and war diaries would be lost or destroyed, or in some cases not kept at all. So it was with the Leibstandarte and Hitlerjugend – their War Diaries for this period do not exist. Readers will no doubt have noticed that fewer details of the fighting are being provided and the beginning of the Soviet offensive sees the picture becoming even more blurred. As we approach the end of the fighting, whole units will disappear from our scene without mention, or come and go like the ghosts they have since become. Every effort has been made to produce a comprehensive image but much reliance has had to be placed on individual memories which may or may not be wholly accurate.

18 – 19 March
(Map 29)

The Hitlerjugend Division completed its assembly around Szabadbattyan during the 18th and then, under cover of darkness, moved to a new concentration area south of Mor. It was under orders, as we have seen, to take part in a I SS Panzer Corps counter-attack, supported by the 356th Infantry Division, aimed at Zamoly. This grandiose scheme, which had little chance of implementation on the scale envisaged, came to naught when stragglers from the 3rd SS Panzer Division Totenkopf began arriving at the HJ Command Post at Balinka around midday on the 19th and aerial reconnaissance reported that the enemy had broken through that Division south of Mor. Most of the 26th SS Panzer-Grenadier Regiment took up hasty defensive positions in the Balinka area in the late afternoon, while Bremer's 12th SS Reconnaissance Battalion blocked crossings over the small canal at Bodajk – a northern extension of the Sarviz (Map 27). Kraas's Headquarters and the 12th SS Flak Battalion set up in Szapar, whilst Martin Gross's armoured group assembled 4km east of that village in close country with woods on both sides of the only road and visibility restricted to less than 500m. Some unspecified sub-units of the Totenkopf Division attached themselves to the HJ at this time and were positioned on the left flank.

The Chief of Staff of the Hitlerjugend Division claims that Müller's 25th Grenadier Regiment and Brockschmidt's 12th SS Panzerjägers were detached to the LAH on the 19th. This would certainly have made sense since the Soviet threat in the Leibstandarte's area of responsibility was the more serious. However, Ralf Tiemann's Leibstandarte History makes no mention of these units operating with the LAH and both units virtually 'disappear' until 27 March, when Meyer describes them in positions behind the Raba river – again under HJ command. We have only three reports of their activities in the intervening period – two provided to Meyer in the early 1980s by Hitlerjugend veterans. One told Meyer that the Jagdpanzers were in action near Inota and the 25th Regiment near Bakonykuti (Map 27) on 19 March, and the other claimed that both units fought 'probably north and north-west of Varpolota' on the 21st. There were no further details. It seems possible therefore that, in the case of Müller's Regiment at least, the delayed withdrawal from the Ozora area (Map 27) resulted in its prolonged separation from the rest of the Hitlerjugend and in the chaotic conditions pertaining at this time, the Regiment moved independently to the Raba. The third report would tend to confirm this, in that two members of Müller's 25th Regiment claim they were fighting in the LAH sector near Herend on the 24th. Certainly, as we shall hear, the LAH was in action in that area on that day.

Soon after the HJ moved into its new positions the first Soviet attacks developed. Balinka was held and six T-34s knocked out but, farther south, Isztimer was occupied by the enemy. Therefore, during the night of the 19th, Priess issued orders for the HJ to attack before first light and retake the village. This turned out to be a mistake because, as we shall see, it ran into trouble and inevitably weakened the 26th SS Panzer-Grenadier Regiment holding the main axis.

Meanwhile, the Leibstandarte, far from preparing for its part in the planned counter-attack, was finding it difficult even to assemble in the Inota area. SS Major Jupp Diefenthal, the commander of the Divisional SPW Battalion, said afterwards:

> The Battalion redeployed through Polgardi to Inota. It arrived on the morning of 19 March. Inota was occupied by the enemy. There was heavy house-to-house fighting . . . with consequent heavy losses. Security was set up east of Inota. . . . There was enemy movement north of the village.[12]

And the War Diary of the 1st SS Flak Battalion recorded:

> After a strenuous night march, the Batteries . . . took up ground role positions north-west and south of Varpalota as part of the 1st SS Panzer-Grenadier Regiment. . . . The 37mm Battery was committed by platoons and located with the Grenadiers on a high plateau in a line east of Varpalota. The German lines were very thinly held there.[13]

The combat, as opposed to total, strength of the LAH at this time is given as 4,214 men.[14] If this figure is correct, it means the LAH was some 60% below the authorised strength of a Waffen-SS Panzer Division on arrival in its new sector.

KG Peiper, which still comprised all the Divisions's tanks and Diefenthal's 3rd SPW Panzer-Grenadier Battalion, assembled behind a security line, set up by the Panzer-Grenadiers, running from Csor to Bakonykuti (Map 27).

During the evening of the 19th, the LAH too found itself fighting off a heavy attack some 4km to the east of Varpalota – eight Soviet tanks are said to have been knocked out. The need to prevent a Soviet advance along the Székesfehérvar–Varpalota–Veszprem road was obvious and Kumm's men were therefore ordered to counter-attack before first light on the 20th and push the enemy away from this vital approach.

As the men of Hitler's Leibstandarte Corps prepared to launch their counter-attacks, they had no idea that their Führer had, on the same day, ordered a 'scorched earth' policy in their beloved Homeland:

> The battle should be conducted without consideration for our own population. . . . Everything . . . which could be of immediate use to the enemy for the continuation of the fight [was to be destroyed] . . . all industrial plants, all important electrical facilities, waterworks, gasworks . . . all food and clothing stores . . . all bridges, all railway

installations, the postal system . . . also the waterways, all ships, all freight cars and all locomotives.

When Albert Speer allegedly protested, Hitler is said to have replied:

If the war is lost, the German nation will also perish. This fate is inevitable. There is no need to take into consideration the basic requirements of the people for continuing even a most primitive existence. . . . Those who remain after the battle are those who are inferior; for the good will have fallen.[15]

The 'good' would, of course, include many members of his Bodyguard Corps.

Wöhler's new command arrangements proved unsatisfactory before the end of the first day. Dietrich requested the return of I Cavalry Corps to his Panzer Army for use in wooded mountains where he was desperately short of infantry, and Balck asked for armoured support from I and IV SS Panzer Corps.[16] Dietrich's request was turned down but Balck managed to retain the 5th SS Panzer Division under his command and, in the event, the 9th SS Panzer Division of II SS Panzer Corps.

The Soviets had been surprised by the tenacity of the German and Hungarian defence in the first three days of their offensive and, as a consequence, they were forced to commit the Sixth Guards Tank Army (Panzer Corps) to battle before a breakthrough on a wide frontage had been achieved. It was these tanks which would now add to problems of I SS Panzer Corps. Hubert Meyer, the Chief of Staff of the HJ, claims I SS Panzer Corps had only eighty-two operational tanks, Jagdpanzers and assault guns available on the 20th to resist Tolbuhkin's advance. His figures, if the nine operational Tiger IIs of the 501st SS Heavy Panzer Battalion are added, match exactly those given earlier in this Chapter.

From Balaton to Raba: 20 – 27 March
(Map 29)

Before describing the next phase of fighting, it is perhaps useful to describe the ground over which it took place. In the case of the Leibstandarte, Varpalota stands on high ground and the area between it and Veszprem is rolling moorland, interspersed with some large quarries. In many ways it would have reminded the men of the LAH of their military training areas in the Fatherland – such as Fallingbostel and Sennelager. Some 5km before Veszprem the ground is completely open, but to the south of the main Varpalota-Veszprem road there were extensive forests. Whilst the defence of the road and the area to its north was a reasonable proposition by day and in good visibility, at night and in poor weather conditions it required far more troops than were available; and of course, the forests to the south of the road presented severe problems for defender and attacker alike.

The LAH counter-attack towards Csor (Map 27) and the hills to its north was due to begin at 0400 hours on the 20th. According to the Divisional History by Ralf Tiemann[17], it was launched on time by Poetschke's armoured group, including elements of Rettlinger's 1st SS Panzerjäger Battalion, but in the face of intense Russian defensive fire. The enemy then counter-attacked along the Székesfehérvar-Varpalota road. A different version of events is presented by Poetschke's Adjutant, Rolf Reiser:

> The enemy attacked before we could launch our own attack. During the early morning the infantry attacked in waves. . . . The attack received massive support from forty tanks . . . . The bitter armoured battle . . . lasted all day. Nineteen enemy tanks were destroyed in the 7th Panzer Company sector. . . . During the afternoon fighter-bombers attacked Inota with bombs and fired on our Panzers. . . . Ivan was able to penetrate into the village. During this fighting SS Lieutenant Wolff's Panzer [commander 7th SS Panzer Company and a Knight's Cross holder] was hit and he was killed. As twilight fell, the situation climaxed dramatically. The enemy infiltrated between our Panzers and pressed hard against our command post. Poetschke decided to give up Inota. He ordered us to break contact with the enemy and withdraw in the direction of Varpalota.[18]

The withdrawal to Varpalota was described by the Divisional commander, Otto Kumm:

> The commander of the Werfer Battalion, SS Captain Menzel . . . reported enemy tanks driving in the rear of his positions [west of Inota] from north to south. . . . Tigers driving along the road in the direction of Varpalota ran into the tanks that were crossing the road and destroyed fifteen of them.
>
> I used a Battalion group from Hansen's 1st SS Panzer-Grenadier Regiment from the main defensive line to comb the forest south of the road – another fifteen enemy tanks were destroyed. In the meantime, the enemy attacked the main defensive line with tanks, infantry and strong artillery support. The front had to be withdrawn to the eastern edge of Varpalota that evening.[19]

The withdrawal of the armoured group to Varpalota was easier said than done because some companies and platoons were out of touch with Poetschke's Headquarters. Werner Sternebeck of the 3rd SS Panzer Company:

> Before midnight we decided to withdraw to Inota. We organised with one Tiger II, then six Mk IVs, followed by another Tiger II [both from SS Lieutenant Jürgen Wessel's 3rd Company]. Making use of the darkness and artillery fire, we reached the eastern edge of the village. The Russians initially took us for one of their own units. . . . We rushed through the village at full speed. Almost at the western edge our lead Tiger had to destroy several T-34s, but we were able to leave Inota unharmed [and reach Varpalota].[20]

Sometime on the 20th Otto Kumm was summoned to Dietrich's Sixth Panzer Army Headquarters. One could be forgiven for thinking that the reason was to discuss the seriousness of the situation – but no, it was to receive Swords to his Knight's Cross! He had been awarded these for commanding the 7th SS Mountain Division in Serbia and Croatia. The Leibstandarte History claims that during this award ceremony there was an air raid and Hein von Westernhagen, the commander of the 501st SS Heavy Panzer Battalion, was mortally wounded by a direct hit on the command post.[21] On the other hand, Wolfgang Schneider, in his very detailed second Volume of *Tigers in Combat*, says the story of the air raid was a cover and that, after being relieved of his command due to illness brought on by strain and old wounds, he shot himself.[22] Whatever the truth, SS Major Heinz Kling, who had commanded the LAH's Tiger Company in 1943 and the 2nd SS Panzer Battalion of Peiper's Regiment in Normandy, took command of what was left of the 501st Tiger Battalion on the 20th.

The ground to the north of the LAH sector, where the Hitlerjugend was fighting, was forested and mountainous. This made it the most difficult axis for the Soviets in their advance westwards and, not surprisingly, they concentrated their main efforts on outflanking the German defence in the open rolling country to the north and south of the Balinka-Zirc road – the only major route through the area and the one being defended by the HJ. This road traversed a series of high ridges, and villages like Dudar, Jasd and Bakonynana dominated the surrounding countryside with perfect fields of fire. To add to the attacker's problems, there were quarries on both sides of the main road. Dudar, standing on a wooded ridge was, and still is, a large mining area.

The Hitlerjugend's counter-attack began at 0500 hours on the 20th and initially made some progress. Unfortunately for Kraas, however, a coincidental Russian move along the Bodajk-Balinka road hit the flank of the HJ's advance and the German attack was brought to a halt. Part of SS Captain Hans Siegel's armoured group, including SPW mounted

Grenadiers of the 3rd Battalion, was ordered to extricate the rest of Braun's 26th Regiment. Siegel describes what happened:

> With four or five Panzers, I rolled along a narrow path towards our objective. . . . Then the valley widened. . . . We spotted ahead of us the outlines of one or more large buildings; a mill? . . . Suddenly [the point vehicle] stopped and immediately fired. . . . Through my headphones, scratchy, the message: 'Achtung! Achtung! Enemy tanks ahead! Out!' . . . Some eight to ten T-34s were sitting, close together, on the path along which we were rolling. Behind the building – dismounted – stood the commanders . . . probably in a briefing with their chief. The luck of war was on our side once again! I immediately ordered the two rear-most tanks knocked out, the two at the point of the column were already burning. The crews fled under fire from our Grenadiers. . . . In no time all the tanks were ours. The radios were still on and one of us, who spoke Russian, took over. . . . 'Hold on comrades, two mechanized corps [Panzer divisions] are on the way to support you!' . . . Our Panzers secured all around. . . . The Grenadiers occupied the hills. We waited, covering the area.[23]

The counter-attack was a success and Braun's Battalions were able to pull back – the Army Group South War Diary confirms that eight Russian tanks were destroyed in this fighting, bringing the I SS Panzer Corps total for the day to sixty-six.

Despite the HJ's apparent success on the Bodajk-Mecser road, the Russians continued to advance on the Division's left flank and during the night of the 20th a village 6km west of Mor was abandoned by Hungarian troops. Elsewhere in the Sixth Panzer Army sector on the 20th, the 2nd SS and 6th Panzer Divisions, after extricating themselves from the area to the south of Lake Valencei and crossing the path of the Soviet advance, moved north towards Dad with the aim of halting the Soviet breakthrough in the Vertes hills.

In Balck's Sixth Army sector, the 1st Panzer Division, during its withdrawal from south of the Lake Valencei, drove back a strong Russian force attacking between the Lake and Székesfehérvar. Later they managed to make contact with units of the 5th SS Panzer Division Wiking still holding on to parts of the town.

On the 21st the Russians renewed their attacks against the Hitlerjugend along and on both sides of the Balinka-Szapar-Zirc road and westwards from Isztimer. At this time Kraas's Division, still less its 25th SS Panzer-Grenadier Regiment and Panzerjäger Battalion, was deployed with the 26th Regiment and Siegel's 2nd SS Panzer Battalion defending the hills on either side of the Balinka-Szapar road at Mecser. To its south, the Headquarters of Hermann Priess's I SS Panzer Corps was located at Tés, with the Corps Escort Company responsible for its protection.

The Soviet attack along the axis of the Balinka-Mecser road could not be held and, although the HJ claimed nineteen tanks knocked out and two captured, Braun's 3rd SPW Panzer-Grenadier Battalion was forced south-west towards Tés and his other two Grenadier Battalions and Siegel's tanks towards Szapar. Hans Siegel again describes part of the action:

> I spotted a column coming down a wooded hill to my right in an extended skirmish line. Through my binoculars I determined that they were our own men. . . . The company chief told me that they were withdrawing as ordered. The Grenadiers were all dead-tired . . . shuffling without looking up. . . . Together with the chief I marched at the point, behind us two Panzers. Then a shout: 'Ivan from the right!' . . . Soviet soldiers . . . came hurtling down from the hill, supported by machine-guns. . . . Along a wide front the hair-raising 'Urraah!' could be heard. There seemed to be no salvation, the ambush had succeeded. . . . But it turned out differently, thanks to those unbelievably brave young Grenadiers of our Division. That shout 'Ivan from the right' was like an order to attack. None of them hesitated, up came the rifles, firing from the hip, hand grenades being thrown. Concentrated fire is returned. . . . They wanted to turn and run back up the hill again – in vain! Our boys had taken hold of them and would not let go again. The nightmare lasted only minutes.[24]

Meanwhile, parts of the 2nd Hungarian Panzer Division defending the sector to the north of the Balinka-Szapar road in the Acsteszer area had been pushed back to the south-west. This exposed the HJ's left flank and the resulting threat, combined with more Russian attacks on Braun's 1st and 2nd Panzer-Grenadier Battalions from the north-east and east respectively, caused Kraas to order them to withdraw that evening directly to Szapar and for the 2nd SS Panzer Battalion to concentrate around the important hill village of Bakonynana. The Hungarians abandoned Csatka at about the same time.

Meanwhile, Soviet troops exploiting the growing gap between the LAH and the HJ, advanced from Isztimer towards Tés where they ran initially into part of the Corps Heavy Artillery Battalion, and later into Brand's 3rd SS SPW Panzer-Grenadier Battalion which, it will be recalled, had been forced there from the Balinka area. In one of the most extraordinary episodes of the day the 2nd Battery of the Corps 501st SS Heavy Artillery Battalion, located 2km north-east of Tés and equipped with 210mm multi-barrelled rocket launchers, was forced to defend its position:

> The Battery chief, SS Lieutenant Hinrich Garbade, learned from indi-
> vidually retreating infantrymen that no more German troops were
> behind them. Garbade reported that to the artillery commander of I
> SS Panzer Corps and requested permission to change position. That
> request was denied and the Battery chief was ordered to defend the
> position in order to allow the Corps staff to withdraw [to a location
> near Zirc]. When the first enemy tanks appeared in the morning in
> front of the position, the two 210mm mortars fired directly at them. . . .
> Some tanks were hit and exploded. Others, however, opened fire on the
> mortars which could not swing round quickly enough. The Battery had
> to give up the unequal fight. The mortars were rendered inoperable,
> the crews withdrew. They were sent into action during the subsequent
> fighting as infantrymen and known as KG Garbade.[25]

Despite the arrival of Brand's SPW Battalion, Tés fell during the afternoon. The Grenadiers were forced back to a hill west of the village and the Corps Escort Company, which had covered the withdrawal of the Corps Head-quarters, into a thick forest 3km south of Bakonynana. There was now a serious possibility of a Russian breakthrough to the main Veszprem-Györ road and Kraas ordered an immediate counter-attack. Four Jagdpanthers (of the 560th Heavy Panzerjäger Battalion), an SPW-mounted Grenadier company from the 3rd Battalion, the HJ and Corps Escort Companies and another unspecified Grenadier Company took part. Three attacks were launched in quick succession – the first at 1700 and the last at 2030 hours. They all failed and three of the Jagdpanthers were lost; personnel casualties are unspecified.

During the late afternoon or early evening another Soviet group moved from the area north-east of Tés and approached Szapar. Since the other two Battalions of Braun's 26th Regiment had yet to arrive in the village, it fell to the HJ's 12th SS Flak Battalion to halt this advance. The action is described by its commander, SS Major Dr Loenicker:

> A major day of action for the Battalion. Massive attacks by the Russians
> on our positions. 1st and 4th Batteries firing directly at attacking
> infantry. We fired explosive and percussion shells and stopped the
> attack. We came under concentrated fire from rocket launchers. . . .
> In the evening [after the arrival of the Panzer-Grenadier Battalions]
> back to Dudar.[26]

By the evening there was no longer a continuous German front in the

Bakony region. The weakened HJ Division – recall one Panzer-Grenadier Regiment and the Panzerjäger Battalion were still 'missing' – was defending a frontage of some 16km running from just west of Tés, through Szapar, to a position 2km north-west of Csesznek. At the southern end of this line the 3rd SS Panzer-Grenadier Battalion with its SPWs, and the Divisional Escort Company with some Jagdpanzers from the 560th Heavy Panzerjäger Battalion in support, were to be found just to the west of Tés; the rest of Martin Gross's armoured group was still at Bakonynana; the 12th SS Pioneer Battalion was in and around Jasd, unaware that they were in the front line; the other two SS Panzer-Grenadier Battalions of Braun's 26th Regiment were defending Szapar; the 12th SS Flak Battalion was in position around Dudar, where it could protect the guns of the 12th SS Artillery Regiment and Kraas's Command Post; and Bremer's 12th SS Reconnaissance Battalion was covering the northern flank of the Division and, at the same time, trying to maintain contact with the attached units of the Totenkopf Division and Hungarians still between Acsteszer and Csesznek.

During 21 March the Leibstandarte came under heavy attack in the Varpalota sector. Hansen's 1st SS Panzer-Grenadier Regiment, with Poetschke's 1st and 2nd Panther Companies, was responsible for the defence of the town and its environs, whilst Siebken's 2nd Regiment, with the 6th SS Flak Battery and elements of SS Major Scheler's 1st SS Pioneer Battalion attached, defended the area between the town and the Hitlerjugend in the Tés area. The fact that the LAH had to provide this significant force on its northern flank reinforces the belief that the HJ's 25th SS Panzer-Grenadier Regiment was not under its command at this time – if it had been, it would have been the obvious unit to provide the link with the HJ. The only reports we have of the 6th and 7th SS Panzer Companies on the 21st are in Veszprem and it seems they were withdrawn there before the other combat units of the Division for maintenance and as a reserve.

The LAH's right flank was covered by elements of the 9th SS Panzer Division Hohenstaufen which was in action near Ösi to the south-east of Varpalota. Inexplicably, and to the intense annoyance of Dietrich and the Divisional commander, 9th SS was still part of Balck's Sixth Army; nevertheless, it kept in close contact with its Waffen-SS comrades.

The first infantry and tank attacks on Varpalota, strongly supported by fighter-bombers, came soon after dawn and intensified throughout the day. Jochen Peiper estimated sixty to seventy tanks were deployed in these attacks.[24]. Although forty-six were claimed by the LAH[25], the Russians began to outflank the town to the north and it became obvious that Varpalota could not be held. Rolf Reiser described the last hours of the fighting in and around the town:

SS Captain Malkomes, commanding the 2nd SS Panzer Company, arrived at the command post at about 1500 hours to report on the worsening situation. According to his assessment the town could not be held through the night. . . . [He was told] to hold until dawn and then withdraw. Thirty minutes later Malkomes' tank quickly returned to the command post. [He] had been killed by a shot to the head [and] was sitting dead in the turret. SS Major Poetschke climbed into the tank in order to lead the last Panzers out of the chaos of Varpalota. . . . The road was already under direct fire and blocked by burning vehicles. . . . Birnschein [3rd SS Tiger Company] and Heubeck [Panther company] reported over the radio: 'Enemy armoured column driving along parallel to Öskü-Hajmasker road in direction Veszprem. Attacking!' Within two hours seventeen enemy tanks destroyed.[27]

The withdrawal to new defensive positions 2km east of Öskü and around Hajmasker began at about 1800 hours. It was covered by the 3rd SPW SS Panzer-Grenadier Battalion, whose commander, Jupp Diefenthal, had orders to pull back to Veszprem once Varpalota was clear. He said later:

Varpalota was in flames! We withdrew south of the town to Öskü which was likewise held by the enemy. . . . We fought to open the withdrawal route to Veszprem. . . . The Battalion moved into position north and south of the main road in order to engage the enemy on the left or the right as they flooded past. There was occasional enemy contact. The width of the Battalion front was 800m. . . . The Russians overtook our forces in the race to the west, particularly in the north. There were disorganised German Army units withdrawing along the main road in the direction Veszprem-Devecser.[28]

It is clear that by this time the other SS Corps under Dietrich's command, Gille's IV SS Panzer Corps, had lost its cohesion. As we have seen, some sub-units of the Totenkopf were attached to the HJ and others were fighting with the LAH. The 5th SS Panzer Division Wiking, which had been fighting a quite separate battle in Székesfehérvar, was forced to give up the town on the evening of the 21st. The southern part of the Sixth Panzer Army's front was clearly beginning to disintegrate.

The fighting had now been raging for six days and in this time the Soviet offensive had advanced an average of only 25km. Unlike, however, the attack by I SS Panzer Corps which had made similar gains in the same timeframe only ten days earlier, it was gaining, rather than losing, momentum. The physical and mental strain of the constant fighting, uncertainty of the situation and fear of capture was beginning to tell on even the most experienced members of I SS Panzer Corps. A member of the 26th SS Panzer-Grenadier Regiment, SS Corporal Martin Glade, later described events during the early hours of 22 March:

> We were at the end of our physical strength. At each orientation stop, comrades dropped to the ground where they stood. . . . A messenger from the Battalion guided us . . . to our defensive sector. . . . He [the Company commander] distributed the Company along a ridge in the darkness. 'Dig in! Dig in!' I heard him shout in the darkness, time and again. We, from the Company HQ, dug shallow holes for ourselves. Mine was the depth of a spade. Then, fatigue overcame me. . . .
> When I woke up again, I was hardly able to get to my feet. I was frozen right through. The sky was turning red in the east. . . . With my frozen fingers I dug in my haversack for a dry bread crust and a piece of sausage. . . . Then I walked along the ridge. . . . Not a tree, not a bush to offer cover! Like dark spots the men lie in small groups . . . they are all still asleep. Hardly any of them still had the will or the energy to dig in during the night. . . .
> A bad feeling came over me. I grabbed my spade, woke the comrades next to me and tried to deepen my hole. . . . Like a bolt of lightning out of a clear sky, Russian fire hit us. It was coming from the left, from the hill where the Pioneers were supposed to be. The effect of the enemy fire was devastating. The Company was in front of the Russians as if on a tray – in full view. . . . I glanced from my cover and was terrified – to the right and left of me, men were lying motionless, silent, strangely curled up – more than half the Company I thought. Last night when we moved onto that damned hill we had been forty-eight.[29]

On 22 March the situation south and south-west of Varpalota worsened considerably. In the Leibstandarte sector the Soviet threat to Veszprem intensified as a tank brigade (Panzer Battalion) with infantry support attacked down the main axis from Varpalota. Since substantial German groups were still trying to fight their way west from the Székesfehérvar area, it remained essential to keep the way open to and through this important communication centre and, while the LAH fought on to the south-west of Varpalota, the 4th Division of I Cavalry Corps struggled to defend a line running north-east from Balatonkenese through Küngös, and parts of the 9th SS Panzer Division covered the Berhida area. This allowed elements of four German Divisions – including the 5th SS Panzer Division Wiking – to escape from the Székesfehérvar pocket.[30]

In the particular case of the LAH, Hansen's depleted 1st SS Panzer-Grenadier Regiment and the remains of Poetschke's 1st SS Panzer Battalion defended the main approach to Veszprem around Öskü, whilst Siebken's 2nd SS Panzer-Grenadier Group covered the approach to the south-west of Tés. The Soviet attack was launched north of the main Veszprem road, through Hajmasker, and it succeeded in splitting the LAH defence – pushing Siebken's Regimental Group north-west towards Zirc and encircling the southern group in the Öskü area. In the afternoon, the Divisional commander, who was with Hansen's and Poetschke's KGs in the south, gave orders for a breakout through Liter and the establishment of a new front on the eastern edge of Veszprem. Without specifically mentioning Max Hansen's Grenadiers, who were of course heavily involved in the fighting east of Veszprem, Rolf Reiser describes what happened to one part of the armoured force:

> After an enemy armoured formation of forty to fifty tanks attacked through Hajmasker towards . . . Veszprem, Panzer Group Poetschke was [ordered] to detour to the south, through Liter . . . attack the enemy, open the road to Veszprem and hold it open. Liter was reached at about 1300 hours. . . . The Panzer Group had a total of sixteen tanks. They were refueled and resupplied with ammunition. At 1430 hours they set out . . . visibility was limited by little acacia woods. . . . The tanks drove along the main road in echelon. . . . Then there were two or three flashes out of the acacia wood to the right and the hollow bellow of T-34 cannon could be heard distinctly. . . . Our lead tank was hit! The enemy tanks broke out on the right from the acacia grove and on the left from the other wood. They had us in a pincer. . . . We screened ourselves with smoke. . . . We lost several more tanks among which was that of the Air Liaison Officer – the Lieutenant came out of his Mk IV like a flaming torch. Finally we reached the western edge of Liter. We had taken heavy losses, seven tanks, several SPWs and killed and wounded with severe burns. We assembled on the north-west edge of Liter and took up defensive positions. We waited to see if Ivan would pursue. He did not![31]

Under the cover of darkness KG Poetschke completed its withdrawal to Veszprem by 2300 hours.

The Soviet attack in the HJ sector continued soon after dawn. Brand's SPW Battalion with some Jagdpanzers and the Divisional Escort Company near Tés received a frontal attack and then another from the west by Russians who had infiltrated to the south during the night – presumably exploiting a gap between the HJ and Siebken's LAH Regimental Group. By 0800 hours both units had been forced back – Brand's men and the Jagdpanzers to Bakonynana where the majority of the Gross's armour was still concentrated, and the Escort Company into the forest south of the village. At 1000 hours the armoured group, including Brand's Battalion, was ordered to pull back to Zirc, which lay in a deep valley to the west, and the Escort Company given responsibility for covering this withdrawal. At 1330 hours, after holding off a strong Russsian attack, it too was given permission to pull out and told to move to Lokut and cover the right flank of the Division. It took until the middle of the night to arrive there. Meanwhile, Kraas's Headquarters had set up in the huge monastery at Zirc.

At Jasd, 4km north of Tés, Taubert's 12th SS Pioneer Battalion had been surprised by a Soviet attack soon after dawn. The 1st SPW-mounted Company managed to pull out with only minor casualties but the others, mainly the 2nd Motorized Company in the buildings of a mill on the east side of a creek, were not so lucky – 120 men were never seen again! The remainder of the Battalion took up new positions on the south-east edge of Dudar.

Braun's 1st and 2nd SS Panzer-Grenadier Battalions managed to hang on in the Szapar area throughout most of the morning, but after Jasd fell there was little option other than to pull back to Dudar. The commander of the 5th Company, Senior Officer Cadet Kunze, was killed during this fighting. By the time the 2nd Battalion reached Dudar, the 5th and 7th Companies are said to have consisted of only five men each and the 6th forty men. The two-Battalion force now amounted to no more than a weak KG.

Dudar itself, protected by the 12th Flak Battalion, came under attack from the north at midday. Six Russian tanks were knocked out for the loss of two 88mm and two 37mm guns before the Flak Battalion was relieved by the 26th Panzer-Grenadiers during the afternoon and sent in an infantry role to new positions 4km south-west of Zirc where it could protect the vital road leading to Penzesgyör. The Artillery batteries of the 12th SS Artillery Regiment pulled back at the same time.

Towards evening Dudar again came under heavy attack and the 1st and 2nd SS Panzer-Grenadier Battalions and Pioneers were given permission to pull back to a position, 2km north-east of Zirc, already held by a sub-unit of the Totenkopf Division. The ever widening gap between the HJ and the LAH was now causing serious concern and, soon after arrival in the new location, Braun was ordered to send the two Grenadier Battalions on to Lokut to protect the southern flank. The few Grenadiers of the 2nd Battalion were carried on an unspecified number of tanks and, after a difficult journey along a conjested road, arrived there early the following morning, with the 1st Battalion catching up later. The Divisional Escort Company, already in the area, was placed under Braun's command.

On the northern flank of the HJ, sub-units of the Totenkopf Division were pushed back towards the Zirc-Csesznek road during the 22nd, but Bremer's 12th SS Reconnaissance Battalion is said to have restored the situation before dark.

Farther north still, the situation was more stable with the 2nd SS Panzer and 6th Panzer Divisions, under the command of II SS Panzer Corps, managing to stabilise the situation between Kisbér and Komarom.

The skies were clear on the 23rd, the weather warm and sunny and by now the ground had dried out, making cross-country movement much easier.

In the Hitlerjugend sector, Brand's 3rd SS Panzer-Grenadier Battalion, with its attached Jagdpanzers, conducted a fighting withdrawal from Zirc back to Penzesgyör. The terrain between the two locations rises steeply and is initially open, but soon after Penzesgyör the road enters hilly country, with thick deciduous woods which were impenetrable to vehicles – reminiscent of parts of the Ardennes. SS Major Dr Loenicker's 12th SS Flak Battalion, 4km to the south of Penzesgyör, fought on into the night of the 23rd with one battery in the anti-tank role and the rest acting as infantry. Five Russian tanks were claimed before it too was forced to pull back to the village.

Braun's 1st and 2nd SS Panzer-Grenadiers and Siegel's few remaining tanks had a relatively quiet morning at Lokut. This small village guards a vital valley leading north-west to Penzesgyör and had to be defended until the rest of the Division had been withdrawn. During the after-noon Russian reconnaissance parties were seen and a full-scale attack developed around 1930 hours. Despite a serious shortage of artillery ammunition, the Germans held on until just after midnight when they also began to pull back to Penzesgyör – the Grenadiers again being carried out on the tanks. Three T-34s were claimed in this fighting. It is of interest that by this time the personnel of the 5th SS Panzer (Mk IV) Company, under SS Lieutenant Gasch, had returned to the Panzer Battalion from the training unit at Fallingbostel in Germany – but without tanks! Some were used to replace casualties and the remainder acted as Panzer-Grenadiers and fought with the tanks.

On the HJ's left flank the Russians broke through the Totenkopf blocking positions near Csesznek, threatening the Division's only remain-ing withdrawal route, Penzesgyör-Bakonykoppany-Beb, from the north-east.

During 23 March Bernhard Siebken's 2nd SS Panzer-Grenadier Group continued its defence of the northern part of the LAH sector. We have no details of its actions – all that is known is that during the day it was forced to withdraw to the hills south of Lokut. The Group seems to have had no contact with the rest of the Division around Veszprem or with the HJ at Lokut. To all intents and purposes it was acting as a completely separate formation.

The southern LAH group, responsible for the defence of Veszprem, still comprised KGs Hansen and Poetschke; it was commanded directly by the Divisional commander, Otto Kumm. The Soviet assault on the town was launched along three separate axes – from Balatonkenese, from Vilonya and from Hajmasker. The LAH was responsible for the eastern and north-eastern approaches and elements of the Hohenstaufen and 4th Cavalry Divisions those from the south and south-east. KG Hansen, with a few Jagdpanzers, covered the roads leading in from Hajmasker and Berhida, while Poetschke's remaining tanks set up on the north-east edge of the town. Twenty Russian tanks were claimed in the day's fighting but as Kumm later described it:

> The Division was thrown out of Veszprem by an armoured attack and pushed back to the eastern edge of Marko [7km to the north-west].[32]

KG Hansen inevitably lost men in the vicious house-to-house fighting, including a Company commander, SS Second Lieutenant Dick. But the 'catastrophe of Veszprem', as Rolf Reiser called it, occurred in KG Poetschke:

> Shortly after 0600 hours we were driving through Veszprem with nine tanks, a radio SPW and two Schwimmwagens. . . . The town was almost dead. Here and there we ran into a vehicle racing through. I drove in a Schwimmwagen with Poetschke to reconnoitre the ground at the edge of the town. The tanks followed. . . . Through binoculars we saw an armoured column advancing from Kadarta [2km to the north-east]. It could have been thirty to forty vehicles. . . . Our tank caught up and Poetschke brought in all the commanders to brief them on the position and situation. The group gathered around near a shed. Suddenly, there was a massive mortar bombardment. One detonanted in the middle of the group! Poetschke was severely wounded – he died a few hours later.[33] Münkemer, Gerdes and Heubeck [platoon commanders] were wounded and three other tank commanders more or less severely wounded. None of them were now capable of action. . . . Meanwhile, the enemy was attacking past Veszprem in the north and blocking the road 8km behind us near Marko. Under the circumstances the tanks, without leaders, were withdrawn and ordered back to Marko. That was the darkest day in our Panzer Regiment.[34]

Werner Poetschke had been awarded Oakleaves to his Knight's Cross only a few days previously – for his performance in the Ardennes and Gran bridgehead offensive. It is strange that a soldier of his great experience, who had already been wounded five times, should have made the mistake of assembling all his commanders in a vulnerable forward area when he could have issued radio orders instead. Needless to say, these latest casualties, following so soon after the loss of the two other Company commanders and Knight's Cross holders – Wolff and

Malkomes – seriously emasculated the 1st SS Panzer Regiment. SS Captain Klingelhöfer took command of all the remaining Mk IVs and SS Major Kling of the 501st Heavy SS Panzer Battalion, not SS Captain Birnschein as stated in the LAH History, led the remaining Tiger IIs and Panthers. Jochen Peiper assumed command of the restructured Battalion himself.

The 24th of March was a clear and unusually warm day with temperatures above 20° Celsius. It was to be the last day in the battle of the Bakony forest – from Lake Balaton, through Veszprem to Zirc, and then on to Korarom on the Danube, the Soviet Armies stood poised to break out into the great western Hungarian Plain. The Forty-Sixth Army was attacking immediately south of the Danube, with Györ as its primary objective; it then planned to advance north-west, past Lake Neusiedler, towards Vienna. On the left flank, the Twenty-Sixth Army had the mission of advancing from Veszprem, through Devecser, to seize Szombathely on the far side of the Raba river (Map 28). The main thrust, however, and the one which was already engulfing I SS Panzer Corps, was in the centre. Here the Fourth and Ninth Guards Armies, strongly reinforced by the Sixth Guards Tank Army (Panzer Corps), were being directed through Papa towards Sopron and Wiener Neustadt (Map 28). The Leibstandarte and Hitlerjugend, now Panzer Divisions in name only, had no chance of stopping them – indeed, as in Normandy the previous August, they were facing annihilation.

The southern KG of the LAH, comprising parts of Hansen's 1st SS Panzer-Grenadier Regiment, reinforced by Diefenthal's 3rd SPW Battalion, the remaining tanks of Peiper's Battalion, and a few Jagdpanzers and Flak guns, was forced to evacuate Marko during the night of the 23rd to 24th. The road between Veszprem and Bakonyjako runs through beautiful woods over a series of ridge-lines and is, today, a most pleasant drive. Not so in 1945! Throughout the day the Germans tried to set up a series of delaying positions at, and between, Herend and Varoslöd but each time they were bypassed. As darkness fell, and after repulsing a frontal attack east of Varoslöd in which seven tanks were claimed, the southern KG finally halted the Soviet advance, 'albeit temporarily', in a blocking position running from Kislöd to east of Ajka. And, on this day for the first time since the Balaton offensive, we have news of the 1st SS Reconnaissance Battalion – its remnants were in position near Urkut, on the right flank, presumably trying to keep some sort of contact with parts of I Cavalry Corps and Gille's IV SS Panzer Corps to the south-west of Veszprem.

Meanwhile, Soviet forces were able to pour through the widening gap between the southern KG of the LAH and the Hitlerjugend. Siebken's 2nd SS Panzer-Grenadier Regimental Group in the north of the LAH sector, rather than risk encirclement, was forced to pull back yet again – to more open ground on the south-eastern approaches to Papa. By evening it was on a line running from Kup to Tapolcafö and on towards Ugod.

Otto Kumm claimed afterwards that he met Hugo Kraas of the HJ during the day to discuss the dangerous gap between their two Divisions.[35] With a combined frontage of over 40km, they agreed there was little they could do about it and that Soviet penetrations between their respective 'strongpoints' were inevitable. He also said that advance parties of the 1st Volks Mountain Division arrived on the 24th with the mission of taking over his part of the front.

By first light on the same day, what was left of the Hitlerjugend's 26th SS Panzer-Grenadier Regiment and armoured group, with the 12th SS Flak Battalion acting as a covering force a few hundred metres to its east, had taken up new positions on a high wooded ridge 700m east of Penzesgyör. The whole force had orders to hold there for at least twenty-four hours in order to allow the vehicle columns of the Division to withdraw along the only road available. This road, to Bakonykoppany, was little more than a river of mud and there was no possibility of resupply trucks moving in the opposite direction with much needed ammunition and fuel for the fighting troops.

At 1030 hours the Flak Battalion fell back under the weight of the first Soviet attack and an hour later a major assault developed with tanks and infantry. This was beaten off and two Russian tanks knocked out. This is not surprising in view of the natural strength of the position; however, following a heavy rocket barrage, a much stronger attack began at 1215 hours and for the first time in the history of I SS Panzer Corps, we hear of panic setting in amongst some of the Panzer-Grenadiers. As they fled, they were mown down by machine-gun fire. The only thing which can be said in mitigation is that they had arrived in that position just a few hours earlier in a state of physical and mental exhaustion and had not had time to dig in properly; even so, it was indicative of things to come. A senior SS Officer Cadet with the 2nd SS Panzer Battalion, Wolfgang Lincke, described his part in this action:

Suddenly, around noon, a signal flare climbed into the sky from the forest. Right away a concentrated rocket fire was directed at our position and the rear slope. At the same time whole hordes of Russian infantry stormed out of the forest. . . . While we were under that effective fire . . . the first of our Grenadiers retreated. Next to me a shell exploded. When I regained consciousness, it became clear to me that I was wounded. Anything but to fall into Soviet hands! . . . The Battalion Command Post was my first safety objective. . . . SS Captain Siegel . . . despite the extremely critical situation, issued his orders in a calm manner. For all his concern about the overall situation, he recognised my poor condition and had me carried quickly into his Command Panzer.[36]

The HJ Divisional Escort Company had already taken up a depth position at Somhegy by 1400 hours and during the afternoon the defenders of Penzesgyör fell back to join it. Hans Siegel describes his experience of the withdrawal:

Along the road to the north, the crate stopped! The engine had seized since the radiator had been shot through. . . . Dismount, bring out the wounded, and blow up the Panzer! SS Captain Bert Gasch, the chief of the 7th Company looked after that. He was shot through the neck doing it. . . . I grabbed another Panzer IV for myself and drove as rearguard until the evening. With two Panzer IVs and a handful of mounted Grenadiers each, we drove from one bend in the road to the next, taking turns providing cover for each other. . . . Our poor Grenadiers were forced to get off the Panzer each time and into the bushes to the right and left of the road . . . so that they would not be endangered by anti-tank fire aimed at us and second, to prevent enemy infantry outflanking us. Those boys fought bravely.[37]

During the withdrawal to Somhegy, SS Captain Alfons Ott's 2nd SS Panzer-Grenadier Battalion was joined by various infantry groups and members of the HJ Divisional Artillery Regiment and medical unit. The ensuing group was designated KG Ott. At the same time a new KG appeared in the forward area, formed from young reinforcements, under the command of SS Captain Karl Hauschild who had been wounded two months earlier. On arrival KG Hauschild immediately prepared a depth position at Bakonybel.

At 1810 hours eight Russian tanks, with infantry mounted, attacked Somhegy and at 1915, under orders, KG Ott fell back to Bakonybel where it arrived at 2000 hours and moved into a reverse slope position behind KG Hauschild. The Divisional Escort Company covered this withdrawal. No sooner had KG Ott arrived at Bakonybel however, than orders were received for the whole Division to fall back to Bakonykoppany. This was occasioned by a Soviet breakthrough between the LAH and Balck's Sixth Army which threatened Papa and the crossings of the Marcal canal at Marcaltö. The German front in Hungary was beginning to disintegrate.

KG Ott pulled out at once, followed by KG Hauschild. The Divisional Escort Company, with Pioneer demolition teams, formed the rearguard. It was ordered to disengage at 0200 hours on the 25th, just as the first elements of KG Ott reached Bakonykoppany after an appalling 10km journey on a route totally congested with vehicles. Hans Siegel, the commander of the 2nd SS Panzer Battalion, was wounded during the withdrawal in an engagement with Russian tanks. His own Mk IV was knocked out.

Kraas called the night of the 24th the 'Wild Night' and Hubert Meyer wrote of it as follows:

The fact that the Division was successfully brought out of the Bakony forest along a single country road, destroyed in many spots, despite being outflanked by the enemy, can be regarded as an extraordinary achievement. The drivers had accomplished indescribable feats during the day and pitch-dark night, expecting the enemy close behind and on the flanks. KG Hauschild [with many new reinforcements] is worthy of particular recognition. The Escort Company proved itself once again during a most difficult situation with unshakeable valour.[38]

Elsewhere on the 24th sub-units of the Totenkopf on the HJ's left flank, were forced back to Papateszer and II SS Panzer Corps, with the Das Reich and 6th Panzer Divisions but still without the Hohenstaufen, defended a line running from Gic, through Réde, to Kisbér and Csép.

In the Hitlerjugend sector things went from bad to worse on the 25th. KGs Ott and Hauschild, in position 1-2km west of Bakonykoppany, were attacked at about 1100 hours and, although they held their ground, they were bypassed to the north. By midday the Russians had taken Papateszer and Csot, and during the afternoon they attacked Vanyola, where Kraas's Headquarters was located. The HJ's artillery gun positions in the same area were penetrated but the enemy was eventually repulsed. Thereafter the Russians swung south and took Beb. This meant that KG Ott was cut off from the rest of the Division but, despite being almost out of ammunition, it managed to fight its way out and join a KG of the Totenkopf located 4km west of the village. The combined force then continued its retreat – and by now it was in full retreat – to Vanyola, where it arrived in the early hours of the 26th and joined KG Hauschild. By this time the Divisional Headquarters had moved back to Takacsi. A proposal that the HJ should be made responsible for the defence of the town of Papa was rejected and the Division told to adopt a front facing east. This was easier said than done for, with the mountains and forests left behind and on flat, featureless ground with no obstacles, there were few places suitable for defence and none prepared. Most of the tanks and other armoured vehicles, which might have made an effective defence possible, had by now been lost through enemy action or mechanical breakdown.

North of the HJ sector, II SS Panzer Corps was forced to give up Gic and Bakonytamsi but managed to halt a breakthrough in the Csép area on the line of the railway running from Kisbér to Komarom.

* * *

The urgent need to close the gap in the Leibstandarte's sector between Kislöd and Tapolcafö was finally recognised on the 25th and Headquarters Army Group South gave permission for the LAH's southern group of KGs to be withdrawn to the Papa area as soon as it could be relieved by the 1st Volks Mountain Division. This was achieved during the day and by 1600 hours the KGs had assembled near Devecser. Unfortunately, at about this time a Soviet attack broke through the 1st Volks Mountain Division's slender defences and both Ajka and a village 4km west of Kislöd were lost. This led to accusations that the LAH had withdrawn before a proper relief had been completed and this was to have unfortunate repercussions. In another serious incident on the 25th, SS Major Heinz Kling, the commander of the 'heavy' element of Peiper's armoured group, and SS Captain Birnschein, one of his Company commanders, were both wounded in an air raid. Despite his wounds, Kling remained in command.

The southern KGs of the LAH were fortunate to get out of Devecser before it too fell in the early evening to Soviet forces moving rapidly north-west through the wide valley south of Ajka. The following day they advanced a further 16km to the west, before being halted by the 1st Volks Mountain Division on the Marcal canal just east of Janoshaza (Map 28).

(Map 30)

By the morning of the 26th the Organisation Todt[39] had prepared the bridges over the Marcal canal and Raba river at Marcaltö and Szany for demolition. The canal was only some 15m wide and could be bridged easily but, together with the river and a railway embankment running along its north bank, it would have constituted a formidable obstacle if sufficient defenders had been available. Sadly for the Germans there were not. The 232nd Panzer Division, which was defending a bridgehead east of the canal at Marcaltö, was a Panzer Division in name only. It had been hastily created from reserve units in January 1945 and promised a Panzerjäger Battalion; however, by March it comprised only two Panzer-Grenadier Regiments and just three operational armoured vehicles! Also acting as a rearguard within this bridgehead were the Hitlerjugend's Escort Company, some of its Pioneers and the last few operational tanks and Jagdpanzers of the Division. They helped to cover the withdrawal of the remainder of the HJ from the Takacsi (Map 29) area. By midnight a new blocking line had been established north-west of the Raba river, near Szany.

(Maps 28 & 29)

The 26th was another bad day for the Leibstandarte. The southern KGs tried to hold the line of the road running from Devecser to Papa but were soon outflanked to the south and in danger of being encircled; at midday they started to withdraw and by last light they too were west of the Marcal canal. Once there, in the area north-west of Celldömolk, they were able to link up at last with Siebken's 2nd SS Panzer-Grenadier Regiment which was already in position south of Kenyeri.

It is clear therefore that by last light on the 26th there were no German units in action to the east of the Marcal canal between Marcaltö and Janoshaza. South of Janoshaza, in Balck's Sixth Army area, units of I Cavalry and IV SS Panzer Corps had also been forced to withdraw to a temporary line ending some 20km from the western tip of Lake Balaton. Elsewhere in the Sixth Panzer Army sector on the 26th, the 2nd SS Panzer Division Das Reich had managed to hold its positions between Kisbér and Komarom but Soviet armoured forces had broken through farther south and, after advancing 20km and capturing Tét, had ended the day threatening the Marcal and Raba crossings south-west of Györ and the withdrawal routes of II SS Panzer Corps.

Far away in his Berlin bunker, Adolf Hitler was completely unaware of the situation just described and had no idea that his prized Waffen-SS Panzer Divisions had already been decimated and were in the process of being routed. As far as he was concerned the front on the 26th, although under pressure, was holding on a line drawn from Komarom on the Danube, through the Bakony forest, to a point about midway on the north shore of Lake Balaton – his information was twenty-four hours out of date. It is hardly surprising therefore that when Army Group South asked OKH for permission to withdraw behind the Marcal canal and for II SS Panzer Corps to pull back into a smaller bridgehead around Györ, he refused and ordered that not one metre of ground was to be given up without a fight. The Führer's refusal reached General Wöhler at 1800 hours – by which time of course the LAH and HJ had already withdrawn across the canal! According to General Guderian:

During the briefing, the Führer was horrified by the plan to occupy a front on the Marcal canal. The front would only become longer [this was true – 50% longer] and would not be able to be held [this was in fact what happened]. . . . The Führer was beside himself about the SS Panzer Divisions.

Long after the war, SS Lieutenant Colonel Otto Günsche, a member of the Leibstandarte and Hitler's Adjutant in March 1945, gave his recollections of events at this extraordinary briefing:

He [Hitler] expressed his bitterness against the leadership in harsh words – especially that of the Waffen-SS formations and even his own

Leibstandarte. It was a horrible situation when . . . the Führer revoked the right of the LAH to wear his name on their cuff bands. Everyone present grew silent. Then Reichsmarschall Goering, who was not held in particular favour at that time, said something to the effect that the Waffen-SS, especially the LAH, had fought bravely on all fronts since the start of the war and had already lost several times its authorised strength. He regarded this measure as unjust and a betrayal of the men, officers and especially Sepp Dietrich. . . . Himmler [Head of the Waffen-SS] spoke no words in defence of the Divisions of the Sixth Panzer Army.

Hitler's anger manifested itself early on the 27th in the form a teletyped message to Headquarters Sixth Panzer Army. It stated that the Führer did not believe that his troops had fought as the situation had demanded and that consequently he was stripping all Divisions in the Sixth Panzer Army of their armbands – this included of course, the LAH and HJ.[41]

SS Lieutenant Colonel Georg Maier, the officer who received the message at Dietrich's Headquarters, said later:

Filled with anger and indignation, I was on the verge of losing my self control . . . when the door opened and Sepp Dietrich came in. I reported, briefed on the morning situation and handed over to him the shocking teletyped message. . . . He read, turned away slowly and bent over the map table, resting on it with both hands in such a way that I could not see his face. He was deeply shocked and moved, and it took him a long time to rally again. Then, after a long interval, still bent over the table, he said in an unusually quiet, almost fragile voice, which reflected deepest disappointment and bitterness: 'This is the thanks for everything.'

Finally he stood up, looked at me with moist eyes, pointed at his sleeve stripe and said briefly: 'This will be kept on. . . . You won't pass on the message to the Corps; inform Kraemer now; we will discuss it when I get back.' . . . Shaking his head, he climbed into his car and drove to the front to his soldiers.[42]

Although Dietrich told his Corps commanders not to pass on or implement the Führer Order, the message soon got out – according to Georg Maier, through Army Group South and Balck's Headquarters. In fact it had no practical significance since all cuff bands in the fighting units had been removed before the move to Hungary as part of the deception plan. In terms of morale however, the veterans who had survived Russia, Normandy and the Ardennes were deeply shocked – in some cases it ended their loyalty to their Commander-in-Chief. On the other hand, their loyalty to one another and to their unit – their last Heimat, as some called it – became that much stronger.

After the war a number of former senior members of the Leibstandarte branded General Balck, the commander of the Sixth Army, as the scapegoat for the infamous Führer Order of 27 March. They claimed that Balck had complained to General Wöhler that his Waffen-SS units suffered from weak command and control, lack of discipline and poor reporting, and that Wöhler had passed these comments on to Guderian, who in turn informed Hitler. It is interesting that, even after this shattering insult, these men could not bring themselves wholly to blame their Führer.

(Map 30)

By the time the 'cuff band' Order reached the Sixth Panzer Army, the Soviets had closed up to the Marcal canal on a wide front and had achieved their first crossings near Celldömolk. At this point the German defence seems to have been powerless to stem their advance, and by midday on the 27th the LAH had been pushed back from the line of the Celldömolk-Kenyeri road to, and across, the Raba river. The Russians even managed to 'bounce' a crossing of that, near Niczk, and only desperate defensive fighting by a few of Peiper's tanks and the 3rd SS Panzer-Grenadier (SPW) Battalion prevented a further breakthrough west of the river at Jafka. Jupp Diefenthal wrote later:

> 27 March afternoon. Personal order from the Divisional commander to hold and secure Jakfa. . . . Reached Jakfa and found allied units, Rumanian or Hungarian, west of the Raba. . . . An understanding was not possible. When they were told to establish a defence with my Battalion, the 'allies' rose as one man and were no longer to be seen. During the night all the Russian attacks against Jakfa were repulsed.[43]

The same day the Soviets also penetrated into the Marcaltö bridgehead, and by late afternoon the 232nd Panzer Division had lost a Battalion and been forced to give up the east banks of both the canal and the Raba river. Unfortunately the bridge over the river was not properly destroyed during the withdrawal and SS Captain Taubert, the commanding officer of the HJ's SS Pioneer Battalion, was ordered to complete the task:

> I was called to the Divisional commander who gave me orders to destroy the bridge personally, effectively and immediately. Darkness was already falling. Together with Senior Sergeant Gauglitz, I went at once to the bridge. The retreating men of the 232nd Panzer Division

came running towards us. I called upon a major to take up a position on the Raba with his men. . . . Two metres above our heads, a four-barrel Flak fired in the direction of the bridge on which three T-34s were already sitting, waiting. With our flashlights, we started to search for a break in the fuse wire and fortunately found the problem after a short time. . . . Then we blew up the bridge across the Raba; the three T-34s dropped into the river.[44]

9km farther north – at Morichida – a similar situation was developing and, since the Hitlerjugend Division was not committed at this time, Kraas was ordered to provide a KG to reinforce the 1st Hungarian Mountain Brigade holding the bridgehead there. It was led by army Lieutenant Colonel Waizenegger, who had just been transferred to the HJ from Hitler's Headquarters, and consisted of the support Companies of Braun's 26th SS Panzer-Grenadier Regiment, Hauschild's Battalion and a few tanks. This additional support still proved inadequate and by the evening the bridgehead had been lost and the Russians were across the Raba in Arpas.

Meanwhile, the rest of the HJ Division had taken up a series of blocking positions behind the Raba, running from just south of Szil to Niczk. Müller's 25th SS Panzer-Grenadier Regiment and Brockschmidt's 12th Panzerjäger Battalion had at last rejoined Kraas's command to give it added strength; elements of the Totenkopf were on the left flank.

Raba to Reich: 28 – 31 March

On 28 March the crisis deepened. By first light the Soviets had established a significant bridgehead across the Raba at Sarvar and it was not long before their tanks, cavalry and infantry pushed into the right flank of the Leibstandarte, causing it to give up Jakfa and pull back towards Hegyfalu and Vasegerszeg. The commander of the Division's SPW Battalion, SS Major Jupp Diefenthal, was severely wounded in this fighting. One of his Company commanders, SS Captain Georg Preuss – a man who had served in every action of the LAH since the beginning of the war and who had been awarded the Knight's Cross for his part in the Ardennes campaign – took over. In the afternoon and evening, more Soviet forces were observed moving north-west from Hegyfalu and the danger of I SS Panzer Corps being outflanked became obvious.

The situation in the northern sector of the Sixth Panzer Army was just as critical. Breaking out of their bridgehead at Arpas, the Russians penetrated into Csorna, cutting off units of the 2nd SS Panzer Division Das Reich, and then turned south to take Magyarkeresztur, scattering the 232rd Panzer Division in the process. The Hitlerjugend, fighting to hold the Raba line from Szil, through Vag, to Niczk, was thus also being outflanked. In the far north the Soviets captured the southern suburbs of Györ.

The only good news of the day was the announcement that Max Hansen, the commander of the 1st SS Panzer-Grenadier Regiment LAH, had been awarded Oakleaves to his Knight's Cross.

By 29 March I SS Panzer Corps was facing annihilation. Its only hope was to pull back as quickly as possible to the protection of what was known as the 'Reich Guard Position' – the mountainous region on what is now Austria's eastern border. On its right flank elements of the Ninth Guards Army, supplemented by tanks of the Sixth Guards Tank Army (Panzer Corps), reached Acsad and beyond that the Twenty-Sixth and Twenty-Seventh Armies had broken through at Szombathely and Körmend and were approaching the borders of the Third Reich itself. The separation of the Sixth and Sixth Panzer Armies was complete.

The Leibstandarte fought desperate battles all day as it fell back from Vasegerszeg towards Lövö, making maximum use of the extensive forests which lie to the south and south-west of the village of Ivan.

In the Hitlerjugend sector, Soviet troops captured Cirak and Gyoro and Kraas's men were forced back into the wooded area north-east of Ivan. Even the Divisional Command Post, 8km farther north at Csapod, found itself under attack and had to withdraw 5km to the west.

By the evening of the 29th, a fortnight after the start of the offensive, Soviet troops were beginning to reach designated German defensive positions before the Germans themselves – there was no longer an identifiable German front line. At last, at 1925 hours, a 'Führer Decision' finally arrived at Headquarters Sixth Panzer Army authorising a phased withdrawal to the Reich Guard Position. With it came also the alarming news that Hitler had replaced General Guderian as Chief of the OKH with General Krebs. As Georg Maier put it:

> The news . . . was received with consternation by the front line troops, particularly the Panzer formations . . . who saw in the Panzer leader Guderian an illuminating example. Faith in the senior leadership dropped further.[45]

The withdrawal continued on 30 March – a day of sunshine and rain and temperatures of 16° Celsius. KGs Hansen and Peiper of the LAH ended the day around Nikitsch (for the first time they were fighting within the territory of the Third Reich) and, during the afternoon, Siebken's 2nd SS Panzer-Grenadier KG pulled back from the Lövö area to Sopronkövesd. Once again a number of immobilized Tiger IIs had to be blown up due to a lack of recovery vehicles; the surplus crewmen fought on as

Panzer-Grenadiers. However, most of the Divisional administrative units managed to get back to the Reich Guard Position during the day.

The Hitlerjugend Division, lacking contact with both the LAH on its right flank and the Totenkopf on its left, tried to hold an 8km line running east from Lövö – a position which was nothing more than a line drawn on a map and which had no defensible features. Whilst the two decimated Panzer-Grenadier Regiments came under attack from the south and the east, the Divisional Escort Company, 12th SS Reconnaissance Battalion and Kraas's Tactical Headquarters also withdrew to Sopronkövesd; and it was at this time that, incredibly, an unknown number of manpower replacements arrived in the Divisional area, together with orders from the OKH that they were to be sent into action at once! The fact that they were naval personnel – mainly from coastal artillery – made no difference, and when Soviet tanks and infantry attacked Lövö at 1415 hours, panic set in. This panic spread to veterans as well and four T-34s overran the fifty or so Panzer-Grenadiers of Braun's 2nd Battalion. The rout was eventually stopped 3km north of Lövö where high ground straddles the Sopronkövesd road.

On the northern flank of I SS Panzer Corps, aerial reconnaissance reported 100 Soviet tanks near Kapuvar and, even more threatening, another forty around Csapod. By last light they had broken through to Pinnye and Nikitsch and Priess's men found themselves manning a line with no defensible features running from Nikitsch to Pinnye and then north to Hegykö.

During the night of the 30th, I SS Panzer Corps, now a Corps in name only, received orders to move back to the Reich Guard Position at Sopron.

Early on 31 March some sixty Soviet tanks of the Sixth Guards Tank Army (Panzer Corps), supported by infantry of the Fourth Guards Army, advanced along the axis of the Kapuvar-Sopron road. The reinforced Ninth Guards Army was on their left, heading towards Wiener Neustadt, and a similarly reinforced Forty-Sixth Guards Army was moving north-west on the eastern side of Lake Neusiedler.

Focusing on our own area of interest, the advance against I SS Panzer Corps soon reached Fertöboz, and another group of sixteen T-34s entered Nagycenk after overrunning some 150 men of the HJ's Pioneer Battalion. Although fifteen of these Russian tanks were eventually knocked out by the Division's few remaining Panzers, Kraas, Hubert Meyer and the Command Post staff were forced to flee cross-country to Deutschkreutz, where the survivors of Müller's Regiment had set up a rudimentary defensive position. They were joined there by three Tiger IIs of the 3rd Company of the 501st SS Heavy Panzer Battalion[46] but it was not long before Deutschkreutz fell too. The Kraas Command Group and the 25th SS

Panzer-Grenadiers moved into the forest west of Harka whilst the Tigers, no doubt with some infantry support, fought a delaying action back along the road to Mattersburg. Meanwhile, the Leibstandarte KGs had withdrawn to a line running from about Lanzenkirchen to Mattersburg in an attempt to set up some sort of blocking position covering Wiener Neustadt. Otto Kumm remembered:

> The Division was withdrawing in the direction of Wiener Neustadt. A large number of Me 262s, the first jet fighter in the world, stood on an airfield which had already been evacuated by the Luftwaffe – they were completely undamaged. We destroyed them with our machine-guns. . . . There were also freight trains with tanker cars of gasoline near the airfield – finally we were able to refuel our last vehicles and Panzers.[47]

Attacks from the south reached Harka by 1145 hours and, despite being delayed by an army Flak unit and some of the HJ's SS Panzer-Grenadiers, the village fell at 1830 hours. SS Captains Ott and Hauschild were both wounded during this fighting; SS Lieutenant Harro Lübbe took over the 2nd Battalion.

Late in the day the surviving Pioneers and Müller's men reached Sopron, together with Kraas's Tactical Headquarters. But there was to be no respite. Sopron lies at the end of a wide valley stretching south from Vienna (Map 28) and it lay at the mercy of the Soviets. In the evening they pushed into the city and some elements even reached Morbisch, 10km to the north-east on the edge of Lake Neusiedler. Throughout the night small combat groups and the last Panzers of the Hitlerjugend fought their way back to, and through, Sopron. On Easter Day, 1 April, the last pathetic remnants of the once proud and powerful Division crossed the border of the Third Reich on the Vienna road. They and their comrades in the LAH had endured twelve days of bitter fighting, conducted under the most difficult and potentially demoralising of all military operations – withdrawal.

For the sixth time in the history of the Leibstandarte and the third in the short history of the Hitlerjugend, both Divisions had been all but destroyed.

NOTES

1. Fourth Gds Army: nine inf; Ninth Gds Army: nine inf; Sixth Gds Tk Army (Pz Corps): three tk; Twenty-Sixth Army: three cavalry, nine inf; Twenty-Seventh Army: two tk, twelve inf (only nine participated); Forty-Sixth Army: one tk, twelve inf (only nine participated).
2. Third Hungarian Army with 1st Hussar, 2nd Hungarian Pz, 23rd, 25th, 76th

& 711th Inf Divs; Sixth Army with 1st, 3rd, 6th, 23rd Pz & 44th and 356th Inf Divs; Sixth Pz Army with 1st SS, 2nd SS, 3rd SS, 5th SS, 9th SS & 12th SS Pz Divs and 3rd & 4th Cavalry Divs.

3. Schneider, *Tigers in Combat* II, p. 266.
4. II SS – ninety-one; IV SS including 2nd Hungarian Pz Div – eighty-nine. Balck's III Pz Corps – thirty-four; 6th Pz Div – thirty-six.
5. It should be noted, however, that at this time the Divs of I SS Pz Corps had the following fighting vehicles in short or long term repair: LAH – fifteen Mk IVs, fourteen Panthers, twenty-four Tiger IIs and eighteen Jagdpanzer IVs; HJ – thirteen Mk IVs, fifteen Panthers and forty-one Jagdpanzers; 23rd Panzer – ten Mk IVs, twenty-six Panthers and fifteen Jagdpanzers or StuGs.
6. Tiemann, *The Leibstandarte* IV/2, p. 231.
7. XXIII Tk Corps.
8. Estimates of its strength vary widely. One Soviet source (IVMV, Vol 10) puts the figure as low as 197, while another (Zavizion, G.T. and Kornyushin, P.A. – 6th Guards Tank Army) gives a figure of 406 tanks and SP guns.
9. Forty-Sixth Army.
10. II Gds Mech Corps.
11. MS # B-139 – Interrogation of Lt Gen Walther Krause, commander Sixth Army Communications Zone, 13 Jun 52.
12. Tiemann, op. cit., pp. 237–8.
13. Ibid., p. 238.
14. Ibid., p. 235.
15. Wilmot, *The Struggle for Europe*, p. 679.
16. War Diary, Army Gp South, 19 Mar 45.
17. Tiemann, op. cit., p. 240.
18. Ibid., p. 241.
19. Ibid., p. 240.
20. Ibid., p. 242.
21. Ibid., p. 244.
22. Schneider, op. cit., p. 266. The exact date on which Dietrich made the presentation to Kumm is open to question anyway. In an interview with Charles Messenger on 1 Mar 86, Kumm said he received his 'Swords' in Vienna on 4 Apr: *Hitler's Gladiator*, p. 171.
23. Meyer, op. cit., p. 300.
24. Ibid., p. 301.
25. Ibid.
26. Ibid.
27. Tiemann, op. cit., p. 249.
28. Ibid.
29. Meyer, op. cit., p. 302.
30. 44th Grenadier, 1st & 3rd Pz and 5th SS Pz Divs.
31. Tiemann, op. cit., pp. 251–2.
32. Ibid., p. 256.
33. Werner Poetschke's body was taken back to the Reich and he was eventually buried in the Mattersburg Military cemetery (Austria). On his gravestone his rank is shown as Major, not Sturmbannführer, thus concealing his membership of the Waffen-SS.
34. Tiemann, op. cit., pp. 255–6.
35. Ibid., p 259.
36. Meyer, op. cit., p. 304.
37. Ibid., p. 305.

38. Ibid., p. 306.
39. Units of civil labour, including men and women from the occupied countries, used throughout the industrial regions and communications system of the Third Reich. It took its name from the head of the Organisation – Dr Fritz Todt.
40. Tiemann, op. cit., p. 264.
41. Ibid., p. 266. Suggestions that this order did not apply to the Wiking and Hitlerjugend Divisions are incorrect.
42. Maier, *Drama zwischen Budapest und Wien*, p. 347.
43. Tiemann, op. cit., p. 268.
44. Meyer, op. cit., p. 307
45. Maier, op. cit., p. 373.
46. Schneider, op. cit., p. 267.
47. Tiemann, op. cit., p. 276.

CHAPTER XXVII

Tales from the Vienna Woods: 1 – 21 April

(Map 31)

The final part of the history of I SS Panzer Corps is by far the most difficult to describe. There are many reasons for this: lack of reliable records, lack of formal military structures, difficult terrain and a multitude of small unit actions which serve to complicate rather than explain the overall picture.

In view of the heavy casualties the 1st and 12th SS Panzer Divisions had suffered in both men and material by the beginning of April 1945, it was fortunate that they found themselves in terrain which required few men to defend it and which largely negated the widespread use of armour. As Werner Sternebeck, the commander of the 7th SS Panzer Company, said later:

The defensive fighting was conducted along the roads in the valleys. There was no possibility of deploying and committing weapons in breadth and depth.[1]

When one visits Lower Austria and the area south-west of Vienna today, the region known as the Vienna Woods, it is hard to believe that the events of April and May 1945 took place there at all. One can more easily imagine the singing of Maria and the von Trapp children than the chatter of machine-guns and the screams of dying and injured men. War is repugnant anywhere but particularly in this place of great and majestic beauty. Fortunately the scars of war have almost entirely disappeared – except perhaps in the minds of those who participated in the fighting.

The actions of the twin Divisions of I SS Panzer Corps in the Vienna Woods during April 1945 can be divided conveniently into four consecutive phases and, rather than risk the confusion which might arise by trying to describe the actions on a daily basis, these phases will be explained in general terms, with a series of vignettes being provided in order to demonstrate particular events and so bring them to life.

The Soviet Offensive

By 1 April the leading elements of the Red Army were less than 30km from the centre of Vienna. Opposing the Forty-Sixth Army between the Danube and the northern tip of Lake Neusiedler were the 2nd SS and 6th Panzer Divisions. To the south of the city, the remnants of Priess's I SS Panzer Corps and the 3rd SS Panzer Division Totenkopf were all that stood before the might of the Fourth and Ninth Guards Armies, supplemented by units of the Sixth Guards Tank Army (Panzer Corps).

Marshal Tolbukhin's plan for the final reduction of Vienna took the Germans by surprise. They expected the Soviets to attack north-west between the Danube and Lake Neusiedler and north between Wiener Neustadt and Eisenstadt, but Dietrich and his staff did not anticipate that the western thrust would swing north-west at Baden, in the direction of Tulln on the Danube, and then turn back and attack Vienna from the west. Tolbukhin was in fact thinking beyond the capture of Vienna. Although he had lost a Tank and a Guards Mechanized Corps (two Panzer Divisions) to Malinovsky for the latter's operations against Bratislava and Brno (in what was then Czechoslovakia), he was still very strong and was already planning an advance towards Germany proper. The way was obvious – along the valley south of the Danube towards St Pölten, Enns and Linz – the line of today's Autobahn.

It was fortunate for the men of the Leibstandarte and Hitlerjugend that in the event, they were brushed aside by Tolbukhin's Divisions and forced into two valleys at the north-eastern end of the Austrian Alps. They thus avoided the bloody street fighting in Vienna which would almost certainly have led to their annihilation or capture.

1 – 3 April
(Map 32)

In the first phase of the fighting south of Vienna, the Hitlerjugend withdrew initially behind the Leitha river in the Ebenfurth sector. But it was far too weak to defend a river line in open country and parts of a Guards Rifle Corps, supported by a Guards Mechanized Corps[2] (Panzer Division), soon pushed it to the west, away from the main Sopron-Vienna road, into the Triesting valley. In the same period another part of the same Rifle Corps and a Guards Tank Corps[3] (Panzer Division) forced the Leibstandarte to withdraw along the axis of the Weiner Neustadt-Vienna road – first to a delaying position behind the Piesting river, and then some 5km westwards up the Piesting valley. One Soviet source[4] claims that by this time the strength of some of the tank brigades (Panzer Battalions) in the Sixth Guards Tank Army (Panzer Corps) had fallen to as low as seven to ten tanks. If this is true, it says much for the performance of the Germans in their retreat from the Lake Balaton area.

By 3 April the twin Waffen-SS Divisions were thus side by side, facing east, on a frontage of no more than 15km. Despite their manpower and material weaknesses, their forthcoming task did not seem too unreasonable. On their right flank they had hastily gathered but fairly substantial forces, including elements of an SS Cavalry Division and an Infantry Division, and they were certainly better off than their comrades in II SS Panzer Corps who were part of the force charged with the defence of Vienna. Anyway the Soviets had no intention of trying to force their way up these narrow valleys and, for the time being at least, they were more than content to seal off the Germans and concentrate their efforts on capturing the capital of the former Austro-Hungarian Empire.

Hubert Meyer's statement that by this time the Hitlerjugend had been reduced to two medium strength Panzer-Grenadier Battalions and only two or three combat-ready tanks or Jagdpanzers, supported by parts of the Divisional Pioneer, Reconnaissance, Artillery and Flak Battalions is misleading. We have a return for 13 April showing the Division with 7,731 officers and men and, since we know that nearly 10,000 members of the Division surrendered to the Americans on 8-9 May, the figure of 7,731 must have been the HJ's combat, as opposed to total, strength. This would indicate that the Division had far more than two medium strength Panzer-Grenadier *Battalions*. It was certainly organised into its four normal KGs: the armoured group under Martin Gross, a Reconnaissance group still under Gerd Bremer, and the two Panzer-Grenadier Regimental groups. We also know from the 13 April return that the Division had nine operational tanks and that an unspecified number of damaged tanks and Jagdpanzers had been towed to repair shops in the St Pölten area.

The Leibstandarte was similarly organised and, on 13 April, had a total strength of 10,552. Rather surprisingly, it received ten new Mk IV tanks during its short time in Wiener Neustadt. Werner Sternebeck remembered:

The 3rd Company was refitted with ten new Panzer IVs and their assigned crews from Linz. Subsequently the Company received a Panzer V [Panther] platoon from an army division and a company of mountain troops. I reported with this KG to the Wiener Neustadt commandant. . . . The atmosphere was truly hopeless, the issue of orders sluggish, inconsistent and lacked conviction. I had the impression that we were facing our last battle and that we, with our seventeen to twenty-two Panzer IVs and Vs could only delay the impending collapse. . . . During the afternoon [1 April] and even after the fall of darkness the enemy probed Wiener Neustadt with tanks and infantry. We were able to repulse each of the attacks . . . and prevent a penetration into the town.[5]

On 2 April the picture changed dramatically:

In the early morning the company of mountain troops was withdrawn without explanation. Our Panzers now stood alone as if on an island, without radio contact to left or right. . . . We stood at the southern edge of the town and the enemy was already penetrating into the north. . . . Finally we were able to drive like hell with the remaining eight Panzers [the army Panthers had been abandoned by their crews after running out of ammunition] through Wiener Neustadt . . . past the surprised enemy . . . and were able to break through to the north. . . . We set up such a good flanking position that we were able to destroy . . . approximately ten to twelve T-34s, without suffering any losses. We then withdrew to the eastern edge of Wöllersdorf. Several fighter-bombers attacked the pursuing enemy armour and gave us a chance to catch our breath. . . . During the fighting in and around Wöllersdorf the remnants of the SPW Battalion were committed under SS Captain Georg Preuss. The local Volkssturm [Home Guard] were not prepared to defend their own homes out of fear of reprisals. The Vienna Woods were entered after Wöllersdorf.[6]

Not everyone was as fortunate as Sternebeck. During the afternoon of 1 April a mortar round hit the Command post of the LAH's Reconnaissance Battalion killing the Battalion commander, SS Captain Wawrzinek, his Adjutant and Signals officer and one of his Company commanders. SS Lieutenant Leidreiter, Max Hansen's Adjutant and a former Reconnaissance Company commander in the Ardennes campaign, took over.

The LAH's Flak and Werfer Battalions were required to act as infantry during this period:

On 2 April a unified front was finally constructed. On that day we were committed as infantry around Felixdorf together with the remaining five 88mm, three 37mm and two 20mm guns.[7]

The Hitlerjugend had to cover two entrances to the Triesting valley – one following the main road through Hirtenberg (not unlike the Amblève valley in the Ardennes) and the other through Grossau. These routes converged at Berndorf but a side road from Grossau led north-west to high ground around Schwarzensee – an area which would see much fighting. The end of this first phase saw the HJ holding positions 2km west of both Hirtenberg and Grossau.

Readers will probably have been surprised to learn that men, ammunition, general supplies and even tanks were still reaching I SS Panzer Corps at this late stage in the life of the Third Reich. Nevertheless, it is a fact that the recovery and resupply systems were still, to some extent, working and there is no doubt that the overall logistical infrastructure within the country was extraordinarily resilient – particularly in view of the Allied bombing. We have heard mention of tank workshops near St Pölten and new tanks being issued from Linz, and we shall hear later of a tank factory near Enns and four new Mk IVs being issued at Kirchberg. Certainly there were ammunition dumps in Upper Austria. Hubert Meyer speaks of 'meagre' supplies, but on 18 April the adjacent Corps on the northern flank had 'ammunition for two days' all-out fighting'[8] and it is unlikely that I SS Panzer Corps was worse off. Meyer speaks also of ammunition barges being unloaded at Melk on the Danube and their contents being hauled to the Division in horse-drawn carts. With regard to petrol, there is an amusing story in relation to the LAH, told by the Maintenance Sergeant of the 7th SS Panzer Company, Rolf Ehrhardt:

> While I was driving along a side road during the night and in fog [12 April], an old Landsturmmann stopped me: 'Herr Unteroffizier, do you know anyone who needs gasoline'? . . . This brave man was guarding several tankers with about sixty tons of the fuel. . . . We had enough to fill all the empty tanks.[9]

4 – 9 April

The second phase of the April fighting saw the development of a major Soviet threat to the west of Vienna. On the 4th, II SS Panzer Corps was pushed back to the line of the Mödling-Heiligenkreuz road, opening up a gap between it and the Hitlerjugend. The following day units of the Sixth Guards Tank Army and the Ninth Guards Army advanced another 12km to Pressbaum – threatening a breakthrough to Tulln on the Danube and the isolation of Vienna. Dietrich, or more likely his Chief of Staff, Fritz

Kraemer, was forced to act. The boundary between the LAH and the HJ was moved northwards in the rather forlorn hope that the latter would be able to close the gap to II SS Panzer Corps' Das Reich Division. Then on the 6th, as the Soviets began their attacks against Vienna from the south and west with their Fourth and Ninth Armies, STAVKA ordered Malinovsky's Forty-Sixth Army to cross to the east bank of the Danube in order to outflank the city from the north. At the same time elements of the Sixth Guards Tank Army and Ninth Guards Army began their first moves towards St Pölten, compelling the Sixth Panzer Army to rush reserve and replacement units into action and to order its senior artillery commander, SS Major General Staudinger, to build up a defensive line on the western flank of the Soviet encirclement. Lack of sufficient suitable troops precluded any chance of attacking this flank.

By the 8th the Germans had managed to establish a fragmentary new front covering the approaches to St Pölten. It ran south from Zwentendorf on the Danube, along the approximate line of the Tulln river, to Laaben. On the same day Major General Schultz took over from Staudinger and his force was rather optimistically named 'Corps Schultz'.[10] At this stage it comprised only three reserve infantry Battalions (two of them made up from SS replacements for the Sixth Panzer Army), two Battalions of an anti-tank Brigade equipped only with Panzerfausts, the well equipped but under-strength 1st Panzer Reconnaissance Battalion, and support from three assault gun and five artillery Battalions. Three Luftwaffe anti-aircraft Battalions were ordered to 'co-operate' with the Corps, which was facing an estimated three Soviet rifle divisions supported by tanks.

On 9 April the Soviets began probing attacks across the Tulln river. The threat to St Pölten and the danger of I SS Panzer Corps becoming isolated in the Austrian Alps was obvious.

As far as the Leibstandarte was concerned this period saw few major developments other than the expansion of its area of responsibility to include the eastern end of the Triesting valley, south of a line drawn from Weissenbach to Grossau. This involved sending a mixed KG, made up from parts of Hansen's 1st SS Panzer-Grenadier Regiment, Peiper's 1st SS Panzer Regiment (mainly Mk IV tanks and his 9th SS Pioneer Company), the 1st SS Flak Battalion and some subordinate artillery to take over in the Berndorf-Pottenstein sector. Once there they were involved in successfully repulsing a series of Soviet probes. SS Second Lieutenant Borchers, of the 9th SS Panzer Pioneer Company, remembered:

We blocked the Berndorf-Pottenstein road. Our Panzers stood behind a curve. Then several Russian tanks rumbled towards us in the early morning. The first two blew into the air 20m from us, the rest ran away. The road was blocked by the wrecks. The mountain rose to the left of the road, to the right was a 100m swamp and the rest of the mountain. Tanks could not pass.[11]

And a member of Hansen's Regiment added his memories:

Some of the platoons were entrenched in a forest north of Pottenstein, some to the west, at the edge of the forest. I set up my 80mm mortars . . . near Pottenstein. From there I was able to conduct blocking fire for several nights because the Russians always tried to assault the northern positions. . . . The point of the forest was also well covered by machine-gun fire. All attacks were repulsed.[12]

In another significant redeployment, part of Leidreiter's Reconnaissance Battalion was moved to the northern flank of the Corps to secure the gap which now existed between it and Corps Schultz and, as another extreme measure, a small KG was formed from the Division's administrative units to fill yet another gap between this new reconnaissance group and the Hitlerjugend.

On the LAH's right flank, in the Piesting valley, the men of Siebken's 2nd SS Panzer-Grenadier Regiment managed to recapture their old positions at the entrance to the valley and, since the Soviets had no intention of advancing west at this point, they were able to enjoy a relatively quiet period until the time came for the final withdrawal.

The Hitlerjugend also formed ad hoc KGs from its administrative units during this period. One, under Lieutenant Möbius, was formed from the Medical Battalion and Ambulance Company and another under Captain Glosser, from the supply troops of the 26th Regiment and 12th SS Flak Battalion. Both these KGs were involved in the early fighting in the mountainous region between Berndorf and Alland. But the main burden of the fighting around and to the east of Schwarzensee fell to the 25th and 26th Regimental KGs. They were able to prevent any further Soviet advances in this sector. SS Second Lieutenant Richter described one episode:

The whole forest was humming and whistling with ricochets. In the meantime our machine-gun had made it to the front and the Russians fled uphill. Suddenly we heard to our rear . . . forceful shouts of 'Urraa'. Obviously all the shooting had woken up another nest of Russians. We were under fire from two sides then, but we were able to keep the Russians at bay. . . . Fortunately we suffered no losses except one wounded man. We continued to pursue our objective: the top of the mountain, the 'Iron Gate'. When we arrived up there we found a massive shelter building. We just made out a few fleeing Russians. On the gate we found a handwritten sign, stuck to the wood with a bayonet, which was later translated at Regiment. It read: 'We have Vienna, we are fighting for Berlin and we are on our way to München.'[13]

By 6 April Gerd Bremer's 12th SS Reconnaissance KG, which had been located west of Heiligenkreuz and tasked with keeping contact with elements of II SS Panzer Corps, had been forced back to the eastern edge of Alland. That evening the Russians captured the town and KG Bremer was forced to pull back again, through Klausen-Leopoldsdorf, towards Laaben. The 2nd SS Panzer Division Das Reich had long since withdrawn towards Vienna and it was to fill this gap between the HJ and Staudinger's troops that the LAH reconnaissance group had been moved to the Corps' left flank.

The Soviet threat in the Klausen-Leopoldsdorf region was the most serious in the I SS Panzer Corps area and on 9 April KG Gross, made up from the HJ's Panzer Regiment, launched a counter-attack which gained a few kilometres and to some extent restored the situation. We have a strength return for the following day which shows the HJ with seven Mk IVs and one Jagdpanzer and the LAH with thirteen Mk IVs, five Panthers and four StuGs. The Corps had another four tanks and three Jagdpanzers under repair.

At the end of this phase the front line in our area of interest can be summarised as follows: from Zwentendorf in the north, through Neulengbach to Laaben, west of Klausen-Leopoldsdorf to Alland, and then south through the Schwarzensee mountains to Pottenstein and on to Wöllersdorf.

Readers may be wondering what, if any, support the men of I SS Panzer Corps were receiving from the Luftwaffe at this time. The only mention in either of the Divisional Histories is by Hubert Meyer of the HJ: 'For the first time in weeks [11th April], a German FW 190 fighter aircraft was observed, flying 30m above our positions'. In fact the Air Fleet covering south-east Germany on 9 April was Luftflotte 4, which numbered only 328 serviceable aircaft out of a total of 440. Of these 154 were day or night ground attack aircraft, sixty-two were fighters and the remainder for reconnaissance.[14] It was a sad fact for the ground troops that by this time the Luftwaffe was a spent force and any aircraft which the fuel shortages did allow to take to the sky, none of which were the Me 262 jets, had little chance against the overwhelming might of the US and Soviet air forces.

10 – 14 April

The most significant events in this third period occurred outside the I SS Panzer Corps area – in Vienna and the Corps Schultz sector. By the 13th the Russians had fought their way into the centre of Vienna and at midnight on that day General Rudolf von Bünau, the Garrison commander, crossed the Danube and the last bridge was destroyed – the Soviets had achieved their immediate goal. Farther west, events in the Corps Schultz area necessitated more regroupings and redeployments for Priess's Divisions.

Between the 9th and 12th Schultz received some sizeable reinforcements[15], but they proved totally inadequate in the face of a Soviet Rifle Corps, backed by a Tank Corps (Panzer Division).[16] As early as the 10th, the Soviets had begun bypassing Neulengbach on its northern side and by the evening of the 12th Schultz's men had been forced back to the Perschling river and both Kappeln and Böheimkirchen were under threat. The following day saw St Pölten fall[17] and the Russians established across the Traisen river. In desperate attempts to halt the enemy advance:

All the physically fit and experienced officers at Corps Headquarters were ordered to turn back troops fleeing across the Traisen river and to get them into positions on the higher west bank. [Engineer] construction Battalions digging in there were employed as covering forces.[18]

By last light on 14 April Soviet troops were 6km west and north-west of St Pölten and Herzogenburg respectively, but the end of this phase saw Corps Schultz, aided by reinforcements, particularly from the 710th Infantry Division, with a more or less continuous front from Krems on the Danube to Obergrafendorf, 8km south-west of St Pölten.

Not surprisingly, the Soviet offensive on the northern flank of I SS Panzer Corps forced Priess to take counter-measures and on the 11th a new KG, known as Task Force Peiper, was formed and given the task of protecting the Traisen and Michelbach valleys against advances from Wilhelmsburg and Böheimkirchen. One group assembled around Rotheau under the command of SS Major Kling. It comprised 'several' Tiger IIs from the 501st SS Heavy Panzer Battalion with the unemployed tank crews from the 501st and Peiper's own Regiment acting as Panzer-Grenadiers. The other group, under Jochen Peiper's direct command, formed up in the Gölsen valley in an area centred on Hainfeld and was made up of the remaining LAH Panthers and a mixed infantry unit of spare tank crews, Preuss's 3rd SPW Battalion and supply personnel. Peiper's front was extended to the east on the night of the 13th to include the Brand sector. Werner Sternebeck's Mk IV tank group, which included several StuGs and Jagdpanzers, remained in the Triesting valley covering the Berndorf-Pottenstein front. It operated in support of an infantry group made up of some of Hansen's Panzer-Grenadiers, a few paratroopers and other stragglers who were glad to find a home. The Division had a total of twenty-two combat-ready tanks at this time and a further forty-six in short- or long-term repair.

Another emergency measure ordered on the 12th had a serious effect on the Hitlerjugend. The left wing of Kraas's Division was being protected by KG Gross (Martin Gross's depleted 12th SS Panzer Regimental Group); included in this were a few Jagdpanzers of Major Goldammer's 560th Heavy Panzerjäger Battalion and some 'quick response' infantry units, including the Corps Security Company. According to Hubert Meyer, Goldammer's KG had also been reinforced with several tanks. In view, however, of the deteriorating situation in the Corps Schultz sector, KG Goldammer was withdrawn at this time for use on the Corps left flank. This placed considerable strain on the Hitlerjugend, which was still responsible for a 25km front running from Laaben to Schwarzensee. A Flak group of 37mm and 88mm guns, which had helped to defend the Berndorf area earlier in the month, had already been withdrawn on the 10th and sent to join KG Gross in the threatened Laaben sector. Some relief was provided on the night of the 12th by the arrival, from Fallingbostel in northern Germany, of the remaining personnel of the Division's 1st SS Panzer Battalion – minus their tanks![19] It had taken them twelve days to reach the Division. The Battalion, under the command of SS Captain Rudolf von Ribbentrop, was equipped with old fashioned K 98 rifles and a few machine-guns; it was immediately sent to reinforce the Laaben sector.

On the 13th the Soviets made a breakthrough in the centre of the HJ front and captured the mountain village of St Corona. This placed them less than 5km from the strategic Gölsen valley and posed a serious threat to the Division and large elements of the LAH. The Gölsen valley was of vital importance since it was the main supply route for the whole Corps, and if the Soviets gained control of any significant part of it, the extraction of units north of the Hainfeld-Altenmarkt section would become extremely difficult.

Since it was now abundantly clear that the HJ's front was too large for the forces available, KG Peiper's front was extended that night, as already explained, to include Brand. At the same time SS Captain Gerd Freiherr von Reitzenstein who, with a small KG[20], had taken over from KG Goldammer, began planning a counter-attack to recapture the St Corona area. This was launched at 1030 hours the following morning and by last light on the 14th, KG von Reitzenstein had reoccupied the positions lost twenty-four hours previously – amazingly, without loss. On the same day part of KG Peiper, known as the Hainfeld Group, was in action on the road leading north-west from Brand towards Böheimkirchen.

Just as von Ribbentrop's Battalion had reinforced the HJ, so SS Major Paul Guhl arrived from Germany on the 13th with six Companies of the LAH's 2nd SS Panzer Battalion – it too was without tanks and organised as an infantry unit.[21] It was committed immediately in the Berndorf sector.

It was on this day that news reached the fighting troops that President Roosevelt had died. It gave rise to much speculation – to the extent that, since it was Roosevelt who had been the first to demand 'Unconditional Surrender', there might now be some hope of a softening in the Western Allies' attitude and that they might demand a halt to further Soviet advances. The Germans even began to think the unthinkable – that the Americans and British might join them in a crusade to halt and turn back the dreaded Bolsheviks. As Hubert Meyer put it: 'Had not the USA gone to war in order to re-establish freedom and democracy in Poland, in Czechoslovakia, in south-eastern Europe'? Nevertheless, he went on to say that he and his commander, on further reflection, had come to the conclusion that:

There was no way around the 'Unconditional Surrender'. The only important aspect left was to safeguard as much German land and as many German people as possible from the Soviets, and to save them for a distant future when the unconditional hatred had been replaced by reason.[22]

He could never have visualised that this would happen within a decade[23] and that in only fifteen years West German tanks would be using old Churchill tanks as targets on a military training area in Britain!

At midnight on 14 April the front line can be summarised as follows: Corps Schultz – from Krems on the Danube, along the eastern edge of the vast Dunkelsteinerwald forest, and then south to Obergrafendorf; next there was a gap of some 6km until Wilhelmsburg, where KG Kling of the LAH was in position; then KG Peiper from Michelbach to Brand; KG Gross of the HJ from Brand to Laaben, KG von Ribbentrop from east of Laaben to the Schöpfl mountain, KG von Reitzenstein in the St Corona sector, KG Bremer[24] in a quadrant 3km south-west of Alland, and then the 25th and 26th Regimental KGs holding a front running roughly south through Schwarzensee to Weissenbach. KG Sternebeck of the LAH and the remnants of Hansen's 1st and Siebken's 2nd Regiments took over again on a line drawn from Weissenbach to just west of Berndorf and south to the Piesting river on the right flank.

The main dangers to I SS Panzer Corps remained obvious: a successful Soviet advance south through the Traisen valley would cut off the whole Corps and a breakthrough into the Gölsen valley from either Michelbach or St Corona would similarly cut off most of the Hitlerjugend Division and a large element of the Leibstandarte.

15 – 21 April

The fourth and final phase of the fighting in the Vienna Woods saw a definite change of emphasis on the part of the Soviets. Because they were already in possession of Poland, Slovakia, Hungary and Rumania and had achieved their desired 'buffer zone' between the western border of the Motherland and their fascist and capitalist enemies, there seemed little point in sacrificing more lives – except for Berlin! With American troops already in Nürnberg and moving on München (Map 24), less than 400km from St Pölten, STAVKA knew that the war on the southern front was almost at an end; even if it did order a major offensive towards Linz in the narrow valley between the Danube and the Alps, its troops were unlikely to get there before the Americans. It therefore made much more sense to go firm on an easily defensible line – like the Traisen valley – consolidate what had already been achieved by clearing up all resistance to the east of that line, and simply wait for the final German collapse. Accordingly, the Ninth Guards Army was placed in reserve and ordered to halt just to the west and south-west of Vienna and the badly weakened Sixth Guards Tank Army transferred to Malinovsky's Second Ukrainian Front. There were no further Soviet attempts to advance west from the St Pölten area after the 14th and, on the 15th, Corps Schultz was able to close the 6km gap between it and I SS Panzer Corps in the Obergrafendorf area without difficulty. Farther north, between 17 and 20 April, there were a series of attacks by units of the Fourth Guards Army against the important Danube town of Krems, but by then parts of the 2nd SS Panzer Division Das Reich, SS Regiment Maehren[25], the rest of the 710th Infantry Division and a medium tank company had arrived in the Corps Schultz[26] area, thus enabling the Germans not only to hold the town but to counter-attack. On the 20th the Soviets abandoned their bridgehead west of Herzogenburg without a fight and went on to the defensive.[27]

The Soviet decision to suspend further attacks to the west and consolidate their conquests east of the Traisen valley had serious implications for the men of I SS Panzer Corps – not least because the Russians were aware that the mountains and woods south-west of Vienna were being defended by members of the hated Waffen-SS.

Initial attempts by the Fourth Guards Army to advance south into Wilhelmsburg on 15 April made little progress against a determined defence by KG Kling of the Leibstandarte, but the following day full-scale operations designed to break into the Gölsen-Triesting valley began and the northern part of Wilhelmsburg fell into Soviet hands. KG Kling, after knocking out eleven tanks, recaptured the lost ground on the 17th, but it took another counter-attack by part of Preuss's SPW Battalion to halt a further Soviet attack after dark.

On the 18th the Soviets bypassed Wilhelmsburg on both flanks and

KG Kling was encircled in the southern part of the town; the eastern wing of the Russian advance reached a point only 3km from St Veit and posed a major threat to the Gölsen valley. At the same time there was a breakthrough at Michelbach by a Soviet tank Battalion, which then turned east to threaten the rear of the Hitlerjugend defences in the St Corona and Laaben sector. KG Peiper counter-attacked successfully and claimed fifteen Russian tanks.

On this same day, the 18th, the Americans reached Regensburg (Map 24) and General Lothar Rendulic, who had taken over command of Army Group South after Wöhler had been sacked, gave orders that some divisions or divisional groups were to be pulled out of the fighting in Lower Austria and prepared for action on the 'Western Front'. 'Divisional Kampfgruppe HJ', as Hubert Meyer describes it, was one of these formations, but it was clear that there could be no question of this order being implemented until the I SS Panzer Corps frontage had been shortened and the situation around St Corona stabilised. In order to achieve this Priess and his Divisional commanders decided that the 26th Regimental KG should be withdrawn from the right flank and moved to the St Corona sector. The LAH was ordered to fill the resulting gap to the north-west of Weissenbach.

The 18th also saw the arrival of SS Lieutenant Colonel Wilhelm Weidenhaupt to take over from Siegfried Müller what was left of the 25th SS Panzer-Grenadier Regiment. He had commanded the 3rd Battalion of the LAH's 1st Regiment in Normandy until being wounded on 8 July.

On 19 April the German front north of the Gölsen-Triesing valley began to collapse. Looking at the situation from west to east: part of KG Peiper managed to halt the enemy at Rotheau, but only with difficulty; Soviet thrusts east of Wilhelmsburg and south from Michelbach succeeded in taking St Veit and Hainfeld until counter-attacks by KG Sternebeck and parts of KG Hansen, both of which had been moved from the eastern flank, forced them back to the north side of the valley. In the centre of the front, despite the reinforcement by the 26th Regimental KG, Brand, Laaben and St Corona all fell. Only on the eastern flank was there little activity.

The crisis continued on the 20th. KG Kling managed to fight its way out of Wilhelmsburg[28] and reform around Rotheau, but during the day the Soviets closed up to the St Veit-Hainfeld road and last light saw the Gölsen valley between those points as the new front line. Vicious fighting took place around Hainfeld itself, with part of KG Peiper attacking from the west and the 2nd SS Panzer-Grenadier Regimental KG from the east in an attempt to reopen the road at that point. A member of Siebken's KG remembered:

We were transported in trucks and SPWs to the eastern outskirts of

. . . Hainfeld. . . . No sooner had we jumped from our vehicles than we were involved in the fighting. We could see the Russian infantry . . . they were attacking in waves across the fields above the town. I was standing next to an SP 20mm four barrelled Flak gun that was firing direct at the enemy with good effect. Likewise a Panther stood near the centre of the village, near a bridge that was prepared for demolition. . . . It was firing to the north-west and belonged to SS Colonel Peiper's unit. The fighting . . . developed into bitter street fighting. It wavered to and fro as the enemy and we occupied halves of the same house.[29]

In the HJ sector near Kaumberg, KG Gross attempted to hold the enemy just to the north of the Hainfeld-Altenmarkt road, but Soviet penetrations south-west of St Corona threatened to cut off the HJ KGs in the Schöpfl area. Hugo Kraas, from his Headquarters at Altenmarkt, ordered a general withdrawal to positions alongside KG Gross. Weidenhaupt's KG just east of Altenmarkt and the LAH KG around Berndorf held firm. As a matter of interest, a few of the buildings in Berndorf still bear the scars of the fighting.

During the 21st KG Kling of the LAH pulled back some 5km to the south-west of Rotheau, while KGs Peiper and Sternebeck continued in action in the Gölsen valley between St Veit and Hainfeld. A counter-attack by Sternebeck's Mk IVs and the 9th SS Pioneer Company to recapture Hainfeld from the west failed and the group was forced to take up new positions south of the valley road. Farther to the east, the 26th SS Panzer-Grenadier Regimental KG, now under the command of SS Lieutenant Colonel Rudolf Sandig[30], also withdrew south of the Hainfeld-Kaumberg road, whilst the rest of the HJ fought on in the triangle: St Corona-Hainfeld-Altenmarkt.

There are 121 unknown German soldiers buried in the cemetery at St Corona. They are unknown because the Russians took away all forms of identification, but there is no doubt that they were members of the Hitlerjugend Division – many of them from KG Möbius, who was himself killed in the fighting in this area on the 21st. Möbius was later described by Hubert Meyer as an 'extremely gallant' officer and one who provided 'exemplary leadership'.

A major problem facing the HJ at this time was the absence of any withdrawal routes between Hainfeld and Weissenbach. In an effort therefore to open up the section of road between these points, KG Gross was ordered to attack from the west and clear the Russian force occupying Kaumberg. Unfortunately for SS Lieutenant Colonel Martin Gross, the bridge 3km west of the village had been blown, blocking his movement. He was blamed for this and the Corps commander immediately sacked him! SS Captain Rudolf von Ribbentrop took over.

By last light on 21 April most of I SS Panzer Corps was south of the road running from Rotheau in the west to Berndorf in the east. The fighting in the Vienna Woods was virtually at an end. The following day was to see the beginning of a painful withdrawal into the Alps and the last battles of I SS Panzer Corps.

As a postscript to this phase it is worth noting that on 17 April it was announced that Bernhard Siebken, the commander of the 2nd SS Panzer-Grenadier Regiment, SS Captain Werner Damsch of the 1st Battalion of the 25th Regiment, and SS Second Lieutenant Konrad Heubeck of the 1st SS Panzer Battalion LAH, had all been awarded the Knight's Cross.

NOTES

1. Tiemann, *The Leibstandarte* IV/2, p. 284.
2. XXXVIII Gds Rifle Corps & IX Gds Mech Corps (Pz Div).
3. V Gds Tk Corps (Pz Div).
4. Zavizion & Kornyushin, *I na Tikhom okeane. . . .*
5. Tiemann, op. cit., pp. 277–8.
6. Ibid., pp. 282–3.
7. Ibid., p. 281.
8. Gen Rudolf von Bünau and Oberst Hans Greiner, MS# B-161, Corps von Bünau (9 Apr – 8 May).
9. Tiemann, op. cit., p. 293.
10. As Note 8.
11. Tiemann, op. cit., p. 286.
12. Ibid.
13. Meyer, *The History of the 12th SS Panzer Division Hitlerjugend*, p. 313.
14. Price, *The Last Year of the Luftwaffe May 1944 to May 1945*, pp. 151–4.
15. As Note 8: two bns of the 710th Inf Div, the 3rd Pz Recce Bn, one AA and two engr construction bns and two Hungarian arty bns.
16. XXXIX Rifle and XVIII Tk Corps (Pz Div).
17. The Histories of the LAH and HJ both say this happened on 15 Apr and quote the Army Group South Daily Report as their source; nevertheless, it is clear from MS # B-161, p. 9, and subsequent events, that the town fell on the 13th.
18. As Note 8, p. 11.
19. HQ Coy, 1st , 3rd & 6th SS Pz Coys commanded by Jauch, Schulz, Minow and Grossjohann respectively. The 5th SS Pz Coy, under Gasch, had already joined in Hungary.
20. Part of the 12th SS Arty Regt acting as inf, a pl of the Div Escort Coy, one or possibly two Gren coys and a Luftwaffe coy.
21. The commanders were SS Lts Jahn, Denker, Stiller, Rattenhuber, Hennecke and Fischer. The latter had been Poetschke's Adjutant in the Ardennes and had been badly burned when his Panther was knocked out in Ligneuville, and Hennecke had commanded the 1st SS Pz Coy in the Ardennes and escaped with Peiper from the La Gleize pocket.
22. Meyer, op. cit., p. 316.
23. West Germany became an independent sovereign state on 5 May 55.
24. Remnants of Bremer's SS Recce Bn and the 26th Regt's SPW Bn.

25. As Note 8. Activated in Mar 45 from instructors and training units of the Moravian SS School, it comprised three bns and a lt fd how bn.
26. General von Bünau, the ex Garrison commander of Vienna, arrived at HQ Corps Schultz on 16 Apr and took command; from 17 Apr the Corps was renamed 'von Bünau'.
27. As Note 8, p. 20.
28. According to Schneider, *Tigers in Combat* II, p. 267, this happened on 18 Apr, with one Tiger having to be abandoned after breaking through a bridge. Tiemann, op. cit., p. 305, says it happened on the 20th.
29. Tiemann, op. cit., p. 304.
30. Readers will recall that Sandig had commanded the 2nd SS Panzer-Grenadier Regiment in the Ardennes.

CHAPTER XXVIII

The Twilight of the Gods: 22 April – 10 May

(Maps 31 & 32)

As the last part of our story has unfolded, readers will probably have noticed that I SS Panzer Corps was operating more and more as a single coordinated entity rather than as two separate Divisions. This was not simply because by April 1945 the combat potential of the Leibstandarte and Hitlerjugend had been reduced to little more than that of two reinforced Regiments; it was much more because the commanders and most of the soldiers stemmed from the same 'family', and knew that as individual men and units they were unlikely to survive on their own – 'My Loyalty is My Honour' had real meaning for these men.

The period 22 to 26 April in the history of I SS Panzer Corps is particularly fascinating because it demonstrates very clearly how, even in the most chaotic and demoralising circumstances such as those pertaining in Lower Austria at that time, highly motivated, well trained soldiers, led by commanders whom they respected, were able to reach levels of military performance to which modern armies can only hope to aspire. The following description will show how the actions of first one Division, and then the other, made it possible for both to withdraw through incredibly difficult terrain, so that both survived to reach safety – even if that safety meant surrender and captivity! It also has to be said that fear of falling into the hands of the Russians was a highly motivating factor in the performance of the members of the Leibstandarte Corps.

The phased withdrawal began on 22 April with the western and central KGs of the LAH pulling back to temporary positions in the mountain valleys on the south side of the Traisen-Hainfeld road. Those in the west withdrew through Lilienfeld towards Türnitz and those in the centre towards Kleinzell and Ramsau. Meanwhile, the men of the HJ struggled to hold on in the Triesting valley between Hainfeld and Weissenbach so as to allow the eastern KGs of the LAH to move back towards Furth and Pernitz.

SS Second Lieutenant Borchers described the withdrawal of parts of KG Peiper and Siebken's 2nd SS Panzer-Grenadier Regiment from Hainfeld:

> We defended the town with three Panzers. . . . Mortars, anti-tank guns and rifle fire would allow us no rest. After the town exchanged hands several times, scarcely a house remained standing. . . . We took up positions 1000m south of the town. The Russians attacked them immediately. The enemy left his dead behind but threw us out of these positions.[1]

And SS Captain Dr Knoll talked later of the withdrawal of his Aid Station:

> Redeployment to Kleinzell. . . . Regimental Aid Station: Kalte Kuchl: one dead, cause of death – hunger! . . . Peiper's Command Post attacked. We still have three Mk IVs and two 20mm Flak guns. Revolting diarrhoea.[2]

SS Lieutenant Stiller also told how his Company reached safety during the night of the 23rd:

> The Company was completely exhausted. . . . Pernitz was reached at 0600 hours in a forced march through the [mountains]. . . . The Russians fired on Pernitz from the . . . hills. The Company continued the march and reached Gutenstein at 0900 hours. Assembled trucks transported the exhausted men through . . . Rohr and Kalte Kuchl to Hölle [not located]. . . . The Company's night camp was a barn with tree branches as straw. It was bitterly cold.[3]

Otto Kumm's Divisional Headquarters in Weissenbach found itself unable to pull out through Hainfeld as originally planned and was forced to withdraw through the mountains:

> A gravel road that led from Weissenbach in the direction of Furth and Pernitz ended . . . as a mountain trail. SS Lieutenant Colonel Ziemssen [the Chief of Staff] had the engineers make it passable for wheeled vehicles.[4]

By the 24th the LAH had established some semblance of a defensive line running from Lilienfeld in the west, through Kleinzell and Ramsau, and then across the mountains to the Pernitz area. This allowed the battered Hitlerjugend KGs to withdraw into the mountains on the south side of the hated Triesting valley. Late on the 23rd the Soviets occupied the Weissenbach-Pottenstein sector.

On 25 April, while the HJ defended the line from Ramsau towards Furth and then south towards Pernitz, the LAH began the construction of a new Alpine defensive position running from Rohr, north-west to Lilienfeld. Most of this ground is well above 1,000m and lay under packed snow. The chronicle of the LAH Flak Battalion recorded:

> The withdrawal became more dramatic from day to day. Through Pernitz-Gutenstein-Rohr-Kalte Kuchl into the Halbach valley [running towards Kleinzell]. The last 37mm guns took up the outer defence while the infantry battle groups occupied the mountain positions. The enemy tried to penetrate . . . into the Halbach valley but he was forced back by a counter-attack. . . . Attacks by enemy infantry were stopped by banging cooking pots together and making cracking noises that echoed in the mountains. This saved ammunition. . . . One 88mm gun which was manhandled into position . . . in the Halbach valley was able to effectively engage the Soviets on the opposing mountain ridges. The remaining three 88mm guns . . . engaged Soviet assembly areas east of Kalte Kuchl with direct fire.[5]

Werner Sternebeck described what it was like for the few remaining tanks:

> We were being compressed in the [Halbach] valley. Only one tank had a field of fire, so we were more and more vulnerable to enemy infantry. It was a desperate, nerve-wracking and ultimately hopeless battle without chance of success.[6]

By last light on the following day, the new defensive line was considered sufficiently organised and orders were issued for the Hitlerjugend to begin its withdrawal to the Tradigist area where it was to reorganise and then take over in that sector from the 10th Parachute Division. This would place the HJ on the LAH's left flank and create a continuous I SS Panzer Corps front running from Rohr, north-west through Lilienfeld to Rabenstein (5km north of Tradigist).

The HJ withdrawal started at 2130 hours and, after appallingly difficult foot marches, the weary soldiers finally reached the road leading to Rohr and Hohenberg where trucks waited to take them back to the new assembly area.

The following two days, the 27th and 28th, saw the HJ reorganising whilst the LAH continued to ward off Soviet patrols and probing attacks. The fighting was limited but ferocious when it did flare up. One Senior Sergeant reported:

Our platoon strength was four NCOs and twenty-three. There was fierce fighting against two Russian companies in the early morning. Losses: three killed, two missing and seventeen wounded. After the battle, which was sometimes conducted hand to hand . . . our platoon had a strength of one and four. . . . I was wounded.[7]

Sternebeck said later that his tanks were withdrawn since there was no longer any ammunition. He went on to say:

Everyone was fighting for bare survival in order to escape falling into Soviet captivity. . . . Comradeship, trust, obedience and even loyalty existed only where people knew each other.[8]

The 'little war in the mountains', as Ralf Tiemann described the last days of the war in his History of the Leibstandarte, could not have been more unpleasant. The Russians used loud speakers to encourage the Germans to desert, the weather was bitterly cold and there was a desperate shortage of food. To counter the Russian propaganda, Dietrich issued a special Order of the Day which included the words:

Our Fatherland is in great danger. . . . Is there one among you who does not have a personal reckoning to settle with the unbridled hordes coming from the Kremlin? . . . You are the Guardians of the Reich, the avengers of all the horrors inflicted on our people, the shield bearers and defenders of a thousand-year military tradition. . . . Long live Germany! Hail our Führer!

But there was no answer to the cold and hunger. SS Second Lieutenant Stiller recalled:

The weather and the hunger were Allies of the Russians. The men lacked any protection from the cold. Their bodies heated the earth bunkers. . . . Our sector had to be carefully controlled. Ivan was not as tired as us and at night we had no contact with our neighbours. In addition the snow muffled all sound.[9]

Meanwhile, during the 27th and 28th, the Hitlerjugend completed its move to the Tradigist valley – a naturally protected and dramatically beautiful area – and began to reorganise into its formal Regiments and

Battalions. What happened next is described best in the words of the Divisional Chief of Staff:

Replacements which had arrived were incorporated. Wounded men returned to their units from the hospitals. Some, who had not fully recovered, 'discharged' themselves since they preferred to be with their units. After a period of rest, the weapons were cleaned and uniforms repaired. Since renewed action was in the future, the replacements . . . were trained in the field and prepared through lectures. The commanders and unit leaders recced the 10th Parachute Division sectors assigned to them.[10]

The relief of the paratroopers took place during the 29th and by last light the new Corps front of some 25km was complete. But in the end the new sector saw little activity and to all intents and purposes the war was over for what was left of the twin Divisions.

1 – 10 May

The news of the Führer's death reached the men of the Leibstandarte Adolf Hitler Corps on May Day in various ways. One SS Lieutenant told his men:

Comrades, the Führer is dead. We will continue to fight here on the front. We have received orders from . . . our Standartenführer [Colonel] Max Hansen, to defend our positions tenaciously until all rear area elements – the aid stations, hospitals, the last elements of the fleeing population – reach security from the attacking Russians. This is an honourable mission![11]

SS Lieutenant Stiller remembered:

We had a new Commander-in-Chief [Admiral Dönitz]. The Company learned of the Führer's death from Battalion. The reaction? Rumours of a cease-fire with the Amis [Americans]. The men endure everything.[12]

But most of the soldiers had no illusions – as a survivor of Leidreiter's Reconnaissance Battalion said later:

We heard on the radio about the catastrophe in Berlin and the death of the Führer. Dönitz spoke words of encouragement, but we knew that our hour of defeat had arrived. Everyone had only one desire – to reach the American lines as quickly as possible.[13]

Hitler's death was certainly seen as a catastrophe by the older and more senior members of the Corps – the ones who, before the war, had stood close to their leader in the Chancellery and at the Berghof. Their relationship had always been special – just as, even today, those who serve close to Heads of State enjoy their privileged positions. As Hubert Meyer put it: the news 'moved them deeply'.

The following day the Hitlerjugend was ordered into Sixth Panzer Army reserve in the Kilb area. Martin Gross had re-assumed command of the Division's Panzer Regiment and, while von Ribbentrop's Battalion remained in position to cover the withdrawal, the rest of the Division pulled out during the night of 2–3 May. The last battle had been fought. The campaign on the Eastern Front in 1945 had cost the HJ 4,376 casualties, of which 1,498 were dead, including one Regimental and seven Company commanders. Thirty-two Mk IVs and thirty-five Panthers had been lost, as well as twenty guns, howitzers and heavy mortars.[14] What was left? Nearly 10,000 men and, according to Meyer, six Mk IVs and nine Panthers combat-ready, as well as thirty-seven guns, howitzers and heavy mortars.[15] As far as the author can establish, the last members of I SS Panzer Corps to be awarded the Knight's Cross were SS Lieutenant Colonel Oskar Drexler, the commander of the HJ's Artillery Regiment and SS Captain Walter Pitsch, commander of the 4th Battery of the LAH's Flak Battalion. Their awards were announced two days before the capitulation – Pitsch's for leading his men in a counter-attack near Schwarzensee on 18 April.

At the same time as he ordered the Hitlerjugend into reserve, Priess ordered all non-operational elements of the Leibstandarte to be withdrawn from the forward positions and assembled in the Türnitz and other adjacent valleys. This included all transport, repair, supply and medical units and heavy weapons without ammunition. For those who remained in the forward strongpoints it was an agonising time:

> Winter continues. . . . Hunger gnaws at everyone. . . . One can see Melk Abbey in the midday sun. Are there Amis or Russians there? . . . During the early morning Russian patrols cause unrest in the Company. If only we could mine the forest trails.[16]

On 7 May Sepp Dietrich, who had lost touch with Rendulic at Army Group South, on his own initiative ordered the 12th SS Panzer Division Hitlerjugend to move into a new assembly area to the south-east of Amstetten. At the same time Hubert Meyer was told to report to his opposite number, Fritz Kraemer, at Headquarters Sixth Panzer Army, located 10km west of Scheibbs. Dietrich was not present. Meyer was told that General Jodl, on behalf of Admiral Dönitz, had offered the surrender of all German armed forces at Eisenhower's Headquarters in Reims and that the necessary document had been signed at 0241 hours that morning. Hostilities were to cease at midnight on 8 May and by that time all troops had to be across the demarcation line between the Americans and the Soviets – that line was the Enns river.

Kraemer went on to thank Meyer, on behalf of Dietrich, for the outstanding actions of the Hitlerjugend and told him to offer the surrender of the Division to the Americans at Steyr that afternoon.

Hubert Meyer describes the afternoon's events in his History of the Hitlerjugend:

> A narrow lane had been opened up through a minefield, marked with white tape. An American jeep guided the car to a sentry at the entrance to a factory. . . . Pistols were handed over. [He and an orderly officer] were driven into the city in an American jeep with an escort. It stopped in front of an hotel in the market square. . . . The American guard at the entrance said, in German: 'Don't worry, everything will work out!' The negotiators were led into a room on the first floor. In its centre stood a large table, covered with maps. There was no other furniture in the room. Three or four American officers were sitting on the floor. A staff officer stood up . . . and [Meyer] was requested to indicate on the map where the Division was located. Then came the question: How many men did the Division have? The answer: 'Ten thousand' was taken in with great delight by the officers sitting on the floor. Bottles and glasses standing around gave an indication that the victory had already been celebrated. That was understandable but it was deeply painful to the negotiators.
>
> The American staff officer announced the conditions: The Division will cross the demarcation line in the Upper Austrian city of Enns on the Enns river on 8 May 1945, from 0800 hours to 2400 hours. Anyone arriving later will go into Russian captivity. All weapons will be unloaded 2km from the river, small arms are to be removed. The ammunition for tanks and guns will follow behind them on trucks. The tanks will point their guns in the air. All vehicles will have to fly white flags.[17]

After Meyer had reported, his Divisional commander summoned his commanders to give them the news and conditions. After ordering that white flags would *not* be flown[18], Kraas made a speech in which he thanked every member of the Division for their valour and loyalty and asked that in memory of their fallen comrades they should maintain their spirit of camaraderie during captivity and during the rebuilding of the destroyed Fatherland. He closed with these words:

> We set out on the bitterest journey of our life as soldiers with our heads

held high. In quiet composure, we will march towards our destiny. We have fought bravely and with integrity in all theatres of war – but still the war is lost. Long live Germany.[19]

Meyer continues his description of the final hours:

On the morning of 8 May 1945 at 0430 hours, SS Major General Hugo Kraas and SS Lieutenant Colonel Hubert Meyer drove with the operations staff and the Divisional Escort Company via Amstetten to Enns. . . . They stopped approximately 1km from the river where the road leads down from the ridge. Along both sides of the road were deep gravel pits. At the left edge of the road (there was a high embankment on the right) stood the Divisional commander, his Adjutant and his Chief of Staff, awaiting the approach of the Divisional columns.[20] The Escort Company buried its weapons in the gravel pits. . . . The commanders reported their units and the troops marched past, mounted, as if on parade, with perfect bearing.

Suddenly, a few Wehrmacht vehicles came out of Enns. Sitting on them were former prisoners from the nearby Mauthausen Concentration Camp with weapons at the ready. They drove along the column and started looting the vehicles. In order to prevent further abuse a Panther was parked in the left lane so that no more vehicles could drive down the column.[21]

It is perhaps ironic that the Hitlerjugend Division was required to surrender at the bridge closest to Mauthausen (8km away) and was forced to ask for protection from the former inmates. Could one be forgiven for suspecting that this was a carefully thought-out scenario on the part of the Americans? Only nine days previously their troops had overrun the infamous camp at Dachau and, in an outburst of anger at what they found, they had 'summarily executed' twenty-one guards, including seventeen SS men.[22] Mauthausen was one of the first concentration camps and some 195,000 men and women were imprisoned there and in its sub-camps between 8 August 1938 and 5 May 1945 – more than 105,000 of them died. According to today's Austrian authorities, when the SS guards fled on 3 May there were 68,268 inmates including 1,734 women, four British and two American citizens. Another 81,000 prisoners were liberated by American troops from the sub-camps and other concentration camps in Upper Austria.

By last light on the 8th most of the Hitlerjugend had crossed the Enns and made camp in the fields close to Enns. Vehicles, guns and tanks were parked separately and lines of American sentries guarded the men. Von Ribbentrop's Battalion was the last to cross the river, just before the midnight deadline, and individual stragglers who were late were turned back. Those who were able swam across the river farther south or found other crossing places. Altogether 9,870 men, including 328 officers and 1,698 NCOs, surrendered to the US 65th Infantry Division. They were only just in time – at 1845 hours three Russian officers from the 7th Guards Airborne Division arrived at the American Headquarters. The leading elements of their Division were only 20km to the east of Enns![23]

And what of the Leibstandarte, which had been given the unenviable task of covering the withdrawal of much of the Sixth Panzer Army? Unbelievable as it may seem, it was still receiving new equipment. On 2 May some forty members of the 501st Heavy SS Panzer Battalion were sent to a depot near Enns with the task of making six Jagdtigers operational[24]; and on the afternoon of the 7th, men of the 7th SS Panzer Company received orders to pick up four brand new Mk IVs from Kirchberg.[25] Two of the Jagdtigers reached the LAH Command Post at Scheibbs but one finished up immobilized and the other as a road block near Waidhofen; the Mk IVs were eventually 'scuttled' in the Enns.

During the night of 7-8 May the men in the forward positions received their orders. They were to assemble south-east of Scheibbs and then move via Waidhofen to the Enns river, 18km south-west of that town. From a school house near Scheibbs, Jochen Peiper sent his last message as a free man: 'The dream of Empire is over! Tonight, with Guhl [commander 2nd SS Panzer Battalion] we face the last enemy.'[26]

A Senior Sergeant in Siebken's Regiment remembered:

> I experienced a spontaneous feeling: there were still Russians to the right, to the left and in front of us – maybe even behind us? Could we expect fairness from the Americans? We suddenly had to think about our fallen comrades, relatives, the columns of refugees and the victims of the bombs. Unconditional surrender made everyone wordless. If yesterday, with gallows humour, we had sung 'Everyone forward', today we are all quiet.[27]

Fear of Russian captivity was now being supplemented by uncertainty about American intentions, but few if any members of I SS Panzer Corps anticipated the hatred felt by all Allied troops for the Waffen-SS. The Germans would complain repeatedly and endlessly that they had never been anything other than combat soldiers and had no knowledge of extermination squads and concentration camps. They had yet to come to terms with the fact that *anyone* who wore SS runes was seen by Allied troops as part of a diabolical machine which had caused endless misery and countless deaths – as a barbarian who deserved to be treated as such. The members of the Waffen-SS would soon discover, to their intense shock, that the Americans had no intention of extending to them the honours and courtesies applicable to normal prisoners of war.

Disengagement from the forward area was accomplished without difficulty and, after five years and eight months of war, the 1st SS Panzer Division began its march into captivity. Amongst the many dead left behind in Hungary and Lower Austria were at least four Battalion and eleven Company commanders. Heavy weapons and equipment were destroyed en route and, as we have already heard, some armoured vehicles were driven into the Enns river. But unlike the Hitlerjugend, which had moved towards captivity as an organised military force, the Leibstandarte found itself split up into unit groups of varying size and competing with countless refugees and Wehrmacht personnel to make the midnight deadline. SS Lieutenant Pulvermüller described what happened to his 4th SS Artillery Battery:

> We drove off by ourselves and blew up the six guns – these were the only ones – at a quarry. . . . A Panther was standing on the road. It used its last drops of fuel to roll into the quarry. We filled it with grenades and ammunition and blew it up with the guns as best we could. Then we moved out to the west in small groups.[28]

The congestion in the Enns valley between Waidhofen and Steyr, caused by the refugees and other fleeing troops, soon brought the LAH columns to a complete stop and it became obvious that few of the units would be able to cross the demarcation line at Steyr by midnight. The commander of the 1st SS Panzerjäger Battalion, Karl Rettlinger, told of what happened to his unit:

> The roads were hopelessly jammed, so the men left the vehicles and reached the Enns on foot. I came upon a footbridge. Peiper and his staff were also there. We crossed the Enns and entered captivity.[29]

The 9th of May was a sunny and warm day but the weather did little to cheer the many members of the Division who had still to cross the river. 'Will the Americans try to stop us?' was the question in everyone's mind. As soon as Otto Kumm arrived in Steyr, he was driven to the local American Headquarters where the commander of the US 71st Infantry Division took him to meet General Rendulic of Army Group South. Major General Wyman's Divisional Cavalry Troop had captured Rendulic in Waidhofen the day before.[30] The latter told Kumm that the LAH was to take up a position on the east bank of the Enns – this was tantamount to ordering him to surrender his men to the Russians! Kumm refused the order and told his units to cross 'the Green border' anywhere they could, preferably to the south of Steyr. Some had to force their way across:

At about 1200 hours we were in Losenstein where we discovered an intact stone bridge. . . . The Americans there refused to let us cross. With the help of several combat-ready tanks in the column, we [SS Colonel Max Hansen and the survivors of the 1st SS Panzer-Grenadier Regiment] crossed the Enns bridge, therefore the demarcation line, at 1400 hours without a fight. . . . During the evening, after the vehicles could go no farther, we set them on fire. We continued marching to the west.[31]

Others, like Rolf Reiser with what was left of the tank group, took a long detour:

Further movement in the direction of Steyr was impossible because of congestion and the bridge there was supposedly blocked by the Americans. Also the Soviets were advancing from Amstetten to Steyr to block the bridge on their side. We decided to take another route. The last four tanks were driven into the Enns and sunk. The 7th Company, approximately sixty men, drove in the opposite direction, to the south, into the mountains in the direction of Altenmarkt. Driving against all the traffic heading to Steyr, our progress was slow, especially since the road was narrow. . . . From Altenmarkt we took the road to the west and . . . reached the 1,050m high village of Winischgarten [33km west of Altenmarkt]. There we made contact with the US Army. A young American lieutenant behaved correctly – we were disarmed and all weapons turned over, but officers were allowed to keep their pistols.[32]

But not everyone was so fortunate. SS Lieutenant Vögler, of Hansen's 2nd Battalion, recalled:

In the smaller villages there were no sturdy bridges, only suspension bridges. These were overtaxed in the desire to escape Ivan. They broke and collapsed with all the men into the icy depths and the rushing waters of the Enns [a large, fast flowing river]. What senseless and desperate actions! However, any exhortations and attempts to stop them were in vain.[33]

Unlike the majority of the troops of the Hitlerjugend who were placed under guard immediately after their surrender, many of those in the LAH were simply waved on to the west. In fact during the period midnight 8 May to midnight 11 May, the US 71st Infantry Division recorded only 3,777 members of the Leibstandarte taken prisoner.[34] Rolf Reiser remembered: 'The march-route was controlled by US military police at all road junctions and in towns', but this was not always so. SS Lieutenant Pulvermüller told how:

The first POW Camp was in a meadow near Steyr. We were able to drive in the three available trucks about 30km outside the camp – the excuse being that we wanted to pick up our Waffen-SS comrades and bring them to the camp. The residents in the towns we passed through could not believe their eyes – so many Waffen-SS soldiers free, and after the capitulation! [After meeting the same US patrol twice] our excuse no longer worked . . . under escort they brought us back to Steyr.[35]

Jochen Peiper took advantage of this lax security to head for his home and family in Bavaria but he was caught and arrested on the 10th by an American patrol. He was only some 30km from his goal! His captors had no idea that he was soon to be branded 'GI Enemy Number One'!

The same lack of control resulted in some actions by the surrendered men which were later regretted. SS Lieutenant Leidreiter of the Reconnaissance Battalion recounted his experiences:

I had seen the massacred German company near Rovno [in the Soviet Union] in 1941. I knew of other stories like that. Therefore I had no trouble making my decision – captivity? Never with the Russians! . . . . We reached the first bridge across the Enns south of Steyr [Losenstein]. . . . On the other side there were two choices – to the north was the road to Steyr – that wasn't even considered. . . . There were many burning vehicles, almost all carrying the sign with the Key [LAH]. Then came the bad time. We took off our uniforms. . . . The uniforms were burned with the VW. It was a wretched moment! There was a forested rocky slope in front of us. . . . The entire slope was swarming with German soldiers and civilians. . . .The higher we climbed the more we discarded from our heavy packs.[36]

Leidreiter remembered meeting Max Hansen as much as two days later:

An officer with a Knight's Cross, in full uniform. . . . The rest of us were going – whether into captivity or to another life – with some baggage, with a blanket, an overcoat or sack with shaving implements – not so Max Hansen. He climbed down the long slope, as always, proud, erect, as if he was going to report with his entire Regiment! . . . What a marvellous and honourable commander![37]

And so, by one means or another, the officers and men of the 1st SS Panzer Division joined their comrades of the Hitlerjugend on the west side of the demarcation line. Soon the vast majority of them would be behind wire, but some managed to escape custody. They, in order to avoid US patrols and armed gangs of former concentration camp inmates intent on revenge, moved in small groups – mainly at night and through difficult terrain; by day they hid in woods, trusting nobody. Not all of them managed to get home and most of those who did were soon picked up by the occupying military authorities.

And what of the first commander of the Leibstandarte and the Leibstandarte Corps – Sepp Dietrich? On 8 May he went to a new Headquarters at Zell am See (60km south of Berchtesgaden) known as OKW South. There he expected to meet its commander, General August Winter, but on arrival he learned of the capitulation and that Winter had gone on to Berchtesgaden. Dietrich told his US interrogators[38] that he tried to follow Winter but that he and his wife were arrested by the Americans before he could do so. Since the place of arrest was Kufstein, some 70km to the *west* of Berchtesgaden, the suspicion has arisen that he may have been trying to smuggle his wife into Switzerland. It is also strange that he made no effort to contact his direct superior, General Rendulic; however, in view of Rendulic's directions to Kumm to stay east of the Enns, it may be that Dietrich suspected that he might be ordered to surrender his men to the Russians and decided to stay beyond reach. Although it would seem out of character for him to have deserted his men, the question has to be asked: why was he not in the Enns-Steyr sector to support his 'boys' in their most distressing hour?

The US Master Sergeant in the 36th Infantry Division to whom Dietrich surrendered, described his prisoner as 'not anything like an Army commander – he is more like a village grocer.'[39]

So ends the story of I SS Panzer Corps in the Ardennes in 1944 and on the Eastern Front in 1945. Our final Chapter will describe what happened to these men after the war.

NOTES

1. Tiemann, *The Leibstandarte* IV/2, pp. 306–7.
2. Ibid., p. 307.
3. Ibid., p. pp. 307–8.
4. Ibid., p. 308–9.
5. Ibid., p. 311.
6. Ibid., p. 309.
7. Ibid., p. 313.
8. Ibid., p. 314
9. Ibid., p. 315.
10. Meyer, *The History of the 12th SS Panzer Division Hitlerjugend*, p. 322.
11. Tiemann, op. cit., p. 317.
12. Ibid.
13. Ibid.
14. Meyer, op. cit., p. 323.
15. Ibid.
16. Tiemann, op. cit., p. 318.
17. Meyer, op. cit., p. 324.
18. Walther, *The 1st SS Panzer Division Leibstandarte, A Pictorial History*, p. 113

has a photograph with the caption: 'Marked with white cloths, vehicles of the "Bodyguard" drive into captivity.'

19. Meyer, op. cit., p. 324.
20. The position described does not exist on the present Route 1 road; however, the area on road number 123a, 5km north-east of the Enns bridge, matches the description exactly.
21. Meyer, op. cit., p. 324.
22. HQ Seventh Army Office of the Inspector General US Army Report dated 8 Jun 45.
23. AAR 65th Inf Div dated 6 Jul 45.
24. Schneider, *Tigers in Combat* II, p. 267. The Jagdtiger was a 70 ton tank hunter derivative of the Tiger II with a 128mm gun and a crew of six.
25. Tiemann, op. cit., p. 319.
26. Ibid., p. 320.
27. Ibid.
28. Ibid., p. 348.
29. Ibid., p. 351.
30. AAR 71st Inf Div dated 2 Jul 45.
31. Tiemann, op. cit., p. 352.
32. Ibid., p. 354.
33. Ibid., p. 352.
34. 71st Inf Div G-2 Periodic Report, which also reports 789 members of the HJ and 316 soldiers of the 560th Heavy Panzerjäger Battalion taken prisoner in the same period.
35. Tiemann, op. cit., p. 355.
36. Ibid., p. 353.
37. Ibid., pp. 356-7.
38. US 7th Army Interrogation Report SAIC/43 dated 11 Jun 45.
39. *Stars and Stripes*, 14 May 45.

CHAPTER XXIX

Captives, Camps and Courts

(Map 31)

During the first few days of captivity, the majority of the Leibstandarte and Hitlerjugend prisoners were held in meadows near Enns and Steyr. Others found themselves in a small Mauthausen sub-camp near Ternberg, 15km south of Steyr. The weather was sunny and warm and, as they still had some rations and tents with them, conditions were reasonable. It was not long though before those at Enns and Steyr were moved to a new camp at Mauerkirchen, 40km north of Salzburg, near the Inn river. Werner Sternebeck described what happened:

The remains of the KG stayed together after being disarmed and marched with the few available vehicles, including the field kitchen, into the camp at Mauerkirchen, which was reached on 12 May. . . . Although we had no weapons and were in close formation, no one tried to beat or steal from us [referring to US soldiers, former concentration camp inmates and Austrian resistance fighters]. . . . Almost the entire Division and our vehicles were kept in the 'open' prison camp in the meadows around Mauerkirchen. . . . The relationship with superiors remained intact and I remember no loss of discipline.[1]

During the short stay in Mauerkirchen and Ternberg, which lasted until about 20 May, the Americans separated the members of the Waffen-SS from other prisoners. Then, while some were marched to what became known as the 'Hunger Camp' at Altheim, 16km to the north-east, and some 4,500 LAH and HJ prisoners to a 'Forest Camp' somewhere on the Enns river, others went directly to the Mauthausen sub-camp at Ebensee, in the mountains 80km east of Salzburg.[2]

There is no doubt that the US authorities set out to break the morale of the prisoners in the 'Hunger' and 'Forest' camps – by severely restricting food, by breaking up units and by separating officers and senior NCOs from the lower ranks. Sternebeck remembered:

The transfer into 'Hunger Camp Altheim', which resulted in the breaking up of the former units . . . automatically caused disciplinary problems. This was what the Americans wanted. An uneasy peace could only be maintained with firmness and weapons.[3]

Hubert Meyer claims that twenty-nine Waffen-SS soldiers died as a result of the 'death march' from Mauerkirchen and the conditions at Altheim.[4]

A soldier of the LAH Reconnaissance Battalion told of his time in the 'Forest Camp' and move to Ebensee:

We lived there in the forest like the ancient Germans. There were almost no rations: one loaf of bread for seventeen to twenty men. Old horses were obtained and eaten. Because of lack of salt the meat tasted terrible. Moreover, it went bad quickly because of the heat. . . . The maggots were scraped off and then it was cooked. Hunger hurts! . . .

On 28 June we were transferred again. . . . our rail cars were pelted with rocks and we were faced by an angry mob. . . . We were received by a large group of former concentration camp residents. All the way to the camp we literally ran the gauntlet, pursued by stones, clubs and raging epithets. We had arrived in Ebensee.[5]

By the middle of August most of the members of the Leibstandarte

Corps had been assembled in two camps at Ebensee. Their treatment, not altogether surprisingly, left much to be desired. Food was short, guards stole personal possessions and the sanitation was primitive. In October both camps was disbanded and the prisoners dispersed. Some ended up in other former concentration camps like Dachau and others in POW camps as far away as France and England[6].

Hugo Kraas, the commander of the HJ, had been moved to a camp just south of Linz, while Meyer and several thousand Waffen-SS soldiers were held in Auerbach Camp No. 24 in the Grafenwöhr military training area.

Kraas kept a diary of his time in captivity in which he noted carefully the poor rations and mis-treatment of prisoners. He claimed that the food: 'was not enough to live on, and too much to die on', and that it was not until July that his complaints reached the right man – a Colonel Georges of the 259th Infantry Regiment – and conditions improved. The 259th was part of the Division to which Kraas had surrendered his Division. He goes on to say that on 6 July the guards who were accused of abusing the prisoners: 'were brought face to face with us so that the guilty could be picked out'.[7]

Hubert Meyer claims that in his camp complaints by the senior German prisoner about the 'unbearable treatment of seriously disabled comrades' which was not in accordance with the Geneva Convention, were met with: 'What do you mean, "Geneva Convention"? You seem to have forgotten that you lost the war!' He claims also that after a visit to the camp by General George S. Patton, conditions improved and American 'C – Rations' handed out; however, shortly after Patton's death in a motor accident conditions again deteriorated.

In mid-August the first screenings for release from captivity began – for those born in 1926 or later. Readers may recall that the Hitlerjugend Division had been formed from boys born in 1926. Then in December it was announced that the entire Waffen-SS was being charged before the International Military Tribunal with being a criminal organisation. This was followed in November 1946 by the removal of prisoner of war status for all members of the Waffen-SS and the announcement that they were henceforth civilian internees in automatic arrest. From then on only those who had been 'denazified' could be released from the 'internment' camps. Special tribunals were established to carry out this 'denazification' and, as they were released, the former members of the LAH and HJ were graded into one of three categories: 'major offender' – which automatically included all officers down to SS major – 'incriminated' or 'fellow-traveller'. The only exceptions were those who had been drafted into Waffen-SS, but even then if the draftee had been promoted to NCO rank he too was 'incriminated'. The grading decided the 'sanction': labour service in an internment camp, monetary fine, prohibition of working in one's profession, or loss of right to vote or to be elected either for life or for a limited period after release.

Most of the LAH and HJ prisoners had been released by the end of 1948 but long before that 'War Crimes' trials had begun before Allied courts. The most famous – or infamous, depending on one's point of view – was held in the former concentration camp at Dachau between 16 May and 16 July 1946. Sepp Dietrich, Fritz Kraemer, Hermann Priess, and Jochen Peiper with seventy men of his Ardennes KG, faced the accusation that they:

> being together concerned as parties, did in conjunction with other persons . . . wilfully, deliberately and wrongfully permit, encourage, aid, abet and participate in the killing, shooting, ill-treatment, abuse and torture –

of US soldiers, including those at the Baugnez Crossroads, and Allied civilian nationals, the exact names and numbers of whom were unknown. The Prosecution alleged that the accused were responsible between them for the deaths of at least 460 Americans and 106 Belgians.

Further details of events leading up to the trial and the trial itself can be found in the companion book *The Devil's Adjutant – Jochen Peiper, Panzer Leader*. Suffice to say here that on 16 July 1946, Peiper, Christ, Diefenthal, Hennecke, Junker, Klingelhöfer, Munkämer, Preuss, Rumpf, Sickel, Sievers, Sternebeck and Tomhardt (all of whom have featured in this book), were sentenced to death by hanging. Twenty-two others, including Dietrich, Knittel and Coblenz, received life imprisonment and the remainder long terms – Priess got twenty years and Kraemer ten. In the event, no one was hanged and all had been released by the end of December 1956.

Three trials of members of the Hitlerjugend Division took place between 1945 and 1949. They concerned atrocities allegedly committed in northern France in 1944 against French civilians and Canadian soldiers and resulted in twenty-one former HJ officers and men being sentenced to death. One of the only two carried out was on Bernhard Siebken, a Knight's Cross holder and the officer who had commanded a Battalion of the HJ in Normandy and the LAH's 2nd SS Panzer-Grenadier Regiment in Hungary and Austria. He was hanged by the British in West Germany on 20 January 1949.

Following their release, many of the former soldiers of the Leibstandarte and Hitlerjugend found life extremely hard and unpleasant. No one wanted to associate with former SS men and so those who were able concealed their wartime service – particularly from neighbours. The only jobs which were easily available were those involving manual labour. One former LAH lieutenant told the author how, after being sentenced to death but released in the early 1950s, he lived with his wife in one unheated room in the Ruhr and the only work he could find was sweeping a factory floor at night. His wife died of hypothermia during their first winter together.

But what of the main characters in our story? What of the men who are regarded by some as heroes and brilliant soldiers and by others as devils in uniform?

Sepp Dietrich was paroled in October 1955, tried before a West German court in 1957 for his part in the 'Night of the Long Knives' and sentenced to another eighteen months in prison. He died in April 1966 and was given a hero's funeral by his 'boys'.

As far as the author can establish, Hermann Priess did not work after his release from prison and died in 1985.

Aged 89, Otto Kumm is still alive. Before retiring he rose to be Deputy Technical Director of the Burda Publishing Company in Offenburg.

Wilhelm Mohnke is also alive, living near Hamburg. He was the last commander of the Citadel in Berlin – the area which included the Chancellery and Hitler's Bunker – and was captured by the Russians on 2 May 1945. After his release in October 1955 he lived quite openly near Hamburg. It is strange therefore that when the author asked to see Mohnke's file in the Public Record Office in London in 1994, he was told it was 'closed', and even after an appeal to the Prime Minister, Mr John Major, the reply was the same: 'the file will remain closed until 2024'.

Hugo Kraas died in 1980 in Schleswig after being a District Director of the Schwäbisch Hall Savings Bank. Shortly before his death he took part in a 'battlefield inspection' in the Ardennes designed to help Hubert Meyer with his History of the Hitlerjugend Division.

One of the best known veterans, Jochen Peiper, was the last to be released from prison. Due to a plethora of books written about him, a cult of adulation has grown up around this 'last of the fallen', as he is known – particularly outside Germany. Although Peiper was undoubtedly a brave and effective soldier, most members of this cult ignore the fact that other Waffen-SS officers, such as Kurt Meyer, were better tacticians and field commanders and still others, like Max Hansen, saw more close combat and were just as revered by their men. Sadly, they also turn a blind eye to the fact that Peiper spent three years in the close personal service of one of the most evil men in history – Heinrich Himmler – a man who addressed him as 'My dear Jochen'![8]

After being sentenced to death for his part in the 'Malmédy Massacre', and spending nearly five years in solitary confinement wearing the red track-suit jacket of a condemned man, Peiper was paroled in December 1956. He worked initially for Porsche but was forced to resign when the workers' union, IG Metall, discovered he was an ex-Waffen-SS officer and a convicted war criminal. He then became an agent for Volkswagen and a liaison officer between the owner/publisher and Editor-in-Chief of *Auto, Motor and Sport*, before retiring to Traves in France in 1972. In 1967 he had told a French newspaper reporter:

> I was a Nazi and I remain one . . . . The Germany of today is no longer a great nation, it has become a province of Europe [prophetic words!]. . . . I shall settle elsewhere, in France no doubt. I don't particularly care for Frenchmen, but I love France. Of all things, the materialism of my compatriots causes me pain.

Peiper died during a fire-bomb attack on his home on Bastille Day 1976. He is buried with his parents, wife and brothers in Schondorf am Ammersee in Bavaria. No one has ever been brought to justice for his death.

Max Hansen ran a cleaning and laundry shop in Niebuell. He spent his last years as a very sick man and died in March 1990 – 'his brain and soul already being in Valhalla', as a comrade put it.

Rudolf Sandig became the director of an insurance company. He was wearing a miniature Knight's Cross, minus its Swastika, in his lapel when the author met him in 1982 – he died near Bremen in 1994.

Huber Meyer is still alive. He reached a leading position in the Agfa-Gevaert Photographic Company in Leverkusen before retiring and writing his brilliant magnum opus, *The History of the 12th SS Panzer Division Hitlerjugend*.

Gerd Bremer was imprisoned by the French for war crimes. He was released in 1948 and died in 1989 after building and managing a bungalow holiday park in Denia-las-Rotas in Spain.

A number of veterans met with tragic ends – Heinz Kling drowned in Lake Constance in September 1951 and Georg Preuss died, destitute and shunned by family and friends, near Luneberg Heath in 1990. Werner Sternebeck was also shunned – by his daughter Sigrid. She claimed that the shock of discovering that her father had been in the Waffen-SS caused her to become a Red Army Faction terrorist and play a part in killing a German politician with a car bomb. She and her father were reconciled shortly before his death in 1990. Rather surprisingly, after escaping the death penalty and being released from prison, Sternebeck managed to gain acceptance into the West German Army and reach the rank of lieutenant colonel.

Jupp Diefenthal returned to his hometown of Euskirchen after release from Landsberg prison and worked in the local finance office. His wife refused to allow him to be interviewed, by Nazi sympathisers or anyone else, and he never attended any Waffen-SS reunions – or 'Treffs' as they are known.

Reunions of Leibstandarte Corps veterans are now held annually. Those in the early days sometimes ran into trouble, with venues being set on fire or coming under attack in other ways, but this did not stop the men who had faced the best that the Americans, British, Canadians and Soviets could throw against them. Nor did it stop small groups retracing their wartime footsteps through the Ardennes[9] and Hungary, and quietly attending the 50th Anniversary commemorations in Normandy.

Most members of the Leibstandarte and Hitlerjugend Divisions felt they were deliberately maligned after the war and that their efforts as soldiers had been misrepresented. Paradoxically, those efforts – and those of many Wehrmacht soldiers – prolonged the war and led to the total destruction of the very things for which they were fighting. The men of I SS Panzer Corps failed to comprehend that through their close association with Adolf Hitler, even if only in name, and by their membership of the SS, even if it was purely the military wing of that odious organisation, they had in the eyes of everyone outside and many inside Germany, forfeited the right to be recognised as honourable men. Most of them had been so brain-washed by Nazi ideology and military jingoism that they had no understanding of the bitterness felt by their former enemies in the West. Milton Shulman interviewed Kurt Meyer, the commander of the Hitlerjugend Division for most of the Normandy campaign, in August 1945. Meyer offered his services to the Allies and said he could raise:

One SS division of about 23,000 men from amongst the German prisoners-of-war. This formation will be named the 'SS Division Europa' and it is to be equipped with Germans weapons and equipment. I will have no difficulty in raising the men for such a unit to take part in the struggle against the East. We will then show you how Germans can fight.[10]

Shulman goes on to point out that:

To Meyer's distorted mind it seemed perfectly logical for British and American troops to welcome as Allies an SS division which represented everything that they had been fighting against for so long.

This was, as he put it, just another example of: 'the disciplined, [German] military mind carried to its logical, uncurbed end.'[11]

For all the hatred which the war had engendered, the practicalities of the Cold War meant that the West Germans had to be wooed by NATO and the East Germans by the Soviet Union. It was not long before the young men of the nation which had plunged the world into the bloodiest war in its history were again in uniform and the dreaded black cross was seen once more on armoured vehicles. No one in May 1945 would have believed that memories could fade so quickly and that in less than thirty years a former senior Waffen-SS officer would be a guest of the British Army Command and Staff College on a battlefield tour in Normandy. Yet this is indeed what happened – in 1974 Hubert Meyer participated in just such a tour without embarrassment to either side. By a strange twist of fate, the German liaison officer to the College that year was Lieutenant Colonel Graf Stauffenberg – it was his father who had attempted to assassinate Hitler on 20 July 1944.

In conclusion, it has to be said that in purely military terms the men who bore Hitler's name and wore the Hakenkreuz and SS runes were remarkable soldiers. They had not 'quit the post allotted by the Gods' and can be seen as the natural heirs of their Teutonic ancestors. As such, their prominent and everlasting place in the history of warfare is assured.

NOTES

1. Tiemann, *Chronicle of the 7th Panzer Company*, p. 170–1.
2. During the war Ebensee housed more than 18,000 inmates at any one time; they worked in an underground armaments plant.
3. Tiemann, *The Leibstandarte* IV/2, p. 358.
4. Meyer, *The History of the 12th SS Panzer Division Hitlerjugend*, p. 327.
5. Tiemann, *The Leibstandarte* IV/2, p. 360.
6. Former members of the Waffen-SS, Luftwaffe and U-boat crews were held in the UK until as late as 1948. The author met one ex Luftwaffe pilot, later the mayor of a famous Westphalian spa town, who reckoned he had been made to rebuild Plymouth 'personally – brick by brick'!
7. Meyer, op. cit., p. 328.
8. Words used in a congratulatory telegram from Himmler to Peiper, concerning his award of the Knight's Cross, dated 9 Mar 43.
9. The author attended two such tours in 85 and 91. The first included Ralf Tiemann, the author of *The Leibstandarte* IV/2, Rudolf Sandig and Werner Sternebeck.
10. Shulman, *Defeat in the West*, p. 343.
11. Ibid., Preface, p. xvii.

Appendix I

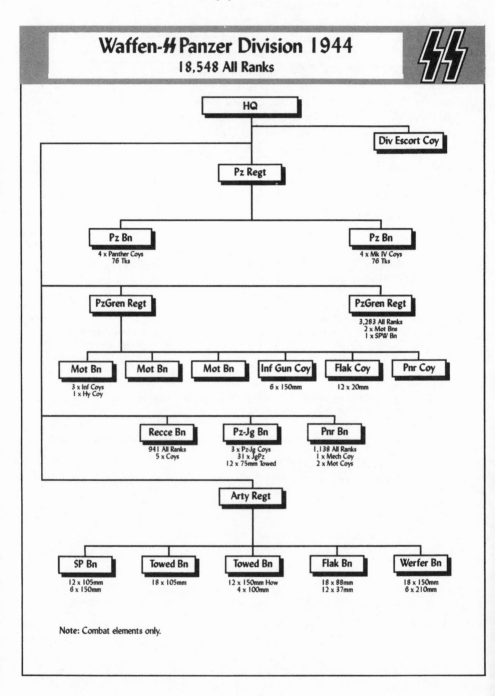

Waffen-SS Panzer Division 1944
18,548 All Ranks

HQ

Div Escort Coy

Pz Regt

Pz Bn
4 x Panther Coys
76 Tks

Pz Bn
4 x Mk IV Coys
76 Tks

PzGren Regt

PzGren Regt
3,283 All Ranks
2 x Mot Bns
1 x SPW Bn

Mot Bn
3 x Inf Coys
1 x Hy Coy

Mot Bn

Mot Bn

Inf Gun Coy
6 x 150mm

Flak Coy
12 x 20mm

Pnr Coy

Recce Bn
941 All Ranks
5 x Coys

Pz-Jg Bn
3 x Pz-Jg Coys
31 x JgPz
12 x 75mm Towed

Pnr Bn
1,138 All Ranks
1 x Mech Coy
2 x Mot Coys

Arty Regt

SP Bn
12 x 105mm
6 x 150mm

Towed Bn
18 x 105mm

Towed Bn
12 x 150mm How
4 x 100mm

Flak Bn
18 x 88mm
12 x 37mm

Werfer Bn
18 x 150mm
6 x 210mm

Note: Combat elements only.

Appendix II

Volks-Grenadier Division
December 1944

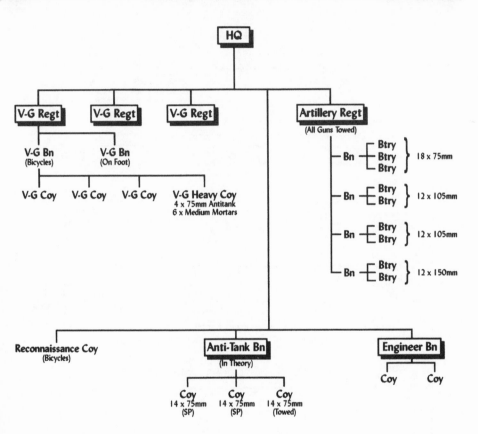

Appendix III

US Infantry Division, 1944

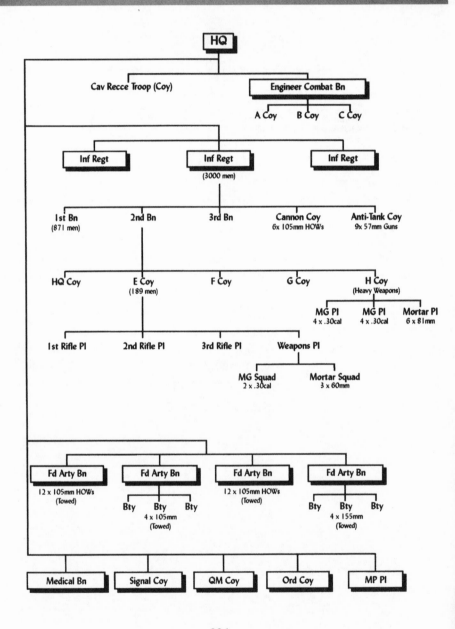

HQ

Cav Recce Troop (Coy)

Engineer Combat Bn

A Coy   B Coy   C Coy

Inf Regt

Inf Regt
(3000 men)

Inf Regt

1st Bn
(871 men)

2nd Bn

3rd Bn

Cannon Coy
6x 105mm HOWs

Anti-Tank Coy
9x 57mm Guns

HQ Coy

E Coy
(189 men)

F Coy

G Coy

H Coy
(Heavy Weapons)

MG Pl
4 x .30cal

MG Pl
4 x .30cal

Mortar Pl
6 x 81mm

1st Rifle Pl

2nd Rifle Pl

3rd Rifle Pl

Weapons Pl

MG Squad
2 x .30cal

Mortar Squad
3 x 60mm

Fd Arty Bn

12 x 105mm HOWs
(Towed)

Fd Arty Bn

Bty   Bty   Bty
4 x 105mm
(Towed)

Fd Arty Bn

12 x 105mm HOWs
(Towed)

Fd Arty Bn

Bty   Bty   Bty
4 x 155mm
(Towed)

Medical Bn   Signal Coy   QM Coy   Ord Coy   MP Pl

296

Appendix IV

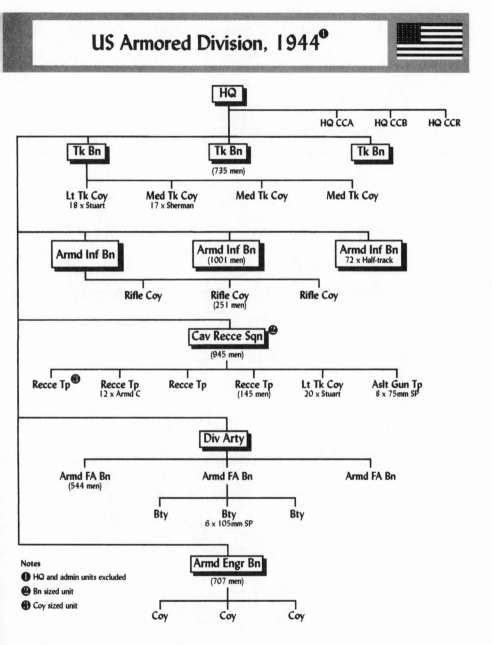

US Armored Division, 1944[1]

HQ

HQ CCA   HQ CCB   HQ CCR

Tk Bn   Tk Bn   Tk Bn
               (735 men)

Lt Tk Coy   Med Tk Coy   Med Tk Coy   Med Tk Coy
18 x Stuart   17 x Sherman

Armd Inf Bn   Armd Inf Bn   Armd Inf Bn
               (1001 men)   72 x Half-track

Rifle Coy   Rifle Coy   Rifle Coy
               (251 men)

Cav Recce Sqn[2]
(945 men)

Recce Tp[3]   Recce Tp   Recce Tp   Recce Tp   Lt Tk Coy   Aslt Gun Tp
               12 x Armd C   (145 men)   20 x Stuart 8 x 75mm SP

Div Arty

Armd FA Bn   Armd FA Bn   Armd FA Bn
(544 men)

Bty   Bty   Bty
               6 x 105mm SP

Notes
[1] HQ and admin units excluded
[2] Bn sized unit
[3] Coy sized unit

Armd Engr Bn
(707 men)

Coy   Coy   Coy

297

Appendix V

1st SS Panzer Division (LAH)
16th December 1944

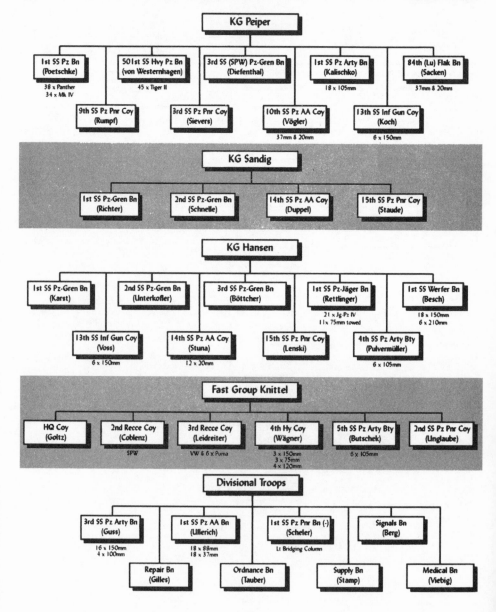

KG Peiper

1st SS Pz Bn (Poetschke)	501st SS Hvy Pz Bn (von Westernhagen)	3rd SS (SPW) Pz-Gren Bn (Diefenthal)	1st SS Pz Arty Bn (Kalischko)	84th (Lu) Flak Bn (Sacken)
38 x Panther 34 x Mk IV	45 x Tiger II		18 x 105mm	37mm & 20mm

9th SS Pz Pnr Coy (Rumpf)
3rd SS Pz Pnr Coy (Sievers)
10th SS Pz AA Coy (Vögler) — 37mm & 20mm
13th SS Inf Gun Coy (Koch) — 6 x 150mm

KG Sandig

1st SS Pz-Gren Bn (Richter)	2nd SS Pz-Gren Bn (Schnelle)	14th SS Pz AA Coy (Duppel)	15th SS Pz Pnr Coy (Staude)

KG Hansen

1st SS Pz-Gren Bn (Karst)	2nd SS Pz-Gren Bn (Unterkofler)	3rd SS Pz-Gren Bn (Böttcher)	1st SS Pz-Jäger Bn (Rettlinger)	1st SS Werfer Bn (Besch)
			21 x Jg-Pz IV 11x 75mm towed	18 x 150mm 6 x 210mm

13th SS Inf Gun Coy (Voss) — 6 x 150mm
14th SS Pz AA Coy (Stuna) — 12 x 20mm
15th SS Pz Pnr Coy (Lenski)
4th SS Pz Arty Bty (Pulvermüller) — 6 x 105mm

Fast Group Knittel

HQ Coy (Goltz)	2nd Recce Coy (Coblenz)	3rd Recce Coy (Leidreiter)	4th Hy Coy (Wägner)	5th SS Pz Arty Bty (Butschek)	2nd SS Pz Pnr Coy (Unglaube)
	SPW	VW & 6 x Puma	3 x 150mm 3 x 75mm 4 x 120mm	6 x 105mm	

Divisional Troops

3rd SS Pz Arty Bn (Guss)	1st SS Pz AA Bn (Ullerich)	1st SS Pz Pnr Bn (-) (Scheler)	Signals Bn (Berg)
16 x 150mm 4 x 100mm	18 x 88mm 18 x 37mm	Lt Bridging Column	

Repair Bn (Gilles)
Ordnance Bn (Tauber)
Supply Bn (Stamp)
Medical Bn (Viebig)

Appendix V (cont)

12th SS Panzer Division HJ
16th December 1944

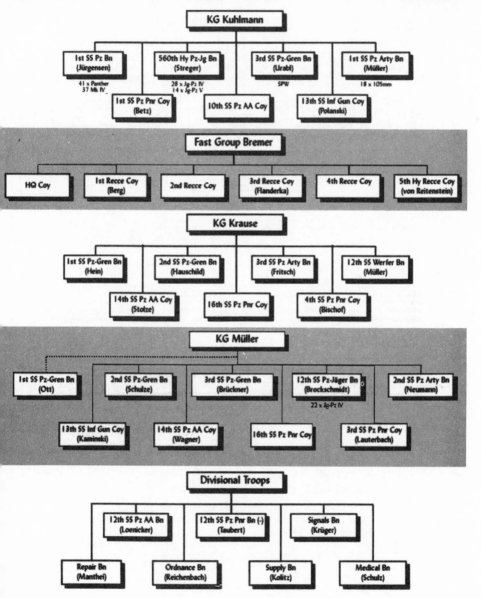

KG Kuhlmann

- 1st SS Pz Bn (Jürgensen)
  41 x Panther
  37 Mk IV
  - 1st SS Pz Pnr Coy (Betz)
- 560th Hy Pz-Jg Bn (Streger)
  28 x Jg-Pz IV
  14 x Jg-Pz V
  - 10th SS Pz AA Coy
- 3rd SS Pz-Gren Bn (Urabl)
  SPW
  - 13th SS Inf Gun Coy (Polanski)
- 1st SS Pz Arty Bn (Müller)
  18 x 105mm

Fast Group Bremer

- HQ Coy
- 1st Recce Coy (Berg)
- 2nd Recce Coy
- 3rd Recce Coy (Flanderka)
- 4th Recce Coy
- 5th Hy Recce Coy (von Reitenstein)

KG Krause

- 1st SS Pz-Gren Bn (Hein)
  - 14th SS Pz AA Coy (Stolze)
- 2nd SS Pz-Gren Bn (Hauschild)
  - 16th SS Pz Pnr Coy
- 3rd SS Pz Arty Bn (Fritsch)
  - 4th SS Pz Pnr Coy (Bischof)
- 12th SS Werfer Bn (Müller)

KG Müller

- 1st SS Pz-Gren Bn (Ott)
  - 13th SS Inf Gun Coy (Kaminski)
- 2nd SS Pz-Gren Bn (Schulze)
  - 14th SS Pz AA Coy (Wagner)
- 3rd SS Pz-Gren Bn (Brückner)
  - 16th SS Pz Pnr Coy
- 12th SS Pz-Jäger Bn (Brockschmidt)
  22 x Jg-Pz IV
  - 3rd SS Pz Pnr Coy (Lauterbach)
- 2nd SS Pz Arty Bn (Neumann)

Divisional Troops

- 12th SS Pz AA Bn (Loenicker)
- 12th SS Pz Pnr Bn (-) (Taubert)
- Signals Bn (Krüger)
- Repair Bn (Manthei)
- Ordnance Bn (Reichenbach)
- Supply Bn (Kolitz)
- Medical Bn (Schulz)

Appendix VI

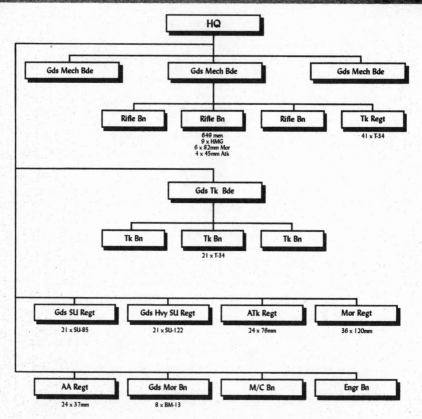

Soviet Guards Mechanized Corps, 1945

HQ

Gds Mech Bde · **Gds Mech Bde** · **Gds Mech Bde**

Rifle Bn · **Rifle Bn** · **Rifle Bn** · **Tk Regt**

Rifle Bn:
649 men
9 x HMG
6 x 82mm Mor
4 x 45mm Atk

Tk Regt: 41 x T-34

Gds Tk Bde

Tk Bn · **Tk Bn** · **Tk Bn**

21 x T-34

Gds SU Regt · **Gds Hvy SU Regt** · **ATk Regt** · **Mor Regt**

21 x SU-85 · 21 x SU-122 · 24 x 76mm · 36 x 120mm

AA Regt · **Gds Mor Bn** · **M/C Bn** · **Engr Bn**

24 x 37mm · 8 x BM-13

Totals: 16,318 men
188 x T-34/85
21 x SU-85
21 x SU-122

Note: A Soviet Tank Corps was similarly organized but with three
Tank Brigades and one Motorized Rifle Brigade. It had
208 tanks and 62 SUs.

Appendix VII

Soviet Guards Rifle Division, 1945
(11,706 men)[1]

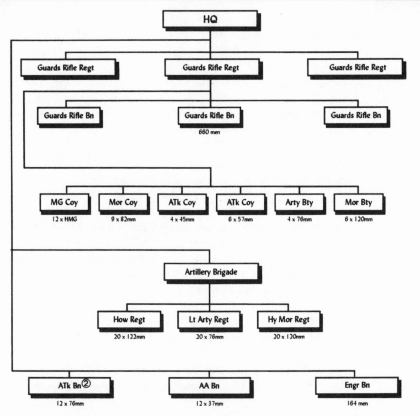

Notes:

① Normal Soviet Rifle Divisions were not as strong; they had
- 2087 fewer men
- 17 fewer 120mm mortars
- 17 fewer 82mm mortars
- 8 fewer 122mm howitzers
- 6 fewer 37mm AA guns and about
- 1500 fewer MGs of all calibers.

② Sometimes equipped with 16 x 76mm SP guns.

Bibliography

In compiling this history my primary sources of information were as follows:

Every available American unit After Action Report for the day in question, supplemented by direct statements, both verbal and written, made by soldiers who took part in, and by Belgian civilians who witnessed, the actions described.

The Histories of the 1st and 12th SS Panzer Divisions and the Radio and Telephone Logs and Daily Reports of Headquarters Army Group 'B' and Army Group South. Further valuable information was obtained through personal interviews with veterans and from interviews carried out shortly after the war by various individuals on behalf of the US Army Historical Branch. The records of these latter interviews are held in the US National Archives and in one case in the British Imperial War Museum. Information on German equipment holdings originated in the Bundesarchiv Germany (Reference RH 10).

Various Soviet Official Histories and other relevant documents originating in the Frunze Military Academy, Moscow.

Books consulted, and in some cases quoted, were:
Bastin Dr, *Bourgomont and the von Rundstedt Offensive*, University of Liège, 1951.
Bauserman, John M, *The Malmédy Massacre*, White Mane Publishing Company Inc, Shippensburg, Pa, USA, 1995.
Blakeslee, Clarence, *A personal Account of WW II by Draftee # 36887149*, Rockford, Michigan, USA, 1989.
Blumenson, Martin, *The United States Army in World War II: Breakout and Pursuit*, (Washington, DC: US Army Center for Military History, 1961).
Bradley, Omar, *A Soldier's Story*, London, 1952.
Cavanagh, William C C, *Krinkelt – Rocherath, The Battle for the Twin Villages*, The Christopher Publishing House, Massachusetts, USA, 1986 and *Dauntless, A History of the 99th Infantry Division*, Taylor Publishing Co, Dallas, Texas, 1994.

Cole, Hugh M, *United States Army in World War II, ETO, The Ardennes: Battle of the Bulge*, Washington, 1965.

Dugdale & Wood, *Complete Orders of Battle of the Waffen-SS in Normandy*, Vol I, Books International, 1999.

Ellis, Chris, *Tanks of World War 2*, Octopus Books Ltd, 1981.

Erickson, John, *The Road to Berlin Vol Two*, Phoenix Giants 1996.

Fontaine, Serge, *Stoumont, La Gleize, Cheneux*, Décembre 1944, Journal Publicité Idéale, 1970 and *Trois Ponts Décembre 1944 Quand les Ponts Volaient en Eclats*, Editions Cadusa, 1992.

Frühbeisser, Rudi, *Fallschirmjäger im Ersatz*, St Vith, 1971.

Gavin, James, *On to Berlin*, Leo Cooper, Pen & Swords Books Ltd, London, 1978.

Glantz, David M, *Art of War Symposium*, US Army War College, Carlisle, Pa, 1986.

Graves, Clifford L, *Front Line Surgeons*, 1950.

Graves, George D, *Blood and Snow – The Ardennes*.

Grechko, Marshal SU A.A., Chairman Main Editorial Commission, *Soviet Official History 1939-1945* (IVMV), Voenizdat, Moscow, 1973-82.

Grégoire, Gérard, *les Panzer de Peiper face à l'US Army* and *Feu-Fire-Vuur*, printed by J. Chauveheid, Stavelot, Belgium.

Hechler, Ken, *Holding the Line*, Office of the US Corps of Engineers, Fort Belvoir, VA, 1988.

Hewitt, Robert, *Workhorse of the Western Front*, Washington Infantry Journal Press, 1946.

Holt Giles, Janice, *The Damned Engineers*, Houghton Mifflin Company, 1970.

Irving, David, *The Trail of the Fox*, London and New York, 1977.

Jung, Hermann, *Die Ardennen Offensive*, Musterschmidt Verlag, 1971.

Kauffman, Robert, *The Red and White Path – One Soldier's Odyssey*.

Lehmann, Rudolf, *The Leibstandarte Parts I, II and III*, J. J. Fedorowicz Publishing Inc, Manitoba, Canada, 1987, 1988, 1990.

Lehmann, Rudolf & Tiemann, Ralf, *The Leibstandarte Parts IV/I and IV/2*, J. J. Fedorowicz Publishing Inc, Manitoba, Canada, 1993.

Lyman, William J Jr, *Curlew History*, The Story of the 1st Battalion of the 117th Infantry.

MacDonald, Charles B, *A Time for Trumpets, The Untold Story of the Battle of the Bulge*, William Morrow & Co, New York, 1985.

Maier, Georg, *Drama zwischen Budapest und Wien*, Munin Verlag, Osnabrück, 1985.

Marshall, S L A, *Bastogne, The First Eight Days*, US Army in Action Series, Center of Military History, US Army, Washington, D C, USA, 1988.

Merriam, Robert E, *The Battle of the Ardennes*, Souvenir Press, London, 1958.

Messenger, Charles, *Hitler's Gladiator*, Brassey's, 1988.

Meyer, Hubert, *History of the 12th SS Division Hitlerjugend*, J. J. Fedorowicz Publishing Inc, Manitoba, Canada, 1994.

Mitchell, Ralph M, *The 101st Airborne Division's Defense of Bastogne*, Combat Studies Institute, Fort Leavenworth, Kansas, USA, 1986.

Officers of the Regiment, *Combat History of the 119th Infantry Regiment*.

Pallud, Jean Paul, *The Battle of the Bulge, Then & Now*, Battle of Britain Prints International Limited, 1984.

Pergrin, David E, with Eric Hammel, *First Across the Rhine*, Atheneum, New York, 1989.

Pospelov, P.N, Chairman Editorial Commission of *Soviet Official History 1941-1945* (IVOVSS), Voenizdat, Moscow, 1960-65.

Price, Alfred, *The Last Year of the Luftwaffe, May 1944 to May 1945*, Arms & Armour Press, 1991.

Pulver, Murray, *Longest Year*, Pine Hill Press, South Dakota, USA.

Radzievskiy A. I., *Army Operations*, Voenizdat, Moscow, 1977.

Richardson and Freidin, Editors, *The Fatal Decisions*, Michael Joseph Ltd, London, 1956.

Roberts, A Eaton, *Fives Stars to Victory*, Atlas Printing & Engraving Co, Birmingham, Alabama, USA, 1949.

Rubel, George Kenneth, *Daredevil Tankers, The Story of the 740th Tank Battalion*, US Army.

Sayer, Ian and Botting, Douglas, *Hitler's Last General*, Bantam Press 1989.

Schneider, Jost, *Their Honor was Loyalty*, R. James Bender Publishing, USA, 1993.

Schneider, Wolfgang, *Tigers in Combat II*, J.J. Fedorowicz Publishing Inc, Manitoba, Canada, 1998.

Shulman, Milton, *Defeat in the West*, Masquerade, 1995.

Skorzeny, Otto, *Skorzeny's Special Missions*, Robert Hale, 1947.

Spearhead in the West, The Third Armored Division 1941-45, Turner Publishing Co, USA.

Tiemann, Ralf, *Die Leibstandarte IV/2*, Munin Verlag GmbH, Osnabrück, Germany, 1987.

Tiemann, Ralf, *The Leibstandarte IV/2*, J.J. Fedorowiecz Publishing Inc, Canada, 1998.

Tiemann, Ralf, *Chronicle of the 7th Panzer Company 1st SS Panzer Division 'Leibstandarte'*, Schiffer Publishing Ltd, USA, 1998.

Toland, John, *Battle, The Story of the Bulge*, Severn House Publishers Ltd, Sutton, England, 1977; and *The Last 100 Days*, Arthur Barker Ltd, London, 1965.

Vandervoort, B H, *Trois Ponts*.

Vannoy, Allyn R. and Karamales, Jay, *Against The Panzers*, McFarland & Co, 1996.

Walther Herbert, *The 1st SS Panzer Division Leibstandarte – A Pictorial History*, Schiffer Publishing Ltd, USA, 1989.

Wilmot, Chester, *The Struggle for Europe*, HarperCollins, 1952.
Yashin, Lt Col V. F., *Study of the Defence by Formations of XXX Rifle Corps in the Balaton defensive operations*, Frunze Military Academy, Moscow, 1988.
Zavizion, G.T. and Kornyushin, P.A., *I na Tikhom okeane . . .*, Voenizdat, Moscow, 1967.

Every effort has been made to obtain permission to quote from letters and from specific books. In some cases the authors are known to have passed away or could not be contacted, and in others publishing companies have ceased to exist or failed to reply to letters.

Unless otherwise attributed the photographs reproduced in this book originate in either the US or German National Archives.

INDEX
PEOPLE

307

Leitner, Karl: 113
Lincke, Wolfgang: 246
Lochbihler, Elmar: 215
Loenicker, Wolfgang: 237, 243
Lübbe, Harro: 256
Lüttwitz, Freiherr von: 147
Mackensen, von: 7
Maier, Georg: 198, 202, 251, 254
Malkomes, Hans: 239, 245
Manstein, Fritz von: 13
Manteuffel, Hasso von: 35, 42–3, 58, 112,
   122, 128, 136–7, 139, 145–6, 159–60, 175
Menzel, Hstuf: 233
Meyer, Hubert – pre-Ardennes: x, 24, 32,
   37; Ardennes: 49, 55–6, 86, 92, 109–12,
   127, 140, 143, 162, 164–5, 169, 172;
   Eastern Front et seq: 179, 182, 190, 207–8,
   211, 215, 217, 230, 232, 248, 255, 260,
   262, 265, 267–8, 270–1, 277–80, 287–8,
   290–1, 293
Meyer, Kurt (Panzermeyer): 20–1, 29, 34,
   290, 292
Minow, Hstuf: 272
Möbius, Lt: 264, 271
Möbius, Rolf: 30, 182
Model, Walter: 26, 29–31, 36, 42, 44, 137–8,
   154–5, 162, 172
Mohnke, Wilhelm: 20–1, 27–30, 36–7,
   42, 47, 54–5, 69, 71, 93–4, 102, 116–8,
   121, 123, 125–6, 131–2, 135, 147, 149,
   180–1, 290
Möllhof, Stubaf: 181
Müller, Siegfried – pre-Ardennes: 37–8;
   Ardennes; 72, 84, 86, 90–1, 127, 129,
   139–45, 161, 163, 166, 169, 171; Eastern
   Front et seq: 182, 195–6, 207, 210, 213,
   216, 220, 222–3, 230, 253, 255–6, 270
Müller, Willi: 37, 181–2
Müller, Oberschar: 166
Münkemer, Erich: 244, 289
Neussbaumer, Heinz: 99
Olboeter, Erich: 33
Opitz, Gottfried: 90
Ott, Alfons: 50, 55, 191–2, 247, 256
Paulus, Friedrich von: 8
Peiper, Jochen – pre-Ardennes: x, 19, 21,
   25, 36, 40; Ardennes: 49, 54–5, 57, 60–4,
   67–70, 73, 77–82, 85, 94–100, 102–4, 115,
   118–9, 121, 125–6, 132–3, 135; Eastern
   Front et seq: 181–2, 189–91, 193–4, 197,
   238, 245, 249, 252, 263, 266, 271, 274,
   281–2, 284, 289–90
Pfeifer, Friedrich: 94, 105
Piegeler, Ostuf: 219
Pitsch, Walter: 278
Poetschke, Werner: 36–7, 49, 68, 70, 81, 98,
   101, 126, 147, 149, 151, 181–2, 190, 192–4,
   197, 206, 217, 233–4, 238–41, 244

Preuss, Georg: 61–2, 68, 82, 102, 120, 253,
   261, 266, 269, 289, 291
Priess, Hermann – pre-Ardennes: 35, 42,
   45; Ardennes: 47–8, 51–2, 54–5, 57–8,
   63–4, 75, 83, 88, 126, 131, 137, 139, 145,
   157, 159–60, 162, 170; Eastern Front et
   seq: 189, 195, 203, 213, 230, 236, 255, 259,
   266, 270–1, 278, 289, 290
Pulvermüller, Ostuf: 282–3
Rattenhuber, Ostuf: 272
Rayer, Rudolf: 98
Reiser, Rolf: 151, 192, 194, 223, 233, 238,
   241, 244, 283
Reitzenstein, Gerd von: 267
Rendulic, Lothar: 270, 278, 282, 285
Rettlinger, Karl: 36, 50, 55, 63, 66, 117, 148,
   182, 219–20, 223, 233, 282
Ribbentrop, Rudolf von: 160–1, 163, 172,
   181, 267, 271, 278, 280
Richter, Karl: 105, 117
Richter, Ustuf: 264
Rien, Ewald: 165
Rink, Herbert: 30, 32–3, 130
Rommel, Erwin: 8
Ross, Hans-Jürgen: 196
Roy, Rudolf: 64
Rumpf, Erich: 96–7, 104, 121, 289
Rundstedt, Gerd von: 6–7, 18, 36, 42,
   137–8, 174, 176
Sacken, Maj von: 49, 102
Sandig, Rudolf: 20, 25, 36–7, 49–50, 76,
   94–5, 102, 117–8, 148, 181, 271, 291
Scappini, Hans: 25
Scheler, Richard: 36, 123, 238
Scherff, Capt: 115–6
Schmidt, Hstuf: 193, 196
Schnelle, Herbert: 104
Schnittenhelm, Ustuf: 113–4
Schultz, Maj Gen: 263, 266
Schulz, Rolf: 272
Schulze, Richard: 63, 65–6, 72, 84, 141–3
Sickel, Kurt: 135, 289
Siebken, Bernhard: 28, 181–2, 206, 209–10,
   212, 217, 219–20, 222, 238, 240–1, 243,
   245, 250, 254, 264, 268, 270, 272, 274,
   281, 289
Siegel, Hans: 181–2, 192, 195–6, 207, 210–2,
   216, 224, 234–6, 243, 246–7
Sievers, Franz: 97–8, 101, 289
Simon, Hannes: 90
Skorzeny, Otto: 43, 52, 55, 58, 71,
   110, 115–6
Sölner, Max: 99
Speer, Albert: 232
Staudinger, Walter: 263, 265
Stauffenberg, Graf: 293
Steineck, Franz: 29, 36
Sternebeck, Werner: 61–2, 64, 67–8, 209,

FORMATIONS AND UNITS

Allied

Army Group
21st: 26–7, 42, 44

American

Army Group
12th: 26, 44, 59, 73

Army
First: 30, 44–5, 59, 72–4, 157, 159, 172, 174
Third: 30, 44, 137–9, 159, 174
Ninth: 42, 44, 59

Corps
III: 139, 147, 154–5, 159, 164
V: 45, 61, 64, 66, 87, 100
VII: 30
VIII: 45, 139, 160, 167
XVIII Airborne: 46, 73, 100, 134

Division
3rd Armd: 100, 141
4th Armd: 147, 153, 155
6th Armd: 154–5, 159–61, 164, 166, 169–70
7th Armd: 59, 76
10th Armd: 59
11th Armd: 154
1st Inf: 59, 65, 91, 112–5, 173
2nd Inf: 45–6, 52, 57–9, 61–2, 64, 66, 72, 90, 113–4, 173
4th Inf: 45
26th Inf: 147
28th Inf: 45, 143
30th Inf: 59, 73, 79, 82, 95, 100, 102, 104, 112, 117, 131, 173
35th Inf: 147–9, 152–5, 159–60
36th Inf: 285
65th Inf: 281
71st Inf: 282–3
82nd Airborne: 46, 73, 82, 99–100, 134–5
99th Inf: 45–6, 53, 56–8, 61–2, 64, 72, 90, 113–4

101st Airborne: 46, 73, 137, 160, 164, 167–8
106th Inf: 45, 76

Cavalry Group
14th: 45, 53, 61, 63, 66, 74–5

Engineer Group
1111th: 73–4

Regiment
9th Inf: 66
26th Inf: 59, 65, 91–2, 107, 114–5, 129
38th Inf: 85
119th Inf: 73, 100
134th Inf: 148, 152, 155
137th Inf: 148, 152, 154, 156
259th Inf: 288
289th Inf: 141, 143
320th Inf: 149, 155
393rd Inf: 45, 56
394th Inf: 45, 53, 59
395th Inf: 45–6, 65
501st Para Inf: 164–5, 167–8, 170
504th Para Inf: 99
505th Para Inf: 100

Combat Command
CCA 3rd Armd: 141–2
CCB 3rd Armd: 100, 104, 173
CCA 4th Armd: 149–50, 152–3
CCR 4th Armd: 137
CCA 6th Armd: 154, 159–61, 164, 168–9
CCB 6th Armd: 160–1, 164, 168, 171
CCB 9th Armd: 45, 67, 76
CCB 10th Armd: 137

Task Force
Britton: 164
Brown: 159–60, 164
Davall: 160–1, 164–6, 169
Harrison: 102, 104, 125, 130
Jordan: 100, 102, 120
Kennedy: 159–61, 164, 167, 169–71
Lagrew: 164

48th VG: 83
89th VG: 63, 90
989th VG: 55–6, 58
990th VG: 55–6, 58, 83, 87
991st VG: 57
5th Para (Luftwaffe): 53
9th Para (Luftwaffe): 54, 91

Brigade
Führer Begleit: x, 139, 148, 153, 159
150th Pz: 52, 55, 71, 110, 115

Kampfgruppe
Bremer: 265, 268
Garbade: 237
Goldammer: 267
Gross: 265, 267–8, 271
Hansen: 50, 54–5, 62, 66–7, 71, 74–5, 93, 103, 110, 121, 148, 151–2, 154, 191–2, 194, 241, 243–4, 254, 270
Hauschild: 247–8
Hupe (Regtl Gp): 189, 191, 193
Kling: 268–71
Krag: 140, 142–4
Krause: 83–4, 87, 91
Kuhlmann: 56–7, 83–4, 87, 91, 106, 109
Möbius: 157, 271
Mohnke: 27–30
Müller: 50, 58, 64–5, 71, 87, 90
Ott: 55, 247–8
Peiper: 49–50, 54, 57, 60–1, 64, 67–8, 71, 74, 76–8, 80, 87–8, 96, 100, 103, 105, 118, 126, 131–2, 135, 190–4, 196–7, 209–10, 212, 221, 223–4, 231, 254, 266–8, 270–1, 274, 289
Poetschke: 147–9, 154, 241, 243–4
Reitzenstein: 267–8
Ribbentrop: 268
Rink: 30–1
Sandig: 50, 55, 67, 76, 94, 110
Siegel; 193
Sternebeck: 268, 270–1, 286
Wahl: 27–8
Weidenhaupt: 271
X: 115–6
Y: 115–6
Z: 115

Fast Group
Bremer: 50, 83, 87, 90,
Knittel: 50, 55, 67, 79, 80, 96, 110

Battalion

Recce
1st SS: 6, 9, 11, 21, 28–9, 36–7, 50, 76, 81, 93–4, 130, 181, 190, 211, 217, 222, 245, 261, 277, 284, 287

2nd SS: 140
12th SS: 21, 27, 37–8, 92, 127, 129, 140, 211, 215, 230, 238, 242, 255, 260, 265, 268
1st Pz: 263
2nd Pz: 128
3rd Pz: 266

Panzer
1/1st SS: 11, 21, 36–7, 49, 78, 98, 148, 206, 217, 240, 272
2/1st SS: 96, 234, 268, 281
1/12th SS: 37–9, 50, 71, 83–4, 87, 90–1, 106, 111, 129, 140, 160–1, 166, 171–2, 181, 267
2/12th SS: 181, 193, 210–1, 216, 235–6, 246–7, 278, 280
101st SS Hy: x, 21–3, 26, 30
501st SS Hy: 49, 51, 68, 80–1, 94, 130, 148, 156–7, 178–81, 190, 201, 216, 221, 232, 234, 245, 255, 266, 281

Sturmgeschütz/Panzerjäger
1st SS StuG: 11, 25, 27, 36
1st SS PzJg; 37, 50, 55, 63, 66, 75, 117, 147–8, 207, 210–1, 219–20, 233, 237–8, 282
12th SS PzJg: 17, 38–9, 50, 63, 65, 71, 83, 91, 111–2, 127, 129, 140, 163, 167, 171, 173, 207, 213, 216–7, 220, 230, 235, 238, 253
560th Hy PzJg: 50–1, 84, 87, 106, 108–9, 111, 129, 140, 163, 166, 173, 180, 190, 202, 211, 216, 267, 286

Artillery
1/1st SS: 49, 80–1, 94, 96, 190
3rd SS DR: 140
101st SS Hy: x, 22
501st SS Hy: 172, 236
1st SS Flak: 11, 36, 148, 218, 231, 261, 263, 275
12th SS Flak: 84, 91, 129, 140, 163, 172, 230, 237–8, 242–3, 246, 260, 264
101st SS Flak: 22
1st SS Werfer: 50, 111, 117, 148, 233, 261
12th SS Werfer: 17, 37, 50, 91, 140, 172, 181
101st SS Werfer: 22
84th (Luftwaffe) Flak: 49, 80, 102

Pioneer
1st SS: 36–7, 117, 123, 219, 238
12th SS: 37, 84, 127, 172, 238, 242, 252, 255, 260

PLACES

317

Gulf of Finland
Lake Ladoga
Leningrad
Lake Ilmen

Map I
The Soviet Union
0   100   400
Kilometres

R. Volga

⊛ Moscow

Minsk

Smolensk

White Russia

Kursk

Zhitomir

Belgorod

Kiev

Ukraine

Kharkov

R. Don

R. Donetz

R. Dneiper

Stalingrad

Odessa

Taganrog

Rostov-on-Don

Sea of Azov

Crimea

Sevastopol

Caspian

Sea

Black   Sea

Georgia

TURKEY

amales 1999

IRAN

Map 2
North West Europe

0   100   200
Kilometres

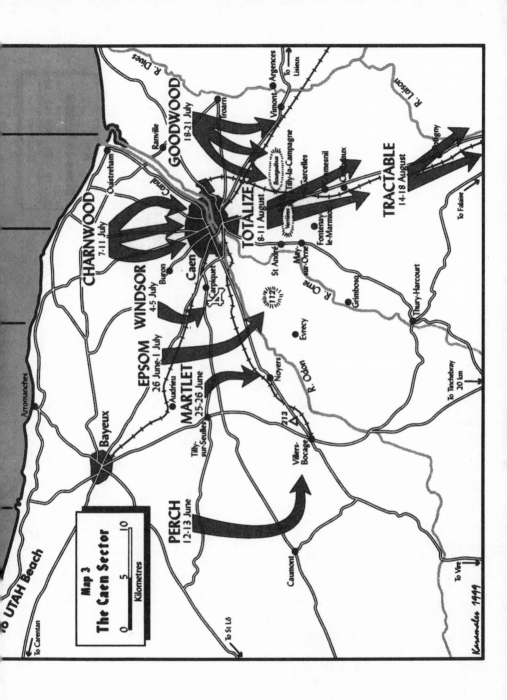

Map 3
The Caen Sector

0   5   10
Kilometres

To UTAH Beach

To Carentan

Arromanches

Bayeux

To St Lô

CHARNWOOD
7-11 July

EPSOM
26 June–1 July

WINDSOR
4-5 July

MARTLET
25-26 June

PERCH
12-13 June

Caumont

To Vire

Ouistreham

Ranville

Canal

R. Dives

GOODWOOD
18-21 July

Troarn

Vimont

Agences

To Lisieux

R. Laison

Caen

Buron

Carpiquet

Audrieu

Tilly-sur-Seulles

Villers-Bocage

213

Noyers

R. Odon

112

Evrecy

St André

May-sur-Orne

R. Orne

Grimbosq

Thury-Harcourt

To Tinchebray
20 km

Bourguébus

Tilly-la-Campagne

Garcelles

mesnil

Fontenay
le-Marmion

Verrières

TOTALIZE
8-11 August

TRACTABLE
14-18 August

oligny

To Falaise

Kaumoler 1999

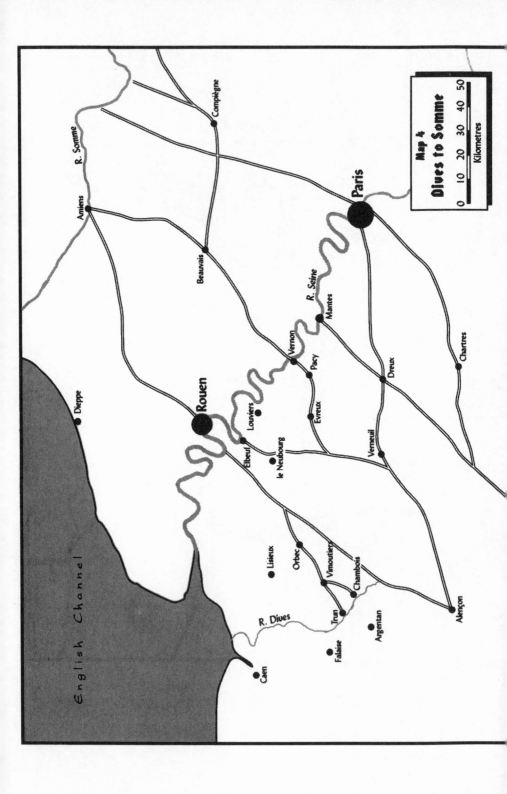

Map 4
Dives to Somme

Kilometres
0 10 20 30 40 50

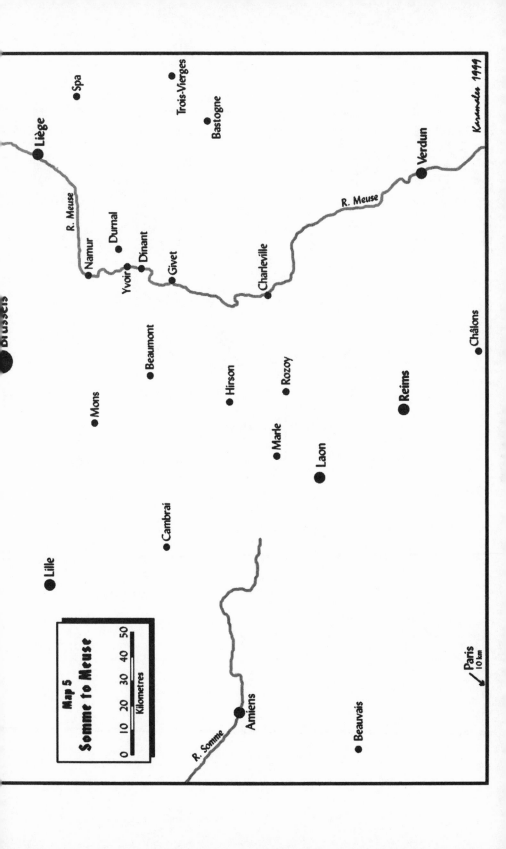

Map 5
Somme to Meuse

Kilometres
0 10 20 30 40 50

Paris
10 km

R. Somme
Amiens
Beauvais

Lille
Cambrai
Mons
Beaumont
Brussels
Liège
Spa
Namur
Dumal
Yvoire
Dinant
Givet
Charleville
Bastogne
Trois-Vierges
R. Meuse
R. Meuse
Verdun
Hirson
Marle
Laon
Rozoy
Reims
Châlons

Kinvander 1999

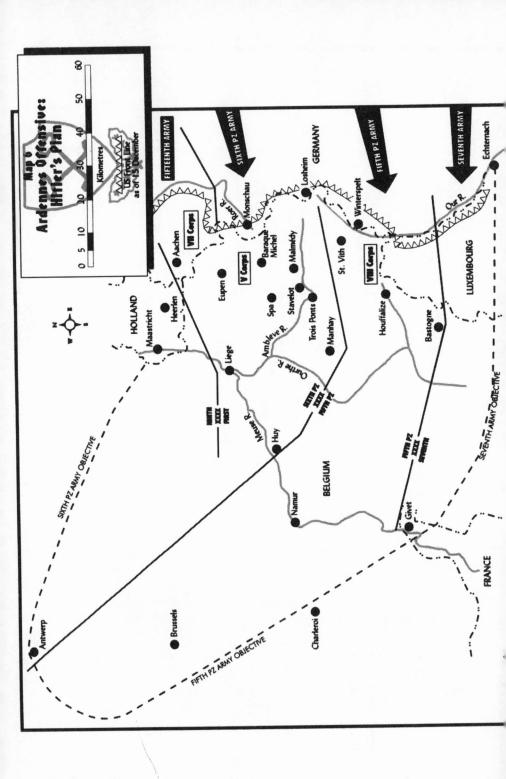

Map 6
Ardennes Offensive:
Hitler's Plan

Kilometres

0 5 10   20   30   40   50   60

US Front line
as of 13 December

SIXTH PZ ARMY OBJECTIVE

FIFTH PZ ARMY OBJECTIVE

SEVENTH ARMY OBJECTIVE

FIFTEENTH ARMY

SIXTH PZ ARMY

FIFTH PZ ARMY

SEVENTH ARMY

GERMANY

LUXEMBOURG

HOLLAND

BELGIUM

FRANCE

VIII Corps

V Corps

VIII Corps

NINTH / FIRST

FIRST / THIRD

THIRD / SEVENTH

Antwerp

Brussels

Charleroi

Namur

Huy

Liege

Maastricht

Heerlen

Aachen

Eupen

Spa

Baraqué Michel

Malmédy

Stavelot

Trois Ponts

Manhay

St. Vith

Houffalize

Bastogne

Givet

Echternach

Winterspelt

Losheim

Monschau

Roer R.

Ambleve R.

Ourthe R.

Meuse R.

Our R.

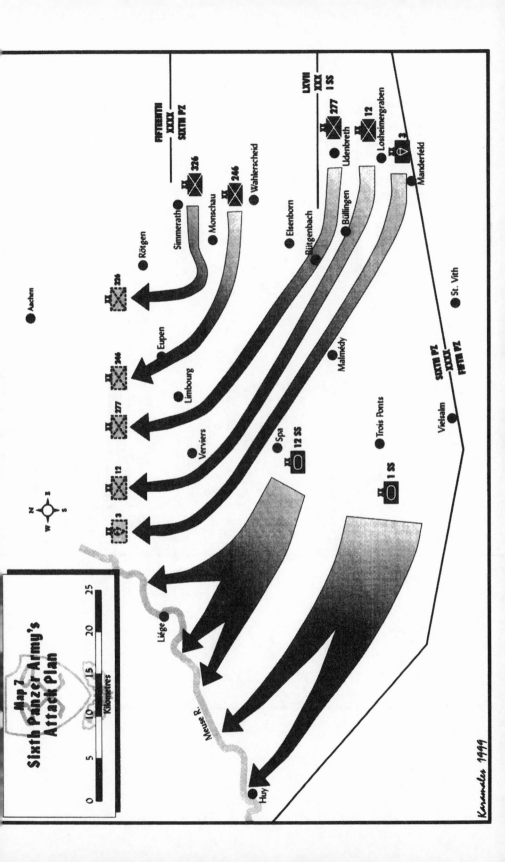

Map 7
Sixth Panzer Army's Attack Plan

Kilometres
0 5 10 15 20 25

Aachen

Rötgen

Simmerath

Monschau

Wahlerscheid

Eupen

Limbourg

Verviers

Spa

Trois Ponts

Malmédy

Eisenborn

Büllingen

Büllingen

Manderfeld

St. Vith

Vielsalm

Liége

Huy

Meuse R.

XXXX
FIFTEENTH
SIXTH PZ

XXXX
326

XX
246

LXVII
XXX
I SS

XX
277
Udenbreth

XX
12
Losheimergraben

XX
3

XXXX
SIXTH PZ
XXXX
FIFTH PZ

XX
326

XX
246

XX
277

XX
12

XX
3

XX
12 SS

XX
1 SS

Karandler 1999

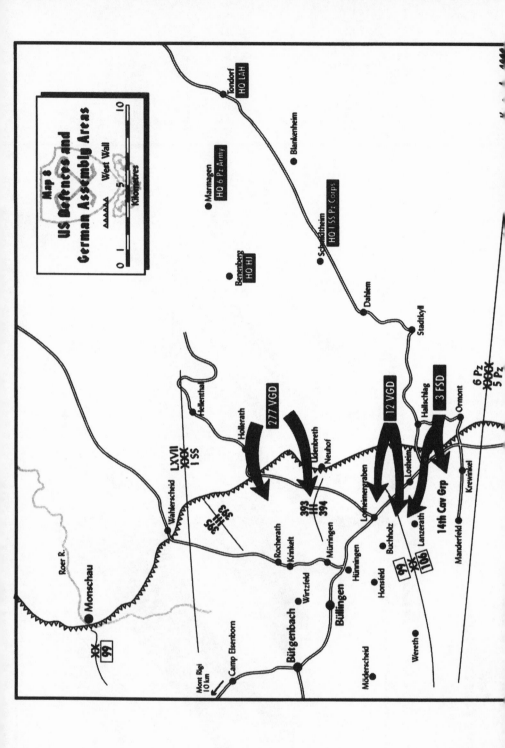

Map 8

US Defences and German Assembly Areas

Kilometres

West Wall

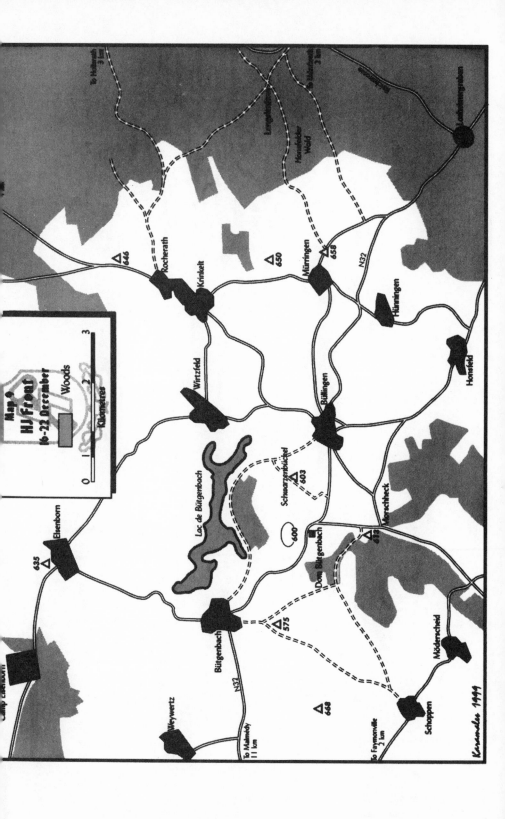

Map ●
HJ/Freat
16-22 December

Woods

0   1   2   3
Kilometres

Kaisander 1999

To Hünningen
3 km

To Hünningen
3 km

Lanzerhopgraben

Langenberg

Rocherath

Krinkelt

Wirtzfeld

Elsenborn

△ 635

△ 646

△ 650

Lac de Bütgenbach

Schwarzenbüchel
△ 603

600

Bütgenbach

Weywertz

N32

To Malmédy
11 km

△ 668

Mürringen

△ 658

N32

Büllingen

Hünningen

Honsfeld

Morscheck

Dom Bütgenbach

△ 575

Schoppen

Möderscheid

To Faymonville
2 km

Camp Elsenborn

Hosselder
Wald

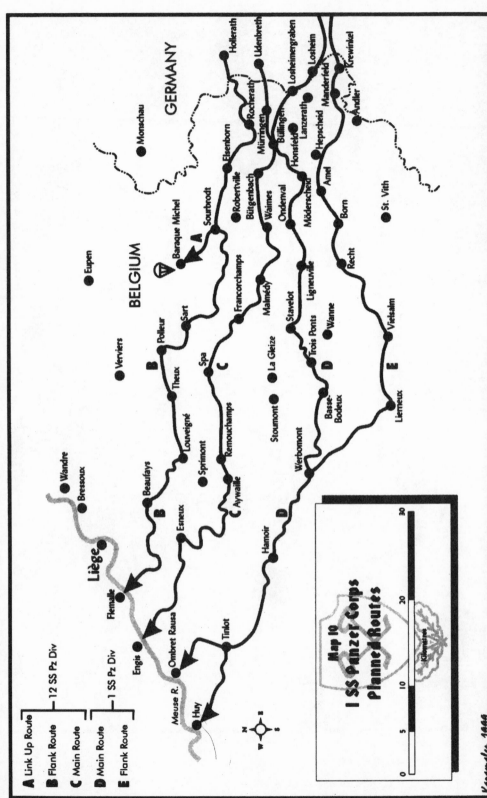

Kesemler 1999

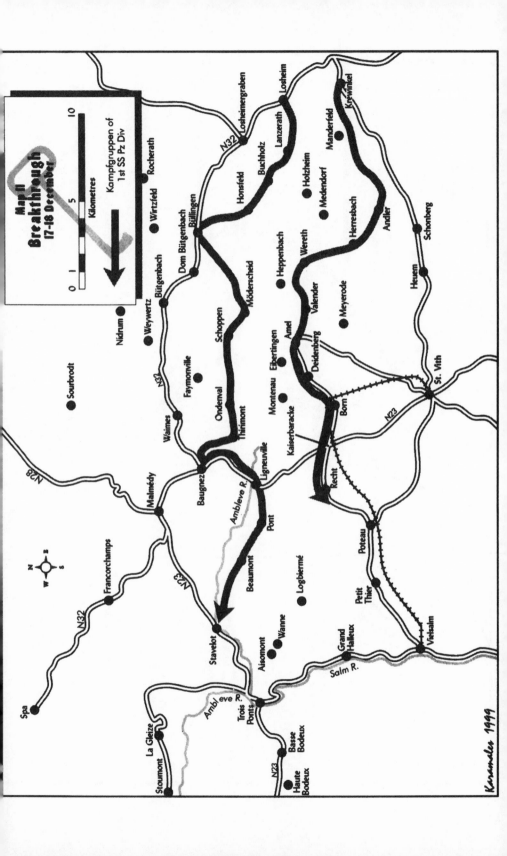

Map II
Breakthrough
17-18 December

Kilometres
0 1   5   10

Kampfgruppen of
1st SS Pz Div

Kasemir 1999

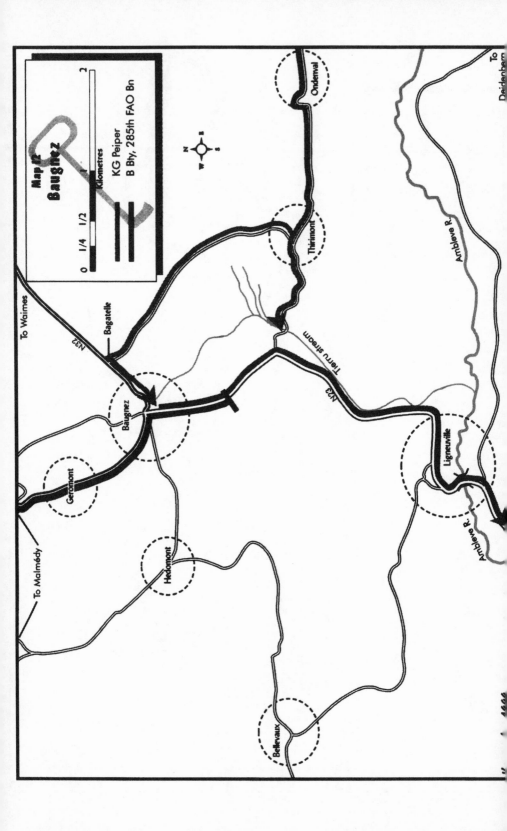

Map of Baugnez

Kilometres

0   1/4   1/2   2

KG Peiper

B Bty, 285th FAO Bn

N

W — E

S

To Waimes

N32

Bagatelle

Baugnez

Tieru stream

N23

Thirimont

Ondenval

To Deidenberg

Ambleve R.

Geromont

To Malmédy

Hedomont

Ligneuville

Ambleve R.

Bellevaux

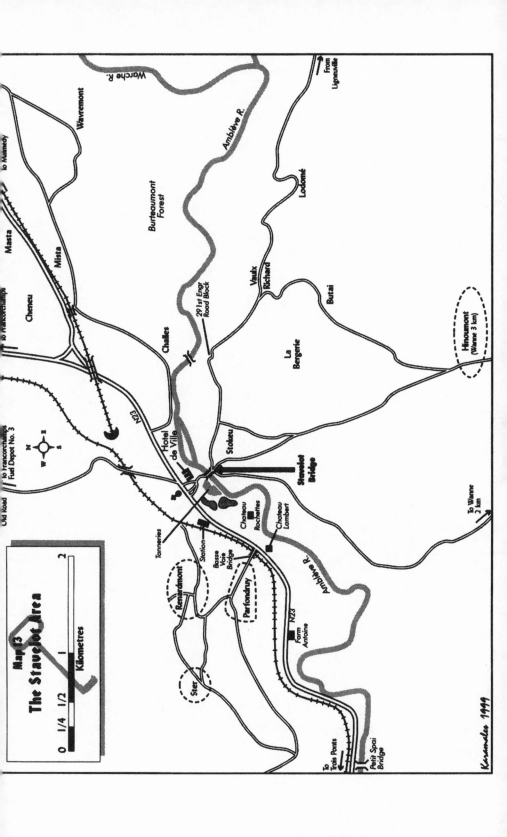

Map 3
The Stavelot Area

Kilometres
0   1/4   1/2   1   2

To Francorchamps
Fuel Depot No. 3

Old Road

To Francorchamps

To Malmedy

Masta

Cheneu

Mista

Wavremont

Warche R.

N23

Hotel
de Ville

Tanneries

Renardmont

Station

Basse Voie
Bridge

Parfondruy

Ster

Chateau
Rocheries

Chateau
Lambert

Stokeu

Stavelot
Bridge

Amblève R.

Burteaumont
Forest

Amblève R.

291st Engr
Road Block

Challes

Vaux
Richard

Lodomé

Butai

La
Bergerie

Hinoumont
(Wanne 3 km)

From
Ligneuville

Farm
Antoine

N23

To Trois Ponts

Petit Spai
Bridge

To Wanne
2 km

Kennedor 1999

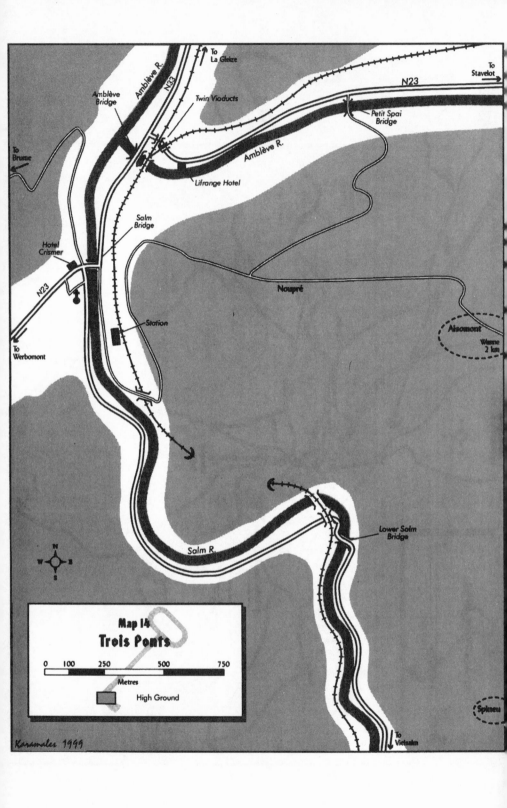

To La Gleize

Amblève R.

N33

Amblève Bridge

Twin Viaducts

To Brume

N23

Petit Spai Bridge

To Stavelot

Amblève R.

Lifrange Hotel

Salm Bridge

Hotel Crismer

N23

Nouspré

Aisomont

Wanne 2 km

To Werbomont

Station

Lower Salm Bridge

Salm R.

Spineux

To Vielsalm

N
W——E
S

Map 14
Trois Ponts

0   100   250   500   750

Metres

High Ground

Karamales 1999

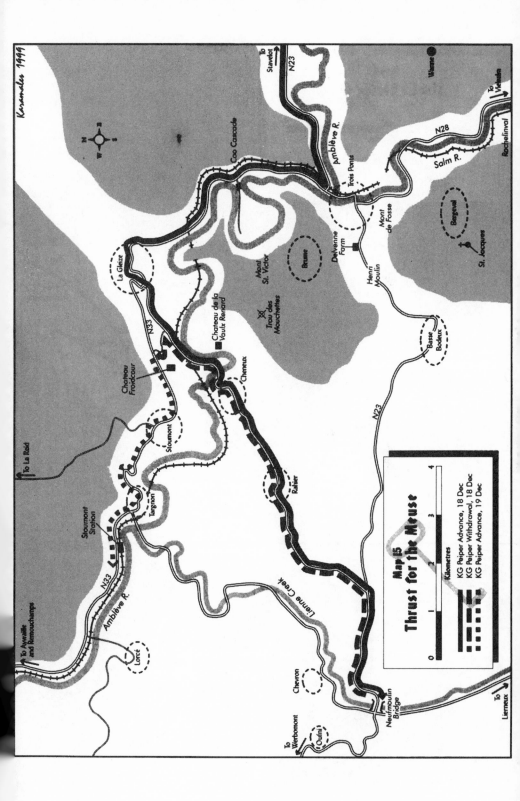

Kampfgruppe 1999

To Stavelot

Amblève R.

N23

To Vielsalm

Coo Cascade

Trois Ponts

Salm R.

N28

Rochelinval

Mont
de Fosse

Delvenne
Farm

Brume

Mont
St. Victor

Bergeval

St. Jacques

La Gleize

Henri
Moulin

Trou des
Mouchettes

Chateau de la
Vaulx Renard

N33

Chateau
Froidcourt

Basse
Bodeux

Cheneux

Stoumont

To La Raid

Rahier

Tergnon

N23

Stoumont
Station

N33

Amblève R.

Lienne Creek

Lorcé

To Aywaille
and Remouchamps

Chevron

To Werbomont

(Oufni)

Neufmoulin
Bridge

To
Liernaux

Map 5
Thrust for the Meuse

Kilometres

0   1   2   3   4

— KG Peiper Advance, 18 Dec
- - - KG Peiper Withdrawal, 18 Dec
▪▪▪ KG Peiper Advance, 19 Dec

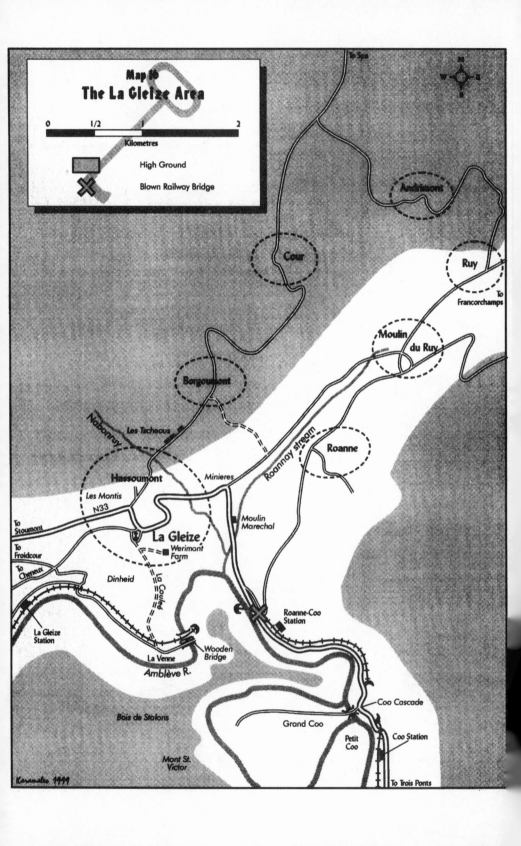

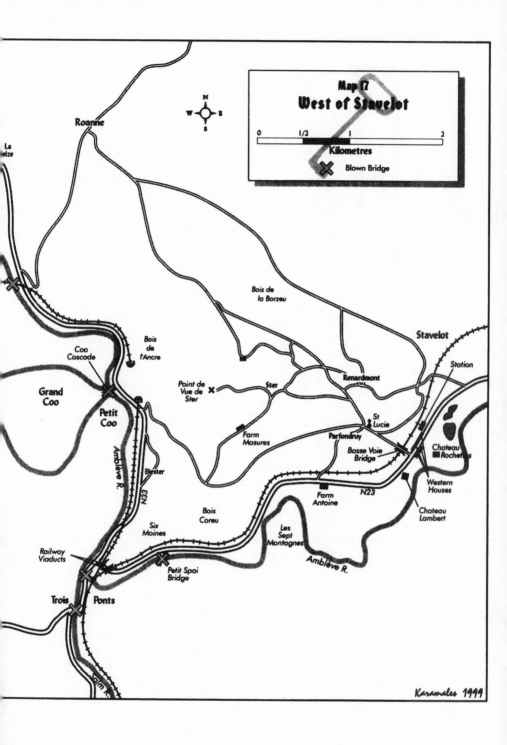

Map 17
West of Stavelot

0   1/2   1   2
Kilometres
✖ Blown Bridge

Roanne

La
Gleize

Bois de
la Borzeu

Stavelot

Coo
Cascade

Bois
de
l'Ancre

Station

Grand
Coo

Point de
Vue de
Ster

Ster

Renardmont

Petit
Coo

St
Lucie

Farm
Masures

Parfondruy

Chateau
Rochette

Amblève R.

Biester

Basse Voie
Bridge

N33

Farm
Antoine

N23

Western
Houses

Bois
Coreu

Chateau
Lambert

Six
Moines

Les
Sept
Montagnes

Ambléve R.

Railway
Viaducts

Petit Spai
Bridge

Trois   Ponts

Salm R.

Karamales 1999

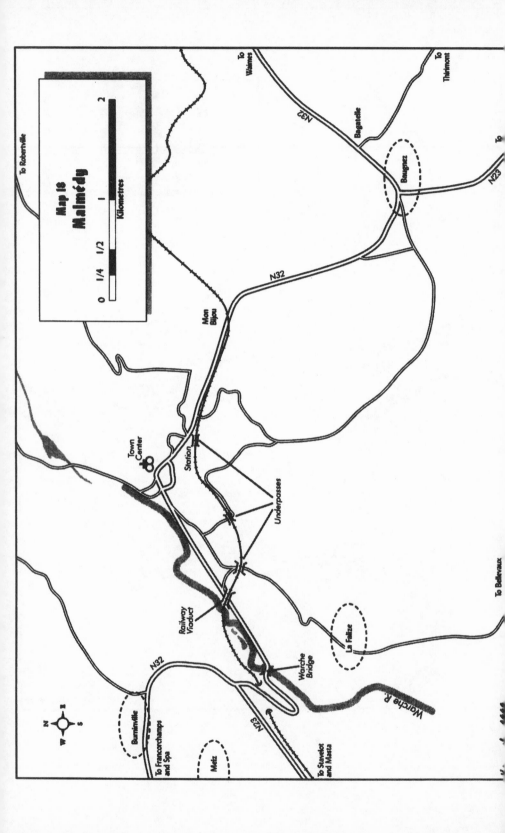

Map 18
Malmédy

Kilometres

0   1/4   1/2   1   2

To Robertville

To Waimes

N32

Bagatelle

To Thirimont

Beauperez

N23

To

Mon Bijou

N32

Town Center

Station

Underpasses

Railway Viaduct

La Falize

Warche Bridge

To Bellevaux

N32

Burnenville

To Francorchamps and Spa

Metz

N23

To Stavelot and Masta

Warche R.

N
W   E
S

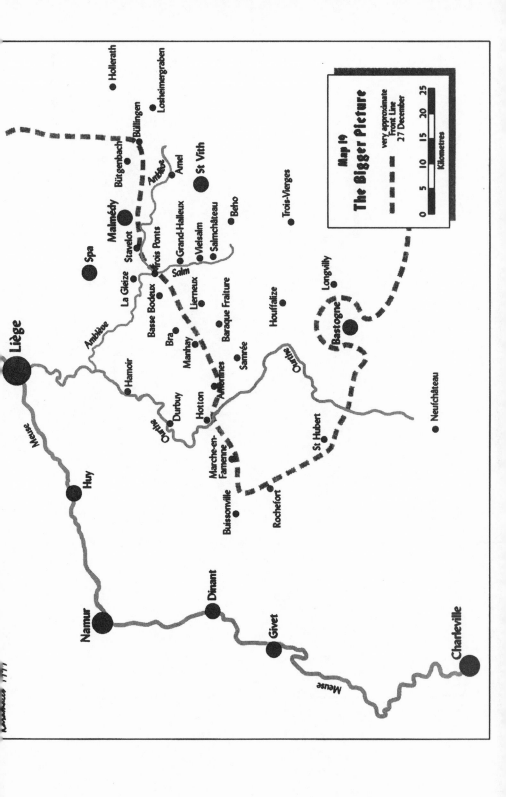

Map 10
The Bigger Picture

very approximate
Front Line
27 December

Kilometres
0   5   10   15   20   25

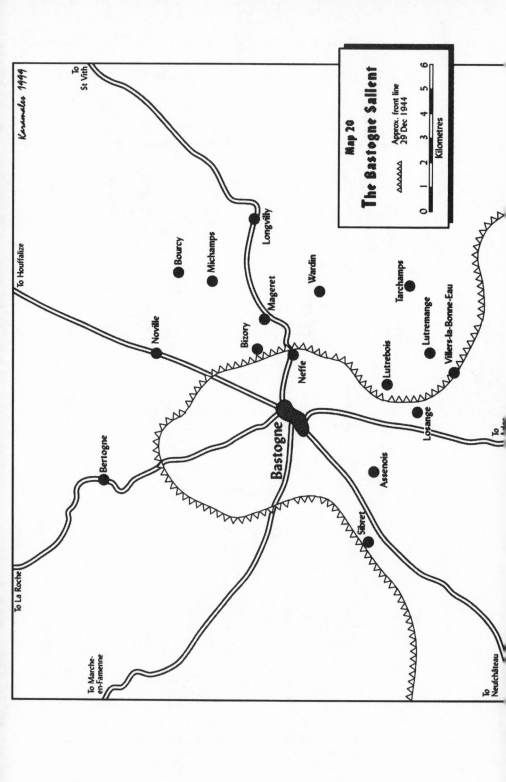

Karsander 1999

Map 20

The Bastogne Salient

△△△△△ Approx. front line
29 Dec 1944

0 1 2 3 4 5 6

Kilometres

To St Vith

To Houffalize

To La Roche

To Marche-en-Famenne

To Neufchâteau

Bourcy

Michamps

Longvilly

Wardin

Tarchamps

Magaret

Bizory

Lutrebois

Lutremange

Villers-la-Bonne-Eau

Noville

Neffe

Bastogne

Losange

Bertogne

Assenois

Sibret

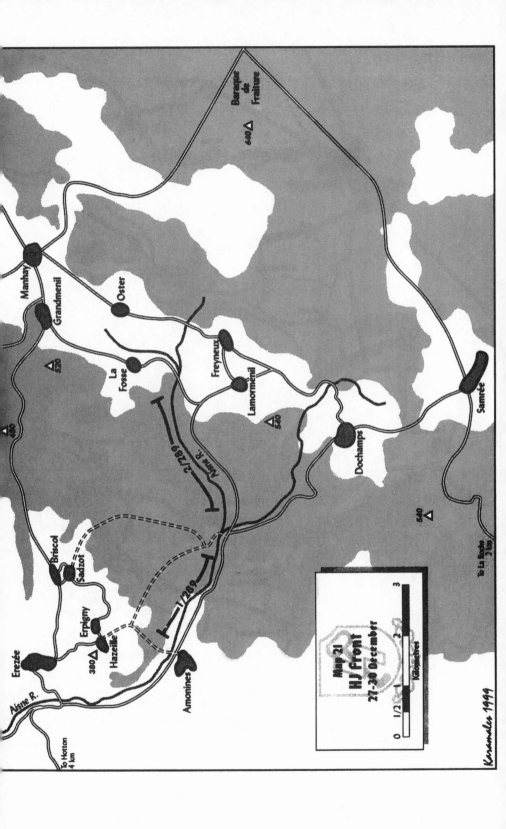

Map 21
HJ Front
27-30 December

Kerninelle 1999

To Hotton
4 km

Aisne R.

Erezée

Bricol

Sadzot

Erpigny

380△

Hazeille

Amonines

1/289

2/289

Aisne R.

La
Fosse

520△

460△

Manhay

Grandmenil

Oster

Freyneux

Lamormenil

540△

Dochamps

540△

To La Roche
7 km

Samrée

Barrage
de
Fraiture

640△

0   1/2   1   2   3
Kilometres

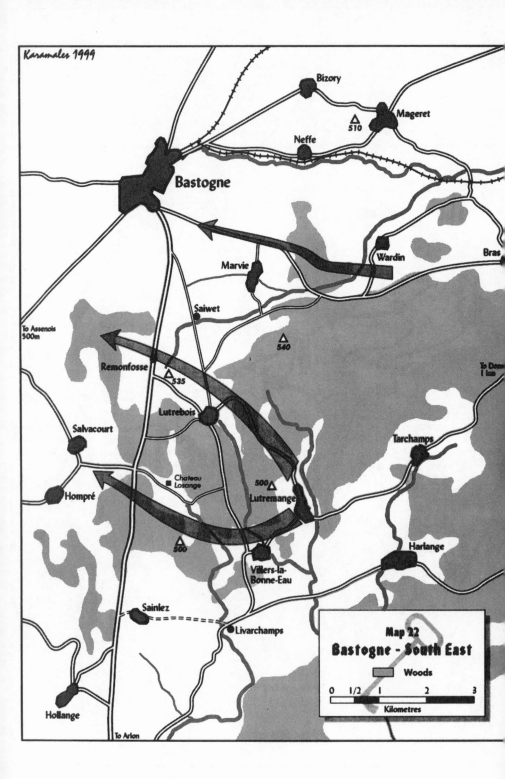

Karamales 1999

Bizory

Mageret

△ 510

Neffe

Bastogne

Wardin

Bras

Marvie

Saiwet

To Assenois
500m

△ 540

Remonfosse

△ 535

To Done
I km

Lutrebois

Salvacourt

Tarchamps

Chateau
Losange

500 △

Hompré

Lutremange

△ 500

Harlange

Villers-la-
Bonne-Eau

Sainlez

Livarchamps

Map 22
Bastogne - South East

Woods

0   1/2   1   2   3

Kilometres

Hollange

To Arlon

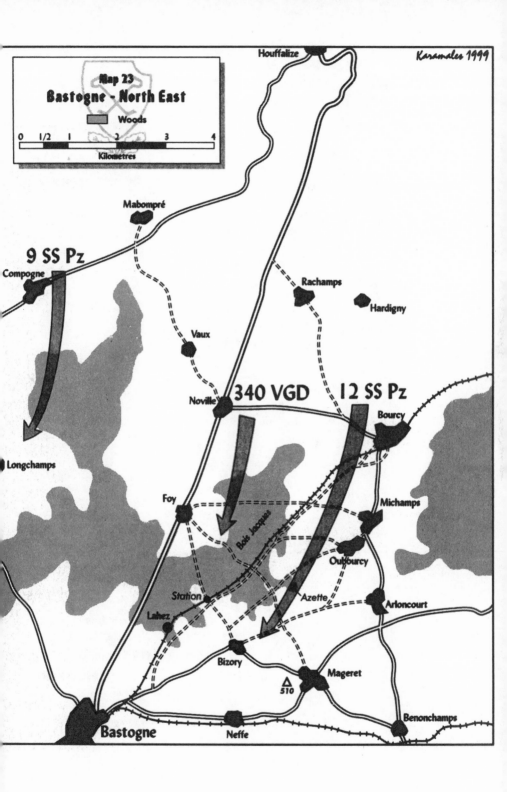

Houffalize

Karamales 1999

Map 23
Bastogne - North East

Woods

0   1/2   1   2   3   4
Kilometres

Mabompré

9 SS Pz

Compogne

Rachamps

Hardigny

Vaux

340 VGD   **12 SS Pz**

Noville

Bourcy

Longchamps

Foy

Michamps

Bois Jacques

Oubourcy

Station

Azette

Arloncourt

Lahez

Bizory

△ 510

Mageret

Benonchamps

Bastogne

Neffe

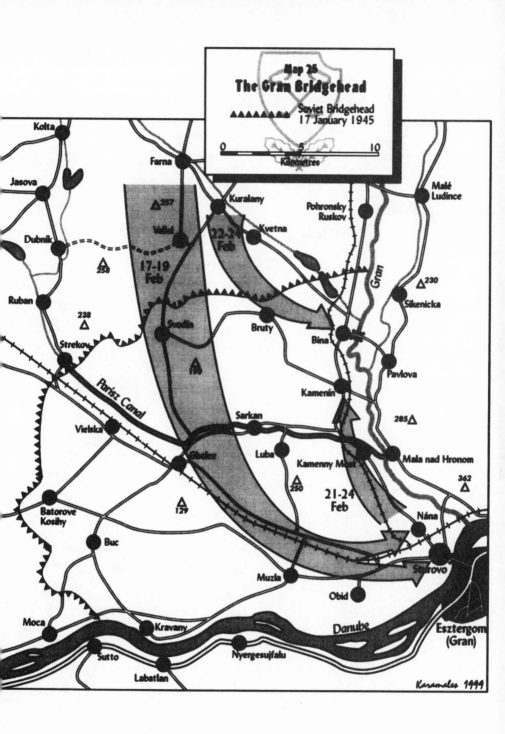

Map 25
The Gran Bridgehead

▲▲▲▲▲▲▲▲▲ Soviet Bridgehead
17 January 1945

0   5   10
Kilometres

Kolta

Farna

Jasova

Kuralany

Malé
Ludince

Pohronsky
Ruskov

Kvetna

△237

Veľké

22-24
Feb

Dubník

△238

17-19
Feb

Gran

△230

Ruban

238
△

Svodín

Bruty

Sikenicka

Strekov

Bina

△190

Pavlova

Parisz Canal

Kamenín

Sarkan

285△

Vielska

Gbelce

Luba

Kamenny Most

Mala nad Hronom

362
△

△129

△250

21-24
Feb

Batorove
Kosihy

Nána

Buc

Štúrovo

Muzla

Moca

Kravany

Obid

Danube

Esztergom
(Gran)

Sutto

Nyergesujfalu

Labatian

Karamales 1999

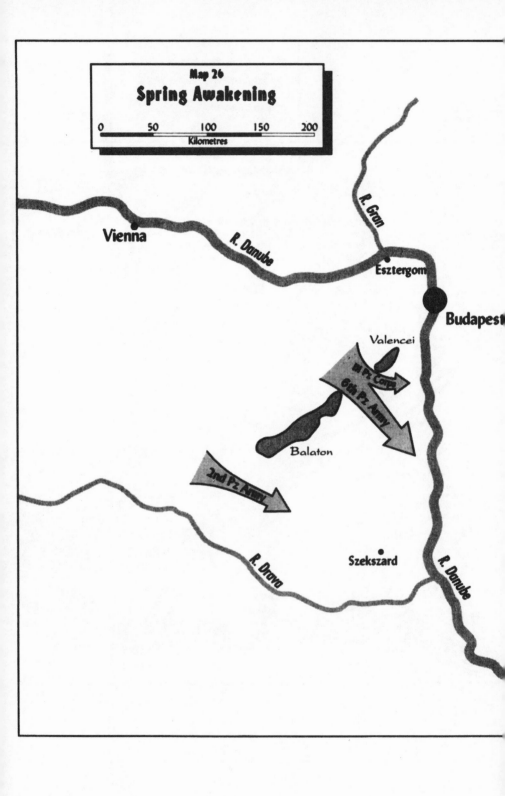

Map 26
Spring Awakening

0   50   100   150   200
Kilometres

Vienna

R. Danube

R. Gran

Esztergom

Budapest

Valencei

III Pz. Corps.
6th Pz. Army

Balaton

2nd Pz. Army

R. Drava

Szekszard

R. Danube

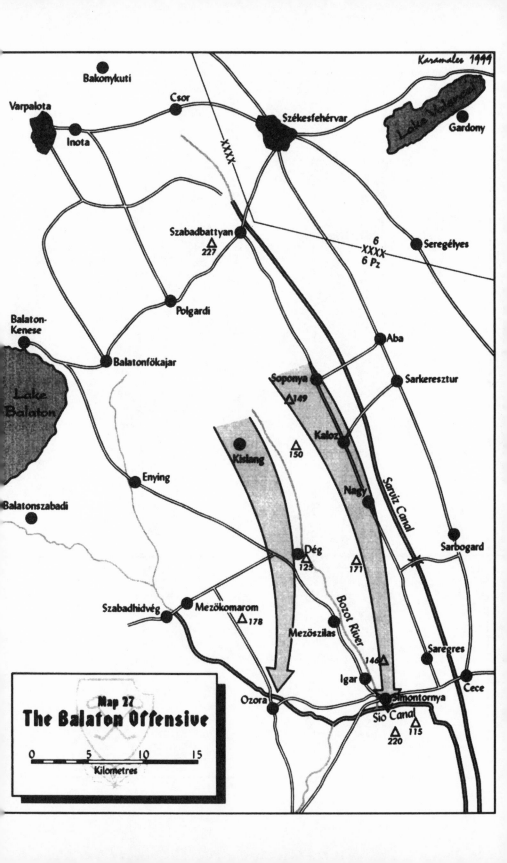

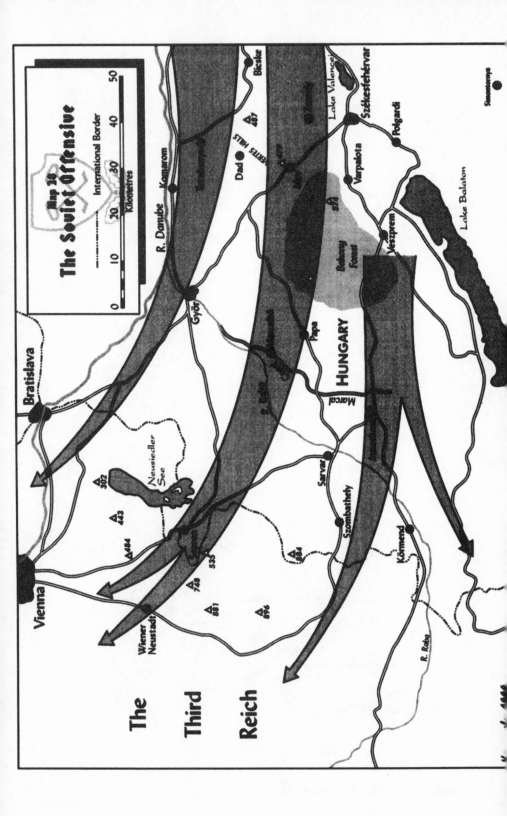

Map 28

The Soviet Offensive

International Border

Kilometres
0   10   20   30   40   50

The

Third

Reich

R. Danube

Bratislava

Vienna

Neusiedler See

Wiener Neustadt

△484

△443

△302

△535

△748

△881

△896

Győr

Komarom

Bicske

Dad ●

GERTES HILLS

△487

Lake Velencei

Székesfehérvár

Polgardi

Varpalota

Veszprem

Bakony Forest

△561

Papa

Marcal

Sarvar

Szombathely

Körmend

HUNGARY

Lake Balaton

R. Raba

Simontornya ●

△484

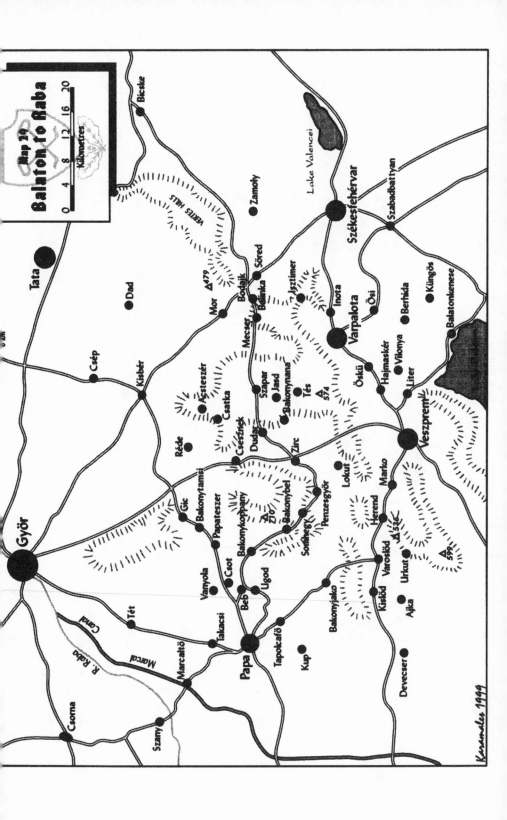

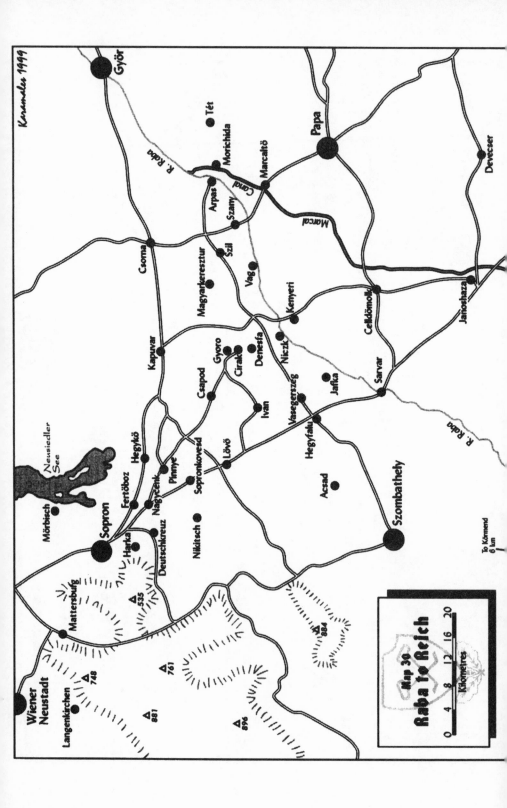

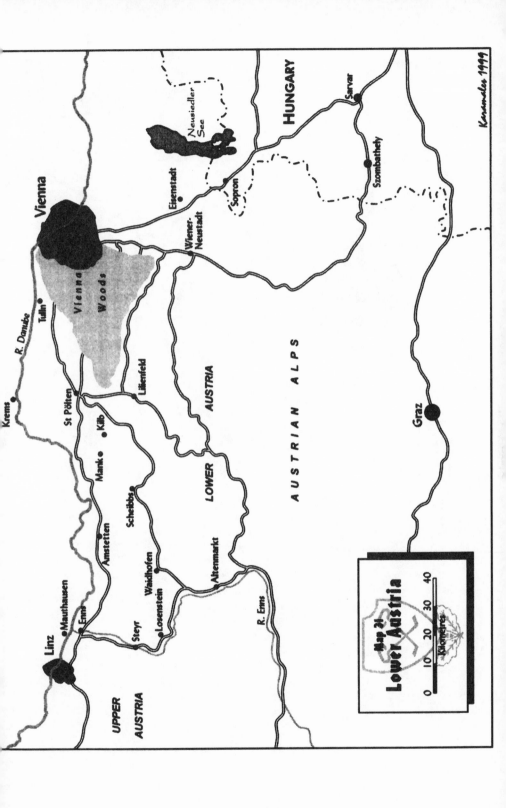

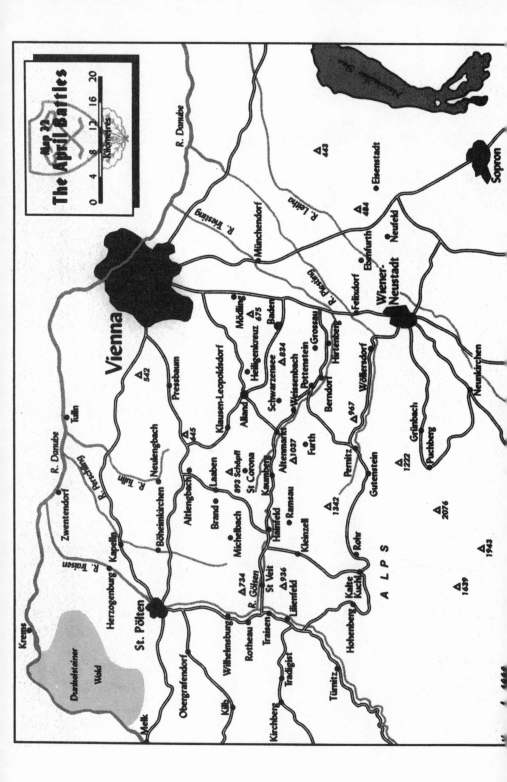

Map 22
The April Battles

0   4   8   12   16   20
Kilometres

R. Danube

Vienna

443

Eisenstadt

Sopron

Neufeld

484

Ebenfurth

Münchendorf

R. Leitha

R. Triesting

R. Piesting

Felixdorf

Wiener-
Neustadt

Neunkirchen

Willendorf

Hirtenberg

Berndorf

957

Grünbach

Puchberg

1222

2076

1943

ALPS

1639

Mödling

Heiligenkreuz 675

Baden

834

Grossau

Pottenstein

Weissenbach

Schwarzensee

Alland

Pernitz

Gutenstein

Rohr

Kalte
Kuchl

Hohenberg

Tümitz

Tradigist

Kirchberg

Kilb

Obergrafendorf

Melk

St. Pölten

Herzogenburg

Kapelln

R. Traisen

R. Perschling

R. Danube

Zwentendorf

Krems

Dunkelsteiner
Wald

Tulln

542

Pressbaum

Neulengbach

445

R. Tulln

Böheimkirchen

Altlengbach

Brand

Michelbach

Laaben

893 Schöpfl
St Corona

Kaumberg

Altenmarkt

1037

Furth

1342

Kleinzell

Hainfeld

Ramsau

734

936

Gölsen

St Veit

R. Gölsen

Lilienfeld

Wilhelmsburg

Rotheau

Traisen